THE
ICELANDIC VOICE
in Canadian Letters

THE
ICELANDIC VOICE
in Canadian Letters
The Contribution of Icelandic-Canadian Writers
to Canadian Literature

Daisy L. Neijmann

Nordic Voices, volume 1

CARLETON UNIVERSITY PRESS

Printed and bound in Canada

Canadian Cataloguing in Publication Data

Neijmann, Daisy L., date-
   The Icelandic voice in Canadian letters : the
contribution of Icelandic-Canadian writers to Canadian
literature

(Nordic voices ; #1)
Includes bibliographical references and index.
ISBN 0-88629-317-0

   1. Canadian literature (English)—Icelandic-
Canadian authors—History and criticism. I. Title.
II. Series.

PS8089.5.I3N44 1997   C810.9'83961   C97-900247-8
PR9197.33.I3N44 1997

Cover Design: Your Aunt Nellie
Typeset: Mayhew & Associates Graphic Communications, Richmond, Ont., in association with Marie Tappin

Excerpts from *What Can't be Changed Shouldn't Be Mourned* by W.D. Valgardson, © 1990,
published by Douglas & McIntyre. Reprinted with permission of the publisher.
Excerpts from "Brothers," "An Act of Mercy," and "The Burning" by W.D. Valgardson
are reprinted from *Bloodflowers* by permission of Oberon Press. The excerpt from
"Capital" by W.D. Valgardson is reprinted from *God Is Not A Fish Inspector* by permission
of Oberon Press. Excerpts from "Celebration," "Beyond Normal Requirement,"
"Trees," and "A Place Of One's Own" by W.D. Valgardson are reprinted from *Red Dust*
by permission of Oberon Press. Excerpts from *Gentle Sinners* by W.D. Valgardson, ©
1980, published by Oberon Press, are reprinted by permission of the author. Excerpts
from "Changeling Poems," "Monkshood Poems" and "Wake-Pick Poems" by Kristjana
Gunnars, © 1981, published by House of Anansi Press, are reprinted from *Wake-Pick
Poems* by permission of Stoddart Publishing Co. Limited, Canada.

This book has been published with the help of a grant from the Humanities and
Social Sciences Federation of Canada, using funds provided by the Social Sciences and
Humanities Research Council of Canada.

Carleton University Press gratefully acknowledges the support extended to its pub-
lishing program by the Canada Council and the financial assistance of the Ontario
Arts Council. The Press would also like to thank the Department of Canadian
Heritage, Government of Canada, and the Government of Ontario through the
Ministry of Culture, Tourism and Recreation, for their assistance.

For Wil and Anneke,

mijn ouders

CONTENTS

ACKNOWLEDGEMENTS

THIS PROJECT WAS MADE POSSIBLE by financial assistance from the Multiculturalism Program of the Department of Canadian Heritage, financial assistance of the Netherlands Organization for Scientific Research (NWO), and by research grants from the Canadian Embassy in The Hague. The project was initiated by the late August J. Fry, who introduced me to Canadian and Icelandic-Canadian literature and inspired me to further study.

I owe special thanks to my mentors Richard Todd and Kirsten Wolf for their tireless and enthusiastic efforts on my behalf, their encouragement, guidance and friendship, and, most of all, for their unconditional faith in this project. I am also grateful to Elrud Ibsch, Christopher Hale, Haraldur Bessason, and Viðar Hreinsson, who have provided helpful commentary and advice, saved me from errors and have generously shared their ideas with me. As well, I would like to acknowledge the assistance of Sigrid Johnson from the Icelandic Collection at the University of Manitoba.

My Icelandic parents Katrín Eymundsdóttir and Gísli Auðunsson have disclosed many of Iceland's secrets to me and have been a source of great assistance and affection, for which I will always be thankful. Michel's brotherly admonitions and unfailing sense of humour have been indispensable for my well-being and sanity.

My greatest debt is to Mark, who suffered most from my obsession but never lost patience or faith. He has been a critical and insightful discussion partner, a pillar of support, and an endless source of love in frustrating as well as inspiring times.

This book is dedicated to Wil and Anneke Neijmann, my parents, with my profound love and thanks for years of generous support and encouragement, and for allowing me to find my own direction in life. Without them, this book would not have been possible.

INTRODUCTION

DURING THE NINETEENTH CENTURY, mass migration took place from Europe to North America. Large numbers of people left their native countries to look for a better future on the North American continent. The United States were the first to attract prospective European immigrants, many of whom used Canada as a port of entry. In 1867, however, the British colony of Canada became a Confederation of five provinces which needed people to settle and develop the western districts it had recently purchased from the Hudson Bay Company. The Canadian government began to develop strategies to entice European immigrants to stay in Canada rather than travel on to the United States by offering free land and travel to a final Canadian destination. After the Mennonites, the first group of non-British immigrants who agreed to stay in Canada were Icelanders. They came in 1873. Immigrants from many other nationalities followed during the end of the nineteenth century and have continued to arrive up until the present day.

While the United States demanded of its immigrants that they become Americans and assimilate into American society, a strategy that has become known as the "melting pot," Canada consisted of two different "founding nations," the English and the French, who settled in segregated patterns and allowed immigrants to do the same. As a result, a large variety of immigrant cultures developed in Canada alongside the "official" culture of the founding Anglo-Canadian establishment. Social currents during the 1960s brought about a renewed political and cultural awareness and interest among immigrant descendents in their ethnic origins, as a result of which multiculturalism became official policy in Canada in 1971. Multiculturalism, or a "mosaic" Canada (as opposed to the American "melting pot"), however, was not only a political step, but also came to constitute a highly cherished Canadian national ideal. Canada's colonial past and its contemporary low profile, in the shadow of the

United States, have long since caused Canadians to feel that they lack a clear national identity. Multiculturalism seemed to offer a solution to this problem. In the cultural search for reflections of a truly Canadian, rather than an adopted, reality, the Canadian mosaic came to play an important role. Gradually, the idea developed that Canada's reality was to be found exactly in its low profile on an international scale and in its diversity of ethnic cultures on a national scale. The position of these cultures on the margins of an "official" national culture was felt to reflect Canada's own marginal position in the world of the great powers. These developments have greatly helped stimulate research in the field of immigrant cultures and ethnic groups in North America, as well as generate a cultural climate in which these groups and cultures have come to be regarded as an important part of the Canadian identity.

This book presents an examination of the literary manifestation of one such Canadian ethnic culture: that of Icelandic immigrants in Canada and their descendents. Until recently, studies devoted to immigrant and ethnic groups were, of necessity, carried out almost exclusively by and for members of these groups, due to language barriers (many sources were in languages other than English) and a general lack of interest among the Anglo-Canadian cultural and academic establishment. This has changed considerably during the last two decades, however. Much important groundwork has been done, especially in the fields of sociology, anthropology and socio-economics, on which many literary and folklorist studies of Canadian immigrant and ethnic cultures have been based. Nevertheless, many *lacunae* remain to be filled in our knowledge about the subject. The Icelandic Canadians themselves have been exceptionally active in conducting studies of their history and literature. Until recently, however, these studies were confined to either early Icelandic immigrant culture or to contemporary works in English by authors of Icelandic descent. While such studies are very important in themselves, what has been lacking so far is a perspective in which the development and transition, indeed the connection between Icelandic immigrant writing and Icelandic-Canadian literature in English, are viewed. This typifies the problems inherent in the study of immigrant and ethnic cultures: they are the product of a dual heritage, two cultures, both of which need to be examined. The main reason for writing this work, therefore, has been to provide an analytical English survey of both the earlier literature in Icelandic and the later literature in English, taking both the Icelandic cultural background and the Canadian cultural context into account. Within this context, I have explored the relationship between literary expression, lived experience and the creative search for identity and place underlying all minority literature.

My choice to focus on one particular group in order to examine in some depth the Old World background of the immigrants as well as the Canadian environment they came to inhabit, is open to the criticism that it highlights ethnic difference, even ethnic segregation. It could be argued that by doing so, the common aspects of the immigrant experience in Canada which transcend most differences are neglected. However, it is my sincere hope that, instead, this work will contribute to a better understanding of how cultures are transplanted and adapt, and how they can survive even as they are integrated in the larger culture that is Canadian. After 25 years of multiculturalism in Canada, no sizeable analytic or comparative work exists on the subject of ethnic-Canadian literatures. This is undoubtedly largely due to the problems inherent in inter-ethnic studies. Scholars face the daunting task of having to examine unfamiliar cultural and linguistic material in order to come to a comparative analysis of patterns of adaptation, cultural retention and other developments which take place after settlement in the New World. Studies such as this, which bring together a comprehensive selection of relevant cross-cultural criticism, are needed to provide a basis for future comparative research on the various immigrant and ethnic groups and cultures.

Icelandic-Canadian literary history shows an intriguing development from the beginnings of an immigrant literature rooted in Iceland and moulded by the Canadian immigrant experience, to the maturing of an Icelandic-Canadian literature both firmly rooted in Canadian reality and concerned with the influence and role of an ethnic culture and identity within that reality. The examination of the development from Icelandic immigrant writing to Icelandic-Canadian literature sheds new light on the nature and function of ethnic culture and calls into question the cultural assumptions underlying multiculturalism in its present form in Canada. Rather than being a quaint and reified relic from an immigrant and Old World past, Icelandic-Canadian culture has evolved into a specific type of New World culture which, although it is informed by Icelandic culture, is firmly rooted in Canadian soil. Although multiculturalism has created a literary climate in which the immigrant and ethnic experience in Canada have become acceptable, indeed fashionable topics in Canadian literature, the development of Icelandic-Canadian literature helps expose flaws in the premises on which multiculturalism is built and raises questions about its effectiveness.

While it may not immediately appear to be the most obvious choice, Icelandic-Canadian literature constitutes an appropriate topic for an investigation into immigrant and ethnic literature. The Icelandic literary tradition is very strong and unbroken; it has enjoyed a wide and deep-rooted popular appreciation and activity in Iceland over the centuries. The beginnings of this tradition are found in Eddic and skaldic poetry and in the Old Icelandic sagas, all of which, as contemporary scholarship increasingly emphasizes, were influenced by the fact that Iceland was itself a colony settled by immigrants from Norway and the British Isles. Literature constituted, in turn, the main cultural baggage of the Icelandic immigrants to Canada during the end of the nineteenth century and the beginning of the twentieth, and it remained the pre-eminent vehicle for cultural expression in the New World, as well as the most important link with the Icelandic past. Without a basic idea of the literary tradition in Iceland, it is very difficult to understand the literary developments among the Icelanders in Canada. I will therefore briefly discuss the Icelandic literary context on which Icelandic-Canadian literature is based before proceeding to Icelandic-Canadian literature itself.

Immigrant literature, although sometimes very nostalgic, often assumes an important social function as well. The immigrant experience causes a profound sense of dislocation and alienation, and requires a re-evaluation of values and traditions, indeed of the self. Familiarity and social stability are traded for chaos and confusion, as ties with kin and country have been severed. As I attempt to show in Chapter II, literature is one medium through which this experience can be expressed and dealt with on a communal level, and through which solutions can be offered. At the same time, the situation in the home country during the time of emigration continued to influence many immigrants. It profoundly affected the way the immigrants perceived themselves and their immigration experience and finally helped locate the immigrants culturally and spiritually in the new land.

The New World culture which grew out of this Icelandic settlement in Canada has received expression in a remarkable body of literature both in Icelandic and in English. As the output of

Icelandic-Canadian authors, especially in Icelandic, has been quite voluminous, I could not include the complete corpus in my analysis. A complete discussion of Icelandic immigrant writing alone would fill many volumes. As a result, only the best known authors could be subject of discussion. Among the immigrant writers these include three poets, Káinn, Stephan G. Stephansson and Guttormur J. Guttormsson; and two prose writers, Jóhann Magnús Bjarnason and Guðrún H. Finnsdóttir. Laura Goodman Salverson is a transitional writer whose work forms a bridge between Icelandic immigrant and Icelandic-Canadian literature. Although she wrote when immigrant writers were still active and was herself moulded by the Icelandic immigrant experience in Canada, she was also the first author who consciously decided to write in English for a Canadian audience. She could be considered part of the Icelandic as well as the Canadian literary tradition, although she has tended to be excluded by both.

I begin my discussion of Icelandic-Canadian literature in English with a brief introduction to the most important developments and characteristics of Canadian literature, in order to provide a Canadian framework in the light of which the later authors can be viewed. Initially, Laura Goodman Salverson's relatively successful venture into English-Canadian literature was not followed up. The decades between 1940 and 1970 were a rather quiet but nonetheless interesting period in Icelandic-Canadian literature. During this time the final transition took place from Icelandic to English, and from immigrant to Canadian. That the completion of this transition did not preclude a continuing influence from the Icelandic cultural heritage is evident from the works of the three major contemporary Icelandic-Canadian writers: W.D. Valgardson, David Arnason and Kristjana Gunnars. Valgardson and Arnason are both fourth-generation Icelandic Canadians who have grown up in the Icelandic-Canadian community. Kristjana Gunnars is a special case, since she is a recent immigrant of half-Icelandic and half-Danish descent who was born in Iceland. She is, therefore, not a member of the Icelandic-Canadian community. Her contemporary immigrant experience, as it is reflected in her work, sets it apart from the works of Valgardson and Arnason as much as it invites comparison with it. My analysis of the works of these authors focusses first on stylistic and thematic influences from the Icelandic literary tradition and then turns to an exploration of the influences of an Icelandic and Icelandic-Canadian mythic consciousness.

In 1969, the Royal Commission on Bilingualism and Biculturalism published volume four of its *Report*, devoted to *The Cultural Contributions of the Other Ethnic Groups*. "Other" ethnic groups meant here, as it generally means in popular use, Canadians of extraction other than British or French. The recommendation of the Commission, based on its findings, was an official recognition and promotion of those contributions, a recommendation acknowledged in the multiculturalist policy statement of 1971. Since then, the research and general attention paid to the cultural expression of heritages different from the French and English has increased considerably. Now, two and a half decades after the political institutionalization of multiculturalism, we can begin to examine the results. What influence has multiculturalism had on Icelandic-Canadian literature? Has it changed the reception and recognition of the contribution of Icelandic-Canadian authors in the field of Canadian literature? I have tried to answer these questions on the basis of a brief analysis of the nature and role of ethnicity for the Icelandic Canadians, the reactions of Icelandic-Canadian authors to the effects of multiculturalism, and to suggest possible reasons why and where, at least for the Icelanders, multiculturalism has failed.

I

OMNIA MEA MECUM PORTO
LITERARY HISTORY AND BACKGROUND OF THE ICELANDERS

INTRODUCTION

THE ICELANDERS who left their country at the end of the last century in order to start a new life on the other side of the ocean were not an exceptional case, but part of a large-scale European migration westwards. However, the Icelandic immigrants were perhaps exceptional in that they left a country which itself had been settled by immigrants from Norway almost a thousand years earlier and had recorded its settlement history in a vast body of literature. Iceland was, in other words, itself an immigrant country. Tomasson (1980), Hastrup (1982) and Byock (1988) are among the scholars who have emphasized this fact and its formative influence on Icelandic culture and society. The implication here is that the emigration to Canada and the settlement of a "New Iceland" were, in a way, a historical re-enactment of the Icelandic past, parallelling and re-establishing historical continuity in the new land.

The significance of an earlier Norwegian exodus for the Icelandic immigrants to Canada is brought out by its pivotal role in the development of a distinct Icelandic-Canadian identity and literary tradition. The symbolic importance for the Icelandic immigrants in Canada of

Icelandic settlement history and the literature inspired by it can be better understood by looking at the cultural climate in Iceland at the time of emigration from Iceland to Canada and by taking into account the profound influence of the immigrant experience. The Icelanders have always been characterized for their historical awareness and their love of literature. The main wave of emigration from Iceland to Canada, moreover, took place during a period that is characterized in Iceland by a fervent nationalism which—significantly—based itself on Icelandic classical culture and history. It is, therefore, natural to assume that the emigrants were highly aware of the fact that they were following in their ancestors' footsteps by migrating to a new country. Most important, however, for the development of an Icelandic-Canadian literary tradition was the fact that Icelandic classical culture validated the Icelandic immigration to Canada and supported the growth of a New World culture and identity without loss of the Icelandic heritage.

The pivotal role of identity creation in immigrant and ethnic literature has been emphasized by prominent writers and scholars such as Mandel (1977), Kroetsch (1985), Sollors (1989) and Padolsky (1991). Indeed, Mandel coined the much-quoted definition of ethnic literature as "a form concerned with defining itself, its voice, the dialectic of self and other and the duplicities of self-creation, transformation and identities" (65). It should come as no surprise that the Icelanders, who have always prided themselves on their literary culture, used writing as the primary medium for the continual re-invention and articulation of their New World identity and to find their place in a Canadian reality. In an attempt to come to an understanding of what has informed and perpetuated the ethnic affiliation of his community, the Icelandic-Canadian anthropologist John Matthiasson has published several articles on the subject of Icelandic-Canadian identity formation. In "The Icelandic Canadians: The Paradox of an Assimilated Ethnic Group" (1979), he developed his ideas about the structural patterns of adaptation among Icelandic-Canadian communities. His ideas provide valuable insights into the formative role of the dynamic relationship between Old World past and New World present in the development of Icelandic-Canadian literature. In his article, Matthiasson relates the Icelandic-Canadian patterns of adaptation back to an Icelandic cultural past by characterizing them as "uniquely Icelandic, reflecting the basic structural features of Icelandic culture dating back to the Viking past and the writings of the sagas" (195).

Matthiasson makes use of the thematic analysis introduced into anthropology by Morris Opler, adding a structural approach in order to analyze Icelandic-Canadian patterns of adaption. Matthiasson finds that the pervasive cultural theme in Iceland is one of contrasts. He calls this theme dualism. Iceland itself is emphatically a country of contrasts, and Matthiasson sees such contrasts reflected in its culture, people and society, although he views the reflection more as a "two-sidedness": "On the social and cultural level, whenever there is one form of an institution, for example, there must also exist another, often identical in form, yet standing in structural opposition to the first" (203). His examples of how dualism operates at various social levels show how both the Icelandic and Icelandic-Canadian communities have always been united exactly by those oppositions that make up their social, cultural and historical structures: cohesion in factionalism, union through the old Icelandic love of debate. As Matthiasson points out, this cultural theme of dualism

helps us understand why Icelandic Canadians, who for more than 100 years have sought to become non-hyphenated Canadians, still exist as an ethnic group in Winnipeg and elsewhere in Canada. The inward thrust created by structural oppositions has worked against the outward pull of assimilation. The debates have concentrated interest inward.... The ultimate example of dualism in Icelandic Canadian culture has been the paradox of a simultaneous drive towards assimilation and cultural retention. The internal factionalism, found on many fronts and a product of structural features brought with them from Iceland has fostered this, and at least in the case of this one ethnic group, helps explain why Icelandic Canadians retain ethnic status within the larger Canadian society. (204-05)

According to Matthiasson, then, traditional Icelandic dualism constitutes the fundamental force of cohesion among the Icelandic Canadians. The dual tendency to preserve the Icelandic cultural heritage and to assimilate into Canadian society is at the core of Icelandic-Canadian culture. This contrast was possible because the Icelanders in Canada were in the unique position of being able to look back to a living culture that itself had been moulded by settlement conditions and that supported assimilation. Icelandic history and culture itself, then, provided the impetus for the birth of a New World culture.

Consequently, any study of Icelandic-Canadian literature remains incomplete unless it is viewed against the background of the Icelandic cultural past that has played such a vital role in shaping the present. Of course, a detailed treatment of early Icelandic literary history and culture would be impossible here. In the following discussion of Icelandic literary history I will focus only on those elements that pertain to Icelandic-Canadian literature and its recurrent themes.[1]

MEDIEVAL ICELAND AND THE DYNAMICS OF IMMIGRATION

Iceland was settled during the ninth and tenth centuries. The settlers are believed to have been mostly, but not exclusively, Norwegians who came either directly from Norway or from other Viking settlements in the British Isles and elsewhere. These centuries were a time of expansion and social change, and people were in search of land or migrated for political or social reasons. Popular legend, however, has it that some noble, proud Norwegian chieftains would rather leave their homeland behind and settle elsewhere in freedom than to sacrifice their independence to a power-hungry, would-be king named Harald Fairhair, who had set out to unite all of Norway under his reign. Thus they migrated to Iceland to build a new society away from royal authority. This legend has lived on in the minds of the people and in their literature on both sides of the ocean. It is of interest here, as it indicates a need among immigrants to legitimize their emigration (Tucker 1989: 8). We will encounter a similar need among the Icelandic emigrants to Canada a thousand years later (see Chapter II).

The chieftains transplanted their households and possessions as well as their culture and traditions. Since the island was practically uninhabited, the settlers were free to claim land for their families and build up a new life and society, based partly on ancient Germanic social structures and traditions that were quickly disappearing elsewhere, and partly on the new environment and challenges the new country offered. They had fled the influence of growing royal authority, and they had settled on an island that was far from the social and political arenas of Europe. The result was a society moulded by the dynamics of immigration that was unique in medieval Europe. Byock (1988) describes medieval Iceland as follows: "What, then, was Iceland? Briefly, it was a society whose development was determined by the dynamics of its immigrant experiences. From these experiences there emerged an innovative social order marked by aspects of statelessness as well as elements of incipient statehood. Features of both ranked and stratified society were present" (1988: 7).

Although there was no true egalitarianism, the legal and social system that developed was probably closer to democracy than any other European political system at the time. Official hierarchies were not established, owing both to the levelling influence of settlement and the traditional Germanic social structure of individual farmers who were free to choose their own allegiances. It was this structure, disappearing fast from Europe, that many settlers sought to maintain. In 930, the *Alþingi*, the National Assembly, was founded. There, in what is often called the first European parliament, old laws were recited and new ones created by the lawspeaker and the thirty-six *goðar* (sing. *goði*; "priest-chieftain") from all over the country. Each *goði* was the leader of a district, but depended on the support of farmers, who were free to change leaders if they felt the need to do so.

The farmers owned their own farms which were largely self-sufficient social units due to the scattered settlement patterns and the uninhabitability of the interior. Having left royal authority and being no longer dependent on Norway, the new Icelanders now accepted only the authority of the laws which they themselves created and upheld. This situation made it difficult, in theory, for any one chieftain to achieve and maintain more power than another. The many *goðar* and the lawspeaker had no executive power; once a law had been accepted or a verdict spoken, the people themselves were responsible for the execution of the law. Lawspeaking, the creation of new laws and the seating of judges, were open to the public so that everyone could remain informed and become involved politically. The position of *goði* was open to all free landowning farmers (*bændr*). It was a system that depended on a strong sense of social involvement on the part of its members.

Since the responsibility for the execution of the law rested with the people themselves, feud formed an integral part of Icelandic society. Wrongs done to one's kin or blood brothers demanded revenge. To restrain the often bloody, violent and endless consequences of feuds, the legal system was geared towards conciliation (Byock 1982: 201). The balance between conciliation and revenge could be very precarious due to the concept of the antagonists' honour involved. Honour was probably the most important element of Norse mentality. The loss of honour resulted in a shame that was worse than death, as expressed very aptly in the medieval poem *Hávamál* ("Words of the High One"):

> Cattle die
> and kinsmen die,
> thyself eke soon wilt die;
> one thing, I wot,
> will wither never:
> the doom over each one dead.
> (*The Poetic Edda* 25)

A Norseman's honour and reputation rested on his fellows' good opinion. Accordingly, there developed an unwritten system of social control which with the help of able and highly regarded arbitrators stimulated people towards legal conciliatory arrangements in feud cases.

Since the settlement of Iceland took place in the pre-literate period, the Icelandic immigrant experience was not documented until much later. However, we may reasonably assume that many memories and experiences were expressed and passed down orally. Not only do several old accounts comment on the importance of oral literature in Germanic society, but it is generally known that story-telling and the composition and recital of poetry occupied an important place among the early Icelanders. Passages in the Icelandic sagas point to the popularity of *sagnaskemmtun* (story-telling as entertainment during festivities and long winter nights), and poetry that bears the traces of oral origins has come down to us in writing.

A veritable explosion of literary creativity in medieval Iceland started roughly a century after the conversion to Christianity in the year 1000 A.D. The remarkable concern in this literature both with life during the first few centuries after settlement and with the mother-country, Norway, suggests a continuous literary tradition as well as a concern with and a deep awareness of the common cultural heritage and history between the New and Old Country. This regard for tradition is clearly expressed in the role literature came to play in the new society. As Haraldur Bessason points out: "One may imagine that nostalgia for Norway provided early generations of newcomers to Iceland with a sharper awareness of their heritage than was the case with those relatives who had never left their native valleys of Norway" (1967a: 54). In one redaction of the *Landnámabók* ("Book of Settlements"), an awareness of the simultaneous influences of the old and the new is expressed:

People often say that writing about the Settlements is irrelevant learning, but we think we can better meet the criticism of foreigners when they accuse us of being descended from slaves and scoundrels, if we know for certain the truth about our ancestry. And for those who want to know ancient lore and how to trace genealogies, it's better to start at the beginning than to come in at the middle. Anyway, all civilized nations want to know about the origins of their own society, and the beginnings of their own race. (*Book of Settlements* 6)

The concern with documentation and learning brought out by this passage is typical of the age in which it was written, the twelfth century. The Icelanders, seeking to avoid the danger of isolation, vigorously maintained relations with European centres of learning which were undergoing a cultural resurgence known as the medieval renaissance. The passage from *Landnámabók* also reveals the concern of the young nation to establish itself culturally in the eyes of the outside world. The genealogies mentioned trace the settlers' families back to important royal or chiefly families in Norway, showing a desire for respect through invoking the history and traditions of the old country. In the words of Stefán Einarsson, the Icelanders kept "one foot ... in the Norwegian homeland" for a very long time (1957: 124).

This awareness of and concern with the cultural heritage was, of course, reinforced by the fact that migration and settlement necessarily involve the breaking of many ties to start anew in a different country empty of culture and traditions. Part of the process of creating a sense of belonging in such conditions is holding on to a common heritage. As time passed and settlement was consolidated, new, local elements gradually found their way into the old tales, beliefs and traditions that had been brought from Norway. Slowly, a new cultural tradition developed which still bore traces of the old culture but was, at the same time, firmly rooted in the new environment.

A large number of scholarly works were produced in Iceland during the twelfth century. Many of these were, remarkably, written in Icelandic rather than Latin; the *Íslendingabók* ("Book of Icelanders"), for instance, which is one of the oldest preserved documents, is in Icelandic, and so is a treatise on the Icelandic language called *Fyrsta málfræðiritgerðin* ("The First Grammatical Treatise"). In the wake of this "age of learning" followed what has become known as the golden age of literature in Iceland: older poetry was written down, new poetry was created, and the renowned Sagas of the Icelanders were recorded. Abroad, in Scandinavia and England, Icelanders had become famous and preferred court poets. Foreign scholars used

Icelandic sources as a basis for their work, because the Icelanders were known for being especially knowledgeable about older Scandinavian history. The Norwegian Theodoricus, for example, who was the first to write a history on Norwegian kings in Latin called *Historia de antiquitate regum Norwagiensium*, and the Danish Saxo Grammaticus, who wrote *Gesta Danorum*, both commented on the "ancient knowledge" that had been preserved by the Icelanders (*Bókmenntasaga* 1: 362). Within a few centuries, the young nation had not only become widely accepted and respected, but even excelled in literary accomplishments. The question why it was the Icelanders who excelled in a tradition common to all of Scandinavia has been much discussed. It seems very likely that both the isolation and the island's harsh climate forced people to turn to their own resources for entertainment. Also, the Icelanders had developed a conscious awareness of their literary heritage as a result of their migration. Moreover, many settlers were, or believed themselves to be, of high rank and had thus either acquired an education themselves or become patrons of artists and scholars. Finally, the spur provided by the unique conditions to which they had had to adapt and the urge to gain respect in the eyes of older, established nations, undoubtedly played an important part in the remarkable cultural development that took place.

OLD ICELANDIC POETRY

The poetry that was composed in Norway at the time of settlement and brought along to Iceland is generally divided into two main varieties, Eddic and skaldic poetry. The Eddic poems that have been preserved are all anonymous and are divided up into two categories: mythological poems and heroic poems. The mythological poems contain stories about the Norse gods and goddesses. While some are very comical, others are of a didactic nature. The most famous didactic poem is *Hávamál*, "Words of the High One," so called because Odin speaks these verses. Its proverbs and wisdom provide some insight into the Norse mentality and way of life during heathen times. The heroic poems, some older, some younger, relate the heroic spirit and ethics of Old Germanic legendary heroes such as Sigurður Fáfnisbani (Siegfried in the *Nibelungenlied*) and Atli (Attila the Hun).

Scholars have found Christian traces in the contents of some of the Eddic poems, but even if their content cannot be said to give us a totally reliable picture of pre-Christian Norse life and ideas, their form takes us straight back to Old Germanic poetry. Most of the poems were written in the alliterative metre called *fornyrðislag*, or variations on it. Their diction was generally simple and straightforward, terse, powerful and pictorial. The Eddic poems have proved an immensely rich source of information not only in Icelandic or Scandinavian studies but in the field of Germanic studies in general. Furthermore, their spirit and form have had a lasting influence on the Icelandic literary tradition. As with many other Old Norse texts, the exact age of the Eddic poems cannot be determined. While the principal manuscript of Eddic poems, known as the *Codex Regius*, dates from 1270-80, the origins of some of the poems are generally believed to date back to a period before the settlement of Iceland.[2]

Whereas scholarly opinions differ on the oral origins of many of the Eddic poems, skaldic poetry was exclusively oral. The poems that have come down to us have mostly been preserved incompletely as verses in prose accounts, where they were often used as historical documents or as a vehicle for the expression of emotion or other personal utterances not readily communicated in the objective, economic prose.[3] Despite their incomplete transmission, the preserved verses can be trusted to be fairly intact as a result of their complexity in metre and diction.

Skaldic poetry differs from Eddic poetry in many respects, yet it relies on the tradition the latter preserves. In the first place, skaldic poetry is not anonymous. In the second place, whereas Eddic poems deal mostly with a mythical or a legendary past, skaldic poetry treats the present. These poems were composed for an actual occasion, either to celebrate a king, a warrior, or a recent battle, or to commemorate an event. One could almost compare them with present-day journalistic accounts, and certainly they had the same function: skaldic poets were medieval historiographers.

Skaldic poetry, however, is widely known not so much for its contents, but rather for its form which is extremely intricate and complex. The straightforward, flexible Eddic *fornyrðislag* has yielded to the so-called *dróttkvætt* metre, consisting of six lines (the variation called *hrynhent* has eight lines), each containing three short and three long syllables, two alliterations and internal rhyme. Moreover, the use of vocabulary is very ornate and intricate. Most characteristic for skaldic poetry are perhaps the figures of speech called kennings. The most rudimentary type of kenning is known is many countries: it is based on a main word plus a modifying noun in the genitive. The kenning thus artistically describes or characterizes something or somebody else (e.g. *unnar hestur* = "horse of the waves" = ship). However, an important feature in the art of skaldic poetry became the construction of variations of the basic form which could extend to the use of five or six modifiers within one kenning.[4] Most kennings were made up of elements referring to Norse mythology. One of the kennings for poetry, for instance, was "Kvasir's blood," alluding to the mythical tale relating how the wise giant Kvasir was killed by dwarfs who collected his blood in a cauldron and mixed it with mead; the person who drinks from the mixture becomes a *skáld*, a poet.

Skaldic poetry was a very popular form of entertainment, a source of news, and could even have diplomatic or political functions. The genre itself lived on until the twelfth century, although its form survived longer in other kinds of poetry. Good poets were in great demand and had chances of becoming highly-respected members of a king's court. The influence a good poem could have on a king is perhaps best shown in *Egils saga* where Egill Skallagrímsson, condemned to death, manages to obtain an acquittal by composing an intricate panegyric for the king.

Nowadays, a poetry as restrictive, artificial and formally oriented as skaldic poetry is does not easily find a favourable opinion. Yet, this form of poetry has been quite influential. First, certain elements lived on in the Icelandic poetic tradition until this century. Thus, they formed a part of the cultural baggage of the Icelandic emigrants. Next, there are indications that certain fundamental aspects of the art of skaldic poetry have once more, in a slightly different form, become relevant in contemporary poetry. For instance, the Canadian poet George Johnston demonstrates what contemporary poets can learn from the art of skaldic poetry, and how it has influenced his own poetry. He points out that "artifice" has acquired a negative meaning in English literature, but at the same time, many North American poets seem caught in what he calls a "sameness," and are uncertain of or limited by their rhythms. His own reliance on the skaldic poets he explains as follows:

Chiefly, effort, however seemingly mechanical, is imaginatively productive. Also, an established form is not restrictive but, on the contrary, full of variety. More specifically, I learned that the metres, syllable-counting, internal rhyme, and alliteration of the scalds were useful in modern English, in whose bone structure Old Germanic characteristics remain. (1982: 6)

OLD ICELANDIC PROSE

Eddic and skaldic poetry rank high, but the peak of literary achievement was undoubtedly reached during the thirteenth century when the major Icelandic sagas were recorded. Indeed, it is remarkable how an isolated, newly-founded nation that had already made itself famous for its poetic exploits at the courts of western and northern Europe should come to excel equally in the composition of such extremely intricate and rule-based poetry and in the plain prose style and mundane subject matter of the sagas. Part of the explanation may be found in considering the settlement history of Iceland and the society that developed from it.

We know that alliterative poetry and song were the "annals" of the pre-literate Germanic peoples, their main vehicle of memorization and all formal expression, whether pragmatic, historical, or literary. Indeed, scholars of oral literature such as Hofman (1977) and Ong (1982) have pointed out that these three features were undifferentiated in oral culture. No clear distinction was made between recent and past events, nor between which part was the result of eye-witness accounts and which was personal opinion or artistic invention.[5] Skaldic poetry developed out of this tradition, and with it an emphasis on form: the function of its content was mixed with, and often overshadowed by, the pleasure the Northern people took in exercises of wit. The strict formal rules that developed made sure that most poems or verses were memorized correctly. In this way they became an excellent means for the oral transmission and preservation of news fragments, but not for narrative.[6]

The traditional alliterative metres such as *fornyrðislag* had been suited to the indivisibility of form and content. With the development of skaldic poetry, form became the main focus of attention. Understandably, the *fornyrðislag* seemed insufficient to express in narrative form the new situation in which the Icelanders found themselves. They needed a new narrative medium tailored to express their experiences in a new country, a new way of life and new developments in society. Prose turned out to be a more suitable medium: its plain, unmetrical directness was an excellent counterpoint to the ornate, grand and aristocratic nature of skaldic poetry, and fully appropriate for the largely unstratified farmers' society that the Icelanders had built up. It was a completely fresh medium for the artistic, vernacular expression of the daily experiences of individuals and families in a rural society. As Auden observed: "Nothing like them [the sagas], as far as I know, had ever been attempted in western literature before, and in the rest of Europe, nothing similar can be found before the end of the eighteenth century" (1968: 59).

Of course, the idea of using prose to this effect did not come to the Icelanders out of the blue. It developed almost naturally out of the cultural developments in Iceland and abroad. Ari inn fróði ("the learned") established a written native prose tradition when he wrote the *Íslendingabók* (a short history of Iceland) at the beginning of the twelfth century. Ari was in this respect a child of his time with regard to his interest in chronological and annalistic documentation, his methods and his critical use of sources. After all, the twelfth century was, in the words of the historian who rehabilitated this period in European history, "one of the great periods of mediaeval historiography" (Haskins 1927: 224). Ari's work bears testimony to the fact that the Icelanders were well-aware of cultural developments in Europe. However, Ari's decision to document the history of his country's settlement and its first years, a history of a rural community without a king, and to do this in the vernacular instead of Latin, is quite remarkable. Contemporary historiographic writing in Europe clearly reflects the highly hierarchical and ecclesiastical structure of European society at the time, and was still mostly written in Latin.[7]

Ari's work attests to the beginning of an Icelandic literary tradition which was rooted in European culture and scholarship, but which did not absorb these influences unchanged.[8] Rather, they were assimilated into a native tradition. In the *Íslendingabók*, Ari traces the genealogies of the settlers back to Norwegian history and briefly accounts the settlement and conversion of Iceland. The choice of subject matter has led to the interpretation among some scholars that Ari wrote this work in order to legitimate wordly and ecclesiastical power in Iceland, as was done elsewhere in Europe (*Bókmenntasaga* 1: 294-95). However, the work is not dedicated to any possible patron, as was the custom, although Ari mentions that two bishops and one chieftain read over earlier drafts of the book. In addition, it seems that the social infrastructure for such legitimation of power had hardly sufficiently developed in Iceland at the time, although this would change. Even if the book would have been used for such purposes, it is quite likely that Ari, being one of the first historiographers, would have been as concerned to provide learned credentials of his country's history in order to claim a place for it among older, established cultures. Certainly Ari's attempt to emphasize that Christians had lived in Iceland before it was settled, in the form of Irish monks who had withdrawn by the time of settlement but had left objects behind, and that the settlers were men and women of noble and ancient lineages, give the impression of a desire to show that Iceland was a respectable, civilized place on both the ecclesiastical and the worldly plane. The fact that the book was written in Icelandic underlines this: it displays confidence in the potential of the language as a medium for scholarship. Moreover, the Icelandic audience it addresses is given a myth of origins in learned prose.

In the course of the twelfth century, vernacular historiography became prominent in Europe, and many chronicles and histories of Icelandic subjects followed Ari's example of a vernacular history of Iceland in the European tradition of learning, such as the *Landnámabók*.[9] At the same time, the influence of Geoffrey of Monmouth's History of the Kings of Britain, *Historia regum Brittanniae* (1135-39), also made itself felt in Iceland. This work showed how the ancient past, ostensibly passed down orally by the people, could be recreated to gain meaning in the present. Its main hero is an individual, Arthur, who is recreated from popular legend to become a mythical leader and founder of a people. Soon, many such histories appeared all over Europe, and the Icelanders were no exception. They may not have had their own king, but they were very active in writing about the kings of Norway and Denmark (the so-called kings' sagas).

The Icelanders also began to write about their own bishops and saints as well as those from other countries.[10] These Icelandic prose works are among the oldest records of vernacular literary works in Scandinavia. They were modelled on European hagiographic writings, but their style and content were adapted to native conditions and taste. As a result, their style is popular and lively, and they tend to be more worldly and realistic than their Latin models. Thus these early religious sagas, as well as the historical writings and kings' sagas, adapted foreign influences to cultural traditions in Iceland. Both types of writing, which were regarded as historiography rather than literature, made possible the development and culmination of a unique literary art form during the thirteenth century: the classical Icelandic saga.

The Sagas of the Icelanders or *Íslendingasögur*, among which are the most famous sagas such as *Njáls saga*, *Laxdæla saga* and *Egils saga*, were written in the thirteenth century. This art form has had a lasting influence on Iceland's cultural history and people to a degree that makes it difficult to imagine the extent of its impact, not least among the Icelanders who emigrated to Canada. Suffice it to say that when Jón Árnason, the Grimm of Iceland, started collecting folk tales, he was often driven to despair by the many informants, mostly farmers and farmers' wives, who wrote down folk tales in perfect saga style. Alver, in a discussion of folklore as a national symbol of the people, remarks: "Iceland ... has such a strong literary tradition that nothing can compete with the sagas as national symbol. We can take comfort in the fact that the sagas are poetry rooted in folk tradition" (1989: 19). Alver here equates Iceland's literary tradition with the sagas, an indication of their impact over the centuries.

The classical sagas exhibit an objective, terse, sober and factual prose style. At the same time, however, this style is so skilfully employed as to call up vivid scenes and character portrayals, and the use of detail is such that it almost seems to invite one to look beyond and add imaginatively to what is left out (Pálsson and Edwards 1970: 2). Although the focus of the sagas is almost invariably on the actions and attitudes of individuals, their thoughts and motivations are seldom given. Descriptions are mostly external, with the addition of some general personal characteristics. Characters speak through their deeds, and it is left to the audience to judge them. Consequently, the sagas excel in a vivid dramatic quality and feature a series of impressive and unforgettable characters.

In contrast to their style, the subject matter of the sagas is generally elusive. In general, one could say that the sagas combine nearly all major native elements, both traditional and immigrant. Whereas they focus on Icelandic subject matter, notably the settlement age, they exhibit at the same time many older, traditional elements. First, they embody the northern Germanic heroic mentality: a character's courage is pitted against great odds, and he must prove his worth by asserting free will, independence and invincibility of spirit against fate. As Gordon has described it:

The heroic problem of life lay primarily in the struggle for freedom of will, against the pains of the body, and the fear of death, against fate itself. The hero was in truth a champion of the free will of man against fate, which had power only over material things. He knew he could not save his body from destruction but he could preserve an undefeated spirit, if his will were strong enough. So the hero resisted to the end, and won satisfaction from fate, in being master of his life while he had it.... It was better to die resisting than to live basely. (1957: xxx)

This explains why the sagas are mainly tragedies. The powerful strain of fatalism which is so bound up with the heroic spirit has a very strong mythical dimension as well. Fate plays a major role in Norse mythology. Some scholars believe that during the last stages of the Viking Age (which included the time when Iceland was settled), or even during the whole of the pagan period in Scandinavia, fate was the only power in which people really believed.[11] A belief in fate still characterizes many Icelanders even after a millennium of Christianity. The heroic and fatalistic spirit of the sagas is reminiscent of the Eddic heroic poems, which carry the oldest inherited memories of the Germanic past. It found its fullest and most unrestricted expression in prose form, however, in the heroic sagas, the *fornaldarsögur*.

Skaldic poetry left its stamp on the sagas in quite a literal way: the sagas used skaldic verses as historical sources or as authorities for certain facts or statements. As was pointed out earlier, skaldic verses were especially suited to preserve brief accounts of events due to their formal complexity, as a result of which they could only be memorized in their original form, as composed by the poets close to the scene of the action. Parts of some sagas were even built around certain verses. A third traditional source the sagas have made use of is that of folk-belief and folk tales, most of which carried leftovers of paganism or other supernatural elements.

The sagas were, then, steeped in traditions the Icelanders had brought from the old country. Yet, the sagas looked to new circumstances for source and inspiration. The conditions in immigrant Iceland helped create a literature of which the thematic concerns differed considerably from those found in contemporary European literary works. Secular European literature consisted of either folk tales or of accounts that bear a heavily aristocratic, political stamp: heroes of noble birth fight for, sometimes even sacrifice themselves for, the service of God or authority or the good of a strictly hierarchal society. The sagas, however, treat individuals defending the honour of themselves and their families, thereby upholding the morality of a small rural society that is widely scattered, largely democratic and has no formal power system. Slaves had initially been brought along to Iceland with the immigrant families, but since it turned out to be more expensive to keep slaves than to allow them their freedom, they were a short-lived phenomenon there. In such a society, the men of high class, the women, the landowners and peasants, all had to work to make a living and to build up a new society. This situation hardly promoted the development of a class system or strong patriarchy.

Having established a society different from others, including the one from which they came, the Icelanders became highly conscious of the structures that maintained that society. They needed to make up for family ties that had been severed with migration. Moreover, everybody had been, and was, involved in the new and largely equal society which, in order to work, depended on its members' involvement and sense of social responsibility. In his discussion of the sagas in the light of the unique society they portray, Auden coined some very useful terms. He said:

The combination of these factors created, for the first and last time in civilized history, a rural democracy: elsewhere, democracy has always been an urban phenomenon. It is not difficult to see why such conditions make a literature of Social Realism possible, and might even suggest the idea of writing it.... Again, in a small almost classless society, and only in such, is it possible to portray realistically the whole of society. (1968: 63)

For the same reason, it was possible to portray characters as rounded, imperfect individuals, fully human and yet recognized only in small, classless communities.

In his discussion of the scholarly debates over the sagas, Jesse Byock has introduced a new approach to saga literature.[12] He suggests that we look at the circumstances in which the sagas originated: a newly-created immigrant society. Since everybody was involved in this society, he proposes that the sagas follow a pattern based on a model of social behaviour. People had built up this unique system, it was a common concern. Consequently, the new Icelanders would have been interested and able to tell each other about how their social system worked in different cases. As Byock points out:

Most narratives of the sagas of the Icelanders deal with material which concerns decision-making, including speculations about moral and ethical topics. It was not only the audience that exerted influence on the saga matter. The narrators themselves came from their ranks. Both the narrator and listener belonged to the same tradition. By splitting up this social environment and looking at the narrator as if he had been a creative writer writing for a small group of literary people, the understanding that we can have of connected medieval sagas which helped people from all layers of the insular society to create a self-image is lost.[13]

The desire of people within a new society to create a self-image is one which is only too familiar to students of immigrant and colonial literatures, and one which received unusually early expression in the sagas. Byock suggests further that the saga-narrator transformed the new social mould into a narrative mould: narrative clusters were combined to make up a longer story, a technique which was built on three narrative parts which he terms conflict, advocacy and solution. In Byock's words: "Taking constant and socially acknowledged behaviour into consideration, the narrator organized these narrative parts in various ways and filled them up with different, often fictive, details. Thus he used these small parts to change a social form over into a narrative form."[14]

The "immigrant nature," so to speak, of saga literature has not been remarked upon only by Byock. Stefanik compares some basic themes and character types in sagas and westerns, and finds that the striking similarities between the two genres stem from the pioneer experience, and from looking back on a heroic formative age when people created laws to stabilize their young nations and fought for justice. Their heroes are, according to Stefanik:

Symbolic culture heroes ... who are larger than life; yet they confront the typical problems of life in these societies and cope with them in ideal ways; or they clearly show up the limits to which a man, even if he is a chieftain-hero, may reach in such a society but which he may not overstep. This might be termed the epic function of the Saga and Western. Both genres serve as vehicles of social comment, as instruments of self-analysis, as a means of constantly re-defining and reinterpreting the Old Icelandic way of life and the American way respectively. (1976: 63)

Durrenberger has likened the Icelandic saga heroes to "natural existentialists"; he attributes this similarity to their life in a new country with an inhospitable environment where they could rely on nothing but themselves. As the pagan system formed part of the social order, not an ideology demanding conformism, people believed mainly in themselves, their own might and main, wit and strength, and did not rely on gods. Having created their laws themselves, people were willing to assume total responsibility for both their own actions and for the execution of those laws. Durrenberger regards the assumption of such responsibility together with the importance of personal honour and exemplary behaviour as being strongly in line with the views of existentialists like Sartre and Camus. He sees the heroism of saga characters as forced upon them by the unromantic, impoverished circumstances they found themselves in:

Their heroism is not in their deeds, but in their approach to life, an approach they did not choose, for there were no alternatives. They were heroes in the same sense that other people of stateless societies are, people who struggle to create meaning rather than to accept it as created; people who confront each other in human terms rather than through bureaucratic structures; people who must live with the consequences of their actions. (1984: 8)

Lönnroth (1970) has analyzed elements of "rhetorical persuasion" in the sagas, claiming that the saga narrators are not as objective as they seem, although they are more restrained than was common in medieval literature: by means of devices he terms "staging" and "stylistic variation," Lönnroth regards the narrator as one who establishes community values. Once again, we notice an emphasis on the social system, which was naturally of great importance to any new society that needs to see its values established, recreated in literature, and its stability maintained.

Icelandic literature developed and thrived in many directions, all of them in one way or another influenced by the fact of Iceland's settlement and its foundation of a new, unique social system. The conscious urge to prove itself equal to more established cultures, the obvious ambition to be well-versed both in ancient Scandinavian lore and contemporary classical European learning, and the concern and pride in native achievement, can all be related to the dynamics of the immigrant experience. Out of the combination of European and native culture, of old and new traditions, grew a prose literature completely new and Icelandic, reflecting the immigrant experience of making a living in a new environment and building a new society.

The writing of the *Íslendingasögur* continued until the fourteenth century. Beside them another type of sagas developed, the *fornaldarsögur* or "sagas of ancient times." These, one could say, continued in prose the narratives found in the Eddic poems in everything but style: they are heroic legends set in different countries and are full of the marvellous and the supernatural. It is quite possible that they are derived from a native story-telling tradition which celebrated ancient heroes and exaggerated their feats and adventures. The *riddarasögur* or romances came to gain great popularity during the fourteenth century and remained popular for centuries. Icelandic prose versions of such popular European literature as the *lais, chansons de geste*, etc., they adopted Icelandic saga and folk tale motifs, and combined them with foreign motifs, primarily French and classical, adapted to Icelandic taste.[15]

The romances have nothing of the native *Íslendingasögur*'s factual, terse style. They are characterized instead by fantasy-like and ornamental qualities, and have many features in common with what we know today as light or popular literature. Indeed, the romances have enjoyed a continuous popularity in spite of severe criticism of their lack of literary qualities. The *riddarasögur* reached their height of popularity during the fourteenth and fifteenth centuries, at a time when Icelandic society had seen many fundamental changes. Iceland had lost its independence in 1262-64 to Norway, although it had been allowed a certain degree of Home Rule, and in 1380 it came, along with Norway, under Danish rule. Consequently, Iceland now owed both obedience and taxes to a foreign king, and the Church had by this time become a major landholder and levied taxes. These changes were merely the inevitable outcome of the impossibility of Iceland's social structure within the larger European social and economic framework, which had become increasingly hierarchical and complex. Iceland was now quickly developing a class system, helped by economic changes, royal authority, and the growing power of the Church. Wealth became increasingly concentrated in ever-fewer hands, while the Black Death, which ravaged Iceland from 1402 until 1404, left a large number of survivors without possessions. Little wonder, then, that the Icelanders felt no particular urge to use these circumstances as a source of inspiration to create innovative or realistic literature. While the wealthy were interested in the foreign types of literature they encountered in trading centres in Norway, Germany and England, the poor preferred escapism, a dream world to brighten up reality. The *riddarasögur*, and the influence they had on later Icelandic poetry and folklore, would also in future centuries help to keep the interest of an impoverished nation in its literature awake and alive.

POST-MEDIEVAL ICELANDIC LITERATURE

Throughout their history the Icelanders have been described as an exceptionally literate people.[16] Indeed, as we saw earlier, nearly all cultural achievements of the early Icelanders were within the field of literature. Although the quality of Icelandic literature declined after the "golden age," literature remained the primary focus of Icelandic artistry on all social levels. Turville-Petre explained the literary nature of Icelandic culture as follows:

Scandinavians of the Viking Age, as indeed of earlier ages, had excelled as visual artists, as is proved by their sculpture, metal-work, and tapestry. But the Icelanders of early times showed little talent in these arts, partly, no doubt, because their volcanic stone was unfit for carving, they had little timber, and no natural source of metal. From the first, the Icelanders found artistic expression in words, and it was the art of poetry and perhaps of story-telling, rather than of sculpture and metal-working, that the settlers brought with them. (1953: 7)

This lack of other means for artistic expression became even more acute after the fifteenth century. Economic decline and loss of political independence robbed Iceland of the ruling class it had gradually begun to develop. One positive consequence of these difficult circumstances was that, under foreign rule, Icelandic society remained largely egalitarian. Moreover, the Reformation promoted the teaching of reading and writing among the people. As a result, literacy remained fairly widespread compared to other European nations at the time. Among the illiterate, poetry and stories circulated orally as they had since the settlement age. Literary activity in Iceland, therefore, never became the exclusive occupation of a literate ruling class. Consequently, the Icelandic literary tradition and folk tradition were closely and inextricably connected; they depended on one another.

In view of this, Sigurður Nordal once made the following claim:

It would not be an absurdity to call Icelanders the most literary nation in the world—not in that they have created the largest number of masterpieces, although they have come a remarkably long way in this respect—but in that no other nation has, proportionally, given literature so much of its strength, so much of its love and affection, no nation has looked so generally to literature for satisfaction and stamina. Possibly the history of mankind does not hold a more palpable example of the extent to which intellectual activity can be a resource of energy and rejuvenation, even when some of the works that are composed, learnt and read, are neither difficult in subject matter nor perfect in form.[17]

Of course, the lengths to which Nordal goes here in his nationalist enthusiasm must be taken with a few generous grains of salt, for this article was written during a time when Iceland was engaged in a national effort to back up its claim for complete independence from Denmark. However, the basic point of Nordal's statement, his emphasis on the continuity of the Icelandic literary tradition and its roots among the common people, is important because the influence of this continuity has often been ignored. It has been, moreover, a considerable formative influence on the development of Icelandic-Canadian culture and literature. Although this period between the fifteenth and the nineteenth century did not produce any major literary works of art, it made possible the cultural revival that took place at the time of emigration.

THE REFORMATION AND ITS LITERARY INFLUENCES

When Iceland officially adopted Christianity, it did so mainly for socio-political and economic reasons. The decision was made to keep unity within the country, to ward off any missionary attacks from the Norwegian king, and to be able to continue trade and other relations with Norway. Pagan people were allowed to practice their religion in the privacy of their homes. The Church and her bishops had very little power to begin with, and although they would eventually gain more, they encountered many difficulties along the way. For many years, paganism and Christianity co-existed, and, being so far removed from Rome's influential sphere, a special type of Icelandic Christianity could develop which incorporated many pagan elements, most importantly from folk-belief, into the Christian religion. This was also one of the conditions which made possible the writing of vernacular, secular prose by clerics. It was only in the fourteenth century that the Church began to gain a strong foothold and exert a larger influence.

The Reformation took place in Iceland during the sixteenth century. The new faith was decreed by the Danish king in 1537, and the last Catholic Bishop, Jón Arason, was beheaded in 1550. The two, now Lutheran, Bishops of Iceland were faced with having to spread the new doctrine and oust the old one among a widely-scattered population which had traditionally practised religion mostly at home owing to the isolation of the farms, bad roads, and weather conditions. Moreover, by nature and tradition the Icelandic people were not much given to dogma and they had continued to regard religion largely as a private relationship between man and his god, as it had been in pagan days.

The fact that Lutheranism finally did take root in Icelandic society was largely the work of three remarkable men, Bishop Guðbrandur Þorláksson and the two pastors Jón Vídalín and Hallgrímur Pétursson. The medium they chose was, inevitably, literature. In retrospect, Guðbrandur Þorláksson must have had an extraordinarily strong sense of how to build a foundation for the new religion in Iceland. The choice of well-written poems of artistic value rather than badly translated texts as a medium would be the only way to appeal to a people traditionally involved in the composition and transmission of literature. Bishop Guðbrandur exercised a virtual monopoly over Iceland's only printing press, and many religious works were published and distributed during his years, including his edition of the whole Bible in 1584. Previously, in 1540, the New Testament had been translated and published in Copenhagen by Oddur Gottskálksson. It was the first printed Icelandic book. The fact that the Icelanders had a Bible in their own language has contributed significantly to the survival of Icelandic as a living, creative language under foreign domination.

Bishop Guðbrandur attempted to provide his people with appealing hymns that were easily learned, and to introduce a corpus of religious poetry to the Icelandic canon in the expectation that it would completely replace the secular. To this purpose he even included some older Catholic poems in his collection of religious poetry. However, his purpose, eventually to eliminate all secular poetry in favour of religious poetry and "improve" the people's taste with more elevating literary fare, soon turned out to be impossible. In his religious fervour, he failed to understand that popular taste cannot easily be dictated. Although Bishop Guðbrandur's efforts played an important part in introducing new elements into Icelandic literature and distributing them among the parishes, the religious works that came from his press could not even begin to compete with the popularity of secular literature.

In the meantime, circumstances in sixteenth-century Iceland had rapidly deteriorated. With the official change from Catholicism to

Lutheranism, the Icelandic Church had lost all her possessions to the Danish king, who now owned almost one sixth of all the land in Iceland, and all commission and taxes went straight into the Danish treasury. In 1602, the king declared the infamous Danish trade monopoly with Iceland. As a result, Iceland became totally dependent on the goods the Danish merchants chose to bring and the prices they chose to ask for them. Never before had the Icelanders been so utterly at the mercy of a foreign authority. As Iceland's climate is harsh and the amount of fertile land limited, its population relied on imports, especially in the event of crop failure. A simultaneous deterioration of the climate meant that starvation occurred when the annual cargo from Denmark was insufficient to ensure survival or proved too expensive. To make matters worse, the Danes proclaimed the draconian *stóridómur* ("great verdict"), the penalties of which for moral crimes were extremely severe.

The consequent atmosphere was one of oppression, poverty and despair. All resistance and all will towards improvement was slowly being squeezed out of the people. Before the Reformation they had been able to fall back on the belief in saints as helpers and mediators. Now there was only the belief in original sin, an ever-angry God and the prospect of hell, the picture of which was repeatedly described in all its gory details by over-zealous pastors. The Icelanders, in other words, had no recourse, since the hopelessness weighing them down in their daily lives was given institutional form in the body of the Church, which, instead of providing spiritual comfort and help, created a general sense of fear and punishment to match their worldly reality. Literature, however, provided an exception. This age brought forth two of the most influential literary figures in Icelandic literary history since the age of the classical saga: Hallgrímur Pétursson and Jón Vídalín. These two writers, both pastors who followed the direction Bishop Guðbrandur had indicated, exerted a great literary influence. Bishop Guðbrandur had done his utmost to introduce a new type of poetry into Icelandic literature, contemporary Lutheran poetry rooted in the German literary tradition. Previously, Icelandic poetry had assimilated foreign influences by adapting them to a native poetic tradition with pagan roots. Moreover, Icelandic translators had always been very free in their interpretations of original texts in order to make them more understandable and attractive to an Icelandic audience. This was no longer possible: poetic forms that carried pagan remnants were considered unacceptable after the

Reformation, and within the Lutheran tradition, textual truthfulness was considered a divine duty as writers were dealing with the word of God. As a result, Icelandic poetic forms and diction had to be adapted to a completely new, foreign tradition with a strong lyrical strain, metres unsuited to Icelandic speech rhythms, and imagery that reflected a religion not yet rooted in Iceland (*Bókmenntasaga* 2: 389-435). Obviously, this could not be accomplished overnight.

A hundred years later, however, the works of Hallgrímur Pétursson and Jón Vídalín accommodated these modes of expression and recreated them into Icelandic literature of great power and beauty which was readily adopted into the popular body of literature. It was not only their literary talents that earned them this popularity, however, but also their messages of hope and support, springing from a profound sympathy and understanding of the conditions people lived in.

RELIGIOUS POETRY: HALLGRÍMUR PÉTURSSON

Hallgrímur Pétursson (1614-1674)[18] was a prolific poet who wrote various kinds of poetry, yet he is mainly known for his *Passíusálmar* ("Hymns of the Passion"). The *Passíusálmar* have seen almost ninety editions since their first publication. Hallgrímur's enduring popularity is a testimony to the fact that out of despair the most exalted art can grow, because the hymns are very much a product of their time as well as a personal expression of hope and suffering. His poetic genius enabled him to lift a mundane subject matter, sprung from the miserable reality of his age, to a level of universal hope.

His interest in and great knowledge of Icelandic classical literature, and his fierce polemical poems against both worldly and clerical leaders gave Hallgrímur's poetry a unique extra dimension and made it popular among the Icelandic people. Moreover, Hallgrímur was steeped in both past and present, native and foreign traditions, and this duality made his poetry innovative. It paved the way for a new direction in Icelandic poetry.

The greatest appeal of the *Passíusálmar* is perhaps the fact that in them Hallgrímur created an image of Jesus synonymous with the suffering people of his nation, and a context recognizable for every seventeenth-century Icelander whose own daily world was filled with enmity, fear, punishment and pain. The narrator is so personally involved with his subject and follows Jesus so closely on his road of suffering that it often becomes difficult to distinguish the two. As the narrator blends in with the figure of Jesus, both come to personify the agony of the Icelandic people.

Hallgrímur's transformation of the story of the passion into an actuality, where Jesus becomes one of the common people who shares their misery on earth, also held a message of hope and consolation: each single step Jesus takes towards his enemies' victory is depicted as one towards redemption and the victory of good over evil. The solace the poet offers through his art is an almost solitary phenomenon in an age characterized by foreign oppression and the threat of divine retribution.

RELIGIOUS PROSE: JÓN VÍDALÍN

The same heights of popularity which Hallgrímur Pétursson had reached in religious poetry were reached by Bishop Jón Vídalín (1666-1720) in religious prose. As the people knew Hallgrímur's poems by heart, so they knew whole passages from Jón's sermons. Jón Vídalín, together with Hallgrímur, formed the final step toward the actual root-taking and acceptance of Lutheranism in Iceland. Hallgrímur had shown the people that the Lutheran faith could inspire poetry of high quality and deep feeling; Jón Vídalín showed how it could work in an Icelandic context and in Icelandic circumstances, and how it could help the Icelandic people.

As was mentioned earlier, the isolation and harsh climate meant that a large part of religious practice necessarily took place in people's homes. After the Reformation, this observance at home received much more attention, as the people needed to be taught the new doctrine to replace the old one. Since the beginning of Iceland's history, the *kvöldvaka* had been a daily tradition on the farms: at dusk outside jobs were abandoned and people gathered in the main room to continue work inside, while one of them would read out loud or tell stories. This was where the old literature was passed on and new literature created. Obviously, if the new doctrine was to be spread among the people, the way to do it was to make Lutheran works part of the *kvöldvaka*. At the same time the Church aimed at eradicating people's interest in worldly literature in this manner.

By the time Jón Vídalín took his vows, many books containing sermons, religious reflections and theological interpretations had been distributed, and the *húslestur* (lit. "house-reading"), the reading of a religious passage followed by discussions and prayer, had become an important part of the *kvöldvaka*. All these religious works were translations from German and Danish books, however, and most of them were highly doctrinal, aimed at a foreign audience, and badly translated.

Jón Vídalín became bishop in 1697, and the work that made him influential was a collection of sermons meant for the *húslestur*, published in two parts in 1718-20, and generally known as the *Vídalínspostilla*. The general estimation seems to be that, since its first publication, nearly every farm in Iceland possessed a copy of the *Vídalínspostilla*. For a collection of sermons amongst a people who consider the private relationship between man and God the main issue in religion and all public formalities (including dogma) a side issue, this is no small achievement (Finnbogason 1971).

Nearly all studies that have appeared on the *Vídalínspostilla* deal with the same issues: its influence, and how Jón Vídalín managed to create such a popular collection of sermons. The basis of Jón's influence and popularity lies in his rhetorical genius, followed closely by his logical, clear reasoning and his awareness of Icelandic realities. Jón Vídalín was a man of intelligence and learning who possessed a quality for which a great traditional respect exists in Iceland: *orðsnilld*, or eloquence, particularly an eloquence infused with practical wisdom. He gained himself the name *Meistari Jón* ("Master Jón"), in acknowledgement of the respect and appreciation in which he was held.

The major importance of Jón Vídalín's oratory within the development of Icelandic culture is that the language used in the *Vídalínspostilla* is, on the whole, very much the living language of its times, although much of the figurative speech and ideas have their basis in Latin and Greek and Church culture. In Jón's days, the official language used was stilted and increasingly influenced by Danish and German. The *Postilla* showed that the living Icelandic language was capable of expressing new currents and ideas without these influences.

The contents of Jón's sermons are, naturally, based on the orthodox Lutheranism of his times, yet in some respects Jón Vídalín was quite unorthodox. As several Icelandic scholars have pointed out, Jón Vídalín had been influenced in his ideas by the radical, pietistic work called *The Whole Duty of Man*, attributed to the English theologian Richard Allestree, which first appeared in English in 1658 and which Jón had translated into Icelandic (Þorleifsson 1945;

Halldórsson 1977; Einarsson 1961). From this work he adopted the view that man himself can work towards his own redemption. Thus Jón Vídalín disseminated a much-needed optimistic doctrine, teaching his parishioners that they could save themselves from eternal damnation, rather than emphasizing only man's hopelessness. This was something the people understood, needed and appreciated.

Although Jón Vídalín did not make any use of the classical Icelandic literature in his *Postilla*,[19] the context and atmosphere in his sermons are firmly rooted in Icelandic reality. The moral climate he envisions and criticizes is Icelandic, and his aphorisms became generally used proverbs. In short, Jón Vídalín's work constituted a final step in the naturalization of Lutheranism in Iceland and gave a new dimension to the Icelandic language as used in a Lutheran religious context.

SECULAR POETRY: *RÍMUR*

The most consistent element in the continuity of Icelandic literature, and the main poetic specialty of the Icelanders are the *rímur* (lit. "rhymes"). *Rímur* were composed from the fourteenth to the twentieth century by every Icelander with any interest in the composition of poetry, but they flourished mostly in the eighteenth and nineteenth century. *Rímur* are narrative poems which combine a popular story line with a highly intricate style and diction that are a continuation of skaldic poetry to a degree, but modified by foreign elements and generic rules dictated by the narrative.[20]

During the first two centuries, *rímur* were composed by anonymous authors. We may assume therefore that the *rímur* were regarded as nothing more than a popular form of entertainment. After the Reformation, poets gradually shifted the focus of their art from telling a story in verse to virtuoso displays of metre and diction. The form of the *rímur* became increasingly complicated, and kennings and other kinds of flowery language began to predominate as they had in the days of skaldic poetry. The narrative was now divided into several groups (*rímnaflokkar*), each of which was composed in a different metre, and introduced by a kind of prologue called the *mansöngur* (pl. *mansöngvar*, from the German *Minnesang*). While in the *rímur* themselves the poet was bound to the storyline, the *mansöngvar* served as a medium for the poet's own message. Originally, they had been used as praise or love poems, but more and more they became a medium for personal or philosophical views and criticisms. Although *rímur* retained their original function of popular entertainment, strict formal rules had made their composition a special art. As a result, the poets' pride in their achievement grew and they started to put their names to their poems. The narratives that were used to compose *rímur* were mostly taken from the sagas, sometimes from kings' sagas and *Íslendingasögur*, but most from *fornaldarsögur* and *riddarasögur*. Some poets also used other foreign tales, for instance "Persíus rímur," based on Ovid's *Metamorphoses*, and *Pontus rímur*, based on the popular German story *Pontus und Sidonia* published in 1483 (Halldórsson 1977: 4; *Bókmenntasaga* 2: 518). We also find folk tale motifs in certain *rímur*, and even polemic *rímur* exist.

The composition and recital of *rímur* developed into a kind of national sport, and for centuries they remained the most popular form of poetry. The increasing emphasis on form gradually turned the *rímur* into mechanical pieces of rhyming without any feeling or inspiration, and with the exception of a few better pieces, most of them are hardly notable poetry. Yet they played a very important part in the literary history of Iceland in more than one respect. First, both the content and the form of the *rímur* ensured that the Icelandic past remained a living part of the present. Second, they provided an opportunity for a people dulled by poverty and misery to retain a form of culture and a sense of beauty, even though the cultural and aesthetical expression was constrained by the formal strait-jacket of the *rímur*. Given the desperate circumstances then obtaining, other poetic forms requiring personal expression would have set free a flood of despair, whereas the strict *rímur* rules provided a form of mental gymnastics which kept the intellect in shape. Third, the Icelanders retained a high command of their language. Fourth, the *rímur* were, together with the folk tales, the most important artistic expression of the people, and as such they have proved an important factor in the continuity of Icelandic literature.

Sigurður Nordal has given an apt description of the role of the *rímur* in Icelandic literary culture:

Icelandic *rímur* are probably the most absurd example of literary conservatism that has ever been noted. It can be said that they remain unchanged for five whole centuries although everything around them changes. And although they frequently have little poetic value and sometimes even border on complete tastelessness, they have demonstrated with their tenacity that they satisfy the needs of the nation peculiarly well. They have brought the people stories that delighted them, in a form that was pleasing to the ear and demanded attention and understanding. They gave each versifier an opportunity to practice his sport, without demanding imagination or originality from him. They were an industry rather than an art.... But industry has always paved the way for art, and if a spark is kept alive, it can always grow into a bonfire. The *rímur* have kept the language rich and in practice, have increased the people's knowledge and understanding of all its resources. Their affinity with skaldic poetry is best brought out by the new metre they have given the Icelandic people for the *lausavísur*, even more perfect than the old classical metres. Four-lined *lausavísur* began to appear during the latter part of the sixteenth century and have hardly flourished more than they do nowadays.[21]

Lausavísur are quatrains in *rímur* metres composed on the occasion, and usually on the spot, of any opportunity which strikes the poet. As Nordal pointed out, they are still very popular. *Rímur* and especially *lausavísur* were also very popular among the Icelandic immigrants in Canada, where they formed an important link with the Icelandic cultural heritage (see Chapter III).

SECULAR PROSE: FOLK TALES

While the *rímur* served the function of exercising the wit and providing a sense of formal aesthetics, the folk tales constituted an outlet for the deepest wishes and feelings of the people. The sagas and *Landnámabók* are living proof that folk tales already occupied an important place in the Icelandic literary tradition at the time of settlement.[22] Folk tales began to be collected on a large scale under the influence of the Grimm brothers in Germany. The first scholarly conducted collection was undertaken by Jón Árnason (1819-1888). He was greatly stimulated and supported by the German scholar Konrad Maurer, who organized the publication of the collection in Leipzig in 1862-64. Although this publication gave rise to a still ongoing series of collections and publications of folklore, numbering up to a hundred or more to the present day, the Jón Árnason collection has so far stood unsurpassed.

Initially, Jón Árnason encountered minor resentment and lack of co-operation due to the indignation of the Church at superstition, the scorn of the Rationalist movement, and to the reserve of the people engendered by their fear of ridicule at their superstition. However, the great public support given to Jón Árnason's work by the father of Iceland's independence, Jón Sigurðsson (1811-1879), helped create a general interest in the project, and gradually Icelandic folk tales came to be regarded and cherished as a national treasure, the reflection and property of the whole Icelandic nation and its history.[23] Indeed, considering the largely egalitarian nature of Icelandic society and culture, this view is not completely unfounded. Many people could read if not write, and were engaged in some form of literary activity, to a degree rarely found in other European countries. As a result, Icelandic folk tales have a far more literary quality, and, additionally, reflect a greater national unity since the nation as a whole was pitted against foreign oppression rather than divided into classes pitted against each other.

The Russian structuralist Vladimir Propp demonstrated earlier this century that folk tales all over the world contain similar structural or narrative patterns and motifs. At the same time, however, these universal tales containing universal themes and patterns are clad in local costumes. Bynum (1978) makes the following remark on the subject of oral narrative patterns: "One must unavoidably deal with fable in its parochial manifestations, because every text of oral fable comes from some particular storyteller in some particular language at some particular time and place. Generic motifs and the designs that hold them together exist only in their myriad parochial variants where fable is actually composed" (78). Although the basic themes of Icelandic folk tales are not unique, it is the various "parochial manifestations" of these basic themes that are of interest in the context of Icelandic-Canadian literature. It is, after all, the folk tales that can provide us with a clearer idea of what gives Icelandic-Canadian works their particular "parochial" or "ethnic" flavour.

CHARACTERISTICS OF ICELANDIC FOLK TALES

Like the *rímur*, Icelandic folk tales bear in many ways the traces of the harsh, often miserable conditions under which their makers and tellers lived, especially during the seventeenth and eighteenth centuries. Many folk tales that emerged at this time reflect the extremism of ideas, which Böðvar Guðmundsson describes so well in the *Bókmenntasaga*:

Thus the age of learning [1550-1750] was made up of different and often incompatible ideas, where individuals were in one word referred to the marvels of creation and in the next forbidden to enjoy them, where it was considered uplifting for man's soul to liken oneself to a dog or swine and at the same time remember that he had been created in God's image, where Satan was at one moment the enemy of God and all His children and at the next he was His creation, instrument and servant.[24]

People were ruled by fear and impotent rage, taking refuge in magic to protect and avenge themselves, at least in their imagination. Hence the name *galdraöld* ("age of witchcraft") given to the seventeenth century. During the eighteenth century, a slight apparent improvement was outweighed by a smallpox epidemic, official corruption, and volcanic eruptions. At the same time, however, the Icelandic people still lived with the sagas in their minds, educating themselves as best they could with help from pastors who were concerned with their abilities to read God's word. Although the country had sunk into physical and mental degradation, it remained steeped in its native culture and familiar with literary style and form.

The background of the larger part of Icelandic folk tales shows a people living in a rugged landscape, enduring an extreme climate, eking a solitary and bare existence off the land and the ocean. No urban centres existed. Iceland's was still a totally agricultural society, and nearly all Icelanders, even many pastors, were farmers, or participated in farming life. Fishing was an extra source of income on the side, not a separate profession. If the Danes are discounted, Auden's description (quoted earlier) of medieval Iceland as a "rural democracy" would also apply to Iceland in later years. The main differentiation in social status, according to Tomasson (1980: 47-49), was that between the educated and uneducated.

Besides being a great source of entertainment, Icelandic folk tales provide a rich source of information on the *Weltanschauung* of the Icelandic people. Hjalti Hugason says: "The religious belief of the people should be seen as a composite system of different and even opposing religious views in which the ideas from pre-Christian times, Catholic medieval views and Lutheran interpretation have been woven together into one compound pattern."[25] Thus, folk tales form a literary repository for the various beliefs and views of the people, both old and new, as much in opposition to as in accordance with the ruling system and its morals. Recent studies have emphasized and analyzed the half-concealed strain of social criticism in many folk tales which, here, function as a literary outlet of the people. These studies draw our attention, for instance, to the views of women and protests against their roles in society.[26] Björn Þorsteinsson has pointed to what he calls rather "daring" elements in folk tales in this respect: he refers to a popular folk tale where the devil is given the role of rector of a Church-run educational institute. Þorsteinsson has characterized the outlook of the folk tale as follows: "The folk tale displays the worldview and view of nature of the child, of the person who is unspoiled by limited scholarship and half-education. In the folk tale are often revealed the clearest poetry and the deepest reality."[27]

One folk-cultural aspect which is important to consider in the view of the "Icelandicness" of folk tales is the age-old belief in and occurrence of what the Icelanders term *dulreynsla*, which may be translated as "psychic experience." Finnbogason is far from being the only one to remark that "the role which these phenomena have always played in the life of our nation is remarkable, what is more, it has for the most part been self-consistent from beginning to end. It is from this role that one of the most peculiar branches of our literature has sprung, our folk-tales."[28] Similarly, a national survey conducted by the University of Iceland in 1975 revealed that about two-thirds of the adult population of Iceland have had psychic experiences, and concluded that "the psychical appears to be a reality also in the thoughts and lives of people today" (Haraldsson 1977: 31). In an article on the results of the survey, it is reported that the most common experiences are psychic dreams, encounters with the dead, and extra-sensory perceptions (also called telepathy or clairvoyance). As I will demonstrate in Chapters III and IV, the phenomenon of psychic experiences, notably psychic dreams, has found expression in both Icelandic and Icelandic-Canadian literature, for, as Turville-Petre remarked: "Among no people in Europe is the cult of dreams so deeply rooted. In no literature are dream-symbols more sophisticated, nor their interpretation more subtle and intricate" (1972: 30).

It has, of course, been pointed out that the use of dreams, especially in Old Norse literature, is at least partly a literary device, but critics seem agreed that the importance that is generally attached to dreams in the sagas, and the extensive use made of dreams (Kelchner mentions 530 in Old Norse literature alone) points to a strong belief in them. Furthermore, folklorists like Chadwick and Sluijter have emphasized that dreams are often presented as a reality: in many cases we need to be told explicitly that we have to do with a dream. Sluijter mentions an example from one of the kings' sagas which shows that dreamlessness in people was considered to be an illness (1936: 40). People who often had portentous dreams were highly respected and often consulted; they were called *draumspakir* ("dream-wise") or *berdreymnir* (clairvoyant, "having clear dreams"), as was, for instance, Njáll in *Njáls saga*.

The persistently strong belief in ghosts in Iceland, expressed in many folk tales, has been attributed to people's fear of the dark during long winter nights spent in isolation, aggravated by mental and physical hardship. Additionally, there was the eerie, open landscape inhabited by howling winds and twisted forms outside, and the "long, dark narrow passages of turf and stone which, in their way, were as choice a haunt of ghosts as the great and gloomy castles of England" (Þorsteinsson 1973: 90). These conditions gave rise to a large diversity of ghost stories among Icelandic folk tales. In many of these tales hatred and fear reign, augmented by envy, greed and stupidity, the latter two always having been despised most by Icelanders. A striking aspect of Icelandic ghosts is that they never lost their tangible, bodily nature. The folklorist Hilda Ellis (later Davidson) has argued that the reality and importance of daily life plus "the Norse passion for turning the abstract and the symbolic into the actual and the concrete can be accounted for the continuing tangible nature of these ghosts" (1943: 147). The most influential and long-lasting among the large range of Icelandic ghosts are probably the personal or family *fylgjur* ("fetches") which follow and haunt a particular individual or family. Some of them became notorious, such as *Írafells-Móri* ("Móri [i.e. masculine fetch] of the people of Írafell"), and a number of them have been reported to have moved along with members of "their" families to Canada.[29] Steingrímur Þorsteinsson has remarked the following about the *fylgjur*: "In Jón Árnason mention is made of 20 such 'fetches,' but there are many more. There is scarcely a district in Iceland without its local ghost. And every family and local ghost has its distinguishing marks, so that one can speak of truly individual and personal ghosts" (1973: 90).

Many Icelandic folk tales express a belief in the magical power of objects. These objects are characteristically objects of learning and literature: verse, certain books, runes and so forth. When one studies the formulas and methods used in magic charms, one finds that they contain a very large number of pagan elements, elements from Old Icelandic literature and runes. As all these sources had been condemned by the Church, they were thought to contain great power, especially when combined with Christian elements. This belief in the power of learning and literature, in the power of the word, gave rise to a phenomenon which is believed to be uniquely Icelandic, the *kraftaskáld* (a poet whose compositions have magic powers).[30] The sagas contain many examples of the physical effects of poetry composed with malicious intentions, which was believed to "bite" the victim. This type of harmful poetry was called *níð*, and heavy penalties were laid down for it in the law. In later years, certain poets were believed to master their art so well that they could work magic with it and disarm evil by the recitation of a poem. Hallgrímur Pétursson was believed to be a *kraftaskáld* and there are many tales about his magical recitations. One of the most famous *kraftaskáld* of the seventeenth century was Jón Guðmundsson, called *lærði* ("the learned") by the people, to the great indignation of many Church servants and formally educated men.[31] Another famous *kraftaskáld* in Icelandic folklore is Kolbeinn *Jöklaskáld* ("Glacier-poet"), who was believed to have outwitted the Devil with his poetry. The Icelandic-Canadian poet Stephan G. Stephansson devoted a long narrative poem to Kolbeinn (see also Chapter III). He once said the following about Kolbeinn: "As distasteful as I find belief in devils, I am nevertheless filled with respect for those men and that nation whose faith in poetry was so great that they dared deliver themselves into the power of what they knew and believed to be the worst of all, with poetry alone as their weapon" (trans. Þorsteinsson 1973: 91).

The influence of literature on Icelandic folk tales has been considerable and far greater than has been the case with folk tales of other nations. This influence shows in the style of the folk tales, as Þorsteinsson has observed:

Embellishment did not appeal to the Icelanders, whose taste had been formed by the plain, objective narrative of the Sagas of the Icelanders. This pithy, laconic style, grounded in a literary tradition of nearly eight centuries, contributed to making the Icelandic folk tales shorter, on the whole, than other Scandinavian or German tales.

But the influence of the saga style extends further. The vocabulary of the tales is larger and richer than might be expected in narratives of this kind, full of proverbial sayings and expressions, and in general more literary than elsewhere. Of course, this is partly due to the writers. But the common people of Iceland have long used a more literary language in their storytelling. (1973: 96)

In addition, we invariably find a very logical reasoning in the folk tales. They exhibit an obvious demand on the part of the audience for clear cause and effect. Matters are not left unsolved, nor are there *deus ex machina* solutions. This points to a direct, strong relationship to reality, also a characteristic of the Icelandic folk tales showing influence from the sagas. Kristinn Andrésson, in a discussion of a novel by Laxness, analyzes the Icelandic requirement of "truth" in literature as being inextricably bound up with identified place names, genealogies and limited exaggeration (1976: 122). In spite of super-natural happenings, invisible worlds and so on, Icelanders seem reluctant to leave the sphere of reality completely. Instead, supernat-ural elements become part of their reality, and seem in many cases to be subject to the same laws as natural phenomena. Not surprisingly, therefore, most folk tales are set in an identifiable framework that serves to ground the reality of supernatural experiences. As in the sagas, such frameworks often consist of genealogies, a familiar locale, verses taught and remembered, or tangible objects left behind.

With regard to humour, two major types may be distinguished. First, there is a continuation of the kind of humour we find in the sagas, in the form of laconic understatement, ironic or witty word-play. Narrators also enjoyed making the most out of a situation which is in itself already comical. Irony and sarcasm are two favourites in this respect.[32] However, in various folk tales this humour is replaced by a more profound tragi-comic strain often approaching the black and the grotesque. Gunnar Benediktsson has analyzed this type of humour as having been the traditional weapon and solace of the Icelandic people in their struggle with oppression and hardship (1950: 238-39). Second, we find the universal theme of poking fun at leaders in the community, such as Danish merchants and pastors, but also at higher and holier servants of God, such as the apostles and saints, the Virgin Mary, and even Jesus himself. The unorthodox lengths to which Icelanders take this kind of humour can be explained by the profound egalitarianism characterizing Icelandic society as a whole: each Icelander regards himself a descendant of a Norwegian chieftain and thus second to none, which makes Icelanders little inclined to respect status.[33]

CREATURES OF THE WILDERNESS: *HULDUFÓLK*, TROLLS AND OUTLAWS

The tales of *huldufólk* ("hidden people") and outlaws together make up the largest part of Icelandic folklore. Belief in these creatures, however, was geographically bound seeing that they were part of the Icelandic landscape, and therefore they could not, ultimately, survive among Icelandic Canadians. Yet even on the Canadian prairies they died, in Magnús Einarsson's words, "a stubborn death" (1991: 404). *Huldufólk* occur in certain Icelandic-Canadian works, notably in Guðrún H. Finnsdóttir's stories (see Chapter III), while outlaws figure prominently in especially W.D. Valgardson's work (Chapter IV). Moreover, the role of these wilderness creatures in Icelandic cosmology is significant for the discussion of mythological aspects in Icelandic-Canadian literature (Chapter IV). I will, therefore, briefly introduce them here in so far as they are relevant to later chapters.

Icelandic elves are named in mythological tales and poems, and it is therefore believed that they were once objects of worship. By the time of the Icelandic settlement, they had already become diminished in status and were soon confused with *landvættir*, spirits of the land. The same process held for the trolls, who are believed to be degenerate forms of the mythological giants. As spirits of the land with mythological associations, the elves and trolls came to inhabit a sphere interposed between human settlement and non-human wilderness. The elves soon became confused with the *huldufólk*, if they were not one and the same thing from the beginning (Aðalsteinsson 1988: 354). They are always referred to as *huldufólk* in folk tales. As the term suggests, they are hidden from man's sight unless they wish to be seen. In contrast to their counterparts in other European countries, these Icelandic elves bear no physical signs of their non-human condition, except for their invisibility. They are exactly like humans in everything, with the exception of their fiercer temper and their supernatural gifts. They are extremely vindictive when wronged, but very generous to those who help them. They live in stones and lead ordinary lives, although they are usually more successful, and therefore richer, than ordinary people.

As the *huldufólk* are a legacy of paganism, the Church often tried to portray them as demonic powers. Some stories still reflect this religious tendency, featuring *huldufólk* as cradle-snatchers or tempters, but most of the stories about them are attractively lyrical. They reflect the wish for company in solitude, and provide touches of feeling, love and beauty in a life devoid of all such things. Many tales tell of love between *huldufólk* and human beings, or of help provided or help requested, in which case the reward is always a precious gift. Some tales tell of the revenge of *huldufólk* after having been wronged. Many tales are interspersed with lyrical verses. The gentle tone and character of these stories and, indeed, of this folk-belief, have made them a favourite, and it seems that the people have always been reluctant to renounce the belief in *huldufólk*. When the Church denounced them, the people responded by making the *huldufólk* Christians. Even this century has shown remarkable examples of a continuing wishful belief in their existence. One famous instance is the re-routing of a section of the national ring-road to avoid the removal of a stone which was believed to house *huldufólk* (Aðalsteinsson 1988: 355). Similarly, belief in them persisted among immigrants in Canada in spite of a changed and unsuitable locale, as we saw earlier.

The trolls are as huge and coarse as the elves are dignified and beautiful. They live in the mountains, and many of them eat human flesh. The so-called "night-trolls" turn to stone when they are caught by daylight: the landscape is full of such troll forms. Most tales are about people being caught by trolls, but some tales also tell of friend-ships between humans and trolls, and the loyalty of trolls in this respect has become proverbial. Although the belief in trolls is long dead, they live on in folk tales and in the form of Grýla, the troll-mother of the Icelandic Christmas lads (*jólasveinar*).

The stories of outlaws, which have their basis in the historical and judicial outlawry sentence that was part of the legal system in Norway and transmitted to Iceland, form a unique group among the Icelandic folk tales. The anthropologist Kirsten Hastrup remarks about the outlawry sentence: "From *Grágás*, the Icelandic law book, we know that outlawry was the strongest possible reaction on behalf of society against individuals who one way or the other upset social order or cultural values" (1986: 305).[34]

Gísla saga Súrssonar is probably the most famous older outlaw saga providing a moving, haunting account of the tragic fate of Gísli. The saga paints a picture of his lonely outlaw existence under the harsh conditions prevalent in Iceland, hunted and rootless, until finally he is killed. Byock points out that the outlaw sagas are the only sagas which deal more with the personalities and psychology of the indi-viduals than with their social dealings and obligations (1982: 192-95). The narrative focusses on the causes and effects of their social failings, for among a small society which recognized law as its only authority there would naturally live a great interest in social deviance or ineptitude and its consequences. These consequences were, necessarily, tragic, for as deviance was regarded as a danger to society, its natural result, expulsion from that society, meant forfeiture of legal protection and community support, and exposure to chaos and wilderness.

How the reality of outlawry and its literary expression in the sagas developed into a popular folk tale tradition which has also found expression in Icelandic-Canadian literature, is best seen by a later transitional work, *Grettis saga*. Still considered one of the Sagas of the Icelanders, *Grettis saga* nevertheless contains an uncommonly large number of folk tale motifs incorporated in many later tales of outlaws. Grettir, who was an outlaw for nineteen years and could only be killed when he had become ill, is no longer simply the noble, tragic outlaw hero whom we find in, for instance, *Gísla saga*. As Hastrup demonstrates, a much greater ambivalence has allowed people to interpret Grettir and his symbolical function in different ways over the centuries.

Grettir's popularity and adaptability is, no doubt, largely due to the many roles he assumes, often conforming to the persona of the trickster figure. Anybody who has read *Grettis saga* will recognize many aspects of Grettir when reading the following characterization that Radin has given in his leading work on the trickster:

He wills nothing consciously. At all times he is constrained to behave as he does from impulses over which he has no control. He knows neither good nor evil yet he is responsible for both. He possesses no values, moral or social, is at the mercy of his passions and appetites, yet through his actions all values come into being. But not only he, so our myth tells us, possesses these traits. So, likewise, do the other figures of the plot connected with him: the animals, the various supernatural beings, and monsters, and man.... Laughter, humour and irony permeate everything Trickster does. The reaction of the audience ... is prevailingly one of laughter tempered by awe. (1956: ix-x)

Indeed, Davidson (1979) has drawn attention to the Norse mythological tricksters, Odin and Loki, as literary models. Additionally, Robert J. Glendinning has studied Grettir's character more particularly in the light of the trickster figure in medieval European literature. He observes:

In looking back on Grettir's character traits, it must be conceded that wit, a sharp tongue, and even guile are characteristics often found in the old saga heroes. Moreover, as an outlaw, Grettir had particular occasion to develop these qualities. But the striking fact about Grettir is that he used his wits less to elude capture than out of sheer waggery. (1970: 61)

Grettir's character, then, and his outlawed condition, as well as the counterpart tricksters in Norse mythology induce us to view Grettir in the light of the trickster figure. Moreover, if we combine some of Karl Kerényi's and Carl Jung's observations of the trickster with Hastrup's analyses, there appears yet another sociological aspect of Grettir as a trickster figure, which will elucidate the further development of the outlaw in popular folklore and cosmology.

Kerényi calls the trickster "the spirit of disorder, the enemy of boundaries," and adds that "nothing demonstrates the meaning of the all-controlling social order more impressively than the religious recognition of that which evades this order" (Radin 1956: 125). The trickster's function, in an archaic society, then, is "to add disorder to order and so make a whole, to render possible, within the fixed bounds of what is permitted, an experience of what is not permitted." His ambiguity is partly explained by his role as a "psychopomp": "messenger and mediator ... hoverer-between-worlds who dwells in a world of his own, a symbol of those divine qualities which transcend mere trickery" (185-89). If we add to Kerényi's insights Jung's observation that the trickster is "both sub-human and superhuman, a bestial and divine being, whose chief and most alarming characteristic is his unconsciousness" (203), we have a psycho-mythological explanation of Hastrup's analysis of Grettir's function and image.

Hastrup argues that Grettir's lasting popularity and relevance within Icelandic folklore and society is due to his function as a mediator between two worlds defined as the social, which is equated with the human sphere, and the non-social, equated with the non-human sphere. These two worlds have their counterparts in Norse mythology in the form of *Ásgarðr*, the realm of the gods of which the human world is a reflection, and *Útgarðr*, the chaotic wilderness outside of that realm. In medieval northern Europe, everything outside the sphere of human society and control was considered "wilderness." Thus, on the mythological plane, the gods, whose existence and that of their civilized and lawful domain are threatened by the doom of destruction in the form of *Ragnarök* (the end of the world in Norse mythology), must continually fight the evil forces from outside which will eventually destroy them.

In his various roles as the outlaw-trickster, Grettir continually crosses the boundaries of the human and non-human, of society and wilderness. He thus continually moves "inside" and "outside." To be able to fulfill this function, Grettir has to play different roles, which Hastrup classifies according to what she calls their "degree of humanity": as a subhuman, Grettir plays in the social sphere the role of the fool or buffoon, the social inadequate, and in the non-social sphere that of the outlaw. As a superhuman, he appears as an exorcist, that is to say a defender of society against evil forces, within the social world; conversely as a culture hero he assumes mythical proportions both resembling the role of Thor as defender of culture and reviving "an old myth of another world of wealth and inexhaustible resources, belonging to non-human space" (294). Kerényi has indeed remarked that when a society is no longer archaic one of the functions the trickster often assumes is that of a culture hero.

What is of concern to us here is the influence of *Grettis saga* and Grettir's image on the popular outlaw tales during the seventeenth century and eighteenth century. These folk tales are, like *Grettis saga*, based on a historical reality and a literary tradition which had developed from it. However, during the later centuries, outlaws became a reality again, although in a slightly different sense: most "outlaws" were in fact people fleeing trials and penalties. During those centuries the *stóridómur* saw to the enforcement of extremely heavy punishments. These fugitives led a hunted existence on the outskirts of the inhabited areas and in the uninhabited interior. Around them tales were spun, patterned on the literary tradition outlined above.

Most outlaw tales tell about either solitary outlaws or outlaw communities located in mysterious, hidden valleys of plenty in the otherwise barren and harsh interior of Iceland. These tales are usually considered the wish-fulfilment of an impoverished peasant society. The hidden valleys offer a bountiful life in freedom, beyond the reach of the ruling foreign powers and social misery. These dreams are clear reflections of a latent hope that a good life could still somehow be found inside Iceland, away from the sphere of the oppressors from "outside." The tales, exemplified by *Grettis saga*, present a positive mirror-image of contemporary Icelandic society. The outlaws frequently take on supernatural qualities characteristic of the other wilderness creatures, the trolls and *huldufólk*, and are therefore both human and superhuman. Social as well as non-social, both in their outlaw-status and in their alternative mirror-image society, they are both inside and apart.

If these outlaws represent the positive aspect, there are a number of other outlaw tales which reflect the dark side of the outlaw-trickster figure and a correspondingly violent projection of Icelandic society. These outlaws attack and rob members of society and often kill as well. Many of these outlaws possess Grettir's legendary troll-like stature and strength, but also his trickster-like baser qualities such as an insatiable appetite (some of them are even cannibals) and limitless greed. Violent and destructive they present a threat to society. The folk tales, in other words, separate the superhuman and the subhuman qualities of the outlaw-trickster into two different types of outlaw tales, the "superhuman" group depicting people's dreams and hopes, the "subhuman" group reflecting their latent but violent bitterness and resentment against a social and judicial system forced upon them, acting out their revenge through tales of outlaws based on real victims of that system.

NOTES

1. For a detailed and up-to-date survey of Icelandic literary history see *Íslensk Bókmenntasaga* 1-3 ([*Bókmenntasaga*]1992, 1993, 1996). For a more elaborate introduction to Icelandic literature in English the reader is referred to Kristjánsson (1988) or Einarsson (1957). Einarsson is still the standard work in English, although it has become outdated in some respects. Kristjánsson is more up-to-date but only deals with Old Icelandic literature.

2. For a collection of recent studies on Eddic poetry see *Edda* (1983).

3. Recently, saga scholars have come to express doubts as to the historicity of certain poetic quotations of which the narrator claims they were external sources but which are suspected to have been composed by later poets or authors. These doubts, however, mostly concern poetic passages which express the emotional states of the protagonist (e.g. in *Gísla Saga* and *Egils Saga*) rather than historical events; see also Dronke (1978); and Poole (1989).

4. For this and a good general introduction to skaldic poetry, see Turville-Petre (1953: 26ff) or Kristjánsson (1988: 83ff).

5. This amalgamation of what nowadays would be called fact and fiction is, according to Steblin-Kamenskij, a characteristic of what he calls "unconscious" (oral or folk) authorship, where "art and truth proper are harmoniously united" (1972). He calls this particular interrelation "syncretic truth." See also Steblin-Kamenskij (1967; 1973). Hallberg (1974) has argued against Steblin-Kamenskij's thesis.

6. This theory has recently been refuted by Lindow (1982), who argues that the fragmentary preservation of the verses has led us to believe that skaldic poetry left no room for narrative, and reckons that skaldic narrative is much like Eddic and saga narrative in its dramatic qualities.

7. From the oldest extant manuscripts we know that it was common among Icelandic scholars to write in Latin as well as in the vernacular. We do not know exactly what the position of Icelandic writers and scholars was towards using the vernacular as opposed to using Latin. However, one gets the impression from the early preserved works that there was an interest in writing in Icelandic from the time when writing was introduced in Iceland by the Church. The Icelanders may well have been influenced by the English in their use of the vernacular, as is suggested by Oleson (1963). Turville-Petre noted that, after the conversion of Iceland to Christianity, the Icelanders were taught to write by English clerics, who devised a system of spelling for them based on their own (1953: 75). During that time, the first half of the eleventh century, Old English had reached its highest point of development as a literary language. Considering the traditional extensive relations between England and Iceland, it is likely that the Icelanders were familiar with Old English literary works such as the *Anglo-Saxon Chronicle*. The decision to compose a historiographic work about Iceland in Icelandic would, in such a case, not have seemed unnatural to Icelandic scholars like Ari. Indeed, in his opening paragraph to the *Íslendingabók*, Ari shows his acquaintance with Anglo-Saxon scholarly works in his references to Bede and his use of the martyrdom of St. Edmund to date Icelandic historical events (Oleson 83-84). At the time of Ari's writing, however, the first part of the twelfth century, the continuity of Old English literature had been broken by the Norman invasion, and England had reverted to Latin as the general language for cultural expression. According to Haskins (1927: 224), European historiographic writing in the vernacular only really begins during the latter part of the twelfth century.

8. Among the European writings that were known in Iceland and exerted a considerable influence on the development of Icelandic literature were Lucan's classical work *Pharsalia* (translated into Icelandic as *Rómverja saga*); extended medieval re-tellings based on "Dares Phrygius'" late classical prose narrative *De excidio Troiae historia* (known as *Trójumanna saga* in Icelandic; the author's real name is unknown); Bede's eighth-century work *Historia ecclesiastica*; and Galterus' *Alexandreis* (translated as *Alexanders saga*) and Geoffrey of Monmouth's *Historia*

regum Brittaniae (*Breta sögur*) from the twelfth century. Other European examples of historiographic writing from the medieval renaissance are Otto of Freising's *Chronicle* and *Gesta*, Robert of Torigni's *Appendix to Sigebert*, Eadmer's *Historia Novarum in Anglia* and William of Malmesbury's *History of the Kings of Britain* and *Historia Novella*.

9. Ari inn fróði has often been credited with the writing of an original *Landnámabók*, but no evidence of such an original has survived, nor is there sufficient conclusive evidence to determine if and how much of it Ari actually wrote (*Bókmenntasaga* 1: 300). Although several redactions of settlement books exist, it has remained customary to speak of the *Landnámabók*.

10. The influence of the earlier religious sagas on the classical sagas, and generally the influence of foreign works on Icelandic classical literature, is even today a subject largely ignored. European medieval studies generally exclude any mention of Scandinavia. Icelandic saga scholarship has traditionally tended to emphasize the uniquely Icelandic qualities of this literature, something that finds its basis in the Icelandic nationalism prior to the Second World War, when Icelandic classical and folk literature played an important role in the Icelandic claim for complete independence from Denmark. Foreign scholars of Old Norse literature have generally followed the Icelandic direction. Gabriel Turville-Petre is a notable exception, and his *Origins of Icelandic Literature* (1953) is still a very important work in this respect. Lars Lönnroth (1965) launched another valiant attempt to break through the insular tendencies of saga scholarship and view saga literature in a broader European framework, as did Dag Strömback (1968). More recently, several studies have appeared which indicate a gradual change, notably *Bókmenntasaga* and, in English, Clover (1982). See also Tómasson (1983), who deals especially with the influence of Latin rhetoric on saga writing and the formal influence of saints' lives, as well as with the largely ignored influence of Catholicism and the Catholic Church on all writers, both historians such as Ari and Snorri, and on saga authors, a point that has been repeatedly raised by Laxness as well (1975). A similar point is raised by Kristjánsson (1981), whose textual analysis aims to show that the style of the saints' lives already combines features of Latin as well as spoken Norse, so that these works must have exerted a formative stylistic influence on the classical sagas.

11. Aðalsteinsson (1988: 395). For a more elaborate and very interesting study see Bauschatz (1982).

12. Saga scholarship has long centered around the question of the origins and development of the sagas. For decades, saga scholars were divided over the question whether the sagas originated and reached their final form in oral tradition (the so-called free-prose theory), or whether they were literary works of art created by individual authors (the book-prose theory). Nowadays, scholars have moved more to the middle ground on this matter and are turning their attention to alternative approaches and aspects of saga literature, of which Byock's anthropological approach is a recent example. For a useful, although somewhat dated, survey of the traditional debate over saga origins see Einarsson (1957: 126-31). Andersson (1967) introduced a structural approach to the sagas which incorporates elements from both the book-prose and the free-prose theory, although it leans more to the latter. For an example of how present-day scholars mediate between and make use of both theories see *Bókmenntasaga* 2: 44-49; and Mitchell (1985). For examples of alternative approaches to saga literature, such as the ritualist-folkloristic approach, see Davidson (1973; 1943); Chadwick (1946; 1968); Bayerschmidt (1965); for a mythological approach, see Greenway (1970).

13. *Flestar frásagnir Íslendingasagna snerta efni sem koma við ákvarðanatöku, þar á meðal vangaveltur um siðferðileg og siðfræðileg efni. Áheyrendur höfðu ekki aðeins áhrif á efni sagnanna. Sjálfir sögumennirnir komu úr þeirra röðum. Þetta tvennt, sögumaður og áheyrendur, tilheyrði sömu hefðinni. Með því að kljúfa þetta félagslega umhverfi og líta á sögumanninn eins og hann hafi verið skapandi höfundur sem skrifaði fyrir fámennan hóp bókamenntamanna spillist sá skilningur sem við getum haft á samtengdum miðaldasögum sem hjálpuðu fólki úr öllum lögum eyjasamfélagsins að búa sér til sjálfsmynd.* (Byock 1990: 34)

14. *Með hliðsjón af óbreytanlegri og þjóðfélagslega viðurkenndri hegðun [sögupersónanna] raðaði sögumaðurinn þessum atburðareiningum á ýmsa vegu og fyllti upp með ólíkum, oft skálduðum, smáatriðum. Þannig notaði hann þessar litlu einingar til að umbreyta þjóðfélagsformi yfir í frásagnarform.* (1990: 35)

15. Examples include *Tristrams saga*, the Icelandic translation of the popular French tale of Tristram and Isolde, the Icelandic re-telling in prose of the *lais* of Marie de France (*Strengleikar*), and the translations of Chrétien de Troyes' *Li contes del Graal* (*Parcevals saga*) and *Yvain ou li chevaliers au lion* (*Ívents saga*).

16. For a discussion of literacy in Iceland see Tomasson (1975); and Laxness (1967).

17. *Það væri engin fjarstæða að kalla Íslendinga mestu bókmentaþjóð heimsins, — ekki í þeim skilningi, að þeir hafi skapað mest af fullkomnum verkum, þótt*

þeir hafi komizt furðu langt í því efni, —heldur af því, að engin þjóð önnur hefur að tiltölu gefið bókmentum svo mikið af kröftum sinum, svo mikið af ást sinni og alúð, engin þjóð leitað þar svo alment fróunar og sótt þangað þrek. Ef til vill á saga mannkynsins ekkert áþreifanlega dæmi þess, hver orkulind og ellilyf andleg starfsemi er, jafnvel þó að sum verkin, sem samin eru, lærð og lesin, sé hvorki höfug að efni né algjör að formi. (1931: xxviii)

18. Here and in further discussions of Icelandic authors throughout this work I shall go by the Icelandic custom of referring to authors by their first name, as Icelanders do not have surnames proper, but patronymics. To avoid unnecessary confusion, however, Icelandic authors are listed by their last names in the bibliography.

19. Different reasons have been advanced for the lack of Icelandic literary influence and references in Jón's sermons. Halldórsson suggests that the frugal style of the Icelandic classical authors could hardly have suited Jón Vídalín's oratory (1977: 56). Magnús Jónsson reckons that in Jón's day, Lutheran pastors and scholars would not have appreciated the native heathen literary tradition belonging to the people, which, at that time, was often used in magical practices (1920). Sigfússon supposes that Jón would have found these works far too heathen in spirit (1956).

20. Although no exact foreign parallel to the Icelandic *rímur* exists, the *rímur* originated alongside the metrical romances in late medieval Europe, which were also narratives in verse recited for popular entertainment. It is quite likely that the Icelanders created the first *rímur* in an attempt to imitate the kind of poetry they had heard recited in trading centres abroad (*Bókmenntasaga* 2: 333-35).

21. *Íslenzkar rímur eru líklega hið fáránlegasta dæmi bókmentalegs íhalds, sem sögur fara af. Það má heita, að þær haldist óbreyttar heilar fimm aldir, þó að alt breytist í kringum þær. Og þó að þær hafi einatt lítið skáldlegt gildi og horfi jafnvel stundum til beinna smekkspjalla, hafa þær með lífseigju sinni sýnt og sannað, að þær fullnægja þörfum þjóðarinnar einkennilega vel. Þær hafa flutt alþýðu manna söguefni, sem var henni til yndis, í formi, sem lét vel í eyrum og heimtaði vakandi athygli og skilning. Þær gáfu hverjum hagyrðingi tækifæri til þess að iðka íþrótt sína, án þess að heimta af honum ímyndun eða frumleik. Þær voru fremur iðnaður en list.... En iðnaðurinn hefur jafnan búið í hendur listinni, og sé neistanum haldið lifandi, getur altaf orðið bál úr honum. Rímurnar hafa haldið tungunni taminni og auðugri, aukið þekkingu og skilning almennings á öllum forða málsins. En bezt hafa þær svarið sig í ætt dróttkvæðanna með því að gefa Íslendingum nýjan hátt fyrir lausavísur, og enn fullkomnara en hinn forna. Ferskeyttar lausavísur fara að koma fram á síðara hluta 16. aldar, og hafa varla áður staðið með meira blóma en á vorum dögum.* (1931: xix-xx)

22. For scholarly studies on folk tale motifs in Old Norse literature see, for instance, Ciklamini (1979); Steblin-Kamenskij (1972); Davidson (1943; 1973) and Chadwick (1946; 1968).

23. For a discussion of the role of Icelandic folk tales in Icelandic nationalism and the struggle for independence see Babcock (1976).

24. *Og þannig var lærdómsöldin samsett úr ólíkum og oft innbyrðis ósamræmanlegum hugmyndum, þar sem einstaklingum var í einu orðinu bent á dásemdir sköpunarverksins en í öðru orðinu bannað að njóta þeirra, þar sem manninum átti að vera það sálarábótaratriði að líkja sér við hund og svín en minnast þess samtímis að hann var skapaður í Guðs eigin mynd, þar sem Satan var ýmist óvinur Guðs og allra hans barna eða hann var sköpunarverk hans, tæki og þjónn.* (2: 517)

25. *Ber því að skoða trúarhugsun alþýðu sem samsett kerfi ólíkra og jafnvel and-stæðra trúarviðhorfa þar sem hugmyndir frá forkristnum tíma, kaþólsk miðal-daviðhorf og lúthersk trúartúlkun hafa ofist saman í fjölþætt munstur.* (1988: 324)

26. Two important recent studies of this particular aspect of folk tales, especially those of elves, are Ingimundarson (1988); and Bjartmarsdóttir (1982).

27. *Þjóðsagan birtist heimsskoðun og náttúruviðhorf barnsins, mannsins sem er óspilltur af skilningslitlum lærdómi og hálfmenntun. Í henni birtist oft hinn tærasti skáldskapur og hið dýpsta raunsæi.* (1962: 191)

28. *Þessi fyrirbrigði hafa að fornu og nýju verið merkilegur þáttur í lífi þjóðar vorra, enda hefir hann að mestu verið sjálfum sér samkvæmur frá upphafi til enda. Af honum hefir að miklu leyti vaxið ein hin einkennilegasta grein bókmennta vorra, þar sem þjóðsögurnar eru.* (1971: 69)

29. In *Confessions of an Immigrant's Daughter*, Icelandic-Canadian author Laura Goodman Salverson relates a haunting and killing in an Icelandic-Canadian family attributed to *Írafells-Móri* (1981: 263); David Arnason tells of Thorgeir's Bull and Mori, fylgjur that fol-lowed immigrant families to Canada and made their appearances in the Icelandic-Canadian Interlake community (1981: 110); in Einarsson's collection of *Icelandic-Canadian Oral Narratives*, several tales are included about sightings of *fylgjur* in Canada (1991: 247-61).

30. Traces of a similar belief in the power of the poetic word can, how-ever, be found in Irish folklore. For this and further information, see Almquist's study of this subject and its development (1961).

31. For a discussion of Jón *lærði* in the light of the poetic tradition of the people see Laxness (1967); and Hreinsson (1992).

32. For a more detailed analysis of humour in Old Norse literature see the chapter on this subject in Hallberg (1962).

33. Finnbogason, in his discussion of this Icelandic phenomenon, referred to the enlightening characterization of Andreas Heusler, a saga scholar, who called the Icelanders "Aristo-Democrats" (1971: 248). See also Turner (1971).

34. In much of my discussion of outlaws, I rely on Hastrup's analysis as presented in her anthropological study of *Grettis saga* (1986). For other, more elaborate discussions of the outlaw in Icelandic history, literature and folklore see also de Lange (1935); Reykers (1936); and Spoelstra (1939).

II

THE SEARCH FOR VÍNLAND THE GOOD[1]
EMIGRATION AND SETTLEMENT IN THE NEW WORLD

THE NINETEENTH CENTURY:
ROMANTICISM AND NATIONAL REVIVAL

SCHOLARS OF ICELANDIC LITERATURE have tended to dismiss the sixteenth and seventeenth century as a period of cultural stagnation and
backwardness which followed an age of literary masterpieces. Only
recently has this disregard come under closer scrutiny. Examinations
show that, rather, it was a period characterized by growth and innovation in spite of declining economic conditions, political oppression and fundamental religious changes. Many new elements were
incorporated into Icelandic literature, which now, for the first time,
also became a medium for self-expression. Icelandic poetry was
enriched with new metres and new modes of poetic expression which
reflected a changed world and new ideology. Similarly, Icelandic
prose was infused with new ideas and a new style and phraseology
that originated with the Reformation and the Renaissance movement
in Europe. Thus, the foundation was laid for future literary developments that would be introduced by the Romantics in the nineteenth
century.

At the same time, popular genres like the *rímur* kept an important part of the literary past alive, both in form and content, while folk tales reflected the ways in which the people tried to cope with the rigours of the present in the framework of past knowledge and experience. They lived with poverty and oppression as climatic and economic conditions gradually deteriorated, and it is surprising to find how much literary activity and growth actually took place under such inimical conditions.

It was only in the course of the eighteenth century that all cultural development came to a virtual standstill. This century saw an unfortunate accumulation of political corruption, bad weather and natural disasters which culminated in the *móðuharðindi*, the terrible famine that followed the Skaptár-eruption in 1773. Living conditions were reduced to the level of mere survival, and the resulting atmosphere was one of apathy and demoralization. Culturally, Iceland began to lag behind its neighbouring countries as all literary development stagnated. Much of the literature that was created during this time bears the marks of the nation's struggle for cultural and physical survival.

Towards the end of the eighteenth century, however, the first indications of change announced themselves. The poet Eggert Ólafsson was in the vanguard of these changes. Under the influence of Enlightenment ideals, he wrote poetry which was aimed at making his countrymen aware of the possibilities of improving their lot. However, his messages still fell largely on deaf ears. It took the revolutionary political and cultural ideas introduced by the Romantic movement, combined with the improved social and economic circumstances of the next century to work any real changes. In Iceland, the events of the nineteenth century which produced this general climate of revival, with its political and social advancements, are inextricably linked to the emergence of Romantic literature and the crucial role it played in the development of these events. Perhaps surprisingly, it was against this same background that emigration to the New World took place during the second half of the century.

THE ROMANTIC MOVEMENT IN ICELAND

During the nineteenth century, literature and politics in Iceland became enmeshed with each other. A nationalist revival took place both on the literary and the political level, setting in motion a long and difficult, but eventually successful battle for independence. In 1830, a group of enthusiastic and ambitious nationalists, among them politicians, teachers and poets, demanded the restoration of the *Alþingi*, the Icelandic parliament which of old was held at Þingvellir and had been abolished in 1800 by Danish decree. At the same time, four of them embarked on the publication of a journal, *Fjölnir* (1835-39, 1844-47), with which to herald the gospel of the Romantic movement.[2] However, their ideas for Iceland and its literature were no longer entirely new. They had been influenced by the lonely voices of two earlier poets, Eggert Ólafsson (1726-1768), and Bjarni Thorarensen (1786-1841), who is now usually called the first Romantic poet of Iceland. While he was in Copenhagen studying law Bjarni attended a lecture by Heinrich Steffens in 1803. This lecture, which marks the beginning of Romanticism in Denmark, greatly impressed Bjarni and inspired him to write poetry.

A number of important features in Bjarni's poetry that we now call Romantic were actually introduced by Eggert Ólafsson, a poet whose name is generally associated with the Enlightenment movement in Iceland. Eggert had studied natural science, and his deep love of his native country had inspired him to beautiful descriptions of Iceland's countryside. He wished to educate his people by making them more familiar with the nature of the land in order to induce them to progress in agricultural methods and in their lives in general. Moreover, since he was principally concerned with educating the people, he cared little for the ornate form and style that Icelandic poetry had called for so far. Thus Eggert introduced both nature poetry and patriotic poems[3] as well as simpler verse forms into Icelandic literature.

Bjarni continued the direction which Eggert had indicated in his poetry. He experimented with looser forms, notably the Eddic metre *fornyrðislag*, and, like his predecessor, he wished his country to be revived and liberated from the curbs on its progress. Bjarni's poetry is infused with a spirit of grim determination and courage. As he was attracted by the terrible, powerful face of nature, so he loved the Icelandic past with its stern Viking ethos and heroes. This shows not only in his use of Eddic metres, but also in the terse, clear-cut, powerful pictures created by his rich imagination. He was so enamoured of this past that it pervades most of his poetry, not least his nature poetry: every patch of land reminds him of its history as described in the sagas, and natural forces conjure up images of the old heroism.

Fascination with the past was, of course, an important characteristic of Romanticism, and as it had always remained a part of Icelandic literature, it was easy for the Icelandic Romantics to invoke it. However, the glorious past was now no longer an escapist amusement, but, on the contrary, spoke directly to the present. Its glories and triumphs became exemplars, for Bjarni, evoking the ideal of energetic prowess and courage. Trials and hardships were to be welcomed as teachers of time-honoured virtues and an opportunity to test and increase strength and stamina, and to keep the youth from the weakening and demoralizing influences of modern city-values and "civilization."[4]

As was pointed out earlier, 1830 saw the first formal declaration of political objectives by nationalist enthusiasts, who had come under the influence of the contemporary European Romantic and revolutionary movements. In 1835 the first issue of the journal *Fjölnir* came out. The introduction to this issue was mostly written by Tómas Sæmundsson, one of the four men who stood behind the publication. In it he explained the aims he and his fellow-*Fjölnismenn*, as they are generally referred to, had set themselves and why. The introduction gives one a good idea of what the Icelandic Romantic movement stood for and the social "evils" it had committed itself to fight. Inspired by the revolutionary movements and liberal spirit of freedom and nationalism that swept Europe in the early nineteenth century, the *Fjölnismenn* abhorred the general atmosphere of inertia in Iceland, especially since the country's increased isolation during the Napoleonic wars had thrown Iceland back on its own resources.[5] This lesson in (relative) self-sufficiency called for action. The *Fjölnismenn* considered apathy, general superstition, isolation and stagnation to be the main obstacles to progress. Centuries of oppression had robbed the Icelanders of the courage and will to improve their situation, not least because the fruits of any action had always gone to the foreign oppressor.

The *Fjölnismenn* suggested four major means to awaken the people, and encourage them to action and struggle for nationalism: utility, beauty, truth and a heightened moral standard. The two first aims became the most important ones. The first one is perhaps the most striking, and also tells us much about the main differences between Icelandic and European Romanticism. It points to the fact that the Romantics in Iceland were, to a certain extent, still under the influence of the Enlightenment, partly because they could build on two earlier poets who had introduced elements that suited the Romantic movement well, and partly because by the time the movement reached Scandinavia, it had already lost much of its vehemence (Jóhannesson 1966: 155-56). The commitment to the Enlightenment ideals of usefulness and progress also indicate the extent to which Icelandic Romanticism was involved in a national political struggle for independence that was actual and real. It gave the movement in Iceland an earthbound and practical character.

In order to inspire their countrymen, the *Fjölnismenn* realized it was necessary to convince them both of the use and the feasibility of their cause. The nation had been reduced to a bare subsistence level for so long that it seemed many had lost all belief in progress. In the introduction of *Fjölnir*, the importance of Icelandic culture and history is stressed. It is pointed out that because of the treasure of their past, their language and their classical literature, Iceland can rightfully claim to the rest of the world to be more than simply a small, impoverished nation. This statement was not unfounded. Owing to the Romantic interest in their own past, many European countries, particularly Germanic ones, had to turn to Iceland for source material.

The introduction to the first issue of *Fjölnir* was preceded by a poem by Jónas Hallgrímsson, another of the *Fjölnismenn*, in which he asks:

> Iceland! gracious Frón
> and hoary magnanimous mother!
> Where are thine ancient renown,
> freedom and valorous deeds?[6]

In this poem, called "Ísland" ("Iceland"), he recalls images of Iceland during the age of the sagas, and compares them to the Iceland of his day: the country is still as beautiful, but the *Alþingi* has disappeared, and the fame of the ancestors has fallen into oblivion. The poem caused great indignation. People thought Jónas had written an epitaph for Iceland. It was, however, a radical attempt to open people's eyes to the beauty of their country, their history, their language, their culture, and Jónas' example was followed until the end of the century.

This has brought us to Jónas Hallgrímsson (1807-1845), also fondly called *ástmögur þjóðarinnar* (translated by Magnus Magnusson as "Darling of the Nation" in Laxness' *The Atom Station*), although

Jónas did not receive this designation until after he had been berated by many of his contemporaries. He was an essential and highly influential figure in both the literary and the political movements in nineteenth-century Iceland, and in the course of the nineteenth century, his stature grew to that of a national hero. Even today, he still inspires great admiration among readers and critics alike. Finnbogi Guðmundsson has tried to explain Jónas' fast growing popularity: "Jónas knew that the first step in the battle for independence was to revive the belief of the people in themselves and their country, encourage them into action and enliven in them an optimism towards life and the future."[7]

Jónas' poetry is characterized by a brilliant harmony between language, subject and form. His style and diction were in themselves simple, and it needed his poetic genius for the right word in the right place to convince a people that had become used to ornate and stylized poetic diction that his was poetry of sheer beauty. One of the aims encompassed in the drive for beauty among the *Fjölnismenn* was to rid the Icelandic language of all Danish loanwords and restore it to its former purity. Therefore, Jónas looked to the everyday language spoken in the country. The result was that, in Indriði Einarsson's words, "he composes one poem more beautiful than the other, and in a language that the angels probably speak when they speak Icelandic."[8]

Most of Jónas' poetry, like Bjarni's, is concerned with Icelandic nature, Iceland's glorious past and with patriotism. But, as Einar Ólafur Sveinsson remarked, whereas Bjarni sees everything in the light of the distance of eternity, Jónas is the poet of detail and the present (1929: 149). As he, like Eggert Ólafsson, studied natural science, he had both the poetic eye and the scientific knowledge to exalt his nature poetry. It taught the people to look at their environment in a different way; it became a world of beauty and sunshine. Similarly he described the people in their daily tasks and transformed them into beauty and poetry without making them any less realistic. In his influential article on the poet, Halldór Laxness explains how Jónas *was* what he described:

In his poems is hidden the glow of the beginning of spring; he goes forth
in the humble nobility of our sense of realism and composes out of the
essence of our consciousness; his life and poetry are a continuous song about
Iceland's fate. Embellishment does not exist with him. He is the singer of our
simple joy as it was the most unclouded during good summer weather, and of

the melancholy long Norse nights with their sleeplessness and anguish. Jónas Hallgrímsson is the crystallization of the Icelandic consciousness. In him the rays of our nature break.... His poems are, in other words, Iceland itself as it has developed in our national consciousness during a thousand years of struggle, but not as poets and prophets saw it, but as the people saw it and felt it, the farmer in the valley and his wife and their people. His poems are the Icelandic soul itself, the way the country has moulded it in the people.[9]

It is for this reason that Laxness and many others consider Jónas to be one of the best Icelandic poets. In many ways, Jónas continued the path that had been cleared by earlier innovative poets, notably Hallgrímur Pétursson: he perfected the gentler, more lyrical strain that had been introduced under the influence of the Reformation and gave it a permanent place in Icelandic poetry. He also created a place in Icelandic poetry for nature in its everyday splendour, for the expression of beauty and rapture, gentleness and nostalgia. His poetry features a simplicity of diction, and foreign metres such as the son-net and terzina, with a less rigid and more musical, flowing pattern than the traditional Icelandic *rímur*-metres.

Jónas Hallgrímsson, then, played a major part in re-invigorating the long-standing, continous Icelandic literary tradition by opening it up to a quickly changing world. In this respect, as in many others, he was a revolutionary. The clearest example of this is his infamous "*rímur*-review" in the 1837 issue of *Fjölnir*. In this review he set him-self out to show the people that *rímur* were bad poetry, a form long dead. Moreover, he claimed that the exercising of this "poetry" stood in the way of the composition and appreciation of other, bet-ter poetry. They hindered the natural progress of Icelandic poetic development. As an example, Jónas used a recent *rímur*-cycle written by the most popular poet of that time, Sigurður Breiðfjörð. The review made Jónas very unpopular, to say the least. A number of people never forgave him, even when his star had started to rise.

This event, however, heralded two important changes in Icelandic literature. First, the *rímur*, which were at the height of their perfec-tion and popularity at this time, began a gradual decline. In many ways, this was inevitable, since the social and cultural circumstances that had remained relatively unchanged in Iceland for centuries and from which the *rímur* had sprung, now became subject to funda-mental changes. Secondly, it was the beginning of an evolving and ever-widening gap between educated poets and popular poets, called *alþýðuskáld* in Icelandic.[10] Before, these two groups, the professionals and the amateurs, had never really been separated. Literature for the Icelandic people had been created by the Icelandic people, some of whom, admittedly, had enjoyed a formal education whereas others had not, but all of them had generally lived a similar type of life and had similar ideas and tastes with regard to literature. From now on, however, the creation of Icelandic literature moved slowly into the hands of a more formally educated group of people.

Although these gradual changes were the most radical in centuries, it would be misleading to suggest that there was no continuity. The Icelandic Romantics did not end the literary tradition, but merely gave it a much-needed change of emphasis. They relied, for instance, strongly on the Icelandic past which the literary tradition had kept alive among the people. No other northern European nation had this direct access to and indeed relationship with its past. Icelandic poetry also remained characterized by alliteration. As Carleton remarks, alliteration was so instilled in the Icelandic poetic consciousness that "poetry simply did not occur to them without the proper alliterative letters. They could not conceive of alliteration as being a limit on poetic expression, it *was* poetic expression" (1967: 66-67). The people took their time to let the new elements sink in and blend with the old. The *rímur* as a poetic genre actually reached its peak at this time in two brilliant cycles by the great unschooled poets of the century, *Tímaríma hin nýja* by Bólu-Hjálmar and the *Núma* by Sigurður Breiðfjörð. In the *Núma*, Sigurður himself expressed his awareness of the limitations of the genre in which he wrote. However, he had had neither the financial means nor the education to avail himself of newer poetic forms and used instead those assets that were at his disposal.

The same was the case for Bólu-Hjálmar, whose poetry is marked by the extreme poverty he lived in and the misfortune that befell him during his life. As he was both a hot-tempered and a very sensitive man, his outlook and poetry were marked by a vehement bitterness bordering on misanthropy. Like Sigurður, he possessed great poetical talent that owed much of its power as well as its limitations to a lack of formal education. Instead, both perfected the only poetical means at their disposal: the traditional genres. Moreover, they offered models to later penniless unschooled poets, among whom were many Icelandic emigrants to North America.

The Romantic period also saw the birth of a modern Icelandic prose tradition with Jónas Hallgrímsson's short story "Grasaferð"

("Going Out Moss-Gathering"). Jónas died young and thus did not follow up on his obvious gifts in the prose field. His example in this direction was followed instead by Jón Thoroddsen (1818-1868). In 1850 the first Icelandic novel, *Piltur og Stúlka* ("Boy and Girl") written by Jón Thoroddsen, was printed. There is no doubt that "Grasaferð" influenced and stimulated Jón to write this novel, but it also has roots in the Enlightenment, the English prose tradition (Scott, Dickens), and, of course, classical Icelandic sagas. As a story, *Piltur og Stúlka* has many Romantic characteristics. It is built on oppositions, black and white, and it makes elaborate use of folkloristic elements. The country-life idyll is idealized everywhere and set against the immorality and "Danishness" of the city, Reykjavík. This shows that Jón Thoroddsen, too, was sympathetic to the nationalist movement: the influence of the Danes in Reykjavík is seen as a threat to Icelandic country culture.[11] The form and style in *Piltur og Stúlka* on the other hand are much more realistic. Jón attempts a very direct, objective style of narrative, making use of predictions and very sharp and entertaining delineations of character, some highly comical, even bordering on the burlesque (Einarsson 1957: 237). In this respect he was obviously influenced by the sagas and by the folk tales that were now being collected.

Romantic literature had made its influence felt and become widely accepted by the second half of the nineteenth century. This was the time emigration started, so that the Romantic influence must be seen as the dominant one at the time the Icelandic emigrants arrived, settled in North America and began to write.

THE NATIONAL SITUATION

The nineteenth century was a time of many radical changes in a society that had hardly known change for centuries. These social changes were possible because of slow improvements in the national situation and the influence of the Enlightenment movement.[12] The cultural climate which developed during the first decades of the nineteenth century formed the basis for the national movement which followed. During the first part of the nineteenth century 82 percent of the Icelandic population consisted of impoverished farmers. It was a period of slightly improved economic conditions, largely due to climatic changes and allowing the larger part of the population the leisure to receive ideas of social and economic progress and change, inspired by the Enlightenment movement. Since Iceland had no native upper class nor a real middle class in the urban European sense, the farmers were really the potential bourgeoisie in Iceland. They slowly became aware of the more democratic atmosphere which had developed in Europe. Moreover, the period of the Enlightenment saw the birth of literary and educational societies as well as periodicals, through which the Icelanders learnt about the struggles taking place in various countries against colonial and imperial powers and for independence and democracy.

When Icelandic students in Copenhagen, under the influence of Romantic ideas, began their call for independence from Denmark, Icelandic society was therefore already prepared for possibilities of change and slowly started to consider and heed the call. National independence would mean economic independence, which in turn meant more profit would come to the farmers themselves rather than disappear into a foreign treasury. The international situation had shown that social change was possible. The nationalists called the farmers up to form reading societies, so that they could become more acquainted with new ideas. In this respect, they could build on the long-standing Icelandic tradition of home education and *kvöld-vaka*. The reading societies, or *lestrarfélög*, formed an excellent means to acquire knowledge in all kinds of fields, to exchange ideas, to nourish independence of thought and action. The newspapers, which were established at this time, became a forum for public ideas and sentiments.

Political interest was thus roused, and the democratic ideals which had been fostered by the Enlightenment movement, supported by the traditionally democratic basis of Icelandic society, created a strong predisposition toward democracy among many Icelanders. Although Icelanders had no right to vote under Danish rule, many did not intend to be excluded any longer from the political developments taking place with increasing speed. They actively participated in whatever way was available to them: they attended district meetings, wrote in newspapers, and drew up petitions, some of which were sent directly to the Danish king.

The fervent nationalists had, then, a network through which they could reach the Icelandic population and convince them of their political ideals. However, centuries of oppression and poverty were not completely to be undone in a few decades. While some people remained sceptical for the time being, many others were at a loss as to how to organize in practice the realization of their hopes for political independence and social and economic progress. All initial attempts at political reforms foundered in Denmark. However, when the nationalists succeeded in re-establishing the *Alþingi* in 1843, the tide turned. In 1848, a young student named Jón Sigurðsson published his famous article "Hugvekja til Íslendinga" ("Essay to the Icelanders"), in which he showed Iceland's legal and historical right to independence in such a convincing and practical way that it became the program in the struggle for independence. It gave form to the national aspirations an increasing number of people had come to entertain, and rallied others who had remained more doubtful to its cause.

In the same year, Denmark acceded to the demand of the people and became a constitutional monarchy. The Icelanders saw their chance and strove to prevent Iceland from being automatically annexed into the new Danish government system. Instead, they proposed a more democratic function for the *Alþingi* with full legislative power. Events throughout Europe at that time had planted a fear of revolution among leaders, and gradually a process was set in motion by which one Icelandic call for reform after another received more serious attention in Denmark. One of these was for a more democratic constitution. The Icelanders in general had become so actively involved in politics, attending meetings and submitting petitions towards new proposals to be sent to Denmark for action, that for them it was only natural to include in their proposals a great expansion of the suffrage (Gjerset 1924: 385). Apart from the activities of the earlier-mentioned *lestrarfélög*, political meetings in the constituencies were very well attended, democratic changes and measures took place in country and Church committees, and more and more free-minded organizations in different fields were founded so as to discuss and influence social issues in a democratic way.[13] In 1854, all trade restrictions were abolished, and different kinds of business and agricultural societies were founded. Nationalism and democracy, then, went hand in hand in nineteenth-century Iceland, and it was in this climate that the culmination of the traditional Icelandic "unschooled poetry" could take place. In this climate, too, many Icelandic-Canadian "unschooled poets" were born and bred, and it was to exercise a major influence on the development of Icelandic immigrant literature in Canada.

During the second half of the nineteenth century, just when the national situation was showing improvement and people had generally replaced their earlier apathy with hope for progress, a series of natural disasters and disappointments in the struggle for independence occurred. In the 1860s, the employment and agricultural situation worsened: the good years had caused an increase of population for which the land could not provide. General weather conditions were declining, a scabies epidemic killed off large numbers of animals, and fishing was bad. In 1868, newspapers reported a general lack of goods with resulting famine. In 1872, a large earthquake occurred in the north (Húsavík and surroundings), and in 1874, Iceland experienced one of the worst winters in living memory. On top of this, a large volcanic eruption took place in the eastern part of the interior, destroying large areas of farmland, killing large numbers of people and cattle, and compounding the disaster with an ash-fall which destroyed crops and killed cattle long afterwards. The 1880s saw continuing bad and cold weather due to polar ice surrounding the island. Large numbers of animals died, crops failed and famine hit the country again. Many people were forced to look to their district authorities for support in order to survive. They were often placed in the care of wealthier farmers to work in exchange for room and board. Families had to be broken up in such cases, as farmers seldom could or would afford to take in more than one person.

In the political field there was only one important event: after two decades of formulating propositions for Iceland's position in the Danish government system Iceland was finally given a constitution and financial independence in 1874. That same year, Iceland celebrated its millenium, commemorated by a visit from King Christian IX and by the official delivery of the constitution. Soon, however, it appeared that the constitution did not allow Iceland the freedom it had hoped for. The Danish king retained an absolute veto over legislative matters, and the *landshöfðingi* (governor of Iceland), who had executive power in Icelandic affairs, was still not responsible to the *Alþingi* but to a Minister of Icelandic Affairs in Copenhagen, who was, however, never appointed. Instead, Icelandic affairs were left to the Danish Minister of Justice. The battle had not been won yet. A long and frustrating struggle still lay ahead, and it was not until 1904 that any further success was gained.[14]

It is against this background, then, that emigration took place. In spite of the hardships, the latter half of the century was characterized by a spirit of enterprise, progress, nationalism and democracy, but the disappointments among many must have been bitter. So it was that in the age of revived hope about a fifth of the Icelandic people sought a better future on the North American continent.

EMIGRATION AND SETTLEMENT IN THE NEW WORLD

EMIGRATION

The idea of emigration as a possible solution for a better future did not, of course, emerge unexpectedly. In 1855, a small group of Icelanders who had converted to the Mormon faith travelled to Utah. This group went independently and for very different reasons than the later emigrants, but the very occurrence of this emigration must have been of influence on later prospective emigrant groups. As we saw earlier, a general spirit of progress and freedom had developed, together with a will to contribute to the improvement of the nation. This spirit of reform, however, was threatened when conditions started to deteriorate, at first in the northern part of Iceland. During the terrible winter of 1858-59, emigration came to be first seriously discussed there. A fear must have arisen that all hope of improvement would be nipped in the bud.[15] At the time, newspapers had begun to publish news of the large-scale migration to North America from other parts in Europe, especially Scandinavia, with the result that Icelandic readers were aware of the possibilities of emigration.

In 1863, a group of men from the north organized an emigration expedition to Brazil, but dealings with the Brazilian government turned out to be difficult, and in the end only 34 people went. From then on up to 1873, a few people went individually to the United States. Only one went to Canada, Sigtryggur Jónasson. The northern Icelandic paper *Norðanfari* now often carried translated articles about Scandinavian settlements in America, and in 1871 an account from a Norwegian emigrant called *Brjef frá Ameriku* ("Letter from America") was translated and published in Iceland, since emigration *er orðið hið mesta áhugamál hjer á landi* ("has become a matter of the greatest interest in our country"), as the Icelandic publisher says in his epilogue. An emigrant Dane, who had lived in Iceland for ten years and then gone to the United States, wrote enthusiastic letters to his friends in Iceland which were eagerly read in the north. Members of this group gathered and organized meetings to examine the possibilities for emigration, and in 1873 the first group of emigrants left Iceland. Although there seems to have been a general wish to stay together as a group, the Icelanders had not agreed on one destination.

Páll Þorláksson, the son of one of the organizing members, had gone ahead to investigate the local situation and make arrangements. He had suggested lodging the Icelanders with Norwegian families in Wisconsin, so that the Icelanders could become familiar with local conditions and work methods before setting out on their own. Páll was in a good position to arrange this since he was an active member and pastor of the Norwegian Lutheran Church Synod. Not all Icelanders, however, were taken by this idea. Icelanders are individualists, and some preferred making their way independently as a group instead of being separated and scattered among what they regarded as "foreigners."

When the Icelanders arrived in Québec, they were met not only by Páll Þorláksson, but also by Sigtryggur Jónasson, who had been employed by the Canadian government as an immigration agent. Canada had become a Confederation of five provinces in 1867, and had bought from the Hudson Bay Company the largely unsettled and vast stretch of land between the Great Lakes and the Rocky Mountains. Canada needed people to settle and work the land, but had hitherto been forced to watch the large groups of immigrants that arrived in Canada travel on to the United States, where most of them had family, friends, or at least settlements of compatriots. The Icelandic immigrants, however, did not have predecessors of any real number to direct them south of the border. Thus the Canadian government had sent an agent to tempt the immigrants with offers of free travel within Canada to their destination, and, as Kristjanson sums up: "temporary quarters, and two hundred acres of free land, on condition of three months residence in the Province [of Ontario]. Should they then desire to move, they were free to go wherever they pleased" (17). Needless to say, no such offers were forthcoming from the United States. As a result, only around thirty people went with Páll to Wisconsin, and about 115 went with Sigtryggur to the Muskoka district in Ontario. Sigtryggur relates in his own account of *The Early Icelandic Settlements in Canada* (1901) how he had been convinced that Ontario would be the best place for the Icelanders and consequently had done most of his scouting there.

THE YEAR IN ONTARIO

In 1873, Sigtryggur was still a young man, in his early twenties, with no formal education. The responsibility of being an official agent and leader of the Icelandic immigrants was a heavy one. Sigtryggur seems to have had an unflagging trust in the promises and goodwill of the Canadian authorities and the Icelanders in turn great faith in Sigtryggur, as it turned out sometimes with disastrous consequences. During their first few years of settlement in Canada, the Icelanders encountered disappointments and hardships no less than those they had left behind. Upon arrival, Muskoka turned out to be a wilderness where none of the promised housing or employment were available. Moreover, the area was not suitable for group settlement, a concern of the Icelanders from the start. Almost immediately they started looking for other possibilities. Their choice fell on a district more to the east called Kinmount where they moved after the winter.

In September of that same year, 1874, a group of 365 Icelandic immigrants arrived. They, too, were met by an agent in order to tempt them to stay in Canada. Most of the members of this group had planned to go to the United States, however, and did not intend to be persuaded to stay by vague promises. They formulated their own conditions, as outlined in Rögnvaldur Pétursson's series of articles on Icelandic national organizations in Canada:

First it was pointed out that the Icelanders should enjoy complete freedom and civil rights equal to those of nationals, as soon as they had fulfilled the residence conditions that were stipulated in this country. Secondly, that they would obtain a suitably large and completely inhabitable area for settlement; and third, that they and their descendants would be allowed without hindrance to keep all their personal rights, their language and their nationality for life.[16]

These conditions were agreed upon, and the newcomers joined the earlier group in Kinmount.

The winter spent in Kinmount turned out to be worse than the one in Muskoka. The Icelanders now formed a large group that had to be accommodated in crowded and inadequate housing, and they had arrived just before winter so that there had been no time to work land or stock up provisions. Furthermore, they were without funds to purchase livestock, and little milk was available. Many people became ill as a result of fatigue from the journey, unfamiliarity with the climate and unsuitable food and drinking water.[17] Labour was difficult to find, and in the spring it turned out the soil in the area was infertile.

The Icelanders realized that there was no future for them in Kinmount, and even Sigtryggur seems to have finally realized that Ontario did not hold many possibilities for a prosperous Icelandic colony. About 200 people left with an immigration agent to try their luck in Nova Scotia. They were given land in an area called Mooseland which they named Markland, the name that Leifr Eiríksson gave to one of the areas which the Vikings discovered in North America (see note 1). However, an exclusively Icelandic colony was still the dream of most of the immigrants, also of those who had left with Reverend Páll to the United States. The possibilities held by the Red River Valley in Manitoba came to the attention of the Icelanders, an area which was attracting many settlers from Ontario at that time because of its fertile land. The province still had large tracts of unsettled land to offer, soon to be opened up as the Canadian Pacific Railway was being built.

An exploration group was formed, which was joined by representatives of the American group on the way. In Winnipeg, they were directed to an area of land outside the provincial border on the west shore of Lake Winnipeg. There, they were provided with a guide and shown around the territory. They were favourably impressed by possibilities of fishing in the lake, by the availability of wood for building and by the absence of grasshoppers in the Lake Winnipeg area. The area was isolated enough for the foundation of an exclusively Icelandic settlement, while on the other hand there were good connections with other areas by way of lake and the CP Railway, which was planned along the southern and eastern borders of the site.

Owing to the pressure of finding a site as soon as possible, the group did not explore long or well enough to consider, for instance, the climate, extreme cold in winter and extreme heat in summer, the heavy soil that was a marsh most of the year, or the absence of more experienced settlers to teach the Icelanders how to work the land. Nor did the leaders show much foresight when they decided to bring the people to the site just before winter, something they should have learnt from their experiences in Kinmount.

THE FOUNDING OF NEW ICELAND

In September 1875 the Icelanders set out on their way to Manitoba. There had been some doubt as to the practicability of the undertaking after the announcement of the good news, as the Icelanders had no money for the journey, and the Canadian government had a funding policy only for immigrants arriving from their home countries and needing to reach their destination in Canada, not for immigrants already in Canada. The Governor General, Lord Dufferin, however, had visited Iceland twenty years before, and had been so favourably impressed by the country and the people that he vouched for the Icelanders and arranged a grant for the trip and their establishment in New Iceland.

The journey was a mixture of hardships due to the over-crowded, slow-moving steamers sailing the lakes, and of optimism among the Icelanders now that they were on their way to their own colony and could start building a new future. In Duluth they were joined by thirteen Icelanders from the United States. Upon arrival in Winnipeg, the Icelanders had to stock up on provisions. They learnt there that the haying that was supposed to have been arranged for them had not taken place, and that they had to leave their livestock behind. Accordingly, efforts were made to arrange employment and find homes for single people and youngsters, especially young girls, as there was a great demand for domestic servants. About fifty people stayed behind in Winnipeg.

The rest of the trip over the Red River was made on flat, square barges that were built for transport of goods but certainly not for people. Some of them ran aground on the way, but the Icelanders were lucky enough to meet and persuade the captain of a Hudson Bay steamer to pull the barges along, on condition that women and children come on board and as long as the weather remained safe; as the Lake was dangerous even for a steamer. They arrived at Víðines (Willow Point) in the late afternoon of 21 October in beautiful Indian summer weather. The next morning, however, there was frost. Although a territorial land survey was conducted, on the basis of which people could claim lots, the early coming of winter prevented settlement or working of the land. People set to work building log cabins to the best of their abilities (despite their unfamiliarity with working with wood, there being no real trees in Iceland).[18] Several families had to live in one cabin. It turned out that the merchants in

Winnipeg had taken advantage of the ignorance and naiveté of the newcomers; because nearly all of the provisions were stale or rotten, food quickly ran short. Moreover, the Icelanders were unfamiliar with the idea, let alone the technique, of ice fishing, and hunting yielded very little. There was a lack of milk, and the first winter in New Iceland was characterized by hunger, scurvy, and cold. That year was one of the coldest winters on record. It went down in Icelandic-Canadian history as "the scurvy-winter."

When the Icelanders had made their claim to the New Iceland territory, the Canadian government had, as promised, granted them exclusive settlement rights and local self-government. New Iceland was situated outside the provincial boundaries and as it were outside the realm of "civilization." "With law the land shall be built," the motto of the Norwegian immigrants to Iceland a thousand years earlier, again inspired the development of provisional legislation and a system of local government. With characteristic pragmatism, and to divert their minds from hunger and cold, the Icelanders used the first winter to discuss and organize those official colony matters which formed the foundation for the official and slightly revised constitution which came into effect in January 1878. A provisional town council of five members was elected that winter and was recognized by government authorities. This council saw to the use and distribution of government funds, surveyed local requirements such as food and seed for spring, and filed for a post office, a road and a school. However, with their traditional keenness for learning, the Icelanders did not wait for the Canadian authorities but set up their own school as they had also done in Ontario. The first school in New Iceland started lessons during the scurvy winter, in 1875.[19] At the same time, people kept themselves entertained in the traditional way of the *kvöld-vaka*, "evening reading" of the sagas and scriptures, as most of them had brought the books they owned even if they owned nothing else. Children who were too young or lived too far from school were taught at home as was customary in Iceland at that time. Rögnvaldur Pétursson concluded that, on the whole, life in the colony differed little from life in the countryside in Iceland (1919: 109). A hand-written newspaper called *Nýji Þjóðólfur* ("New Þjóðólfur") was circulated, of which an uncertain number of issues appeared.

In the spring, people could move onto their lots and start working the land. Because of the Icelanders' unfamiliarity with nearly all agricultural techniques and tools except for that of cutting grass with a short scythe, however, the process of clearing and cultivating the land did not go smoothly and many crops failed. As the immigrant historian Þorsteinn Þ. Þorsteinsson worded it: "because we had only learnt how to live in Iceland, and never in North America, which did not know how to deal with us, nor we with it, at first."[20] Considering the conditions which the Icelandic settlers had lived through in Ontario and encountered again in different forms in Manitoba, the fact that a considerable number of people managed to survive their first year in New Iceland was, however, an achievement in itself. As Kristjanson pointed out: "In the circumstances, mere survival would have been no inconsiderable achievement, for the people had much to learn, and the learning process was one of trial and error. Undaunted they had endured the rigors of a climate new to them, restricted diet, and some deterioration in health conditions in the spring" (42).

In the summer of 1876, Sigtryggur returned with what is often referred to as the "Large Group" of new immigrants. After one of the worst volcanic eruptions ever in Iceland, in 1875, many people had lost their land and possessions and about twelve hundred decided to emigrate. Their means of transportation to Winnipeg were steamers, box cars and barges, which, along with the immigration sheds, were not designed for such large groups of people. Not only had the new emigrants no time to become adjusted to the climate and food, but the conditions of their journey were atrocious. In a letter sent home from New Iceland in 1877 one of the pioneers of this group, Björn Jónsson, described the journey. His laconic style highlights the sorrow revealed in his accounts with poignancy:

The inland journey was long and difficult, although it was worst on Lake Superior and Lake Huron, because the crowding was intolerable and everything was bad. We finally got here on 21 August.... Many of the people were ill during the boat trip, especially the children, the longer the trip lasted, mostly of a stomach disease. About 50 died of both groups [they travelled in two groups], both on the way and just after we had arrived here. Most of the victims were young, and many people suffered great losses. I lost my youngest child the day before I arrived here.[21]

Shortly after the arrival of the Large Group in New Iceland, the first symptoms of disease appeared but were not recognized for what they were. By November 1876, a smallpox epidemic was raging through the entire colony. As many families lived together in small cabins there was hardly any hope of stopping the illness. To make matters worse, the cold was severe, and the colony was placed in quarantine. As a result, the Icelanders were completely dependent on their own resources with little hope of finding work within the colony except caring for the sick. Moreover, although the epidemic was over in April, the quarantine was only lifted in mid-July. Until that time, the Icelanders could not sell any of their catches or produce, they could not go out to find work, and seed arrived too late for spring planting. The total number of deaths is estimated at around one hundred.

Although morale was understandably low, the Icelanders continued a far-seeing organization of the colony, partly as a distraction from the epidemic and its consequences. Again, the matter of local government was publicly discussed. The colony had already been divided into four districts or *byggðir*, for each of which elections were held in February 1877. Each district had a leader, a *byggðarstjóri*. All four districts together formed the *Vatnsþing*, the "Lake Parliament," which had its own council made up of the four district leaders plus a fifth member who was the *þingráðsstjóri*, the "Parliament Union Leader" and at the same time the colony leader. Sigtryggur Jónasson was elected *þingráðsstjóri*. The New Iceland constitution was remarkably democratic for its times. It gives a clear indication of what the Icelandic people had objected to or been dissatisfied with in the ruling system in Iceland at the time, as has been suggested by Jakob Jónsson (1943). Clearly, such nineteenth-century ideals of democracy and freedom as a more humane and less humiliating poor-relief had found their way into the political structure of New Iceland.

The vote was given to every male of eighteen or older with an unblemished reputation, regardless of means or social class. The constitution contained a special chapter concerning the duties of the colony members for the general good. For instance, every male older than 21 had to perform two days' tasks toward road upkeep every summer and pay $2 into a "road fund." There were special subsidies for widows and orphans. The district councils had similar duties to perform for the common good. The colony leader combined social leadership with liaison between the colony and the Canadian authorities. A council of arbitrators was established to settle disputes. If no conciliation was achieved, five men would be appointed to judge the case. Various of these aspects in the social system of New Iceland closely resembled those from Icelandic society during the settlement age, notably the use of the old Icelandic word *þing* rather than the modern Icelandic *sýsla* for "district," the enlistment of a council of arbitrators in case of disputes before judges were called in, and the absence of a penal code. While it is true that the medieval Icelandic republic had a penal code of sorts, it lacked executive power. Jakob Jónsson has argued convincingly that the reason for the absence of a penal code in both medieval and New Iceland is to be found in the pioneer conditions which moulded these settlement societies. According to Jónsson, people simply did not expect crimes to occur, nor final judgements to be disobeyed, since the performance of neighbourly help and other social duties was, if not compelled by feelings of honour, enforced by the watching eye of the community. Such a situation precluded the necessity of a penal code: "It may truly be said that in such a trial all life is dependent on the fact that people can trust each other. To receive a villainous reputation or to have lost the trust of others because of dishonour could in itself alone be enough punishment for anyone who experienced this, even though there were no instructions for it in a few laws."[22] Kristjanson has furthermore observed that the New Icelanders modelled the division into districts on the Ontario county system with its division into townships, so that the political organization of New Iceland may be said to have been influenced by both the Old World and the New, in order to suit local conditions. As mentioned earlier, the constitution would officially come into effect in January 1878.

During the winter of 1876-77, the same winter of the smallpox epidemic and when the New Iceland constitution was devised, the Icelanders also began discussing the possibility of founding an Icelandic newspaper. It was a popular issue among a people with a great traditional fondness for the written word, and soon a printing press was ordered from the United States. In spite of delays caused by the difficulty procuring the special letters in the Icelandic alphabet, in June 1877 the press arrived. In the meantime, a board of directors had been founded, and at a time when illness raged and there was a shortage of almost everything, enough shares were sold to finance the undertaking. In September 1877 the first issue of the paper, significantly named *Framfari* ("Progress"), appeared. It was printed in a log cabin. In total, 75 issues would appear over two years.[23] Kristjanson has well expressed the uniqueness of the publication: "The founding of a paper less than two years after the arrival of the first settlers in the colony, in a community of some fifteen hundred people, the majority of whom were destitute, and in the year of a devastating epidemic, is surely a unique achievement in the history of journalism in America, or anywhere else" (60).

During the same time when the idea of *Framfari* was born, another important matter to the colony came under discussion that was to have far-reaching consequences for the settlement and its history. The people had expressed a desire to have their own pastor, form their own parish and build churches in New Iceland. They knew that in North America there was no state church, and that they were now themselves responsible for church organization. Earlier in this chapter mention was made of those Icelanders among the first group of emigrants who went to the United States under the leadership of Páll Þorláksson. He had gone ahead in 1873 to make arrangements for them. Páll had been trained for the ministry at Concordia, St. Louis, which was run by the Missouri Synod Lutherans, who were known for their religious conservatism. He was ordained by the Norwegian Lutheran Church Synod, which had also helped him with his arrangements for the Icelanders. Páll was dedicated to helping the Icelandic communities in North America, and had come to New Iceland when the Large Group arrived in order to conduct baptisms and burials as well as divine services for the colony. He had also offered his services as a future pastor to the colony, in which case he would be supported and paid by the Norwegian Synod. He had then left again to resume his duties in the Icelandic community in Wisconsin.

However, elements in New Iceland resented the idea of being served by what they viewed as a "foreign" church organization, particularly because of a rising nationalist feeling after centuries of Danish oppression. Moreover, it was well-known that, although Páll himself was considered an eloquent, devoted man and was generally well-liked, the Synod to which he belonged was very conservative and strongly upheld the literal interpretation of the Bible. As an alternative, the Reverend Jón Bjarnason was put forward. In 1874, he had conducted a divine service on the occasion of the national celebration of Iceland's millenium for Icelanders in the New World in Milwaukee (see also below). *Séra* Jón, as he was commonly known,[24] was an orthodox man, but along the lines of the more liberal Icelandic Lutheran Church which believed in the spiritual interpretation of the Bible. During the service in Milwaukee, he had stressed the importance of the Icelandic community's upholding its national heritage.

The problem now arose that each minister had his supporters. Since the most distinguished members of the community, including Sigtryggur Jónasson, who were greatly revered for their leadership and support of the colony, favoured Jón Bjarnason, he was in the end invited to become the colony's pastor and was offered a salary to be paid by the parish. This did not conclude the controversy, however. Factionalism developed within the colony to the extent that members of the two parties, the *Pálsmenn* and the *Jónsmenn*, would even cross the street to avoid each other. And *Framfari*, being in the hands of the same leaders who had extended the invitation to *Séra* Jón, periodically inflamed the controversy further.

The religious dissension reached its climax in the autumn of 1877. Páll had made himself familiar with the conditions in New Iceland during the times he visited the colony to conduct services there. During his autumn visit in 1877, he gave his support to a letter written to the Norwegian Synod to ask for financial help. The letter, which was signed by a number of *Pálsmenn*, was delivered by Páll on his arrival back in North Dakota. When the news of the request for assistance reached the leaders of the colony, it caused an outrage among them, for their policy had been to keep the colony isolated and self-sufficient, and to make it a matter of general pride to start paying off the government loans as soon as possible. Thus, the leaders sought to prove that the colony could be an asset, rather than a burden, to Canada. As for the hardships, the colony leaders appear to have strongly pushed the idea that the Icelanders were a traditionally tough nation which had managed to survive through the ages with an "if it does not kill you it makes you stronger" mentality. This appears, for instance, from the lecture which Sigtryggur Jónasson held before the Manitoba Historical and Scientific Society in 1901, where he omitted all mention of hardships and disappointments, or of mistakes that were made, merely wishing to show that the Icelandic settlers had proved worthy of the loans and favours of the Dominion.

The eventual result of this religious dissension was that, in April 1878, most of the *Pálsmenn* left New Iceland for the Red River Valley in North Dakota, where Páll had discovered a more promising settlement area. Páll had never believed in the potential of New Iceland for prosperity from the moment he had seen it. His views must have influenced his supporters in their realization that they had no especial ties to New Iceland. In spite of what the colony leaders said, it clearly could not offer them the better future for which they had left

Iceland. The gravity of this blow to the leaders of the colony is obvious from Sigtryggur's reactions in the April issue of *Framfari*. Not
only did it end the dream of one exclusively Icelandic colony on the
North American continent, it was also an indirect criticism of the
leadership of the colony and of its ideals of proud nationalism. In
his reaction, an editorial in *Framfari* entitled "Are the Icelanders Born
to Everlasting Hunger and Suffering," Sigtryggur set forth his ideas
about the necessities of hardship to harden the people and accused
Páll of having made Icelanders into "spiritual paupers" (1878: 176).
Here, Sigtryggur expounds his idea that being a true Icelander means
looking at suffering and hardships as something that "toughens and
hardens" people, rather than something that should be allowed to
reduce them to "parish paupers" and "common beggars." Indeed,
the tenor of the editorial is quite disparaging toward those immigrants who had had to rely on welfare in Iceland and, so Sigtryggur
assumes, were looking to do the same in Canada.

In his biography of Páll, George Houser suggested that
Sigtryggur's inflexible and vehement stance in the dissension was
rooted in the fact that Páll's actions revealed poignantly what he himself could never admit: that he had chosen the wrong piece of land
for the colony. In Houser's own words: "What was even more galling
for Sigtryggur was that his judgement had been called into question.
He was not a man who could admit graciously that he had made an
error in leading his countrymen to this inhospitable site. But the fact
was there" (1990: 146-47). Houser's work is one of the first studies in
English to expose the underlying factions and motives of the New
Iceland colony leaders, who had traditionally been presented uncrit-
ically to the outside world as celebrated heroes. In fact, when contemporary documents are studied, it appears that the colony leaders
quickly began to regard themselves as a kind of ruling class among
the immigrants. In his reminiscences, for instance, pioneer Simon
Simonson criticizes the fact that the leaders had ensured the best lots
of land for themselves before giving others the opportunity to claim
their land (1946). They also held all influential positions in the colony:
in the council, the editorial board of *Framfari*, and the Church, since
Séra Jón had aligned himself with the leaders. Moreover, Sigtryggur
Jónasson was not only leader of the colony but also the colony's representative in its dealings with the Canadian authorities and, consequently, distributor of funds and collector of loans. Thus, the leaders
were in a position to construct a myth about the Icelanders as a proud,

hardy and culturally superior people (see below).[25] Through the baptism and burial services he conducted in New Iceland, Páll, on the other hand, had witnessed the misery that many of the less fortunate immigrants endured. His concern was not so much the image and nationalism of the Icelanders as it was the improvement of their situation.

Séra Jón Bjarnason, however, became the popular Church leader of New Iceland, and, later on, the leader of the Icelandic Lutheran Synod. This Synod encompassed nearly all Icelandic church communities in North America, and therewith he officially sealed over the breach, although even *Séra* Jón's supporters had to admit that, later in life, he became increasingly fundamentalist and intolerant. *Séra* Páll was equally revered in the Icelandic community of North Dakota as its founder and father. He died a very early death in 1882, at the age of 33, having sacrificed his delicate health to the services of the community.

A chapter that has remained almost completely ignored in Icelandic immigrant historiography is that of original native presence in the New Iceland area. Sandy Bar Salteaux had lived in the area since the seventeenth century, and settlement rights had been granted to the Icelanders on the assumption that the outstanding Treaty No. 5, which would relinquish local native land claims, would soon be signed. In fact, the Treaty was not signed until 1876, and as a result relations between Salteaux and Icelandic settlers were problematic, especially with regard to the contested northern border of the colony (Brydon 1997). The poet Guttormur J. Guttormsson, who grew up near the northern border, is one among few who has documented the actual displacement of the Salteaux as a consequence of Icelandic settlement (in his poem "Indiána Hátíð," "Indian Festival," discussed in Chapter III) as well as the invaluable assistance they generously offered the invading settlers until most of the band died from smallpox in 1877 (for instance in his essay "Tveir Þættir," 1975). The theme of individual native-Icelandic relations and the general plight of native peoples in Canada does, however, regularly surface in Western Icelandic literature and popular lore (see Chapters III and IV).

The history of New Iceland does not end here. The ensuing events, however, are of less relevance to the field of Icelandic-Canadian literature. Suffice it to mention briefly here that further hardships, such as a great flood in 1879, led to another general exodus in 1880 and 1881. Many new Icelandic communities were founded, most importantly in the area around Lake Manitoba, to the northeast of New Iceland, and the area in between Lake Manitoba and Lake Winnipeg, generally called the Interlake area. Many people also moved to Winnipeg, where a thriving Icelandic community developed. Winnipeg became the capital and cultural centre of the Icelanders in North America. In 1881, New Iceland was left with only 250 inhabitants, although this number increased again with newly arriving immigrants.

The settlement in Markland, Nova Scotia, did not succeed. The piece of land the Icelandic settlers had been given contained infertile, stony soil, and although they seem to have developed a great fondness for the area and the people, they eventually had to leave. Nearly all of them moved to the Red River Valley. The Markland settlement, however, has lived on in the writings of the Icelandic immigrant author Jóhann Magnús Bjarnason, who will be subject of discussion in the next chapter. The Icelanders in Wisconsin never quite felt at home there. They moved early, mostly to Minnesota and later to North Dakota. From there, a small group of farmers moved on to the Red Deer area in Alberta, among them the poet Stephan G. Stephansson (see Chapter III).

It is rather ironic that the major settlement of the Icelanders turned out to be less prosperous than the other Icelandic settlements in North America. Nevertheless, the ideal behind the colony of New Iceland has been of extreme importance from the beginning, and somehow the New Iceland area appears to have continued embodying this ideal up to the present day, even though the Icelanders have moved far and wide over the continent since. This ideal is what has kept the Icelanders together as an ethnic unity independent of distance and national borders.

At this juncture, it seems appropriate to point to an important development among the Icelandic immigrants which forms a bridge between this section and the next. This development involves the self-image of the Icelandic pioneers, and the ways in which it was influenced by reactions to the emigration in the home country. This self-image exerted its own influence on the development and outward appearance of the Icelandic immigrants in Canada, and explains, for instance, the ideological underpinnings of the religious dispute.

As was mentioned previously, emigration from Iceland to North America started in 1873. It continued in waves surging and ebbing until the beginning of the present century. During this time, the reactions of the Icelanders who did not leave varied considerably. Although no specific study has been conducted on this topic, Helgi Skúli Kjartansson touches on the subject in his dissertation on the emigration of Icelanders to North America (1976: 94-104). He notes that, at first, the reactions were rather negative among those who did not consider emigrating. Those who left were regarded as traitors and cowards who abandoned the country exactly at a time when the battle for independence was being fought and the people needed to stand together. As emigration continued and the domestic situation worsened, the people who remained seem to have grown used to it and accepted it. Their emigrant compatriots came to be known as *Vestur-Íslendingar*, or West Icelanders.[26]

However, the numbers of people emigrating during the late 1880s took on such large proportions that a fear arose that the country would bleed to death with all its manpower disappearing, since single and young people were then leaving rather than complete families, as had been the case before. The battle for independence was stagnating, the farmers were complaining of a lack of farmhands and workers, and more and more farms fell desolate at a time when the nation was finally showing a keen interest in enterprise. The nationalists who had tried for so long to get the country back on its own feet now watched its people disappear.

The consequent reactions to the emigrants and emigration were quite bitter and violent during those years. A deep distrust had grown towards agents and emigrants who visited the country, especially as the latter were sometimes paid by agents to entice people at home to emigrate as well. A vitriolic polemic was conducted in 1888 between two writers, Benedict Gröndal and Jón Ólafsson. Of these, the first was outspokenly opposed to emigration, whereas the latter had been an emigrant himself. Although newspapers were divided over the issue, the most widely-read ones were adverse to emigration. This resentment only really subsided in the 1920s by which time the degree of emigration had become inconsequential.

Many emigrant Icelanders were keen to be kept informed of all that happened in Iceland, especially when they could not yet speak English and had not yet developed any ties with their adopted country. By way of letters from friends and family at home and through Icelandic newspapers the Icelanders in Canada learnt about the growing opposition in their home country to emigration. Accusations made against Icelandic emigrants as being traitors, rabble and cowards, rubbed salt into the wounds of many. Uprooting, nostalgia and pioneer hardships had made the immigrant experience painful enough. In addition, during the 1880s and 1890s many poor Icelanders were shipped to Canada by district authorities to reduce welfare costs. Little wonder, then, that a cooling of sentiments developed during this time between Icelanders at home and their compatriots in North America (Pétursson 1933: 67). The peak of Icelandic resentment was reached at the end of the nineteenth century, at exactly the time that the worst initial hardships among the emigrants were coming to an end. Most of them had learnt how to survive in their new environment, so that more attention could be given to other matters, such as the documentation of the settlement experience, and the future of the Icelandic heritage in Canada. Considerations about the social position of Icelandic immigrants and their descendents in an anglo-centric Canadian society occupied the minds of many West Icelanders. It is hardly surprising that in this climate, the resentment emerging in Iceland was felt in Canada as a betrayal, especially so since the Icelandic immigrants had to deal with Anglo-Canadian prejudices against "foreigners" at the same time. The influence of Icelandic and Canadian attitudes toward the West Icelanders on the immigrants' self-image at this time has, therefore, been considerable.

These developments have resulted in the gradual creation of what I have brought down to three important Western Icelandic myths. These myths concern the West Icelanders themselves, their history and their position towards their old and their adopted country. They arose as formal defences, justifications of conduct and position, and as a legitimation of the Western Icelandic immigrant reality. They involve what Greenway has explained as "the spontaneous reconstruction of the past to support the factual nature of the values of the present. In a sense this creative act of the mythic imagination is mythopoesis, but the expression of the mythic imagination is not limited to literature, nor is it an act of conscious creation" (1977: 20). As a result, the large majority of Western Icelandic literary and non-literary writings are concerned with a reconstruction of both Nordic and Western Icelandic history, in order to validate the Western Icelandic situation of the present.

The earliest part of Icelandic history lent itself perfectly to the intermingling of factual and mythic images because of its immigrant nature: the settlement of Iceland was re-established as the symbolic matrix of Western Icelandic immigrant history. Thus, the Icelandic emigration to Canada could be legitimized through both the historical and the mythic fact of Iceland's origins. The original settlement of Iceland became the *illud tempus*, the sacred origins of the group, of which the emigration to Canada was a re-enactment, what Greenway calls a "historically symbolic event of origin" (13). This Western Icelandic reconstruction of the ethnic past conforms to Greenway's definition of social myth: "Social myth may be defined as the intermingling of mythic images and rational inquiry in the apprehension of human value. As such, the constructs of social myth retain myth's quality of being objectively real to the believer, but the reality must be sustained by an appeal to scientific validation.... Thus the value truths of social myths are assumed to be facts" (63). Indeed, we find that any references to the past, whether in a historical or a mythic sense, are presented as rationally if not scientifically validated, and carry a definite note of belief on the part of the author. Three myths derived directly from the Western Icelandic social myth are an essential feature of the self-image of the West Icelanders, and as such permeate a wide variety of Western Icelandic writings.

The first myth is of a historical nature. It is primarily concerned with the historical settlement of Iceland and the Norse discovery of the American continent. Its main claim is that the Icelanders have never lost their Viking spirit of proud independence, noble courage, and, most importantly, what they term *útþrá*, which Lindal translates as the innate yearning "to reach beyond" (1967: 100). When emigration is viewed or presented in this light, it takes on an ancient glory and has at the same time become a natural, almost inevitable consequence of both history and ancestry. This myth allows the West Icelanders to retain a sentimental nostalgia for the home country without being disturbed by memories of resentment harboured against them in contemporary Iceland. Moreover, it is a very attractive picture for non-Icelandic Canadians and Americans, who, if they do know anything about Iceland at all, are most likely to have acquired their knowledge through the sagas. For the many North Americans who have no idea of Iceland, it provides a very romantic and stereotypical image. Many Western Icelandic writings display this emphasis on Viking Iceland, such as the historical surveys by Lindal and Kristjanson, innumerable articles by, for instance, Beck and a large number of novels and poems by early and later writers.

The second myth is based on the geographical and social circumstances in Iceland during the nineteenth century and before. It suggests that the country's climate, its general tendency to natural disasters and its social inertia made life in Iceland intolerable. Those who strive for freedom and success, therefore, have no other choice than to leave Iceland. This view seems to have been especially popular during the earlier decades of the Icelanders in North America. We encounter it, for instance, in Sigtryggur Jónasson's editorial as well as in several poems published in *Framfari* (*Bókmenntasaga* 3). The most obvious representative of this myth about the geographical disadvantages of Iceland would be Þorsteinsson's otherwise elaborate and well-documented standard history on Icelanders in North America, the *Saga Íslendinga í Vesturheimi*. Þorsteinsson spends almost one whole volume in a series of five (three written by himself) describing natural disasters in Iceland.[27]

The third myth derived from the Western Icelandic social myth is compensatory. It is concerned with actions rather than theoretical explanations, with any action, in fact, which serves to prove the worthiness of the West Icelanders as both Icelanders and Canadians. Many books and articles list the achievements of West Icelanders in numerous fields. Complimentary remarks made about West Icelanders by others are repeated many times while Iceland is incessantly and emphatically promoted as a country with a glorious past and an unsurpassed cultural tradition and literacy. In short, West Icelanders must be portrayed as outstanding in both Icelandic and Canadian spheres. Sigtryggur Jónasson's ideas are an early manifestation of this ethnic pride in Canada. The ambition to be both the best Icelanders and the best Canadians has, in practice, served the West Icelanders well, although, in written works, it has sometimes tended toward overcompensation bordering on national arrogance. A good example would be Jónas A. Sigurðsson's article "Vestur Islendingar" (1929), which attempts to show that Icelanders are the best in everything they do by the sole virtue of their nationality. The compensatory urge has been so widespread that it is still quite difficult to find works by Icelandic Canadians which give a less idealistic and more realistic picture of the West Icelanders as a group throughout their history in North America. It has, in some cases, led to the exclusion or dismissal of members who did not conform to the ideology, such as, for instance, the author Laura Goodman Salverson (see Chapter III), and to the suppression of native presence in Western

Icelandic historiography and myth. Those who wrote more critical works about Icelandic Canadians were certainly not the more popular for it, such as Gunnsteinn Eyjólfsson, Stephan G. Stephansson, the non-immigrant Icelander Halldór Laxness (in his short story "Nýja Ísland") and, to give a more recent example, W.D. Valgardson (see Chapter IV). When *The Icelandic Canadian* magazine published the translated reminiscences of Simon Simonson, the translator Kristjanson thought it necessary to defend the colony leaders and community spirit from Simon's criticisms. Kristjanson says the following about Simon's account: "Since it is written from the autobiographical and not the broad historical point of view, other accounts of the time and place must be kept in mind in order to obtain a true final impression" (1946: 55). Although he does contend that Simon is "at times justly critical of the leaders," Kristjanson hastens to defend the colony leaders over their choice of the colony site, a choice severely criticized by Simon: "It should be borne in mind that at the time when the site of the settlement was chosen, it was proposed to build the main line of the Canadian Pacific Railway through Selkirk." Kristjanson then proceeds to list the achievements of the colony members during the first years, probably to counteract Simon's criticisms of a perceived lack of community spirit.

It is important to keep these myths in mind when reading material by West Icelanders about West Icelanders or about Iceland, as they pervade many works, especially earlier ones. In some typical writings, it leads to a dramatic, almost sentimental tone. In others, it is less obvious, and sometimes even combined with a more critical attitude which is, nevertheless, presented with the utmost care. After all, it was generally regarded as a Western Icelandic task to nurture a very delicate national identity and self-image which were being resented on the one side and threatened with extinction on the other. This nurturing process will be our next consideration.

THE PRESERVATION OF ICELANDIC CULTURE AND IDENTITY DURING THE FIRST DECADES

Many Icelandic-Canadian books, articles and accounts would like us to believe that the Icelanders were absolutely determined to preserve their culture and nationality from the moment they left their native country. In reality, national awareness and a general conscious urge to preserve and promote the national heritage are more likely to have developed as a result of the conditions prevailing during the first years in the Canada, and as a consequence of the psychological shock and feelings of alienation which the emigrant experience entails. Bergsteinn Jónsson suggests that the reading societies, especially in the North of Iceland, may have provided prospective emigrants with useful information on life and conditions in North America (1975: 34). It is, however, unlikely that any source could have prepared these people for the actual experience of having to make a mentally and physically fulfilling life, in a chaotic, foreign and therefore apparently hostile environment. After all, Iceland is an island, and while people may have read about foreign countries, many would never have experienced any contact with foreign people or surroundings.

Consequently, it may well be that the Icelandic emigrants had become aware of certain economical and geographical conditions prevailing in North America, but whether they could have realistically foreseen any need to formulate structures and organizations to protect themselves from psychological and cultural shock or to preserve their culture, seems doubtful. Mossberg has remarked on the clash between the idea of the New World on the one hand, and its reality on the other:

The immigrants could only conceptualize the attractions offered by America—the *idea* of property ownership, the *idea* of religious freedom, the *idea* of democracy and a classless society. Before they actually made the voyage to America, they could not define these ideas in terms of daily events of their experience. They could only understand these concepts in terms of the conditions they rejected in Scandinavia. But the immigrants' emotional and spiritual lives were rooted in concrete experiences in the home country. They could think about religious freedom in America, but they could not experience the emotional associations of that freedom, the way that they could re-experience, each time they entered a particular village church, the emotions they felt when they were married or when they were confirmed. They had to sacrifice the emotional associations inextricably bound to an immediate sense of place. They were keenly aware of this sacrifice and experienced it as a profound sense of loss. (1976: 113)

That the idea of an exclusively Icelandic settlement in North America was born and discussed in Iceland, as, for instance, Rögnvaldur Pétursson suggests (1919: 101), does not necessarily contradict this assumption; it indicates a natural and practical desire, first, to stay together and help each other in an environment where people could safely resort to their native language and customs in spite of their residence in a foreign country and, second, to counteract the effects of homesickness.

Indeed, it seems that the ideal for which New Iceland came to stand, the preservation of Icelandic culture, language and nationality in one homogeneous Icelandic settlement, was mostly the work of a small group of colony leaders, notably Sigtryggur Jónasson. Their reasons for the unflagging encouragement of nationalism were, if not motivated by personal betterment, probably ascribable to concerns for the pioneers' psychological need, especially in the distressing circumstances in which many of the Icelanders found themselves, and to a fear of the Icelanders becoming scattered and lost in the larger North American society. National pride, linked to images of Viking ancestry with its ideals of courage, defiance of fate and yearning for freedom and new horizons, were celebrated themes for nineteenth-century Icelanders. Now they were to inspire the immigrants with the will and strength to persevere in the face of the many disappointments they had suffered, and were also to provide them with a popular cause to unite and fight for, so as to counterbalance the fact of their emigration.

Most importantly, it was only now, after the first pioneer hardships, that this ideal struck a chord. It was a noble cause to strive for together, as well as a promise of a psychological support structure in a foreign world. Nationality was no longer an unconscious attribute that could be taken for granted: it was becoming a conscious construct in need of preservation and fostering. The Icelandic writer Einar Hjörleifsson Kvaran, who spent a number of years among the West Icelanders as a newspaper editor, had this to say about Western Icelandic nationalism when he was back in Iceland:

But the love of the West Icelanders for their old native country is, of course, of a special kind. It lacks some of those aspects that make up the patriotism of people here.... The practical aspects of that patriotic feeling disappear more or less. The romantic aspects, however, become proportionally stronger. The feeling is almost exclusively of a romantic nature.... Their joy at all honour, all respect, all the fame of their country and their people double. The love for its poetry and language multiply. And the memories of their native country bloom up in their souls, refined, transformed, longed for in the illuminated ocean of their own love. Yet although it has lightened up around those memories, the colours are not clear. The hardships of the individuals and the hardships of the people have cast a faintness over them, the same faintness which rests, so to speak, on all Icelandic thoughts and emotions. The Western Icelandic love of Iceland is a plant which is rooted in the innermost part of their souls, in that part where most things which are dearest and most beloved grow. However, as this plant is fed exclusively, so to speak, by their romantic nature, and thus not connected to the work done for the upbringing and honour of themselves and their nearest, the flower is so astonishingly delicate. It never lives long on earthly warmth alone, the warmth from its own roots. It needs nursing....[28]

As Ingibjörg Ásta Gunnarsdóttir suggests, they were no longer simply Icelanders, they had become Icelanders with a mission: that mission was to be an Icelander in a non-Icelandic environment (1987: 50).

Bergsteinn Jónsson has remarked on the incredibly tenacious nature of the dream of a New Iceland among the immigrants when viewed from the Old World. He reminds us that: "there the Icelanders could for a while again hold on to their language, culture and nationality in peace. People should be careful not to underestimate the spiritual burden which rested on these people's shoulders while they were forced to move around amongst unfamiliar, curious and sometimes plain hostile foreigners." [29] Here, Jónsson indicates the development of the dream of a New Iceland from an initial practical concept, a means to retain the familiar, to a psychological need rather than a nationalist ideal in a confusing, strange new context. Þorsteinsson points to the same development when he says:

The poverty was nothing compared to being cast out of their ancient, thousand-year-old home, which they knew—and loved dearly in spite of everything—into an unknown world, which required many long years to become acquainted and familiar with, and which had to be to their liking in all respects for the rest of their lives. In many ways they were like fish out of water in American society, but in their own associations and society they lived again in their old world and kept their heads high. It was, therefore, of the utmost necessity to be able to found a general colony before anything else.[30]

Furthermore, Jónsson's reminder to those in the Old World points to the difficulty of envisaging this immigrant experience.

The beginning of the nationalist movement among the Icelandic immigrants is generally dated at the national celebration of Iceland's millenium, 2 August 1874, in Milwaukee, then a cultural centre for the Icelanders in the United States. In Iceland, celebratory services were held all over the country at King Christian IX's request, and a group of enthusiastic Icelanders in Milwaukee had undertaken to organize a similar service on their side of the ocean. The service was lead by *Séra* Jón Bjarnason, who had been teaching at Luther College in Iowa for a year. The importance of this national celebration in Milwaukee is not so much due to its form or size, for at that time, there were only about 350-400 Icelanders on the continent. Neither was it remarkable that the Icelanders still felt closely enough linked with their native country to celebrate the event. Emigration had just begun, and it is only natural that these newly emigrated Icelanders still felt connected to Iceland. Rather, it was Jón Bjarnason's speech during the service which made the celebration a significant one for the history of Icelandic nationalism in North America. In this speech, he strongly emphasized the link between religion and nationalism, which he rhetorically described as a continual link throughout Icelandic history. He ended his speech with the following emphatic reminder to the Icelanders in North America:

We did not come here in order to rid ourselves of our duties to the nation which God has connected us to with holy and exalted bonds of descent. Anyone, who forgets his native land or thinks himself too good to preserve that of his nationality which is good and divine, for the sole reason of dwelling in a foreign country and finding his livelihood there, comes very close to forgetting God. It is only a short and quickly-taken step from casting away one's nationality to casting away the faith of one's forefathers. True Christian love of one's country does not fill the heart with contempt for other nations than one's own; it does not blind the eyes to the superiority of foreigners in so many respects, nor for one's own poverty, drawbacks and lack of education.[31]

In a Canadian context, one need only think of the example of the Québécois to realize how powerful this relation between religion and nationalism can be.

The influence of Jón Bjarnason's speech was not immediate. It is true that shortly after the celebration the first Icelandic national society was founded, the *Íslendingafélag* ("Society of Icelanders"), but this society was short-lived, as most Icelanders moved away from Milwaukee and later from Wisconsin. In addition, many of the immigrants were too busy learning the ways of the country, adjusting, and building up a new life, especially during those first years. After all, this was what they had come to the New World for: to find a new and more prosperous future. The stimulating talk of a few leaders about national pride worked well enough in times of hardship and severe disappointments, but there is very little indication indeed that this talk was taken to heart when the situation was improving. On the contrary, many accounts of the more prosperous times mention very quick assimilation and a tendency among many to adopt everything North American. Along with this went a denial of the Icelandic nationality, which was seen as a stumbling block rather than an asset or object of pride.[32] Rögnvaldur Pétursson also pointed to the possibility that those who were more nationalistic may have found themselves unable satisfactorily to organize a nationalist society or to formulate and achieve its goals (1933: 78). This is not at all improbable; as we saw earlier, many people in Iceland found themselves faced with the same problem as they attempted to co-ordinate their struggle for independence.

As the New World community grew, finding itself increasingly able to devote time and interest to other pursuits, so various social and cultural structures were set up. Naturally, these resembled the ones at home, for they were the only structures known to the Icelandic pioneers. Moreover, the familiarity of these structures acquired a special, deeper meaning in a foreign environment. Additionally, the West Icelanders would have begun to feel a spiritual need which the New World environment, empty of history, culture and myth as it seemed to the emigrants from an Old World country, could not fill with its own alternatives, except for quick money-making.[33]

It is in this context that we should see the growing importance of religion among West Icelanders, who went from a State Church to the North American system of free Churches. This change demanded a much greater involvement on the part of everyone who felt drawn towards the practice of religion. Apart from the build-up of their own free Church, the responsibility for decisions about Church matters and organization now lay with the parish members. People therefore had to consider and vote on issues that, before, had not been their responsibility. Religion thus became an excellent arena for various clashes of opinion, and, in this way, took the place of politics at home. In an attempt to explain why the Church has had a much more extensive meaning for West Icelanders, Einar Kvaran pointed out: "As their whole Church organization is built on free contribution, that organization becomes a matter that is incredibly close to people's hearts."[34]

Churches were invariably at the forefront in the development of community life. Because pioneer conditions did not allow for much money to be spent on separate buildings for various community activities, divine services were usually held in the same building as social events such as debates, meetings and dances. As a consequence, Church activities and social events were not considered to belong to two different spheres. The Church was, on the contrary, an initial and inseparable part of a larger body of social activities in the pioneer communities which served the spiritual and cultural needs of the people, a part which demanded active involvement. Moreover, services were held in Icelandic, so that the Church and its concerns, such as Sunday schools and Church publications, became the focus of the preservation of the Icelandic language and culture.

Against this background it is not difficult to envision how Jón Bjarnason's speech during that first Icelandic service held on the American continent, with its strong emphasis on the close link of religion and nationality, came to reverberate in people's minds. Under the powerful leadership of the charismatic *Séra* Jón, the Church became one of the strongest, if not *the* strongest body of Icelandic nationalism in North America. It is for this reason that many societies, clubs and organizations concerned with the preservation of the Icelandic culture and nationality were closely bound to or in co-operation with the Church. Through them and the Church, the notorious Western Icelandic factionalism found a natural outlet for its energies among an immigrant group whose members have been characterized as being at the same time the most sociable and the most discordant of people (Árnason 1923: 98; Houser 156; Þorsteinsson 2: 328).

As was pointed out earlier, the Icelanders had become acquainted with democracy and its methods of social improvement and change during the nineteenth century. It had been only a brief acquaintance however. As a consequence, we see an eagerness among the West Icelanders to found societies of all kinds to organize their lives in the best and most democratic way possible. However, we also see growing pains, especially during the first decades. No one was quite sure as to the goals and how these could be achieved. As a result, different opinions abounded and clashed violently, especially with regard to nationalist societies.

Those societies mainly concerned with the practical and burning issues of the day usually held out the longest. Most of them came into being during the pioneer days, when help and co-operation were matters of survival. For instance, in Winnipeg the *Íslendingafélag* ("Icelandic Association"), later renamed *Framfarafélag* ("Progressive

Association"), was most importantly occupied with the reception, assistance and keeping track of new Icelandic immigrants. Ladies Aid Societies developed in nearly every Icelandic community, concerning themselves with community care, education and social events of various kinds. More often than not, these societies were closely linked with the Church, and contributed greatly to the preservation of Icelandic culture. The longevity of some of them is striking in comparison to other societies.

Rögnvaldur Pétursson distinguishes three main tasks which characterize all societies that align themselves with the cause of preserving the Icelandic culture in North America in some way or another. First, there is the upkeep and preservation of the Icelandic language, its religion, culture and customs. As a second task he names the aim of leading the Icelanders to recognition and fame both within and outside the Icelandic community. The third goal is their support, both spiritual and material, of Icelanders in the New World, to preserve their independence and their rights (1919: 99).

When one looks at the history of the national organizations in North America, the first two surely became the most prominent tasks. They also point to an important and characteristically Western Icelandic issue: the fervent ambition of West Icelanders both to preserve their native culture and identity and to become the best possible citizens of their adopted country. This ambition is evident from the strong compensatory urge among West Icelanders discussed earlier in this chapter. As I suggested there, this ambition can be traced to the immigrants' perceived predicament in being simultaneously resented by their compatriots at home and despised and threatened by their new North American neighbours. It is far from unnatural to react in such a situation with a strong urge to prove oneself the best in both worlds and thus worthy of respect rather than resentment or contempt.

The ambition to be both good Icelanders and good Canadians, together with the tendency toward factionalism, also forms the basis of John Matthiasson's theory, introduced in Chapter I, on dualism as an Icelandic cultural theme. We find attempts to harmonize the dual Western Icelandic ambition in the argument that by preserving what is characteristic for them as Icelanders they will be the better Canadians. Only as good Icelanders are they in a position to offer their adopted country anything of value, namely their cultural heritage, in return for their adoption. If instead, they only live to imitate native North

Americans, they will always remain the lesser because they are not North Americans, and they will lose the opportunity to make their mark.[35]

The third goal observed by Pétursson points to the influence of the democratic farmers' and reading societies in nineteenth-century Iceland, the prototypes of most of the Icelandic national societies in North America. This becomes even more clear if we look at the types of national societies and the names and key-slogans they carry. Nearly every Icelandic community, for instance, had a reading society which bought books and circulated them among its members. It is also remarkable how many societies, like their counterparts in Iceland, carried the word "progress" (*framfari*) or "education" (*menntun*) in their names or listed goals. Many societies were involved in the organization of lectures and discussions.

These societies appealed to the people and became an important part of their social life in the new country, for they continued a popular development which had started in Iceland. Moreover, with their aims for progress and education, they fulfilled a mental and cultural need, and at the same time paved the way for progress and prosperity in North America. Since the societies were built on Icelandic models, and since their activities, conducted in Icelandic, were concerned with either Icelandic issues or issues relevant to West Icelanders, they also played an important part in the interest in and preservation of Icelandic culture.

One society deserves special mention here, *Hið íslenzka menningarfélag* ("The Icelandic Cultural Society"). This society was founded in the Icelandic community in North Dakota in 1888 in reaction to the conservative religious climate under the leadership of the Norwegian Synod pastor Páll Þorláksson. Among the initiators and founders of the society was the poet Stephan G. Stephansson, who will be discussed in the next chapter. The slogans of this society were *Mannúð, Rannsókn, Frelsi* ("Humanity, Research, Freedom"). In terms of affiliation, the influence of the American Freethinkers, and especially of Felix Adler's *Ethical Cultural Society*, has been convincingly argued elsewhere (Halldórsson 1961: 23-24; Jóhannesson 1966: 231-37). The Cultural Society wished to increase knowledge by critical reading, study and discussion, thus liberating the mind to make way for progress and a more humanitarian outlook on life (Bessason 1967b: 50-51).

The influence this society had was considerable and long-lived, even though the society itself rapidly declined when many of its members moved away. At first, it caused much vehement criticism and dissension, since it was critical of the Church, which was seen as hindering man's pursuit of progress and freedom because of its emphasis on the uncritical and a blind belief in dogma and creed. However, its emphasis on humanitarianism and progress through self-education was to become a great influence on a number of "unschooled" Western Icelandic writers (*alþýðuskáld*), especially those with a bent towards socialism, such as Sigurður Július Jóhannesson, Þorskabítur and Guttormur J. Guttormsson. In addition, many of those sympathetic to the Society's criticism of the Lutheran Church were later to form their own Unitarian Church. In fact, the Unitarians founded a Cultural Society in 1906 with similar goals and in memory of the original Cultural Society.

As time went by, the Icelandic societies concerned with nationalist issues became more organized and more conscious of their goals and how to achieve them. This was, of course, in large part due to more experience in the New World, but possibly also because the interest among West Icelanders in the preservation of their cultural heritage slowly increased. Rögnvaldur Pétursson (1920) shows that, after the blind rush for assimilation during the first two decades, certain events kindled a renewed nostalgia and interest in things Icelandic. Among these events were the World Exhibition in Chicago in 1893, which celebrated the 400th anniversary of the "discovery" of America by Columbus. This raised discussion about Leifr Eiríksson's discovery and increased world interest in Icelandic history and documents, enhanced by the display by Denmark of a copy of one of the Icelandic saga manuscripts at the Exhibition. The respect and appreciation shown on a world-wide scale certainly increased the self-confidence and pride in their heritage among the West Icelanders.

Another event which rekindled an interest in preserving the national heritage was the first national celebration of the West Icelanders, the so-called *Íslendingadagurinn*, held in Winnipeg in 1890. It was one of the biggest events ever in Winnipeg, and its positive reception in the Canadian press exerted a stimulating influence on Icelandic nationalism. The contribution of the various Western Icelandic communities towards a memorial statue in Iceland to commemorate the 100th birthday of Jón Sigurðsson in 1911 was not only proof of their interest and willingness to remember and contribute to their communal heritage but awakened an interest in Iceland and its history among their younger members.

In the course of time, many new societies were founded to safe-guard the Icelandic heritage and promote community activity, also among the younger, English-speaking members. When they put their minds to it and the issue was important enough, the Western Icelandic community as a whole could accomplish impressive feats, such as the establishment of the Chair of Icelandic at the University of Manitoba through community effort and money the better to preserve and promote Icelandic culture. However, continual factionalism has pre-vented these societies from organizing themselves on a larger scale. To name but the most (in)famous examples in the history of Western Icelandic factionalism in later years: another religious split between the Lutheran and the Unitarian Church; contention over Western Icelandic participation in the First World War; and disagreement over whether a Western Icelandic presence at the celebration of the millenium of Iceland's *Alþingi* should be financially supported by Canadian authorities, eventually causing the rival groups to travel to Iceland on two separate ships. When I attended the annual con-vention of the Icelandic National League in Winnipeg in 1990, my impression was confirmed that, still today, factionalism is an integral and active component in the Icelandic-Canadian community. During this convention, the INL's suggestion of closer co-operation to bring the various Western Icelandic societies and communities closer together under one umbrella organization was declined.

The question may arise here whether the Icelandic immigrants can and should be seen as one ethnic community regardless of the Canadian-American border. While there seems to be no conscious policy or general opinion regarding this question among West Ice-landers, the impression one receives is that the 49th parallel hardly exists in the Western Icelandic community consciousness. For all the discord among West Icelanders, Canadian or American nationality never appears to play a role. Western Icelandic cultural and com-munity activities seem to be conducted without regard to national borders. Obvious examples are American-Icelandic writer Bill Holm's close affiliations with the Icelandic-Canadian community, and Kristjana Gunnars' remarks in her introduction to the collection of Icelandic-Canadian short stories explaining her reasons for including Bill Holm in the collection (1989: xiv).

Some of the most important means of uniting the Western Icelandic community all over the North American continent and of fostering its sense of nationality and community have been the numerous Western Icelandic newspapers and journals. They have also played an essential role in the preservation of the Icelandic cultural heritage. Richard Beck has referred to them as the *lífstaug* ("lifeline") of all communal efforts (1957: 7-12). Rögnvaldur Pétursson has summed up their meaning for the Western Icelandic community:

How great the importance of the papers has been for the preservation of the Icelandic language in North America becomes clear when the contents and subject matter they have carried are studied. Since they have come out, there has hardly been anything concerning the Icelanders ... which has not been mentioned. They have carried weekly news from all Icelandic settlements, and, in doing this, have connected people even in the most faraway places of the continent. If some undertaking was being planned, the papers had to bring up the matter so that organization could be achieved among the scattered settlements. In them have written those who have received recognition as writers, whether in poetry or prose....

It is to be doubted whether the collection [of these writers] would have been so large if there had been no papers. Although the subject matter was often poor, it should be kept in mind that, by coming out every week and being distributed to 5000 homes, with each postal journey the hour was postponed by yet another week when, in these homes, Icelandic was no longer read, and all the while neither the language nor the national consciousness could be lost. Without the papers, the Icelanders could surely not have been called an ethnic group, or a national whole within the American society. They would only have been a certain number of individuals, a kind of lost family members, about whom stories would have been told that they once existed, but no stories that they ever survived.[36]

Considering the great respect and fondness for the written or composed word that has always characterized the Icelanders, it is hardly surprising that language and literature became the two major manifestations of Icelandic culture in North America. The important function of language and literature among the West Icelanders also explains why newspapers and journals became such essential carriers and promoters of this culture, and were of such importance in the Western Icelandic community. The number of Western Icelandic newspapers and journals is too large to be treated here. Richard Beck gives a very good survey (1928), and for a brief but useful survey in English, the reader can turn to either Kristjanson's or Lindal's history of Icelanders in Canada, or to Einarsson's *History of Icelandic Literature*.

The largest and most influential newspapers were *Heimskringla* (founded 1886) and *Lögberg* (founded 1888), both based in Winnipeg. They amalgamated in 1959. The paper still appears weekly under the name *Lögberg-Heimskringla*, and as such is one of the oldest ethnic newspapers in Canada. Before the amalgamation, the two contributed to Icelandic discord, as one was founded in opposition to the other, as a result of which, in Jane McCracken's amused words, "some interesting alignments emerged": one paper (*Heimskringla*) supported at the same time the Conservative party and the Unitarian Church, while the other (*Lögberg*), in response, aligned itself with the Liberal party and the Lutheran Synod (1982: 158). Kristjanson mentions how the papers used to "relish a disputation": "In days gone by the weeklies engaged in many a heated controversy; not only did they reflect controversy; they stirred controversy" (1990: 496). Controversy, however, reflects an interest in the concerns of the Western Icelandic community and culture; it no doubt kept people interested and cleared the air in a fairly healthy way. In addition, as was mentioned by Rögnvaldur Pétursson, the papers were a vital outlet for the Icelandic writers and poets to whom we will now turn our attention.

NOTES

1. Vínland is the name given to one of the lands sighted and explored by Leifr Eiríksson around the year 1000 as related in the so-called *Vínland sagas*, *Grænlendinga saga* and *Eiríks saga rauða*, the other two being Markland and Helluland. Vínland is described in these sagas as a place of plenty, where wheat and grapes grow wild, ready to be picked and eaten, and is referred to in the *Hauksbók* manuscript as Vínland the Good (Magnusson and Pálsson 1965: 7-43, 93n). The areas were later identified as being parts of the North American continent. In 1960, the Norwegian explorer and writer Helge Ingstad and his wife, the archaeologist Anne Stine Ingstad, discovered the first authentic Norse site found in North America at L'Anse aux Meadows, Newfoundland. This site, which has since been excavated, turned into a National Historic Park and declared a UNESCO World Heritage Site, is now generally assumed to be the location where Leifr built houses (*Leifsbúðir*) from where the area named Vínland was explored (H. Ingstad 1969; A.S. Ingstad 1985; Wallace 1996).

2. In my account of Romantic literature in Iceland I rely on the following works: Sveinsson (1929); Jóhannesson (1966); Einarsson (1919); Carleton (1974).

3. The Icelandic term for what I have here translated as "patriotic poems" is *ættjarðarljóð*, which means literally "poems of the native earth" or, even more literally, "of the earth of one's family," which gives them a more applicable and less offensive meaning.

4. Bjarni was probably influenced in this respect by the climatic theory of Montesquieu which claims that people are moulded by the climate they live in. Bjarni portrays the harsh side of Icelandic nature as natural to and in harmony with the national character of the Icelanders. He sees the ideal state of harmony between Icelandic nature and the Icelanders in the past. For this insight I am indebted to Páll Valsson, University of Iceland, winter 1991/92.

5. Gjerset (1924) argues that, while Icelandic Romanticism had its inception in the Romanticism of Germany and Denmark, it derived its main strength and impetus from the revolutionary movements of the time, notably the American Declaration of Independence (especially its message of liberty and human rights), followed by the French Revolution and its Republic Constitution, the Spanish Constitution of 1812, and, perhaps most importantly, the Norwegian Constitution of 1814. The introduction of the Romantic movement in Iceland coincided, moreover, with the July revolution in France in 1830.

6. *Ísland, farsælda frón / og hagsælda hrímhvíta móðir / hvar er þín fornaldarfrægð,/ frelsið og manndáðin bezt?* Trans. Guðmundur J. Gíslason (*Icelandic Lyrics* 1930: 49).

7. *Jónas vissi, að fyrsta sporið í frelsisbaráttunni var að endurvekja trú þjóðarinnar á sjálfa sig og landið, hvetja hana til dáða og glæða með henni bjartsýni á lífið og framtíðina ...* (1967: 153-54)

8. *Hann yrkir hvert kvæðið öðru fegurra, og á máli, sem englarnir að líkindum tala, þegar þeir tala íslenzku.* (1919: 60)

9. *í ljóðum hans er fólgin glóð upphafs vors; hann geingur fram í auðmjúkri tign raunkendarinnar og yrkir út frá kjarna vitundar vorrar; líf hans og ljóð er óslitinn saungur um íslensk örlög. Skreytni er ekki til í honum. Hann er saungvari vorrar einföldu gleði einsog hún var skýlausust í góðviðri á sumrin og hins dapra norræna langnættis með andvökum sínum og angist. Jónas Hallgrímsson er kristallur íslenskrar vitundar. Í honum brotna geislar eðlis vors....*

   Ljóð hans eru með öðrum orðum Ísland sjálft einsog það hefur skapast í þjóðvitundinni á þúsund baráttuárum og þó ekki einsog skáld sáu það og spámenn, heldur einsog þjóðin sá það og fann, bóndinn í dalnum og kona hans og fólk þeirra. Ljóð hans eru hið íslenska sálarlíf sjálft einsog landið hefur skapað það í þjóðinni. (1972: 21-22)

10. *Alþýðuskáld* literally means "poets of the people." In the Icelandic literary tradition, the poets referred to by this name composed almost exclusively in the conservative, popular genres of poetry. They lacked formal schooling due to poverty, and are therefore often referred to in English as the "Unschooled Poets" or the "Unschooled Farmer-Poets." The *alþýðuskáld* composed for an audience which suffered circumstances similar to their own, and many of them were known for the fierce social criticism and radical political views expressed in their poetry. See also Beck (1950: 61-73); and Hreinsson (1992).

11. McTurk (1991) suggests that Jón Thoroddsen was inspired by Jón Þorláksson's translation of Milton's *Paradise Lost*, which introduced the pastoral tradition into Icelandic literature. McTurk, using Bloom's Freudian theory that every writer feels intimidated by his/her predecessors and therefore seeks to move away or react against them, sees this as providing a way out for Jón Thoroddsen of the traditional heroic saga pattern and its dominating influence on Icelandic prose literature.

12. For this brief historical survey I have relied on the following works: Guðmundsson and Karlsson (1988); Jónsson (1958); *Öldin sem leið* (1956); Derry (1979); Mowat (1990).

13. For an illuminating account of one of the larger and more influential of these reading societies among farmers in northern Iceland, and the political radicalism it harboured, see Höskuldsson (1970).

14. Iceland obtained home rule in 1918, and complete independence was gained in 1944, when Iceland declared itself a Republic and severed all formal ties with Denmark.

15. Pétursson (1933). For the following account of the emigration I further rely on the following works: Bergsteinn Jónsson (1975); Þorsteinsson and Oleson (1940-53); Houser (1990); Kristjanson (1990); Jóhannesson (1966); Halldórs frá Höfnum (1926).

16. *Var það fyrst fram tekið, að Íslendingar skyldu njóta fullkomins frelsis og borgararéttar jafnt við þarfædda menn, strax og þeir hefði fullnægt búsetuskilyrðum, er áskilin væri þar í landi. Hið annað, að þeim væri fengið hæfilega stórt og í alla staða byggilegt svæði fyrir byggðarlög sín; og hið þriðja, að þeir fengi óátalið að halda öllum sínum mannréttindum, tungu og þjóðerni, þeir og niðjar þeirra um aldar og æfi.* (Pétursson 1919: 103)

17. Elford claims that "there were twenty-four deaths among the Icelanders, and of eight children born, five died" (1974: 54; no source mentioned). The diary of pioneer Simon Simonson (1946), states that 30 children died in Kinmount and some adults, about ten, mostly elderly.

18. In an article which he called "Tveir Þættir" ("Two Stories"; 1975), the Icelandic-Canadian poet Guttormur J. Guttormsson recounts many humorous anecdotes about how the Icelanders learned to adapt to their new environment. They were taught many skills by the native people who lived in the area.

19. For this and more elaborate information on the history of Western Icelandic education see Ruth (1964).

20. *því okkur hafði aðeins verið kennd að lifa á Íslandi en aldrei í Vesturheimi, sem kunni ekki að fara með okkur, né við með hann, svona fyrst í stað.* (Þorsteinsson 1951: 14)

21. *Landferðin var löng og erfið, þó verst væri á vötnunum Superior og Huron, því þar voru óþolandi þrengsli og allt illt. Við komum hingað loksins 21. ágúst.... Margt af fólki var veikt á sjónum, en börnin því meir sem lengur var ferðazt, mest af magaveiki, svo eitthvað 50 dóum af báðum flokkunum, bæði á leiðinni og fyrst eftir að hingað kom, flest ung, og höfðu margir um sárt að binda. Ég missti yngsta barnið mitt, daginn áður en ég kom hingað.* (Björn Jónsson 1975: 69)

22. *má segja með nokkrum sanni, að í slíkri eldraun sé öll lífstilvera undir því komin, að menn geti treyst hver öðrum. Það eitt að fá á sig níðingsorð eða glata trausti annarra sökum ódrengskapar, gat vafalaust orðið alveg nægileg refsing fyrir hvern, sem fyrir því varð, þó að ekki væru til fyrirmæli um það í nokkrum lögum.* (126)

23. The value of the paper as a historical source of pioneer history in Canada has recently been recognized in the translation and publication of all issues in hard cover in English: *Framfari 1877-1880* (1986).

24. *Séra* is an Icelandic ecclesiastical title corresponding to "Reverend" in English.

25. Icelandic-Canadian historians such as Walter Lindal tried to historically validate this myth (1967; 1969). Lindal refers the idea to Arnold Toynbee, *A Study of History* (1947), especially to the chapter called "The Virtues of Adversity."

26. The term "West Icelanders" was adopted by Icelanders and Icelandic immigrants alike, and is still in use among many Canadians and Americans of Icelandic descent. The term "Icelandic Canadian," indicating a Canadian of Icelandic descent, seems to be a more recent one, which has probably developed as ethnicity within Canadian society has become more pronounced and acknowledged. The latter term has a much wider use, since the term "West Icelander" is largely unknown outside Icelandic circles. Neither term carries pejorative associations.

27. For reactions in Iceland to this belief see Jóhannesson (1966);
    Laxness (1941); and *Öldin sem leið 1861-1900* (1956: 210).

28. *En ást Vestur-Íslendinga á sinni gömlu ættjörð er vitanlega nokkuð sérstaks*
    eðlis. Það vantar í hana suma af þeim þáttum, er mynda ættjarðarást manna
    hér á landi.... Praktísku þættirnir í þeirri tilfinning hverfa að meira eða minna
    leyti. En rómantísku þættirnir verða að því skapi sterkari. Tilfinningin verður
    nær því eingöngu rómantísks eðlis.... Fögnuður þeirra út af öllum sóma, allri
    virðing, allri frægð lands og þjóðar tvöfaldast. Ástin á skáldskapnum og tungunni
    margfaldast. Og endurminningar frá ættjörðinni stíga upp í sálum þeirra, fágaðar,
    ummyndaðar, langaðar í ljósshafi þeirra eigin kærleika. En þótt bjart sé orðið
    yfir þeim endurminningum, eru litirnir ekki skærir. Raunir einstaklinganna og
    raunir þjóðarinnar hafa varpað yfir þær fölleik, hinum sama fölleik, sem hvílir
    svo að segja yfir öllu íslenzku hugsunar og tilfinningalífi. Ættjarðarást Vestur-
    Íslendinga er planta, sem á rætur innst í sál mannanna, á því sviði sálarlífsins,
    þar sem flest það grær, sem mönnum er bezt gefið, inndælast og elskulegast. En
    af því að sú planta fær næringu svo að segja eingöngu úr hinu rómantísku eðli
    mannanna, stendur ekki í sambandi við störf þeirra sjer og sínum til uppeldis og
    sóma, þá er blómið svo undur undur viðkvæmt. Það lifir aldrei lengi á jarðhitanum
    eingöngu, hitanum frá sínum eigin rótum. Það þarf aðhlynning.... (1895: 30-32)

29. *þarna gátu Íslendingar enn um hríð fengið í friði að halda tungu sinni, men-*
    ningu og þjóðerni. Ættu menn að varast að vanmeta það andlega farg, sem á
    fólki þessu hefur hvílt, meðan það hraktist athvarfslaust meðal ókunnugra,
    forvitinna og stundum beinlínis fjandsamlega útlendinga. (1975: 38)

30. *Fátæktin var ekkert hjá því að vera kastað út úr sínum forna, þúsund ára*
    heimi, sem þeir þekktu—og unnu flestir heitt þrátt fyrir allt—og inn í ókunnan
    heim, sem útheimti mörg og löng ár að kynnast og þekkja, og alla æfina að fella
    sig við að öllu leyti. Í mörgum skilningi voru þeir eins og fiskur á þurru landi, í
    þjóðlífi Ameríku manna, en í sínum eigin felögum og samlífi, lifðu þeir aftur í
    sínum gamla heimi og héldu höfði hátt. Þess vegna var sú nauðsyn öllu öðru
    meiri, að geta sem allra fyrst stofnað allsherjar nýlendu. (2: 237)

31. *Vér ættum ekki að vera komnir hingað til þess að skjóta oss undan skyldum*
    vorum við þá þjóð, sem drottin hefir tengt oss við helgum og háleitum ætternis-
    böndum. Hver, sem gleymir ættjörðu sinni eða þýkist yfir það hafinn, að
    varðveita það af þjóðerni sínu, sem gott er og guðdómlegt, af þeirri ástæðu að
    hann er staddur í framandi landi og leitar sér þar til lífsviðurværis, það gengur
    næst því að hann gleymi guði. Það er stutt stig og fljótstigið frá því að kasta
    þjóðerni sínu til þess að kasta feðratrú sinni. Sönn kristileg ættjarðarást fyllir
    ekki hjartað með fyrirlitningu á öðrum þjóðum en sinni eigin; hún blindar ekki
    augun fyrir yfirburðum útlendinga í svo mörgu tilliti, né fyrir sinni eigin eymd,
    ókostum og mentunarskorti. (Bjarnason, 1946: 217).

32. Indirectly, this subject often comes up in Western Icelandic literary works, where it is either put in the form of a warning or treated with the utmost contempt, for instance in several poems by Stephan G. Stephansson, and stories by Jóhann Magnús Bjarnason and Guðrún Finnsdóttir, all of whom will be discussed in the next chapter. Obviously, this tendency is common among most immigrant groups and not unique to West Icelanders. However, it is mentioned here because the reality seems to have been contrary to what many later Western Icelandic accounts would have us believe.

33. That the replacement of their native culture with the "cult of Mammon" was a not uncommon reality among the West Icelanders appears from several literary works as well as essays, such as a number of poems by Stephan G. Stephansson, notably "Á Ferð og Flugi," O.T. Johnson (1935); and Skuli Johnson (1948: 23).

34. *Af því að öll hin kirkjulegu fyrirtæki þeirra eru byggð á frjálsum framlögum, verða þau fyrirtæki mönnum næstum því að segja ótrúlega hjartfólgin.* (1895: 26)

35. This argument is found pervasively in, for instance, the following works: Jónsson frá Sleðbrjót (1920); Johnson (1935); Sigurðsson (1929); Lindal (1967; 1969).

36. *Hve stóra þýðingu blöðin hafa haft til að bera fyrir viðhald íslenzkrar tungu í Vesturheimi verður ljóst, þegar farið er að skoða innihald þeirra og málefni, er þau hafa haft meðferðis. Naumast er það nokkuð, er Íslendinga hefir snert ... síðan að þau fóru að koma út, að um það sé eigi getið. Fregnir úr öllum íslenzkum byggðum hafa þau flutt vikulega og með því tengt saman fólk er búið hefir á hinum fjarlægustu stöðum álfunnar. Ef um eitthvert fyrirtæki hefir verið að gera, hafa blöðin orðið að bera þau mál upp til þess að samtök næðust með hinum dreifðu byggðalögum. Í þau hafa ritað þeir sem viðurkenningu hafa hlotið sem skáld, hvort heldur í bundnu eða óbundnu máli....*

   Er eigi að vita hvort það safn hefði jafnstórt orðið, ef engin hefðu blöðin verið. Þótt oft væri efnið fátæklegt, ber þess þó að gæta, að með því að koma út á hverri viku og heim á 5000 heimili var, með hverri þeirri póstferð þeirri stund frestað—um viku—að á þessum heimilum yrði eigi lengur lesið íslenzkt orð, og á meðan gat hvorugt tapast, tungan eða þjóðernismeðvitundin. Án blaðanna hefðu Íslendingar áreiðanlega eigi geta talist þjóðflokkur, eða þjóðernisleg heild í hinu ameríku þjóðfélagi. Þeir hefðu orðið aðeins ákveðin tala einstaklinga, einskonar týndar kynkvíslir, er sögur hefðu gengið um að verið hefðu til, en engar sögur gengið um að nokkru sinni hefðu lifað. (Pétursson 1920: 112-13)
   For other discussions of the role of the immigrant press among immigrant groups see also Furuland (1987: 290-98) and Tuttle Marzolf (1987: 299-319). Although these discussions focus on other

Scandinavian immigrant presses, much of their information also sheds light on the Icelandic immigrant press.

III

"WITHOUT A POET YOU AND YOURS/
WILL DISAPPEAR AND LEAVE NO TRACE"[1]

ICELANDIC IMMIGRANT LITERATURE

INTRODUCTION

En týnt er ekki tungumál,
þó torkennt sé og blandið,
hjá fólki, er verður sína sál
að sækja í heimalandið.
þó hér sé starf og velferð vor
og vonin, þroskinn, gróðinn,
er þar vort upphaf, afl og þor
og æskan, sagan, ljóðin.[2]

THIS CHAPTER DEALS with Western Icelandic literature, by which I
understand the literature written from an immigrant perspective in
the Icelandic language and tradition, and with the first transitional literature, written in English but still characterized by the immigrant
perspective and closely associated with the Western Icelandic tradition. The term "Western Icelandic" derives from the Icelandic *Vestur*
Íslendingar, and while some Icelandic Canadians today still use it to

refer to Icelanders in Canada and their descendents, it seems to me to be a more appropriate term for immigrant Icelanders whose native culture is Icelandic rather than Canadian. I have therefore chosen to limit my use of the term in the framework of literature in this way to facilitate distinction between immigrant literature and later literature in English written by Canadians of Icelandic descent, which I believe is more appropriately termed "Icelandic-Canadian."

In volume four of the *Report* of the Royal Commission on Bilingualism and Biculturalism, a volume dedicated to the contributions to Canadian culture of ethnic groups other than English or French, the cultural legacy of the Icelandic immigrants is described as follows:

A small and hardy group of Icelandic settlers, who faced the hardships of pioneer life, transplanted into the new world their rich literary tradition, especially their love of poetry. In relative terms, no other cultural group, including the British and French, has produced so many poets writing in such volume. Although a large portion of this work may have no lasting literary value, it demonstrates that the Icelandic appreciation of poetry has survived in Canada despite adverse conditions. (1969: 205-06)

The *Report* next makes mention of the considerable number of self-educated farmers among these poets, and continues:

Icelandic prose has had a much smaller following but it has included a wide range of writing—fiction, short stories, plays, memoirs, and fairy tales for children. Icelandic literature serves as a cultural bridge between the old and new worlds. The few Canadians not of Icelandic extraction who can appreciate it give it unqualified acclaim.

These remarks together with the words of the Western Icelandic poet Stephan G. Stephansson quoted above point to some very characteristic aspects of Western Icelandic literature. The Royal Commission notes its quantity and range, stressing the preference for poetry and the bridge it forms between mother and foster country. Earlier in the *Report*, "a deep involvement with Canada" is mentioned (204). Stephan G. Stephansson's poem implies a similar dual involvement, indicating the different functions and associations each country carries. Canada incorporates the new reality, the new source of livelihood and welfare, the daily environment. However, it stands for more than mundane values: it also contains the future, with hopes for growth and development. Iceland, on the other hand, still holds the souls of its far-away children. Iceland constitutes not only the beginning, the cradle of youth and childhood memories, it remains a powerful mythological source. Moreover, Iceland embodies history and poetry. If Canada stands for a glorious future, then, Iceland represents the glorious past with all its legends, myths and values. As the quote from the *Report* implies, the immigrants find themselves in uneasy suspension between the two countries that claim their loyalties.

These conflicting elements can all be found in the literature of the immigrants. The effects of deracination and emigration caused the immigrants to become more consciously aware of the existence of their common nationhood and cultural identity. Their first need was therefore to establish what, if anything, they wanted their culture to constitute in the New World. Naturally, they turned to what they perceived as relevant to them in their new situation. In their choice they were also influenced by the discussions concerning culture and nationhood that had swept their mother country in its battle for independence. These had stressed the role of the Icelandic language and the values of its past, especially its literary past. Language was, of course, the most obvious link to the mother country. It contained the whole literary and oral tradition and history, and was the clearest possible proof of loyalty to Iceland. As the poem "Móðurmálið" ("The Mother Tongue"; 1960) by S.E. Björnsson reveals, to the immigrants the Icelandic language was *arfurinn dýrsti frá ættlandsins strönd*, the most precious inheritance of the motherland. It was the symbol of the native earth, their country, the faith of the people now as well as previously, and the relics and achievements of their ancestors. In their new environment, language was also, of course, a powerful means of exclusive communal bonding for the immigrants.

Literature had always constituted the most vital part of Icelandic culture. Traditionally, it had been practised by an exceptionally wide social range of the population. Icelanders in the New World therefore had at their fingertips an obvious medium for the expression of such fundamentals as group pioneer experience, introspection, novelty, bewilderment and relation to a completely new social and geographical environment. Another relevant factor is the Icelanders' likely awareness of the high regard in which the Anglo-Canadian establishment held literary activities, compared to cultural manifestations of another, more traditionally folkloristic type.[3] This would explain why even Western Icelandic and Icelandic-Canadian folklore took on an almost solely literary expression.

Language and literature, then, became the focus of Icelandic culture in the Western hemisphere, and the main vehicle for the preservation of that culture and the fostering of a national group identity. Mossberg has explained the specific functions of immigrant literature:

> Many of the early novels and stories serve the combined functions of travelogue, guidebook, farmer's almanac, and textbook on how to survive the immigrant experience. The fiction was actually a tool for providing knowledge. Immigrants read it to gain information about how to respond and behave in their new environment. The literature recreated situations that were common to the group experience. Therefore these novels provided invaluable practical and psychological support since the immigrant's own experience was anticipated, reinforced, and validated. (1976: 113)

It is for this reason, Mossberg claims, that earlier immigrant literature reads like a "documentary report," in its attempts to define the nature of the group experience, and only becomes more imaginative in its dramatization of alienation, confusion and the process of having to re-establish one's values. Viðar Hreinsson, who has studied early Western Icelandic literature (1993b), finds that during the first decades in Canada, the poetry printed in newspapers was mostly traditional poetry as it had been composed for centuries, or an echo of Romantic poetry in Iceland. The bulk of publications consisted of practical writings (containing information on issues such as immigration, education, religion, and conditions in Canada), classical or later sagas (for instance *Páls saga biskups* and *Hungurvaka*, both of which are Old Icelandic bishop's sagas, and *Hellismanna saga*, a late Saga of the Icelanders), and translations of popular foreign literature, much of which was also read in Iceland at the time (Jules Verne's *Around the World in Eighty Days* and Fergus W. Hume's *Murdered in a Coach*). As in medieval Iceland, instructive, traditional and translated writing formed the foundation for the gradual development of a new literature. Stephan G. Stephansson, who was the ultimate embodiment of the pioneer poet, once described how the immigrant writer must settle twice over, once in the physical and once in the literary wilderness, in order to build something new. In order that this process may proceed, the pioneer first needs to clear his field before he can really see it and begin to work with it. Indeed, it was only during the last decade of the nineteenth century that literature began to be published in book form, thereby giving an artistic expression to the immigrant experience which earlier writing had either avoided or suppressed.

When dealing with immigrant literature, it must be borne in mind that the immigrant experience is one of immense psychological cost. It involves uprooting, a constant awareness of loss and insecurity in all fields of life, the departure of friends and kin and everything familiar. It is an experience that requires not only the creation of a new home, but also the redefinition of the old values and the self, wrenched from the context of history, ancestry, legends and place. They have to be translated into a new world from which the immigrant is alienated: "the barriers that cultural differences pose may be more formidable than those presented by even the harshest physical environment," and "the experience of being foreign has the potential for working a significant transformation at the deepest level of an individual's sense of being," Lewis and Jungman note (1986: xiii-xviii). "Somehow it has come upon me, / I've no fatherland," Stephan G. Stephansson mused in his poem "The Exile."[4]

In the case of the Icelanders, feelings of guilt and inferiority played an important part in this experience as well. The new immigrants had been accused by the fellow-countrymen they had left behind of treason and cowardice. Moreover, they were looked down upon by anglophone Canadians as "foreigners," uncouth strangers who spoke an incomprehensible language and did not know the (Anglo-Canadian) ways of the country. These experiences had a profound and lasting influence on the immigrants and must have added to their feelings of loss and alienation. It is here that the ethnic myths discussed in the previous chapter enter Western Icelandic literature.

Mossberg has remarked that many writers were actually involved in the cultural activities of their group. This certainly applies to Western Icelandic writers. Thus, as Mossberg has pointed out, they were closely aware of the tolls that the immigrant experience exacted:

As active participants in their communities, the writers were intimately aware of the problems of the group, such as alienation, and were therefore committed to the necessity of preserving the group identity....

But the immigrant writers ... were also trying to fill a cultural—and one might even say spiritual—void in the lives of later generation immigrants torn from the old world values, and alienated from the new. The writers wanted to present an alternative vision to the materialism they viewed as the base of the modern American value structure most immigrants were aspiring to. (115)

The purposes and functions Mossberg sees as serving Scandinavian immigrant literature do indeed correspond to those found in most Western Icelandic literature, and not solely in prose works, but also in poetic ones. Western Icelandic literature variously reflects or recreates the immigrant experience and provides a support for those facing this profound upheaval.

However, Western Icelandic literature is also unique in other respects, some of which I noted in the introductory quotes of this section. First, poetry was the medium most favoured. Secondly, Western Icelandic literature was produced in very large quantities and by a remarkably large percentage of the whole community. Communal participation in literature included reading and discussion, but most importantly composition. We get a clear idea of this from part of a letter which the author Jóhann Magnús Bjarnason sent to his friend Stephan G. Stephansson:

"Good Lord" (says my neighbor, old Jón Sveinsson, whenever he mentions his brother Benedikt's politics), and "good Lord!" say I when I think of the many thousands who compete for the title of poet. I rarely open a newspaper without finding somebody "illustrating his name," as the priest puts it. All the magazines come monthly replete with a brand new author, and it's impossible to step into a neighbor's house without running into a budding poet. There are about forty families around here and I think every fifth man and woman is thought to be a poet (by the people).... Gunnsteinn lives nearby; people call him a "competent poet." Þorsteinn Borgfjörð owns land two miles from my house; people call him a "national poet" (as clever as Jón J. Eldon). Jón Guttormsson's sons are here also; both are called "poets of quality." Then there is Haraldur, Pastor Sigurgeir of Grund in Eyjafjörður's son; he is considered one of the "major poets" of the Western World. I could also count a certain Sigurgeir Einarsson, Jón Stefánsson and Baldvin Halldórsson. Andrés Jónsson Skagfield has moved to Selkirk, and in Selkirk every other man is considered verbally gifted. There is such a swarm of poets in and around Gimli that it is amazing. Even Thompson and Guðni write poetry. Poets are everywhere: most teachers are poets; all Icelandic clergymen in the West write poetry, except Rev. Jón; everyone who has been to school in Iceland writes as soon as he comes to this country. I know two fellows who took up poetry writing for the first time when they were well in their sixties; one of them now has almost half a trunk full of manuscripts. Finally there are the *wandering poets*—it is pure torture to run into them. (Guðmundsson 1982: 42)

Thirdly, Western Icelandic literature could to an important extent and in a unique way draw on the Icelandic literary past. This past served several functions. In the first place, the past had received world-wide acknowledgement and acclaim, and thus provided a source of pride in the Icelandic heritage and a demonstration to the Canadian population of the high "cultural status" of the Icelanders. In the second place, an important part of the Icelandic literary heritage was exactly concerned with the effects of immigration and the dynamics of an immigrant frontier society. In Chapter I, I explained that one can find, for example, indications of national ambition stemming from immigrant feelings of inferiority towards older and established countries reflected by Old Norse literature similar to the Western Icelandic ambitions discussed in this chapter. Furthermore, there was a similar fascination with introspection, with the developments within the new society being created, the problems it faced and their solutions, and its individual inhabitants, who all participated in its creation. Kirsten Wolf (1991) demonstrates that the tensions within the saga-writing society were a main cause for the outburst of literary creativity during that period just as the tensions within Western Icelandic immigrant society led to its voluminous literary output.[5] Wolf convincingly argues that Western Icelandic authors chose from their literary past those elements that were relevant for their present situation. She discusses the Western Icelandic hero figure in this light, whom she sees as the embodiment of traditional and romantic ideals and virtues from the saga past, but recast in the topical context of the Icelandic immigrants in North America. The traditional virtues are shown to create for the hero both a respected place within his new social reality, and a worthy outlet and expression of his attachment and loyalty to his native country and heritage. As Wolf puts it:

These examples, to which many more could be added, show how the immigrant writers portrayed their compatriots. With very few exceptions they are brave, noble, upright, conscientious, and proud of their old country, their people, and their traditions. In these heroes the hopes and aspirations of the Icelandic immigrants found a true expression, and it is clear that the authors wrote them, in part, to combat the social and economic inferiority of the Western Icelanders.... The hero functions to provide a bridge linking the cultural heritage of the past with a new culture in the process of being shaped by a new environment. The hero offers a framework of established values, thus yielding a sense of security that has its roots in past tradition but which finds solid application within the present in a newly-adopted environment. There is, to be sure, an apparent strain of romanticism running through these works that aids in shaping the character of the hero, but beneath this romanticism must reside a core mirroring self-perceptions, real or imagined, and thus expressive of a cultural need. The literature and its heroes thus celebrate both loss and renewal, as it seeks to translate into the new cultural environment the best values offered by the old. (442-43)

Since in saga literature, Iceland was pre-eminently an immigrant society, it is hardly surprising to find in the Western Icelandic context a similar occupation with the process of translating the old values and heritage into the new situation and environment, i.e., the dynamics of adaptation and preservation. The cultural tensions resulting from this process seem a plausible cause of the outburst of the tremendous literary output both in saga Iceland and in immigrant Canada.

WESTERN ICELANDIC POETRY

Alt er hirt og alt er birt / aldrei hlé á leirburði ("All is collected and all is published, / never a break from bad verse"), remarked the pseudonymous poet Káinn in an epigram about the Western Icelandic literary scene. Similarly, in a discussion of the Versemakers' Society in Winnipeg (*Hagyrðingafélagið*), the poet Guttormur J. Guttormsson (1966: 159) mentioned the observation of an Icelandic journalist that Western Icelandic society was the *Eldorado leirskáldanna*, the "Eldorado of bad poets." Although these characterizations are hardly flattering, they point to the widespread literary activity in the community and the willingness of Western Icelandic newspapers and publishers to give everybody a chance to pour out their thoughts and experiences in the most traditional and respected manner for Icelanders.

In her study of culture shock and narrative creativity, Barbara Kirshenblatt-Gimblett concludes that "situations of multilingualism and multiculturalism, where worldviews, cultures and languages clash and undergo massive and rapid change, unleash the creative energies of immigrant raconteurs" (1976: 113). In other words, the fact that the Icelandic immigrants showed a keen and widespread desire for narrative expression of their experiences is in itself a fairly common occurrence. However, what *is* remarkable about the Icelanders is that they showed a decided preference for literary forms of expression, especially poetry, rather than folkloric, notably storytelling. "Poetry was a way of life for the Icelanders who came to Canada. You would as soon admit you had no sense of humour or were without intelligence as admit that you were not a poet," Icelandic-Canadian writer David Arnason says in order to give an indication of the strength of the desire to compose verse (1981: 94). Poetic activity provided a strong link with the culture and tradition of Iceland while at the same time serving as a channel for the immigrants to vent and come to terms with their manifold feelings and observations.

There are many varieties of Western Icelandic poetry. One large group is that of occasional verse. It includes, for instance, obituary and wedding poems, toasts and honorary poems. They are numerous, and although most of them are of little aesthetic quality, they played an important social function and constitute unique cultural and historical source material. There are, of course, a few notable exceptions, among which Stephan G. Stephansson's famous "Úr Íslendingadags Ræðu" ("From an Address on Íslendingadagur") stands out. The largest group in number is probably that of the *lausavísur* or epigrams. These quatrains are subject to particular stress and alliteration patterns, are often composed on the spot, and generally carry a sting in their tail. Magnús Einarsson suggests that by and large, the folklore of West Icelanders is contained in either these verses or in anecdotes, but, since versifying was much more popular, the verses are in the majority. They depict daily scenes and events, often wittily, with a preference for the off-beat or off-colour, so that they give a lively picture of Western Icelandic life and society (1975: 22). They are, however, also put to a more supernatural use. In these cases, the old Icelandic belief in the power of the spoken word, especially in poetry, finds re-application in the New World. Einarsson mentions examples where *vísur* are used for *níð*, to harm or "bite" the victim, or to call on superhuman agents, and instances where *vísur* came to people in their dreams. The phenomenon of the *kraftaskáld* apparently did not die during the emigration.

Lausavísur should not be regarded as an inferior form of poetry, however. As in Iceland, they were actively composed by such major poets as Stephan G. and Guttormur J. Guttormsson. The poet who is probably best known for his epigrams in North America is Káinn, whose work I will discuss below. His poetic talent made his epigrams of lasting value, and he could therefore be called a literary representative of the genre. Káinn also represents the clearest example of a kind of poetry which was not at all widespread in Iceland, but flourished among the West Icelanders: humorous poetry. In Iceland, solemnity was expected and respected in poetry, excepting perhaps to a certain degree the epigrams. The West Icelanders were probably influenced in this respect by the humour and entertainment that was current in North America. However, this new, light type of humour was sometimes blended with the Icelandic love of the incongruous also found in many folk tales.

There is also a clear strain of social satire in Western Icelandic poetry, which is linked to the large number of poems that are concerned with social problems and social criticism. We have seen that the Icelanders brought to the New World an awakened sense of social awareness and responsibility and a strong desire for democracy. On both sides of the ocean, this climate allowed the development of an idealistic radical-mindedness among some in the literary sphere, supported by the Icelandic tradition of the *alþýðuskáld* and stimulated by the Realist movement in literature. Nearly all Western Icelandic poets of any importance subscribed to a greater or lesser extent to this strain. Many of them were influenced by the writers at home who developed out of this climate, most importantly by the poet Þorsteinn Erlingsson, the most radical of these.

Another large body of poetry is lyrical in tone and subject, echoing mainstream Romantic poetry in Iceland at the time. This poetry reflects the nostalgia and homesickness and the romantic haze of memory gradually enshrouding Iceland. There are many odes to the mother country, the beauty of the countryside and the mother tongue, and the glory of her past. Many of these are heavy with the pain of loss, or sometimes mixed with regret or guilt at having left. However, while many lyrical poems looked to Iceland, this was not universally the case. Quite a few poems describe the new country, its landscape in various seasons, and the pioneer environment. These poems, unlike those about Iceland, are optimistic, often celebrating the hopes of the immigrant which are seen embodied in the country. Hreinsson has observed a developing pattern of self-representation especially in these lyrical poems:

The poetry that deals directly with emigration is monotonous and repetitive, no matter whether dealing with the departure (and many poems express sorrow over the departure), the motherland or the New World. A certain pattern of self-representation is developed, repeated again and again, in part or as a whole: Icelandic nature and history is glorified, its present state lamented, the emigrants view themselves as seeking freedom, parallel to the settlers of Iceland and the Vinland explorers. The new country ... is glorified and a wish is expressed to participate in the glorious progress of the New World. Poets created an embellishing ideology, seen in the bulk of the poetry, which consisted of a general tendency to suppress the hardships and the negative aspects of the emigrant experience. (1993b: 8)

Finally, there are poems that deal with past events. Among the earlier poems especially, these are invariably set in the Icelandic past and were composed in the traditional Icelandic *rímur*-style. Later poets, however, would make use of their new situation and environment. Sometimes these are poems about the recent pioneer past, sometimes about Iceland's past, but in most cases the past is used to shed light on the present. Many poems about the pioneering days are concerned with the price the immigrants had to pay for their new home, and the responsibility this involves for their descendants. Others are more in the "immigrant style" as outlined above, using the Icelandic past to recreate and deal with the immigrant experience. Generally we can say that the closer the past is to the present, the less rigidly traditional is the form.[6]

We see, then, that, in subject matter, Canada has gradually been assigned an important place, although the mother country is still very prominent. However, Iceland is no longer a clear presence; it is an ideal, a memory which, to be sure, evokes profoundly vehement emotions, but has lost the touch of the present as reality has become fused with the pain of homesickness and the blur of nostalgia. Canada has become the reality, the present, the future, which now permeates all experiences. Gísli Jónsson has aptly described this literature as being both "a threnody of the disappearing generation and a cradle song of hopeful youth" (*líksöngur hverfandi kynslóðar og vögguljóð vonbjartrar æsku*; 1913: 45).

As regards form and metre, however, Iceland still stood on much firmer ground. In my discussion of Icelandic poetry I pointed out that form was an integral and traditional factor in the Icelandic literary tradition. Jóhann Magnús Bjarnason once complained that "Icelanders will always be more infatuated with the frame of the picture than with the picture itself...."[7] While Western Icelandic poetry does show the formal effects of the Romantic movement in Iceland, it seems much less affected by North American influences in this respect. It is not unlikely that, to the form-loving Icelanders, North American poetry was simply too "light." In his ode to Walt Whitman, for instance, Þorsteinn Þ. Þorsteinsson expresses his regret in the last lines that "America's greatest spirit" should not possess the beauty of sound nor of poetic art which locks itself in one's heart (*Vestan um haf* 170). Similarly, Sigurður Július Jóhannesson expresses an abhorrence of poetry without any form or rhyme, which he sees as a disgrace rather than an honour to one's country (1951). Poetry without form or poetic diction was simply not poetry to Icelanders, who, after all, genuinely believed in the power of the poetic word.

In general, one could say that Western Icelandic poetry displays a mixture of traditional Icelandic, Romantic and Realist influences. Roughly speaking, the Romantic influence is most prominent in the lyrical poems, the traditional form in the poems concerned with the Icelandic past, and the Realist influences in the social poems. However, not everywhere is the distinction this clear.

Many poets were unschooled farmers, representatives of a long-standing and unique tradition of Icelandic *alþýðuskáld* in the Western hemisphere. In the previous chapter it was pointed out that the *alþýðuskáld* in Iceland reached the perfection of their art during the late Romantic period. It is the influence of this state of the national poetic tradition that is most in evidence in Western Icelandic poetry— the combination of complicated, traditional poetic metre and diction, and crystal-clear, deeply emotional and lyrical expression. Moreover, the influence of the social and political climate, especially among farmers in the north of Iceland, is clearly discernible in the many poems with a social message. The extent of its influence appears from the fact that the *alþýðu*-tradition has continued in Canada until this day, although it is now dying out.[8] Additionally, in the hands of the best poets, this "unschooled" poetry is adapted and attuned, opened up to the new environment and world of experience.

The New World, then, makes its greatest contribution in subject matter. Form was too traditionally ingrained as yet, only a few poets occasionally experimenting with it. The result is a unique type of poetry all its own, both within the Icelandic and the Canadian poetic tradition, although clearly still more Icelandic than Canadian. It reached its peak through the poetic talents of Stephan G. Stephansson and Guttormur J. Guttormsson, and, to a slightly lesser extent, through Káinn.

KÁINN

Mín eru ljóð ei merkileg
mínir kærir vinir!
En oft og tíðum yrki' eg
öðruvísi en hinir.[9]

Thus did the Western Icelandic poet Káinn or K.N., pen name of Kristján Níels Júlíus Jónsson (1860-1936), once describe his poetry. And although the majority of his poetic references to himself or his art are caricatures, one can detect here two important clues to Káinn's poetry: it is different from that of the other poets, and it is mainly concerned with "unremarkable" subjects or events.

In many ways, Káinn's poetry can be regarded as a more literary form of Western Icelandic folk poetry. This suggestion is based on Káinn's almost exclusive use of the traditional folk genre, the *lausavísa* or epigram, and his subject matter, which is usually the daily life and environment of the Western Icelandic community in its widest sense. In addition, Káinn was very popular. It has even been suggested that he was the most widely cited poet among West Icelanders during his time. His poems were on nearly everybody's lips and thus became the people's property (cf. Holm 1990: 2).

Káinn emigrated in 1878 and initially settled in Winnipeg, where he spent the first part of his immigrant life before moving to the United States. Even after he moved, Káinn often visited Winnipeg and surroundings, and remained an active part of the Winnipeg Icelandic cultural scene which, in turn, formed the subject matter of numerous of his poems. Káinn's first poetry collection *Kviðlingar*, the only one published during his lifetime, was published in Winnipeg in 1920, and many of his poems appeared in Icelandic-Canadian newspapers and journals. These facts, together with the prominent place he occupies in Western Icelandic literature, constitute the reasons why Káinn is included for discussion here whereas other authors who lived south of the Canadian border are not.

The fact that Káinn ranks among the best Western Icelandic poets is due to his poetic deftness within his genre, the apparent ease with which he captures the essence of a situation or person and transforms it into a highly comical and well-crafted epigram. Moreover, his poetic transformations often place the subject in a slightly different, surprising light which finds its roots in Káinn's sharp yet sympathetic understanding of human nature and life. His best works are serious or tragi-comical, containing worldly wisdom or a profundity underlying what at first sight appears merely funny and superficial. Such is Káinn at his best. There are also many ditties to his name which will be forgotten, dependent as they are on the time and place in which they were composed, but his better works are numerous and good enough to have earned him a place in the literary history of the Icelanders on both sides of the ocean.

Káinn occupies a special place in both Western Icelandic and Icelandic literature, in that he is the only really humorous poet. Icelandic poetic history contains humorous pieces, but all by essentially serious poets. Poetry is traditionally regarded by Icelanders as a solemn, serious and powerful form of art. The same is the case for the Western Icelandic poets. While Stephan G. Stephansson and Guttormur J. Guttormsson also wrote light, comical works, they are not chiefly comic poets. It is very likely that in this respect Káinn was influenced by his North American environment.

Although Káinn stood on the one hand firmly in his native poetic tradition, writing solely in Icelandic, using traditional Icelandic forms and utilizing Icelandic poetic and cultural references, he was on the other hand open to the influences of his new environment and employed them readily and deftly. His subject matter is the Western Icelandic community in which he lived and its natural environment. Káinn first resided in Winnipeg and Duluth, and finally settled down in Pembina County, North Dakota, in 1893. He delighted, moreover, not only in descriptions of Western Icelandic life but also in its verbal expressions: he often interlaced the Icelandic with English words and expressions, and used many typically Western Icelandic words, usually English words adapted to Icelandic, such as *baslari* (from "bachelor," "Baslara-vísa" 242) and *bríta* (a half-*breed* woman, in "Engar Refjar" 285). A typical example of Káinn's humour in an unexpected final twist and bilingual wordplay is the following verse called "Brúin," "the Bridge":

> *Þó Atlantshafið skilji sundur óðul vor og lönd*
> *þú yngissveinn og góðumborna jómfrú,*
> *nú tökumst við í hendur og treystum kærleiksbönd*
> *og tengjum saman þjóðina með "home"-brú.* (141)[10]

Paul Sigurdson, the Icelandic-Canadian poet and translator who translated some of Káinn's poetry in 1990, shows an instance where Káinn managed to corrupt the English as well:

Hjartakær með hárið klippt
hjá mér situr frúin.
Ef hún væri ekki gift,
yrði "something duin." (251)[11]

Elsewhere, Sigurdson remarked on the "clever verbal manipulations K.N. was capable of, and how ingeniously he was able to blend the two languages opening up virgin territory to give himself wide range for his inimitable flights of fancy" (1990: 4).

If we take into consideration the battle that was being waged among the nationalistic West Icelanders and the emphasis which had been laid on the role, the beauty and the purity of the Icelandic language by the Romantics, it is not difficult to imagine the consternation that Káinn's witty language mixing caused among purists. Káinn himself makes a comic reference to this in a poem called "Bréf til Jónasar Hall" ("A Letter to Jónas Hall"):

Mér er erfitt brag að byrja og brag að enda —
eg veit ei, hvar það kann að lenda.

Gætið ykkar, góðir hálsar, gleðin dvínar, —
sit eg hér með sorgir mínar.

Er hér komið eitt af stærstu Íslands tröllum —
Goðmundur frá Glæsivöllum.

Heyri' eg sagt hann hati enska heimsku prjálið
og hengi þá sem "mixa" málið.

Mér er kannske málið skylt, en má ég spyrja,
á hverjum hann ætti að byrja.

Mér og Páli mun hann fyrstum meina' að sálga,
og hengja' okkur á hæsta gálga.

Honum þarf að hegna fyrir heimsku slíka,
ég held það ætti' að hengja hann líka. (52)[12]

From a later verse to the "Goðmundur" whom Káinn here compares to one of Iceland's biggest trolls, in which he kindly asks him to greet his beloved native fjord ("Til G. Finnbogasonar" 108), we may gather that Guðmundur Finnbogason took the joke well. This

is indeed the remarkable feature of Káinn's poetry which distinguishes it from many other humourous Icelandic verses: it is almost
completely without malice. Káinn's humour was based on a sharp
and alert sense of judgement and therefore won him popularity
rather than enmity.

Káinn's exceptional use of two languages in his poetry may well
have originated from an open-mindedness sprung from what seems
to have been an equal love for his foster country and his native country. While it is true that Káinn wrote a few touching poems about
Iceland which betray deep feelings of nostalgia, his main focus was
on the Dakota environment and the Western Icelandic community in
North America in general. Western Icelandic subjects abound in his
poetry, far outnumbering Icelandic subjects, and while he usually
pokes fun at many of them, a certain number of his poems reveal a
profound attachment to his new environment. If we compare, for
instance, the following two poems, we glimpse in the first the natural
feelings of loss and nostalgia of the immigrant reminiscing, but in the
second we see that such feelings have not blinded or distorted Káinn's
view or feelings for the beauty and qualities of the New Land:

[Untitled]

Svo dreymi þig um fríðan Eyjafjörð
og fagrar bernskustöðvar inn' í sveit,
því enginn hefir guðs á grænni jörð — —
í geislum sólar — — litið fegri reit.
Enn upp' á Brattahjalla hóar smalinn,
og hjörðin kyrrlát þokast framan dalinn. (ix)[13]

"Minni Dakota-byggðar"

Að minnast þín, byggðin, sem mér er svo kær,
er maklegt, þó tíðin sé naum;
þess krafðist ein íslenzka konan í gær,
sem kom til mín aðeins í draum.

Þó vanti þig fossana, firðina og margt,
sem fjallkonan gat okkur veitt,
það bætir upp akranna skínandi skart
og skóglendið voldugt og breitt.

Þú sveltir ei börn þín, sveitin mín kær,
og sólskínið lætur þeim falt;
allt, sem þau þarfnast, í görðunum grær,
og Guð hefur blessað það allt.

Þú gafst okkur fríðastar meyjar og menn,
sem mest hefur samtíðin dáð,
og vindurinn hvíslar í eikunum enn,
að ekki sé hámarki náð. (185)[14]

Although the immigrant eyes still see through comparative glasses as it were, interpreting the new environment in comparison with the old rather than in its own right and noticing what is "lacking," Káinn is quick to discern and acknowledge unfamiliar beauties and features which in his view make up for those lacks. Moreover, he then inverts this process by openly admitting to Iceland's negative side to which the New Land, in its turn, compensates. Thus, he sets the two countries on an equal footing. Káinn is unique in this respect. Although the Icelandic immigrants were from the start eager to adapt to and adopt the New Land, Iceland was still always either foremost in their minds and hearts or denied and forgotten. Káinn on the other hand, although an immigrant like the others, seems to have been truly a man of two countries.

Recently, the contemporary Icelandic-American poet Bill Holm has emphasized the importance of Káinn to present generations:

This remarkably unremarkable man can tell us something with his life and work, and with the perceptions of, and stories about him that still persist two generations after his death, about the inner life of the pickled-in-amber immigrant culture that persisted for a few generations in every ethnic group. It had amputated the old world but didn't have time enough in one life to grow the new one inside itself. K.N. Julius wrote Icelandic salted with English words, peppered with the malapropisms of immigrants who attached Icelandic inflections and phonemes to English words, and new world meanings to unsuspecting ancient Norse words. (1990: 2)

Káinn indeed makes an innovative use of "Western Icelandic" in his poetry. Both through this and through his apt and witty descriptions we get a unique and fairly accurate description of Western Icelandic immigrant life devoid of ethnic ideology and myths. Through his exceptional sense of humour and poetic skill, Káinn managed to become popular in spite of his sometimes mercilessly witty caricatures of "Western Icelandicisms," which left their subject exposed to good-natured ridicule.

As an example of Káinn's hilarious and brutally honest portraits and verbal snap shots in the field of Western Icelandic nationalism we find "Já" ("Yes"):

> Já, íslenzkir viljum við vera
> á Vesturheims iðgrænu sléttum;
> og hvor annars byrði að bera
> við bróðurhönd hver öðrum réttum;
> og eins þótt það kunni að kosta
> kjaftshögg og barsmíð á stundum;
> með þjóðernisrembing og rosta
> menn rífast og skammast á fundum. (105)[15]

Here, Káinn first imitates the clichés of the ideological style of Western Icelandic poetry with its grandiose images of the Icelandic nationality on the glorious North American prairies, where all Icelanders stand united and help each other unconditionally. In the last four lines he proceeds to pull the ground from under this ideology by exposing the factionalism and jingoism the nationalist myth attempts to hide. Along similar lines he exposes Western Icelandic factionalism and duality in the following epigrams:

> Þetta er ekki þjóðrækni
> og þaðan af síður guðrækni,
> heldur íslenzk heiftrækni
> og helvítis bölvuð langrækni. (180)[16]

> Gleymd er okkar gamla sögueyja,
> grafin, staursett, lá mér við að segja.
> Enskan hefir alltaf nóg að segja,
> íslenzkan má halda kjafti og þegja. (175)[17]

One of the mainstays of the Western Icelandic myths was traditional Icelandic literacy. Káinn mercilessly toys with his perceptions of the daily reality of this idealized literacy:

> Nú er ljóðalöngun
> landans burt að hverfa;
> fæstir fróðleiks þorsta
> feðra og mæðra erfa.

> *Þegar eg kom með kverið,*
> *keypti' hann það með illu,*
> *las ekki í því línu,*
> *en lét það upp á hillu.* (162)[18]

Like many of his fellow Western Icelandic writers, Káinn loathed hypocrisy, blind fanaticism and social injustice, and often pointed his arrows at narrow-mindedness, prejudice and superficiality. The Church and its servants became a popular subject of abuse for Káinn in this respect. When a wealthy pastor in the neighbourhood was given a horse, Káinn wrote:

> *Tíðum hér á tölti eg sést;*
> *til þess eru líkur,*
> *gefið mér þeir hefðu hest, — —*
> *hefði' eg verið ríkur!* (14)[19]

A missionary once came by while Káinn was cleaning the floors and forking manure in the stables. When Káinn remained silent during his fervent preaching, the missionary finally asked him about his faith. Káinn answered

> *Kyrrassa tók eg trú,*
> *traust hefir reynzt mér sú.*
> *I flórnum því fæ eg að standa*
> *fyrir náð heilags anda.* (159)[20]

In the poem called "Messafallið" ("The Failure of Services"), Káinn ironically describes the effect of the zealous efforts of pastors on the religious life of the community:

> *Klerkarnir sínar kirkjur vígðu;*
> *konurnar margar syndir drýgðu.*
> *Dansholur allar opnar stóðu,*
> *inn í þær landar þétt sér tróðu.*
> *Á sunnudögum þeir sváfu og hrutu,*
> *um sáluhjálp ekkert heilann brutu,*
> *og andskotinn gat nú orkað þessu,*
> *að enginn maður kom til messu.* (263)[21]

From his poetry it is clear that Káinn was never a man of means. He earned a meagre living working as a farmhand and a gravedigger, and never had much fortune nor good luck. His compassion and empathy with the poor and unfortunate in life and his aversion of social injustice were based on his own experiences. He had received very little formal schooling, although he made up for this by extensive reading. Káinn, therefore, belongs to the tradition of the *alþýðuskáld*. One of his most poignant polemic poems is "Við Gröf B.B." ("At the Funeral of B.B."):

> *Eg held þú myndir hlæja dátt með mér*
> *að horfa' á það, sem fyrir augun ber.*
> *Þú hafðir ekki vanizt við það hér,*
> *að vinir bæru þig á höndum sér.*
> *En dauðinn hefir högum þínum breytt*
> *og hugi margra vina til þín leitt;*
> *í trú og auðmýkt allir hneigja sig,*
> *og enginn talar nema vel um þig.* (38) [22]

Káinn liked to compare his own life and fate with that of the prodigal son ("Týndi Sonurinn" [167], "Eg hefi ei auðinn elskað" [vii]), and most of his poems about himself which are not in jest reveal a fairly bitter tone. He was drawn towards the bottle, and the many Western Icelandic Temperance groups averse to seeing the reputation of Icelanders among Anglo-Canadians tarnished by insobriety, were a thorn in his side. Once he answered a woman who lectured him about his drinking:

> *Gamli Bakkus gaf mér smakka*
> *gæðin beztu, öl og vín,*
> *og honum á eg það að þakka,*
> *að þú ert ekki konan mín!* (281) [23]

It is likely that we owe some of the clearest glimpses of Icelandic immigrant life, stripped of mythic and nostalgic hues and rooted in a good-natured humour and perceptiveness, to Káinn's conditions in life. In the poem "Gunnars-saga hin nýja" ("The New Saga of Gunnar"), Káinn subverts the famous and deeply moving scene in *Njáls saga*, where the hero Gunnar looks at the beauty of his native hills on his way from Iceland into exile, and is so touched that he refuses to leave, which he knows will cost him his life:

> *Gunnar vildi heldur "go to" hel*
> *en heima vera á fóstur-jarðar ströndum.*
> *Þar hafði hann skotið hafísbjörn og sel,*
> *hámera-stóð og æðarkollu á söndum.*
> *Lifandi-dauður lengi bæði og vel*
> *lék 'ann sér glatt með himinbornum öndum.*
> *Í Vesturheimi þoldi hann þrauta-él,*
> *þrældóm og skort, með ótal fleiri löndum.*
> *"Hugljúfa samt ég sögu Gunnars tel."* (272-73)[24]

This poem is not only quite disrespectfully tongue-in-cheek with regard to the literary reference, it also parodies two very sensitive Western Icelandic issues: the new Gunnar preferred to leave his native hills, and his ultimate fate was no great improvement on what he left behind.[25]

However, Káinn's aversion to nationalist ideologies and hypocrisy did not blind him to the positive aspects of the Western Icelandic immigrant community. His toast to the old Winnipeg Icelanders, for instance, reveals fond memories of the pioneer days when hope counterbalanced all mishaps:

> *Eg þarf ei því að leyna,*
> *að þó var stundum kalt,*
> *en gleðin gekk um beina — —*
> *og guð veit hvað ég meina,*
> *því vonin vermir allt.* (67)[26]

Ultimately, Káinn's sense of humour always balanced out his views, and helped others as well as himself come to terms with the difficulties of the immigrant experience.

STEPHAN G. STEPHANSSON

Stephan G. Stephansson (1853-1927), or Stephan G., as he is usually called, has been the subject of extensive praise in the realm of Icelandic and Western Icelandic literature. The Icelandic scholar Sigurður Nordal called him "the greatest man among all Icelandic poets past and present" (*mesti maðurinn meðal íslenzkra skálda fyrr og síðar*; 1939: lxv); the Canadian scholar Watson Kirkconnell called him "Canada's Leading Poet" (1936: 263); the American scholar F. Stanton Cawley called him "the Greatest Poet of the Western World" (1937: 120);

and many Icelanders fondly call him *Kléttafjallaskáldið*, "Poet of the Rocky Mountains." No matter how literally these statements should be taken, there is at least a definite indication that to those North Americans who understand Icelandic the greatness of Stephan G.'s best works is as clear as to the Icelanders themselves, who generally consider him one of their best poets.

Stephan G.'s status was recently acknowledged by his adopted country when his house was opened to the public and declared a historic site in 1982. In the wake of this followed a study in English about Stephan G., his times, his life, and a few comments about his poetry (Jane McCracken: *Stephan G. Stephansson: The Poet of the Rocky Mountains*, 1982), and a selection of existing translations of poems (*Stephan G. Stephansson: Selected Translations from Andvökur*, 1987). In 1988, a modern translation of a selection of his works by contemporary poet Kristjana Gunnars was published: *Stephan G. Stephansson: Selected Prose and Poetry*. Unfortunately, further appreciation and attention in Canada has been hampered by the fact that he wrote only in Icelandic and, moreover, that he is extremely difficult to translate: "You are so Icelandic that English simply won't have you," Hjörtur Leó once exclaimed in a letter to him (Guðmundsson 1982: 9).

However, even if the form and diction of his poetry cannot be completely captured in English, more translations, more widely distributed, would make their content more accessible. It would then at least become clear that Stephan G. cannot simply be dismissed or ignored by Canadian mainstream critics as just another immigrant poet who tried to reconstruct an Old World past without regard for Canadian reality and place, writing only about his homeland or his victimization as an immigrant in Canada. His appeal is too comprehensive, his mind too unfettered, his experience too Canadian for such a limited approach. As Haraldur Bessason points out: "The language ... will pose a problem for many, but [the] wholesome view of humanity defies the limitation of both language and geography" (1967b: 76). David Arnason has attempted to draw a wider attention to Stephan G.'s contribution to Canadian literature:

First ... he dealt in an intense way with Canadian phenomena and Canadian experience; he captures it in a way that can break through even the most inadequate of translations. Second, he was the first poet in Canada, writing in any language, who wrote out of a modern sensibility.... It is commonly believed that others had to express those feelings first before we were able to deal with them. Stephansson, however, is proof that this was not the case, and it is important that his work be available in English translation. (1982: 61-62)

Moreover, New has recently acknowledged Stephan G.'s contribution to Canadian literature in mainstream Canadian circles, when he included Stephan G. in his *History of Canadian Literature* as one of the writers in Canada's other languages who "deserves special mention." New briefly discusses Stephan G. in the light of contemporary developments in Canada. He notes:

While conventional in his use of rhyme, Stephansson ... championed non-traditional causes: pacifism, the Bolshevik Revolution, the United Farmers Party—though a disillusionment with political parties rapidly set in. Through language and theme, he resisted the anglophone norms while at the same time committing himself to the local political culture. The "realist" movement essentially worked at the ramifications of this distinction. (1989: 156-57)

It is one of the exceptional features of Stephan G. that his poetry strikes a deep chord among Icelanders while, at the same time, it reveals his Canadian experience and environment. Moreover, as he speaks from both realities, he transcends, as Bessason aptly states, their cultural and geographical boundaries and speaks to us all. He possessed the gift of moulding any cultural or local subject in his poetry so that its particulars become animated before our eyes, taking on a universal meaning that touches our lives as human beings.

Stephan G.'s main theme is life as it is, as it should be, and our role in it as human beings. His ideas and approach to this theme were moulded by various influences. First of all, Stephan was influenced by his native country, which he left when he was twenty years of age. By that time he was, as he himself said, "already formed and unable to yield to outside pressure" (1988: 20). However, his keen interest and eager mind anxiously swallowed all that went on around him in the New World, whether this was with regard to landscape, his social environment, or in the intellectual sphere.

Because of the extreme poverty of his parents, Stephan G.'s formal education was almost non-existent, to his own great grief. His parents, however, were nevertheless book-loving people, and they taught him what they could. His father was a member of a reading society for a few years, and many people in the neighbourhood owned books. With his early passion for knowledge and literature, the young Stephan read whatever he could borrow, mostly the Bible,

Icelandic sagas, some Icelandic poetry, and the *Vidalín's postilla*. These formative years later proved essential for his writing, as Stephan never had enough money to buy copies of these books and, consequently, had to draw on his memory.

Although Stephan G. did not begin to write seriously until much later, these Icelandic influences moulded him to a considerable extent, reinforced as they probably were by nostalgia and by the fact that he lived exclusively in Icelandic communities in North America. He composed solely in the Icelandic poetic tradition, drawing mostly on the Eddas, the *alþýðu*-tradition and certain individual poets such as Egill Skallagrímsson, the tenth-century poet and hero of *Egils saga*, and Bjarni Thorarensen.[27] These were the kind of works in Icelandic literature that most appealed to him and formed a kind of poetic framework within which he created his own style. He adapted and experimented with form, but only within this framework. As a result, he can, stylistically speaking, be regarded as a rather conservative poet, albeit otherwise original and progressive.

His originality comes out most strongly in his diction, his subject matter and his imagery. Indeed, it is in these fields that the influence of the New World becomes important. His experiences as a pioneer, his working with the land, and the extensive reading he did reaching from topical issues in newspapers and magazines to American litera-ture, formed a different, late kind of New World education for him which, if it could no longer change him as he himself claimed, at least influenced the development and shaping of his outlook and ideas. From his letters it is clear that Stephan G. tried to keep informed as much as possible about the currents and developments in literature. He discusses his readings of contemporary English and American writers like Emerson, Stevenson, Kipling and Hawkins in a letter to fellow Western Icelandic writer Jóhann Magnús Bjarnason (*BOR* 1: 4 Jan. 1899), and of modernists such as T.S. Eliot (*BOR* 3: 1 Sept. 1924). According to the poet himself, however, he had no favourite writers among the ones he read, and he was far more interested in their ideas than in any other aspect of their writing. Stephan G. was too much of an individualist to be attracted by any one movement or writer, as appears from the following passage in his letter to Jóhann Magnús Bjarnason:

Yesterday I read "The Waste Land." I came away from it disconcerted but not surprised. I have experienced the smell of "symbolism," "impressionism," "futurism," "Cubism," "Dadaism," and all sorts of poetic "gripes" before this. Most of it is lacking in enjoyment for me and impossible to fathom. That's not to say it offends me. Some of it has existed for a very long time. Now, however, it has become the only and inedible fare, although it might turn into some kind of food. Poetry should in any case never be allowed to stagnate in the same old puddle. (Guðmundsson 1982: 54)

Indeed, it was to a large extent due to the outlook he developed in the North American intellectual and social climate that Stephan G. was alienated from the Western Icelandic community. Whereas he was, on the one hand, deeply concerned with tradition and the preservation of the Icelandic cultural heritage, he was, on the other hand, a radical who believed that drastic changes were necessary to make this world a better place. The seed of his radicalism might well have been sown by the cultural atmosphere of the farmers' reading societies; it grew to fruition under the influence of American transcendentalism, the freethinkers' movement and international movements such as Marxism and socialism. Most influential in this respect were Stephan G.'s readings of Robert Ingersoll, Felix Adler, William Channing, Karl Marx, and Charles Darwin.[28]

Although Stephan G. was, on the whole, quite active within the Icelandic communities, his views as set forth in his poetry which appeared in Western Icelandic papers and magazines often caused criticism or a stir. On two occasions, his views caused so much antagonism that the large majority of the Icelandic community in North America turned vehemently against him. The first time this happened was because of his radical views with regard to the Church, which culminated in the foundation of the Icelandic Cultural Society, described in the previous chapter. The second time it was because of his outspoken opposition to the First World War and the participation of Canadians, and more specifically Icelandic Canadians.

Stephan G.'s position, then, can be seen at the same time as one of international exposure and of exile. He was highly aware of and concerned with contemporary currents and events, yet he was exiled, to a varying extent, from those with whom he had affinities: Iceland was no longer home, Canada was not yet home, and the Western Icelandic community, at least the larger conservative part of it, rejected him.[29] This sense of displacement we find widely reflected in his poetry, although nowhere as clearly as in "Útlegðin" ("The Exile"):

Ég á orðið einhvern veginn
ekkert föðurland,
þó að fastar hafi um hjartað
hnýtzt það ræktarband,
minn sem tengdan huga hefur
hauðri, mig sem ól,
þar sem æskubrautir birti
bjørtust vonarsól.

Fóstran gekk mér aldrei alveg
í þess móðurstað.
Það var eitthvað, á sem skorti —
ekki veit ég hvað —
og því hef ég arfi hennar
aldrei vera sagzt.
Þó hefur einhver óviðkynning
okkar milli lagzt.[30]

However, we also find this displacement in, for instance, his alternate adherence to and rejection of tradition and in his shifting perspective from the local to the universal, from nationalism to internationalism, from past to present (Gunnars 1988: ix). It is, after all, natural that someone comparatively deracinated should make life, mankind and the world his place and his community: *öll veröld sveit mín er*, he says ("the whole world is my region," *Andvökur* 2: 73). Nevertheless, Stephan G. felt himself so closely bound up with his native literary heritage that he remained, as Viðar Hreinsson notes: "unaffected by modernist fragmentation and scepticism towards ideas and language.... his integrity is an interesting contrast to modern alienation" (1993a: 13). In other words, while some of Stephan G.'s ideas expressed in his poetry clearly show affinity with modernist sensibilities, such as the collection of fierce anti-War poems *Vígslóði* ("Battle Field"), he was far removed from modernism in other respects. The movement he himself felt closest to in spirit was the Realist movement (*BOR* 1: 72, 85).

The most essential theme in Stephan G.'s poetry is that of the pioneer in the widest sense of the word. In this respect his New World experience was one of the main formative aspects of his work and ideas. Stephan G. settled three times over in North America: first in Shawano, Wisconsin, then in Dakota, and finally in Markerville, Alberta, where he remained for the rest of his life. Packing up and leaving worked land behind to start all over again is difficult enough when it only happens once, and we may begin to see why the pioneering experience became such an all-important theme for Stephan who was three times a pioneer. Once settled in Alberta, Stephan G. had to provide for a family which came to include eight children. He was poor when he came to North America, and he never became wealthy. He spent his days working the land, keeping animals and building up a farm that could provide for the family. When he settled in Markerville, this area on the Red Deer river-bank was still a frontier area, an isolated wilderness. The Icelandic community which developed there during his day remained small compared to most others.

As a result, Stephan G. lived a culturally isolated life. Moreover, his cultural occupations, reading and writing, were confined to the evenings. If we look at his total output, 2000 pages of poetry and 1400 pages worth of letters and essays, it may become clear why his poetry was published under the name *Andvökur*, which has been translated as "waking" or "sleepless nights." Although his poetry is very uneven in quality, it certainly does not need the excuse of the circumstances under which Stephan G. wrote. It merely makes his achievement all the more incredible.

Although he kept himself informed of the cultural, social and intellectual events and currents of the times to a truly surprising extent, Stephan G.'s life was, from beginning to end, quite literally rooted in the earth. He was a pioneer farmer, and it is as a pioneer farmer that he considers life around him and speaks to us in his poetry: *Ég er bóndi, allt mitt á / undir sól og regni* ("I am a farmer, all I own is / under sun and rain"; 217). As a pioneer farmer, Stephan was daily involved in the struggle of man against the primal forces of nature, the struggle for life, the creation of an existence in the wilderness. It is this experience that he makes archetypal in his poetry: man as a creative power, man who creates his own history, man who is both master and servant of the primal forces of existence. As he sees life as all-enveloping and engaged in a continual, unending process of becoming, he sees work as man's role, for which his reward is the contribution to progress formed by the fruits of his toil. That this role was one that demanded hard work, struggling and endurance he accepted as natural, as part of the deal. After all, it also involved its own reward, its own victory: to have fought for the progress of human existence and to have made one's mark. In this way, Stephan G. gave meaning to the conditions of his own life and that of the majority of people. With his poetry, he created a lasting monument to honour all working men and women (Kristjánsson 1953). As a natural consequence of his outlook, Stephan G. had three main enemies: those who live off the fruits of other people's work and creation, those who serve destruction and those who attempt to hinder progress. This should explain Stephan's severe criticism of capitalist forces, warfare and organized religion (Þorsteinsson 1953: 31).

His heroes are those who work towards progress. They can be revolutionaries, fighting for a better world in the past or the present (Nicodemus, Jón Sigurðsson) but they need not be so glorious. Many of his heroes are those who rise above their circumstances, no matter how miserable or looked-down upon they may be. They are isolated figures who manage to make the very best out of what they have, people who will not be brought down by difficulties or poverty but will, instead, defy their circumstances and regard them as a challenge (*ekki láta baslið smækka sig* ["not let difficulties fell one"]; examples are "Sigurður Trölli," and Kolbeinn in "Kolbeinslag"). Stephan G. also sees heroism in those who have been underrated by the spirit of the times, the people who were misunderstood and trodden on because of blind dogmatism, superstition or conservatism (such as "Jón hrak" and Ragnheiður *litla* in "Á Ferð og Flugi").

Thus Stephan G. made the pioneer experience, with its trials and seeming hopelessness, into a contribution to progress and a better world, even though pioneers generally do not live to see the fruits of their contribution. He realized that life is too short, and that people are like farmers who do not live to harvest their crops, but who continue work, knowing that those who come after them will enjoy the fruits of their work:

> *Við höllumst að sjón, ekki sögum,*
> *oss sýnist nú örvænt um flest!*
> *En enn mun að ákveðnum lögum*
> *við aldarhátt þroskaðri fest:*
> *að hugsa ekki í árum, en öldum,*
> *að alheimta ei daglaun að kvöldum*
> *— því svo lengist mannsævin mest.*

> *Ur árgöngum vortíða og vetra*
> *það vitinu sjálflærast fer*
> *að umskapa ið bezta í betra,*
> *að byggja upp það farsælast er.*

Það er ekki oflofuð samtíð,
en umbætt og glaðari framtíð,
sú veröld, er sjáandinn sér. (215)[31]

In this world-view characterized by progress and pioneering, Stephan G. combined Old and New World views: while his firm belief in the evolutionary forces of an all-encompassing life immediately bring Darwin and Marx to mind, there are also echoes of the heathen outlook of the Viking Age and the Eddas, with their materialist emphasis and their heroism of defying the odds to fight chaos and destruction. Moreover, while his recognition of life as a fated struggle which has to be fought alone and which challenges one's daring and vigour are reminiscent of Iceland's history and the Norse tragic heroic view, Stephan G.'s view of work as a creative force and a blessing and his firmly optimistic faith in the future and in progress resemble socialism, and even, as McCracken has suggested, the Victorian work ethic (1983: 40-43).

Stephan G. was extremely concerned with the message of his poetry. At the same time he realized full well that, frequently, the large scope of his message tended to weigh down the light flow of his lines, making them heavy-going, crammed with ideas. The most common criticism of his poetry has therefore always been that of obscurity. Stephan himself was aware of this fact, but he lacked the time to polish his poetry, and he found the thought unacceptable that the message might suffer in the polishing process: "It is true that what you call 'unclear' on my account is 'turf.' I have worn myself out trying to cut it down it better, but then the thought would be lost," he says in one of his letters (*BOR* I, 164).[32] In the poem "Áin" ("The River") he sees the river as his companion in whom he recognizes a similar tendency to force its way through where necessary:

Og loks, er hafðir losað þig,
þú lagðist söm og áður
svo tær og hrein í hroðinn stig
sem heiðblá silkiþráður —
sem hugsun stór og sterk og frjáls,
sem styrkir mig og gleður,
en bryzt í rofum ríms og máls
og röngum stuðlum hleður. (120)[33]

The deeply felt humanity in his message, however, and the beautiful imagery in which he clothes it, make his occasional obscurity forgiveable. His belief in the message of poetry finds its roots in the traditional Icelandic belief in the power of the poetic word. Stephan G. probably succeeded best in combining the expression of his philosophy and idealism with aestheticism in the poem "Kveld" ("Evening").

Stephan G. made the power of poetry the subject of one of his most famous narrative poems, "Kolbeinslag" ("Kolbein's metre"). "Kolbeinslag" is one of Stephan's poems set in the Icelandic past by way of sagas or folk legends. Stephan G. was, through his close affinities with the poetic *alþýðu*-tradition, directly linked to Iceland's literary past, from which he, moreover, drew ambition and strength rather than merely nostalgia. "Kolbeinslag" is based on an Icelandic folk tale about the *alþýðuskáld* Kolbeinn who agreed on a poetic contest with the devil and won. In Stephan's poem, Kolbeinn becomes the archetypal Icelandic *alþýðuskáld*, the poetic figure with whom Stephan felt most affinity. The figure of the *alþýðuskáld* stands at the same time as the representative of the Icelandic people who, throughout their history of poverty and struggle, had only one weapon left: literature. This weapon kept them from degenerating into a subhuman level of existence. In the poem, Stephan G. created a devil who is reminiscent of the leaders in society who live off the misery and poverty of their people. The devil sets out to rob Kolbeinn, and thus the Icelandic people, of their last weapon, literature, so that they can be utterly subdued. Kolbeinn does not understand that this is the real object the devil seeks to gain with the poetry contest until the very end. When he realizes what is at stake, he can only think of one solution: he invents a new poetic metre, to which the devil cannot answer. Kolbeinn saves the Icelandic nation with the little it has at its disposal: flexibility. Thus Stephan G. turned this poor, simple *alþýðuskáld* into a pioneer who clears the road to freedom and cultural progress (Friðþjófsson 1961: 165).

To fit the subject of the Icelandic *alþýðuskáld*, "Kolbeinslag" was composed in a variation on the complicated form and diction of a *ríma*. However, Kolbeinn is also a pioneer, and to fit his pioneer reality Stephan G. included Canadian idiom in the poem as well, as for instance in the following passage:

> *Þó að spör á "eld" og "örk"*
> *yrðu kjörin ferða,*
> *axarför í bjarkabörk*
> *benda á örugg leiðarmörk.* (68)

Haraldur Bessason observes:

An imperfect rendering of this verse follows: "Although the pioneer's course of travel is neither shown by burning beacons nor lavishly praised in authors' writings, the 'axe-marks' on the 'birch trees' show us the way."

This verse from Kolbeinslag is not included here because of its high literary merit; rather it is an interesting example of metaphorical use where trail blazing in Canada is neatly linked with the poet's search back into the literary history of Iceland. It shows us clearly how perfectly Stephan G. Stephansson had adapted himself to the difficult role of an Icelandic Canadian. (1967b: 75-76)

It is one of the striking characteristics of Stephan G.'s poetry that he uses the love for his native country and cultural heritage as a creative source in his contribution to the future and progress of his foster country. It was the best way he knew to serve both countries well without betraying either of them or himself. After all, the man who made the whole world his region knew at the same time that *heimsborgari er ógeðs yfirklór* ("a world patriot is the poor excuse of antipathy"; 125), as he says to his foster country:

> *Svo vermdu þá, Kanada, í kjöltunni þinni*
> *upp kólnaða frændsemd og ættjarðarminni!*
> *Ver frjálsust, ver hollviljuð hugsjónum ungu,*
> *ver heimaland sérhverrar þjóðar og tungu!*
> *Þó aðskotaloftunga ofhrós þér segi*
> *ef ættjörð hann svívirðir, trú honum eigi,*
> *því hann bæri, ef á reyndi, sæmd þína í sjóði,*
> *hans sjóndeildarhringur er laustekin gróði —*
> *það innræti flýtur með flugumanns blóði.* (95)[34]

Canada, in other words, will be best served by those who remain loyal to their native heritage. Stephan G. was not the only Western Canadian author who had such early multiculturalist ideals for Canada's future, as we will see.

In his narrative poem "Á Ferð og Flugi" ("En route"), Stephan G. paints a lively picture of the prairies in pioneer times as well as of his fellow Icelandic pioneers. The poem is very critical, both of the Church and of the Western Icelandic community, and was therefore not received equally well everywhere when it came out in 1900. However, its imagery and descriptions of the prairie landscape and pioneer communities give it lasting value, and challenge those who believe that no one in Canada described a Canadian landscape in and on its own terms before 1950.

In contrast to "Kolbeinslag," "Á Ferð og Flugi" is written in light, smoothly flowing lines which, although they do contain the inevitable Icelandic alliterative patterns, are especially suited to Canadian subject matter: they convey the speed of the train as it is rolling through the flat prairie landscape, the rush of the people who are out to make a fortune quickly in the mining town of Golden and are just as quickly brought down, and the shallowness of the crowds who have shaken off their past to live in a present of materialism and appearances:

> *Því siðir og hugsanir dagsins í dag*
> *þar drottna með óskoruð völd,*
> *sem frumbyggðin sprettir upp fortíðarlaus*
> *og fóstruð af samtíðar öld.*
> *Og framförin mikla og menningin hér*
> *við minningar ei hefur töf*
> *ef endistu að plægja, þú akurland fær,*
> *ef uppgefst þú: nafnlausa gröf.* (134)[35]

In this mercenary world of the present, characterized by the rush for survival and quick money, the real gold that lies hidden in less obvious and accessible places, such as in the heart of Ragnheiður *litla*, is all too easily passed by or ignored. Ragnheiður is an Icelandic girl whom the narrator briefly meets twice on his travels. The poem traces the misfortunes of this girl. She is the daughter of poor immigrants who has to work for an English family in the city. She faithfully sends money home to her parents, and on her visit to the Icelandic community she donates a great sum of money and helps to collect more for a church building. However, after a while, when she has lost her attraction as an "English" city girl, she leaves for the city again.

When the narrator sees Ragnheiður again after many years, she has become a disreputable woman with an English name. During the train accident that follows she saves the life of a baby, thereby losing her own. The Icelandic pastor who is also on the train refuses to hold a funeral service for her because he is afraid that her reputation will sully his. However, when the rich mother of the baby offers to pay for a funeral, the pastor readily complies. When the narrator visits Ragnheiður's grave, he finds a stone with only her English name on it and that of the lady who paid for her funeral. Stephan G. himself characterized "Á Ferð og Flugi" in a letter: "I think I have set the

small picture that I drew of an Icelandic 'pioneer-woman' in a framework of pioneer history, the landscape and life in pioneer towns, as
far as possible in brief poetry."[36] In this poem he drew a realistic
picture of a situation many West Icelanders knew either from experience or from their environment, but preferred to keep quiet about.
Ragnheiður symbolizes those Icelandic immigrants who lost all contact with their compatriots and nationality, and, having no education
to fall back on and having grown away from their native culture,
often ended up on the less reputable side of society. Her antitype in
the poem is the pastor, a poignant example of those Icelanders who
so wanted to be respectable that they became slaves to local public
opinion. In this respect, "Á Ferð og Flugi" is also a poetic confrontation with, in Stephan G.'s words: "the feeling that most of us have in
common, to try and stand as far away as possible from those who
have been a shame to our nation...."[37]

   "Á Ferð og Flugi" is, then, a poetic study and description of the
prairies, of pioneer life and of Icelandic pioneers. It vividly and accurately conveys the atmosphere and the landscape. Stephan G., however, devoted many more poems to his foster country than this one,
possibly more than to his native country. It is true that he ends "Á
Ferð og Flugi" with the following lines:

> — Til framandi landa ég bróðurhug ber,
>   þar brestur á viðkvæmnin ein,
> en ættjarðarböndum mig grípur hver grund,
>   sem grær kringum Íslendings bein.
> Ég skil, hví vort heimaland hjartfólgnast er:
>   öll óhöppin og ólánið það,
> sem ættkvísl þín beið, rifjar upp fyrir þér
>   hver árhvammur, fjallströnd og vað.
> Og það er sem holtin sjálf hleypi í mann þrótt,
>   þar hreystiraun einhver var drýgð,
> og svo er sem mold sú sé manni þó skyld,
>   sem mæðrum og feðrum er vígð. (167-68)[38]

However, this does not mean that Stephan G.'s loyalty to Iceland prevents him from developing a different kind of bond with his foster
country:

> Landið, sem mín vígð er vinna,
> vöggustöðin barna minna!
> Ég hef fellt í lag og línu

> Ljóðið mitt í grasi þínu.
> Yfir höfuð yrkir mitt
> aftur seinna grasið þitt.
> Hjarta og hugur er
> heimabundið þér.
> Met ei við milljón dali
> mætur, sem á þér ég hef,
> stuðla ei í stef
> hrós þitt í hundraða tali. (128-29)[39]

In a different way, then, Stephan G. formed a "home-bond" with Canada, based on something deeper and more lasting than just the dollar. Many of his Canadian poems convey a profound communion and companionship between the poet and the natural scene around him. As a farmer from a rugged, northern country, he had no illusions about the romance of nature. He knew nature in all its primal force and indifference to man. However, this does not cause him to back away in awe of nature's power. They work together, for better for worse. In fact, Stephan G. preferred nature in her grimmer guise:

> En klakann og mjöllina met ég þér betur,
> því mjallar og klakans ég fósturbarn er.
> Og ég á ævinni oftast nær vetur
> einn fleiri en sumrin mín — hvernig sem fer.
> ...
> Ég veit það er lánsæld að lifa og njóta,
> að leika og hvíla, sem hugurinn kýs.
> En mér finnst það stærra að stríða og brjóta
> í stórhríðum ævinnar mannrauna ís. (103)[40]

To Stephan, nature was part of the great scheme of life and progress, just as he was himself. Nature tells him things about himself, about life, about mankind. Thus his nature poems usually contain some universal message or idea, while at the same time immortalizing Canadian natural scenes in an unforgettable way. His poem "Greniskógurinn" ("The Spruce Forest") is an impressive ode to the spruce trees which grow where nothing else can grow, and adorn the winter landscape, never bending to the frosty storms. The unbending spruce trees remind Stephan of all the people who are like them, living where no-one else wants to live, deprived of warmth, but firmly rooted in hope. Similarly, he has given poetic expression to the majesty of the Rocky Mountains in "Klettafjöll." In this poem, the Rocky Mountains become the image of *Valhöll* ("Valhalla"), as Stephan links the conventional image of Canada as the land of hope with the Norse mythological dream-world.

Stephan G. Stephansson, then, gave voice to his profoundly humanistic ideas and ideals, based on both his Icelandic heritage and his New World experiences, in poetry that has immortalized both the Western Icelandic pioneer experience in Canada and the Canadian landscape. As a Western Icelandic pioneer-farmer, he combined the best that he found in his Icelandic heritage and his Canadian life, and transformed it into a unique kind of poetry that has greatly enriched the Icelandic poetic tradition, and that will, one hopes, one day be more easily accessible to Canadians.

GUTTORMUR J. GUTTORMSSON

Guttormur J. Guttormsson (1878-1966) is frequently mentioned along with Stephan G. Stephansson, not only because the two have many things in common with regard to circumstances, outlook and poetry, but also because they are considered the two best poets among the West Icelanders. Whereas Stephan G. is generally considered to be the better of the two, Guttormur occupies the unique position of being the only Western Icelandic poet who was born in Canada, three years after the emigration of his parents in 1875.

Strictly speaking, Guttormur should not be discussed in this chapter, as he was not an immigrant nor did he have a direct personal experience with Iceland. However, Guttormur wrote only in Icelandic, and wrote, moreover, almost solely in the Icelandic poetic tradition about the Icelandic pioneer and immigrant experience. Although his position gives his work a special dimension and identity, it nevertheless belongs to Western Icelandic literature in atmosphere, point of view and content, as well as in language. In fact, Guttormur is the one known example we have of the West Icelander whom the nationalist immigrants ideally had in mind in promoting the preservation of the Icelandic heritage in the Western hemisphere: Guttormur was moulded by his Canadian environment, yet steeped in Icelandic culture. He was a Canadian citizen, but grew up on a New Iceland farm on the northern Manitoba frontier.

Guttormur's parents lived through all the trials of pioneer New Iceland and paid for it with an untimely death: his mother died when he was seven, and at sixteen he was an orphan. First due to poverty, then to the necessity of working for a living, he only enjoyed four years of formal schooling. This lack of schooling remained with him as a profound and painful source of regret during his entire life, although, according to good Icelandic tradition, he more than made up for it by extensive and varied reading. In all likelihood it also allowed him to keep Icelandic as his first language, although he was virtually bilingual. As he spent all his years in Icelandic communities, and nearly all of his adult years on the farm of his parents, he found himself in the position of being a true West Icelander: not quite Icelandic, even less quite Canadian, but a unique combination.

Stephan G. Stephansson and Káinn were young men when they emigrated, already moulded by life in Iceland. Although they were both, in their own ways, open to the New World, they were aware of a loss, which ultimately made their view a retrospective one, and of a gap between two worlds that needed to be bridged. This is reflected in their writing, as we have seen. Guttormur is also keenly aware of these two worlds which inform his life and writing, but his view is that of the son who stands in the middle of the bridge, hesitating and torn, the cultural influence of the one world as real to him as the geographical influence of the other. Moreover, he is faced with the spiritual gap which separates the two. This is where he differs importantly from Laura Goodman Salverson, whom I will discuss below. Laura Salverson was also a pioneer's daughter and also bilingual, but with English as her first language, and Canada as both her geographical and her cultural first-hand reality. For her, Iceland was an ancestral image which informed her life, while for Guttormur, it was a mother culture which informed his life. As a result, Guttormur's poetry is a curious and intriguing blend of Icelandic poetic tradition and diction encompassing what is essentially Canadian subject matter: a Canadian landscape, and a Canadian immigrant past and present.

One of Guttormur's main themes is the poetic recognition and expression of Icelandic pioneer history in Canada. In this respect, Guttormur's works belong to second-generation immigrant writing as analyzed by Mossberg. I outlined earlier how Mossberg saw first-generation immigrant writing as works designed primarily to guide and support as well as to document group experience: "how to survive in the New World with an Old World past." By the time Guttormur started to write, most of the Icelandic settlements had been established. As Mossberg notes:

These later writers, therefore, have an historical perspective on their subject when they are writing about the pioneer generation; but they were themselves very much a part of the second and third generation, and all their incumbent problems. The writers are extremely conscious of the link between generations, and their fiction can be viewed as a drama of experiences typical to individual generations, rather than individual persons. Although the immediacy of the living, personal responses are provided by characterizations of individuals, heroes and heroines of specific novels are representative of a whole generation of the immigrant group. By making the different generations the protagonists, the writers gain a sense of historical continuity that provides a tone of epic import to the story of the social group. (1976: 114)

Moreover, Mossberg sees this literature as focussing on "the issues which the writers felt would determine the fate of the immigrant":

The writers look at the pioneer generation and are astounded by the scope of their achievements—and the sacrifices necessary for what these forbearers accomplished. The characters create energy and productivity, for they are shown concentrating on the goals of planting, building, and developing. The accomplishments of the first generation serve as a focal point of pride for other immigrants, though that pride is muted by a sense of sacrifice and tragic loss. (115)

This analysis, even though it speaks of fiction, is a very apt description of the many poems which Guttormur devoted to the Icelandic pioneer past. It is, perhaps, only fitting that a child of pioneers should be concerned with what he knows to be the direct past of his own and future generations, rather than that of an Old World left behind.

One of the chief differences between Guttormur and his fellow Western Icelandic poets, then, is that whereas they are informed by the loss of the mother country, Guttormur is concerned directly with the loss and tragedy involved in the pioneer experience. After all, the pain which informs the Old World memories of the first generation has been supplanted by the romance of imagination and tales among later generations. Instead, Guttormur feels and expresses the pain involved in the memories of the pioneer experience.

Guttormur's first published book of poetry (in 1909) consisted mainly of the narrative poem "Jón Austfirðingur" ("Jón of the East Fjords"). The name of the poem is suggestive of Guttormur's own father, but it is really a poetic account of the pioneer experience of one man personifying the generation of immigrants to which Guttormur's parents belonged. It is a deeply tragic poem which focusses on tribulations and sacrifices, and although it ends on an optimistic note for the future, its main message seems to be that the new country was acquired at a very high price.

The poem consists of eleven sections or chapters, which follow a pattern that is common to much immigrant literature. It begins with a rather pastoral description of the Icelandic home in the countryside ("Heima"). Then follows the exodus ("Vesturförin"), which is here attributed to the wiles and deceptive talk of an immigration agent ("Evangelíum"). The fourth chapter covers the settlement ("Landnámið"), and the following four chapters are concerned with the tribulations, the physical and psychological cost, epitomized by three major New Iceland disasters, the smallpox epidemic, the flood and a forest fire. This middle part of the poem constitutes the testing or initiation phase ending in a spiritual death, symbolized by the death of Jón's daughter Guðrún in chapter nine ("Guðrún"). She is the Old World child, *síns fósturlands ímynd*, who dies at the hands of her deceitful, murderous New World husband. In the last two chapters, however, a kind of harmony is re-established when the completely broken and disillusioned Jón finds his hopes revived through Guðrún's son, whom he brings up. The son embodies the hope of the future and the union of old and new. The poem ends on the following note:

> *Og fólkið með íslenzkan framfarabrag*
> *við framtíðarhorfurnar sættist,*
> *og byggðin fór stækkandi dag eftir dag,*
> *og draumurinn smám saman rættist.*
> *— Þó mörg hafi framkvæmdin farizt,*
> *er fólgið í reynslunni manns:*
> *Að aldrei til einskis er barizt*
> *í óbyggðum Norðvesturlands.*[41]

Guttormur's first publication received mixed reviews, and it is indeed a flawed, though promising youthful work. However, from his second collection of poetry, *Bóndadóttir* ("Farmer's Daughter"), onwards, we see the typical "Guttormian" characteristics developing: a striking originality and mastery of rhyme-scheme, symbolism and wit. However, these characteristics do not manifest themselves in every poem. This is, perhaps, not so strange for a poet who was poised between two cultures and, therefore, did not really belong to either of them. The balance is a precarious one, and only in his best works does Guttormur achieve and sustain it. Inevitably, these are nearly all poems which reflect either Guttormur's personal situation or feelings, or his own past, surroundings and concerns. As Sveinn Skorri Höskuldsson points out, Guttormur never really considered himself free enough to become the poetic experimenter that was so obviously in him, as he felt responsible for the preservation of the Icelandic cultural heritage (1980: 81-82). In this sense, too, Guttormur is typical of the second-generation immigrant writer.

Guttormur's sense of poetic diction and form was moulded by the Icelandic tradition, in spite of his wide reading of English and American literature. Guttormur faithfully sticks to complicated patterns of alliteration, rhyme and metre. However, he follows not only Icelandic models, but also foreign ones, or he even makes up his own. Moreover, Guttormur had a natural gift for using complex forms and rhyme-schemes so that, on the whole, they do not impede but rather enhance the beauty of his poems. Gísli Jónsson once remarked that if the Icelandic words *hljóð* ("sound") and *ljóð* ("poem") were of the same origin, they embraced each other again through Guttormur (1949: 78).

An example of such a typically Guttormian mixture of cultural influences, of old and new, is found in what is probably his most famous and popular poem, "Sandy Bar."[42] In this poem he expresses the same message as in "Jón Austfirðingur," but in a much more sophisticated and effective manner. The poem is named after a graveyard in New Iceland where victims of the smallpox epidemic were buried. In the poem, the narrator visits this graveyard, where atmosphere, nature and lingering ghosts mingle into what becomes an apocalyptic vision of the pioneer experience. The poem is written in the form used by Edgar Allen Poe in "The Raven," which adds to its haunting atmosphere. The clustering rhyme pattern of "The Raven" and "Sandy Bar" is non-Icelandic, but is combined in "Sandy Bar" with Icelandic alliterative patterns (Kristjanson 1990: 491). Moreover, its poetic diction is very Icelandic, as are its natural and literary images. The natural scenery, however, with its towering trees and wild thunderstorm, is Canadian.

In "Sandy Bar" the uneven bargain of the pioneers is again recalled, this time poignantly described through images of broken hearts and broken strength as the pioneers built the road to the future with the breath of death in their necks and the haunting fear of not being able to finish their work. As lightning lights up the graves, the narrator realizes that the pioneers awaited no gratitude or glory, not even the satisfaction of a job finished, only a grave and a forgotten name. As, in the climactic last stanzas, the natural surroundings seem to re-enact the tragedy of those pioneers, the elements suddenly blend together to form a vision which links the pioneers to the deeds and glory of the ancient saga heroes through an allusion, first to *Valhöll* ("Valhalla") in stanza VIII and then to the phenomenon of the *vafurlogar* in stanza IX. *Vafurlogar* are flames which were believed to shine over graves that contained a treasure. In the case of the pioneers, the treasure is their "golden muscles," the strength which enabled them to work, suffering and brokenhearted, on a job they would never finish. However, it is only this transitory, physical aspect that is contained in the graves in Sandy Bar. In the last stanza, the sky suddenly breaks open and shows a star-ridden arch of heaven, and the narrator realizes that the eventual pioneer settlement is achieved and enjoyed in heaven rather than on earth.

Guttormur's subject matter, however, covers a much broader range than only the pioneer experience. He was a poor self-educated New Iceland farmer who relied for his Icelandic reading on local societies that provided him with Icelandic sagas as well as contemporary Icelandic literature. Thus, his circumstances were those of an Icelandic *alþýðuskáld*, and Guttormur's poetry does indeed have many features in common with this tradition. One of these has already been mentioned: composition faithful to the patterns of a long-standing poetic tradition. However, in Guttormur's case, this feature receives a powerful new dimension due to his position as a second-generation immigrant poet who is concerned with the preservation of his literary heritage within a larger majority culture, and who, therefore, consciously composes in order to preserve and, possibly, sustain.

Another feature Guttormur has in common with this tradition which thrived so well among Western Icelandic poets is the influence of both Romanticism, a sensitive, lyric strain we find in many nature and contemplative poems, and of the radical social reform strain which can be traced back to the influence of the Realist movement on the Icelandic farmers' reading societies. It is mostly in Guttormur's nature poems, however, that we see an important difference between Guttormur and his first-generation fellow poets: Guttormur's nature poems are invariably set in Canada rather than in Iceland and describe his direct natural environment. An exception are the poems he wrote during his visit to Iceland in 1938.

Guttormur's nature poems are seldom only descriptive or an invocation of a certain feeling or atmosphere. In most cases, they form an occasion for the contemplation of a much more profound, universal issue or theme which then, in turn, becomes reflected in the natural scene. An example is his poem "Góða nótt" ("Goodnight"), in which he begins by picturing nature as a cosmic made-up bed ready for mankind to fall asleep in so as to find rest and regain vigour. Then he turns to all those who wrecked their ships in life and drifted past its beauties, and asks the peace and quiet of night to descend on them to cool their wounds and bring them the dreams that they never achieved in life, so that they will wake up without cold and fear but see the sunshine.

Another example of a nature lyric by Guttormur which brings out more clearly his Canadian-ness, is the thirteenth poem in the cycle "Á víð og dreif" ("Far and Wide"), in which he pictures Indian summer as an Indian girl:

> *Indíána sumar er svanni*
> *með svart og mikið hár,*
> *koparlitt, æskuslétt andlit*
> *og ylhýrar dökkar brár.*
>
> *Hárið er skammdegis húmið*
> *að hníga með stjörnuglans,*
> *hörundsliturinn haustleg*
> *hálmbleikja akurlands.*
>
> *Laufum með regnbogalitum,*
> *litum hins dýrasta ríms,*
> *skýrðist hin prúða og prýðist*
> *perlum daggar og hríms.*
>
> *Svo kastar hún laufakjólnum.*
> *— Kuldi fyrir' dyrum er —*
> *Í kríthvíta ísbjarna kápu*
> *klæðir hún sig og fer.* (319-20)[43]

Although this description is a particularly gentle one in Guttormur's oeuvre, it still ends with the sudden icy cold of winter. It is a striking characteristic of Guttormur's poetry that he always sees a deeper universal meaning under the surface, which frequently exposes a grim truth. It is here that a tragic vision comes out in Guttormur's poetry.

This deep sense of a grimness lurking behind the face of things, the poignant awareness of the fleeting nature of all beauty in life, is one that is found very widely in Icelandic literature. Among some writers, it finds expression in an undying, sometimes almost naive, hope and belief in the coming of these fleeting moments and an intense enjoyment of them while they last. Jónas Hallgrímsson is the major representative of these gentle "spring poets," as they are sometimes referred to, and through his genius this expression found a defined and lasting place in the Icelandic tradition. Of the Western Icelandic writers, one might count Þorsteinn Þ. Þorsteinsson, Einar Páll Jónsson, and Jóhann Magnús Bjarnason among these voices of spring.

The more traditional expression, which goes back to the fatalism in Old Norse literature and mythology, is however a tragic one, the voice of the "doom of *Ragnarök*," based on the inevitability in life of tragedy and cruelty, which will, eventually, destroy everything. This voice of doom has its origin not only in Icelandic mythology, but also in Icelandic reality. In Guttormur's case, it originates, too, in the reality of the Icelandic immigrant experience. The traditional response to this view has always been to face up to tragic fate with defiance, without a thought of yielding to it, however great the odds. This is the background of the traditional ideal of valour and courage in Icelandic culture, which regained so much of its importance for the immigrants in their pioneer struggle. Guttormur himself remarked on the two different strains in Icelandic literature in a letter to Kirkconnell:

There are two strands in Icelandic poetry: the one hard and strong, the other soft and feminine. The former is Northern, derived from the Eddas. The latter is Southern, derived from the German Romantic poets. I have always been more attracted by the Northern element in the Icelandic poets, especially in Bólu-Hjálmar, Bjarni Thorarensen ... Stephan G. Stephansson.... (Kirkconnell 1939: 109).

Stephan G. called these two strains the *silkiþráður* and the *stuðlaberg*, "the silk thread" and "the alliterative rock" (*BOR* 1: 160).

The main focus of Guttormur's tragic poetic vision is social injustice, which is another feature that links Guttormur to the *alþýðu*-tradition. His protest is characteristically voiced through satire, absurd paradox and black humour. Although part of his protest is—like Káinn's—rooted in personal bitterness, Guttormur's black humour and satire have a more grimly serious dimension and are not nearly as harmless as Káinn's. Compare for instance Káinn's epigrams above with the following epigram by Guttormur:

> *Fylgi sníkja flakkar tveir,*
> *fárra en ríkra vinir.*
> *Plata, svíkja og pretta þeir*
> *pólitíkarsynir.* (346)[44]

Here, too, the joke is hidden in wordplay. In Icelandic, the word *pólitíkarsynir* is a perfectly innocent word meaning politicians. However, if one translates the word—*tíkarsynir* literally into English, the reference suddenly changes to "son of a bitch" and the humour of the poem blackens (Höskuldsson 1980: 77).

This, however, is one of Guttormur's more vitriolically outspoken epigrams. Many of Guttormur's polemic poems take on a subtler form, making them both more universal through the symbolism he employs, and more effective. An example is "Vatnið" ("The Lake"), where he gives a lyrical description of the serene beauty of a lake. Through its clear waters, however, we suddenly catch glimpses of the merciless tyranny exercized by the greedy, bloodthirsty pike over the smaller fish, which are eaten one after the other. Guttormur leaves no doubt as to the symbolic reference of the poem as the small fish call out to unite in order to stand strong and demand freedom and peace by the power of international law. Guttormur's faith in the executioners of the law is made clear as the pike comes and eats every one of the fish.

Guttormur's sympathy is always with the duped and lost in life. In the witty "Bölvun lögmálsins" ("The Curse of the Law") he powerfully universalizes the plight of the farmer, as he tells how the hardworking Esau, providing his family with food from the land, is cheated by his lazy brother "Kobbi" ("Jake") who lives a wealthy life off the fruits of other people's labour. The poem ends thus:

> *Og allt af skal blómgast hans verzlun og vald*
> *án vinnu og líkamans sveita,*

og frumburðarréttur hins fátæka gjald
sé fyrir hans bauna að neyta.
Og prífast hann einn af öllum skal
og einn vera feitur og glaður.
Frá bændum að eilífu blessun stal
sá baunaverzlunarmaður. (166)[45]

That he was concerned not only with his own community is clear from the poem "Indíána Hátíðin" ("Indian Festival"). Guttormur knew Indians from his early days on his parents' frontier farm. Guttormur's descriptions of native people are realistic, tainted neither by hostility nor by a romantic idealism. He wrote some illuminating accounts about the encounters of Icelanders and Indians and the cultural misunderstandings between the two (1975: 75-92). Guttormur was well aware of the fact that the Icelanders had been assigned to a strip of land that was not "white man's land" (see also Chapter II). His understanding for the Indians' plight is expressed in the above mentioned poem of which follow here the last two stanzas:

— Undir hulning fati flettum,
flæmdum út á lífsins sand,
varnað þess að rísa réttum
reikað verður þeim um land,
land, sem þeir ei lengur eiga,
land, sem rændir voru þeir,
land, sem þeir með leyfi mega
líta', en ekki hóta meir.

Hallur steikistaur við loga
stendur, rekinn gegnum hund.
Er í skrokkinn skeyti' af boga
skotið, þá er matmálsstund.
Flöium beinum fold er setin.
Flátt að mæla sérhver kann.
Hvítur rakki, öllum étinn,
á að tákna hvítan mann. (208)[46]

One of Guttormur's most moving and personal poems about the painful acquiescence to a fate where dreams and ambitions have been thwarted in life, has found universal application through its original symbolism:

Hugsjóna minna hunangsflugur
hafði ég um minn lífsins vetur
lokaðar, náttaðar nótt og degi,
niðri í kjallara sálar minnar. (156)[47]

In this poem, called "Býflugnaræktin" ("Bee-keeping"), the image of the narrator's ideals as bees which have, of necessity, been locked away in the cellar of his soul to await his life's summer, is carefully developed into a powerful climax: as the wait for life's summer continues, the bees reach the point of near starvation, and when the narrator finally opens the cellar-door, he is viciously attacked by the desperate animals. He has to bear the scars for the rest of his life: *Líti ég smáður við leiða og örkuml, / líkari hröpuðum engli en manni* ("Loathesome I feel in my mutilation, / Less like a man than a fallen angel"; 1939: 114).

The symbolism of the poem discussed above originates from Guttormur's native environment, as bee-keeping was not practised in Iceland. Similarly, "Indíána Hátíðin" is, as regards subject matter and imagery, a Canadian poem, and even "Bölvun lögmálsins" is more directed toward the farming situation in Canada than in Iceland. Yet, the language and tradition in which they were written are Icelandic. Guttormur must have been aware of the fact that he wrote for a very limited audience, more limited even than that of Stephan G. and Káinn, as much of his subject matter was, and is, as alien to the Icelanders as the Icelandic language is to Canadians. Although Guttormur acquired a certain degree of fame among the Icelanders, who invited the poet over to Iceland as a national guest, his reputation rests more on the pride of his cultural achievement and the recognition of genuine poetic talent than on a real understanding of his poetry. Arnór Sigurjónsson, in his introduction to the collection of Guttormur's poetry, admits:

Among Guttormur's poetry there is a wide variety of aspects that are little or unknown to us here in Iceland. This concerns both the subject matter itself and the understanding and opinions of the writer which appear unfamiliar to us, as well as the atmosphere which is enveloped in the subject matter and its treatment.[48]

Thus, Guttormur's position is not just a unique but also an isolated one. The only people who really could understand his poetry were the West Icelanders themselves, that is to say the ones who still understood Icelandic.

There are a few poems which express Guttormur's awareness of his dual reality, but one can only really feel the isolation resulting from it in the desire for a union of the two realities evident in these poems. One such poem is "Íslendingafljót," named after the river close by Guttormur's farm, which is called in English "Icelandic River." This is yet another poem which reveals Guttormur's use of symbolism. Guttormur pictures the river as the body which separates the two shores of his two worlds. However, the shores are connected through the trees which grow on each shore, as they spring from the same roots, shake hands through their touching branches, and are subject to the same natural laws. Guttormur feels this connection to be so strong, that if a tree on one side would fall, the one right across from it would automatically fall along with it. As long as nobody uproots these trees, he says in the last stanza, and water from life's source will feed them, they will continue to live and hold hands over the river.

The belief in such a strong connection between the Icelandic and Canadian realities, especially by the time when this poem was published (in 1944), seems almost a willful contradiction of the reality of the day: West Icelanders were developing their own immigrant culture separately from the development of Icelandic culture. Instead, this belief seems to point at Guttormur's emotional need to bridge the duality of his own reality. Similarly, in the poem "Kanada," Guttormur pictures Canada as a princess and Iceland as a prince who are united in marriage and establish a kingdom. Their children, although they speak a different language, are united in origin and soul.

In Guttormur's poetry, then, we find the immigrant trials and experience epitomized, past and present. Having been born and raised an immigrant son of New Iceland, Guttormur found himself in a unique but isolated position, in that he belonged to two worlds, two realities, and yet to neither. Through his poetic talent he has painted a powerful picture of his and his community's experience of the Canadian immigrant reality, choosing at the same time his own poetic isolation by writing solely in Icelandic in a wishful attempt to preserve his Old World heritage from extinction in the New.

WESTERN ICELANDIC PROSE

Whereas Western Icelandic poetry covers a wide variety of topics in which both Iceland and Canada are represented, Western Icelandic prose is almost exclusively concerned with the new situation, the immigrant experience. This theme is not only in accordance with the general tendency in Scandinavian immigrant literature in North America as analyzed by Mossberg, but also with the Icelandic literary tradition itself. As outlined in Chapter I, medieval Icelandic society developed its own prose medium, the saga, for the expression of its immigrant experience.

Unlike its poetic counterpart, Western Icelandic prose could not build on a continuous native prose tradition. *Piltur og Stúlka*, the first extended prose fiction of modern times in Icelandic, was only published in 1850. However, it could build on a native immigrant literature, an established tradition, and in this respect it probably found itself in a unique position. We saw earlier how Wolf has demonstrated the transformation of this tradition to fit its new context. Accordingly, Western Icelandic prose has as its subject matter the West Icelanders themselves, as Einar H. Kvaran pointed out: "The writers are describing these people, their inner life, their conditions and surroundings. They are noticeably rooted in reality. Their descriptions are straightforward, clear and true."[49] Kvaran's remark about the realistic nature of these works, however, calls for a qualification. The immigrant experience entails utter confusion and bewilderment, as security and familiarity are left behind and the old reality is superimposed on, and at the same time clashes with, the new. The Western Icelandic authors were immigrants themselves, and their view of the outside or "foreign" reality is, therefore, inevitably slanted. Their recreation of the immigrant experience sought to provide practical and psychological support through the redefinition of an old native value system, showing how it might work in the new context. Such a redefinition is an attempt at recreating a certain amount of security which allows the immigrant to deal with the experience. The realistic nature of Western Icelandic prose works for modern readers depends, therefore, very much on the extent to which the old value system and its transfer to the New World are romanticized. However, with regard to the descriptions and recreations of the Western Icelandic group experience themselves, Kvaran's analysis is correct: these descriptions are often painfully realistic. Mossberg refers to this realism as a necessary process of "de-mythifying" the pioneer experience (113).

Kvaran's analysis also indicates an interest in the inner life of the immigrants. In this respect, Western Icelandic prose differs from its medieval counterpart, which was focussed on social and ethical developments, on outer rather than inner life. This difference may in part be owing to the fact that the West Icelanders moved to a country which was already settled, so that they had no part in the social, political and legal build-up of the country. While it is true that New Iceland was its own republic to begin with, this was only for a short period of time (1878-1887) and no longer the case when prose was being written. As a result, the focus turned inward for its expression of group experience. What is more, this change is likely to have been influenced by the literary developments of the time. When Western Icelandic prose began to be composed, the influence of the Realist movement had made itself felt. It is only natural that Western Icelandic writers would be influenced by this movement, as its goals and ideals, contrary to those of Romanticism, lent themselves especially well to prose, and thus provided a contemporary narrative framework. With its concern for the moral and social role to be played by literature, the Realist movement provided, moreover, a suitable literary framework for the expression of the social reality of the West Icelanders. The immigrant experience called for a re-examination and re-establishment of group values, a moral code and a possible cultural direction for the immigrant group to take.

The old Icelandic narrative tradition itself, that is to say the sagas, displays a clear tendency towards realism. Even the Romantic Jón Thoroddsen, the author of *Piltur og Stúlka*, employed a relatively realistic style and form in which to clothe his romantic story. In this he was influenced by the early Dickens, just as the Western Icelandic author Jóhann Magnús Bjarnason was. This combination of outer realism and inner romanticism readily accommodated a Western Icelandic literature which dealt with an outer reality, based on actual experiences in the New World, as well as an inner reality, based on nostalgia and tradition from the Old.

JÓHANN MAGNÚS BJARNASON

Jóhann Magnús Bjarnason (1866-1945) contributed to nearly all genres of Western Icelandic literature, from poetry to fiction to articles, essays, speeches, letters, and even a diary.[50] He has, however, become popularly known mainly for his novels and short stories. He is one of those few Western Icelandic writers who gained popularity on both sides of the Atlantic and knew his collected fiction would be published in Iceland, although the collection did not actually appear until after his death. It consists of two volumes of short stories, three novels and one collection of fables and fantasy stories.

Jóhann Magnús was born in Iceland, and left for Canada with his parents shortly after the volcanic eruption of 1875. As he emigrated at a very young age, he had only been partly moulded by the culture and surroundings of his native country. We can clearly see the result from his works: while Jóhann Magnús consciously lived and experienced the emigration and settlement in Canada with actual childhood memories of Iceland, his experience was more coloured by childhood enthusiasm and optimism than that of his older compatriots. His memories of Iceland were vaguer, and he grew up and received his education in Canada so that he did not suffer from a similar degree of cultural alienation.

All his life, however, Jóhann Magnús remained true to the Icelander in him: he wrote exclusively in Icelandic, and was deeply concerned with the preservation of Icelandic culture and traditions in Canada. This preservation, along with the immigrant experience, form the major themes of his works. The influence of his New World education and environment are nevertheless very clear in his works. Jóhann Magnús had an open eye and an open mind. He was a philanthropist who had as his greatest interest human nature: its outer quirks, its inner sufferings and its innate goodness, in all of which he had an undying faith. Although his first concern was with the Icelanders, his interest extends to all human beings, especially the unwanted, ignored, trodden-on and unfortunate. In his works we find a large collection of individuals from different ethnic and social backgrounds, already reflecting the ethnic mosaic that Canada was developing.

Jóhann Magnús was a widely read man, not least in English and American literature. Among his favourites was Charles Dickens, whose influence is obvious in his works. Jóhannes P. Pálsson remarked, in a memorial article on Jóhann Magnús: "What enchanted him must have been the human kindness and the justified anger of Dickens against the injustice and mercilessness of the social system; in other words, the realism of this writer."[51] Realism was, however, an unsteady influence on Jóhann Magnús' writing. His first publications *Sögur og kvæði* ("Stories and Poems"; 1892), *Bessabréf* ("Bessi's letters"; in *Heimskringla* 1893-94) and *Ljóðmæli* ("Collection of Poetry"; 1898) were within the Realist tradition.[52] They depicted the Icelandic immigrant environment as he knew and observed it, and contained a fair amount of social criticism and satire based on his deeply felt sympathy with the victims of society. These poems and stories caused indignation in the community: he was accused of having ridiculed and slandered identifiable community members. The knowledge of having hurt people's feelings induced Jóhann Magnús to adopt an utterly fanciful, romantic style instead, such as we find in his novel *Brazilíufararnir* ("The Brazil Farers").

Not all of Jóhann Magnús' works exhibit such extremes, however. His best-known stories are a combination of both. All are set in an Icelandic immigrant community or revolve around Icelandic immigrants. These works yoke an outward realism with an inward romanticism; that is to say, whereas the framework and setting of the story are so credible and true-to-life, that they give his works historical as well as fictional value, the values, perceptions and moral messages represented by the characters and events are romanticized.

Jóhann Magnús' main works illustrate the earlier mentioned analyses of both Mossberg and Wolf. Mossberg held that early immigrant writing mostly recreated group experience in order to provide practical and psychological support by the reinforcement and validation of this experience, while Wolf suggested that Western Icelandic writers, like their predecessors in the saga-writing age, reach back to the heroic past of the original Icelandic immigration and settlement in order to recover an ancient, tested moral code of honour and behaviour and show its reapplication and relevance in the context of the present. While the recreation of the immigrant experience requires realism among an audience familiar with it, the revival of a traditional moral code involves, almost inevitably, a certain degree of idealization.

Jóhann Magnús spent all of his adult life in Western Icelandic communities where he worked as a teacher in public schools. His job and his great love of children undoubtedly contributed to the general tone of voice and point of view found in his books. It resembles alternately that of an innocent, enthusiastic child and that of a gentle teacher. He believed that the child's eye often saw clearer than the eye of a grown-up:

Children sometimes get strange ideas about what is going on around them, and they regard these ideas as doubtlessly true. Yet, although they do not notice it, these ideas are still based on clear and sharp perception. I have frequently noticed since I have reached maturity, that most children look closer for the causes behind events in everyday life than most adults.[53]

Many of his stories have indeed been enjoyed by youngsters. Richard Beck (1977) compared Jóhann Magnús' fantasy-stories (*ævintýri*), which Jóhann Magnús himself preferred to call "fables" (*dæmisögur*), to Lewis Carol's *Alice in Wonderland* and Selma Lagerlöf's *Niels Holgerson's Fantastic Journey*.

The gentleness underlying the social criticism and realism of Jóhann Magnús' works, rooted in a belief in the beauty of life and in the innate goodness and innocence of man, reminds one very much of the author of *David Copperfield*. Indeed, the novel *Eiríkur Hansson* seems modelled on this favourite work of Jóhann Magnús'. Although *Eiríkur Hansson* is largely autobiographical, the protagonist Eiríkur has many characteristics in common with David Copperfield as a boy: the child-like innocence which is at times endearing, at times funny in its clumsiness or its unconscious sanity and sharp perceptions, but also at times annoying in its sentimentality and saccharine.

In this respect, Jóhann Magnús is removed from the Icelandic tradition with its profound emotions masked by a tone of restraint. He is closer to the softer strain which was introduced into Icelandic literature by the Romanticism of Jónas Hallgrímsson, although Jóhann Magnús often outdoes the Icelandic Romantics with his sentimentalism. In a review in *Heimskringla* (13 April 1899), Stephan G. characterized Jóhann Magnús very accurately when he remarked that he was "no Viking who expects to sail the seas and attack at every peninsula; he is rather a pioneer who cultivates his flower garden in the woods at the water's edge...."[54] In a personal letter to Jóhann Magnús, Stephan G. added:

I know well, that the story-telling of Dickens is not good Old Norse; he is too long-winded, petty, insignificant and unbearably sentimental for many. It was exactly this sentimentalism, which now receives sharper criticism, which moved the everyday people the most. I am not taken with these good or bad points of you two either; I am too Norse.[55]

This posed a problem for Jóhann Magnús; he knew that he was no Viking by nature and that the Norse style did not suit him, but he was also well aware of the fact that Norse literature and the idealized stereotype of the freedom-loving and adventurous Viking had become an essential part of what was seen by Canadians and Western

Icelanders alike as constituting the Icelandic culture and nationality. He must have felt himself caught here between his nature and his commitment to the preservation of his native heritage. Passages in two letters by Jóhann Magnús hint at his awareness of this duality as he "excuses" Dickens for falling short of the standard set by Norse writers, and attributes the distance between him and Icelandic writers to the influence of English Victorian writers on him in his youth (Beck 1977: xviii).

Jóhann Magnús' realism, then, was rooted in his Canadian education and immigrant experience rather than in the radical realism of the Icelandic farmers' reading societies or the Icelandic *alþýðu*-tradition. It is a Dickensian realism, critical but romantically hopeful and optimistic, clothed in a largely Dickensian, straightforward but often long-winded narrative style.

Jóhann Magnús' social criticisms deserve some extra attention here, since they are clearly based on the immigrant experience. Although he is not blind to the general signs of social injustice in his Canadian environment, as is evident, for instance, from the long list of social evils which Eiríkur spots in Halifax (*EH* 273-75), Jóhann Magnús' main purpose seems to be to serve as the mouthpiece of the immigrants in Canadian society. His fiction betrays an awareness of the silenced and excluded position of immigrants, who, even if they do speak English well enough to express their experience, lack a willing and understanding audience, and who, even if they have managed to make a decent living, always remain simply "foreigners" to the Anglo-Canadian establishment. For the average Canadian, immigrants formed an alien class of people outside their social sphere, and they showed no regard whatsoever for their nationality and cultural heritage. Thus they deprived the immigrants of their dignity. After having met the Dutch immigrant son, Hendrik Tromp, Eiríkur Hansson makes the following remark: "We became the best of friends immediately. Perhaps we were attracted to each other so quickly because we were both to a large extent foreigners, and we soon sensed that our other Canadian-born school-mates regarded us as plain *foreigners*, although they were on the other hand pleasant and nice to us."[56] Interestingly, Hendrik is described as a foreigner, even though he is Canadian-born and speaks English without an accent. The reason seems to be that Hendrik makes it no secret that he is of Dutch descent and that he is proud of it:

Hendrik Tromp was a true Dutchman who loved his country and people with all his heart, and regarded his mother tongue and the literature of his people above all other tongues and literatures. He was proud of the military fame of his forefathers and could trace his ancestry back to grandpa Van Tromp, the great Dutch naval officer. Hendrik knew all exceptional Dutch folk tales, and never got tired of telling them.[57]

Most of the characters in Jóhann Magnús' fiction are non-British immigrants who are proud of their descent. As a reaction to the situation in which most immigrants found themselves, Jóhann Magnús reverses this situation by making immigrants heroes simply because they are immigrants, and by making pride in their nationality a virtue of almost heroic proportions. In turn, Anglo-Canadians are given mostly subordinate roles, and nearly all of them seem to be without any past or pride of culture; they are portrayed as being Canadians and nothing else.

The pride which the immigrants in Jóhann Magnús' works take in their nationality is characteristically based on heroic ancestry and an ancient national culture. This heritage is often presented as both a source of dignity and of cultural and moral provisions for life's journey which are universally and eternally relevant and applicable. In the story "Íslenzkur Ökumaður" ("An Icelandic Coachman"), the wandering Jew says to the Icelander Hrólfur:

You have more strength and talents than you realize. Good old stony Iceland has given you good provisions for your life's journey, which you have never used since you came to this country—it has given you a valuable treasure which you have never been able to appreciate. These hidden forces I now want to wake in you, these provisions and this treasure you will have to use now whenever the opportunity arises.[58]

Jóhann Magnús speaks not only for immigrants of European descent, but for Jewish immigrants ("Gyðingurinn gangandi," "The Wandering Jew"), Syrians (Aron Hassan in "Farandsalinn," "The Travelling Salesman"), and for Inuits (in "Karl litli," "Little Karl") and Indians and métis (Í Rauðárdalnum, "In the Red River Valley"[59]). Moreover, many protagonists are put in a situation where their racial prejudices are proved wrong ("Gyðingurinn gangandi," VE 100; Í Rauðárdalnum 340-41). Two of the fables in the collection Gimsteinaborgin ("The City of Jewels") refer to the existence of racial discrimination of Jews and Native Canadians, which is shown to be based on nothing but prejudice alone ("Mannvinur" and "Ættarfylgjan," "A Philanthropist" and "The Family Fetch").[60]

It is remarkable that, while most of Jóhann Magnús' ethnic characters hold their own culture and nationality in the highest regard, they consider national pride in people of other descent to be a virtue:

"Are you not an Eskimo then?"
"No, I am an Icelander."
"Wouldn't you rather be an Eskimo?"
"What I like best is being what I am, namely an Icelander."
"What do you know!" said the little girl. "I thought all children wanted to be Eskimo-children—What do you know!"
"I know that you are still a good guy," said the Eskimo-boy, "I know you're still a great guy even though you are not an Eskimo."[61]

Moreover, all immigrant characters support each other and empathize with each other's feelings of national pride, homesickness and the desire to meet other fellow countrymen, as is shown, for instance, by the friendship of Hendrik and Eiríkur, which is all but hampered by each boy's pride in his own cultural heritage.

Jóhann Magnús thus seems to have had in mind the kind of mosaic society based on ethnic preservation and tolerance which Canada began to promote as its own in the 1960s. Unfortunately, however, we generally get no more than glimpses of the characters in Jóhann Magnús' fiction. The lively descriptions are exterior and remain typifications of individuals. They are described by their outer quirks and peculiarities rather than by individual character or an emotional life. Thus they remain flat, doing little more than personifying national stereotypes and their creator's moral and social message, although some of them are entertaining nevertheless.

This is also true of the many Icelandic characters in Jóhann Magnús' fiction. They mostly remain either just narrators (Erlingur in Í Rauðárdalnum) or are personifications of the heroic virtues of their nation. Eiríkur could be counted as an exception, but then he is largely autobiographical. In accordance with his own ideal, Jóhann Magnús' pride in his nationality tends to exalt it above other nationalities, although never at the expense of his respect for them. As Jóhannes P. Pálsson remarked: "Although Magnús found something good in all people, regardless of nationality or skin colour, the Icelanders topped them all. It was almost as if he saw Icelandic nationality as an innate virtue."[62] Thus, the Icelanders in his fiction nearly always exceed other people, either on a physical or a psychological level or both. Furthermore, they are personifications of a traditional code of honour and behaviour. They represent time-honoured virtues such as *drengskapur* ("magnanimity"), independence, honour and pride in their national heritage. They are modern, New World versions of the old saga heroes, whose virtues still find application in their new context.

Kirsten Wolf discusses this aspect of Jóhann Magnús' fiction in the light of the story "Íslenzkt heljarmenni" ("An Icelandic Giant") in her earlier mentioned article. Another example would be "Boy Burns," which is about an Icelander who becomes the victim of the xenophobia of one of his fellow-mineworkers, an Englishman by the name of Ben Killam. Ben blows up a shed with explosives in the hope that Boy Burns will be blamed and fired. His scheme backfires and Boy Burns demands a public apology, as he feels his honour has been stained. If Ben will apologize, he is quite willing to forgive him, but Ben refuses. Finally, during their last meeting when Ben still refuses to give Boy Burns "satisfaction," as Boy calls it, Boy Burns pronounces a curse over him. Although it takes place in a multicultural Canadian setting, the whole atmosphere of the story is very saga-like, with its emphasis on honour and noble-mindedness and with the fulfilment of a curse, in keeping with the Icelandic belief in the power of the spoken word.

Although Jóhann Magnús' fiction might at a first reading seem excessively nationalistic, it should be seen in a larger context which makes it inoffensive and even understandable, if sometimes tedious. First, it is counterbalanced by the representation of a large number of other ethnic groups which, amongst each other, show tolerance, understanding and support. Second, it should be seen as an urgent response to the situation of the West Icelanders (and also that of other ethnic groups who, however, did not belong to Jóhann Magnús' audience). In the profound psychological confusion characteristic of the immigrant experience, the West Icelanders needed a code of behaviour and a sense of direction as well as a validation of their feelings. Jóhann Magnús found such a code in the Icelandic past, which at the same time served the purpose of ensuring the preservation of the Icelandic heritage. Third, Jóhann Magnús seems to have responded to the prejudice which existed against foreigners in general, and to the general ignorance about Iceland and its culture in particular, which account in part for the tendency toward total assimilation among Icelanders who felt embarrassed or hindered by their nationality. Jóhann Magnús' works are full of "outsiders'" reactions to the declaration that someone is an Icelander, and although these are generally comical, it is not difficult to see how Icelanders could become self-conscious about their nationality.

In the fable "Íslenzki drengurinn grátgjarni" ("The Icelandic Cry-Baby"), an Icelandic boy cries about the reactions he continually gets in response to his name, his nationality and his native country. In the story, the root of this problem emerges as ignorance, which can be cured with education. Other stories, too, show that Jóhann Magnús sees no excuse for shame for or denial of one's nationality. On the contrary, the fable "Sessunautur miljónamæringsins" ("Sitting by the millionaire") strongly denounces it and "Kínverski kaupmaðurinn og spánverjarnir" ("The Chinese Merchant and the Spaniards"), like *Séra* Jón, equals it to the renouncing of God. The ethnic myths I introduced in the previous chapter are thus widely present in Jóhann Magnús' works.

Jóhann Magnús has told the story of the Icelandic immigrant experience in several of his short stories, but most importantly in his *Eiríkur Hansson*. This novel follows the pattern of what might be called the archetypal immigrant novel: home idyll, reasons for emigration, journey across the Atlantic, settlement, problems and hardships encountered and, finally, new life and prosperity in the New World. The novel is told from the point of view of a young boy, who is seven years old at the time of emigration to Nova Scotia. His memories of Iceland are, therefore, scanty and vague, although they become his most beautiful and treasured ones:

And what I remember from those years, I find now to have been so bright and so much fun, all so *peculiarly* bright and fun, nothing unpleasant or bad. And when I go back in memory to my native district ... I feel it must be the most beautiful place by far which exists under the sun, and Iceland the most magnificent country in the whole world.[63]

The novel is very optimistic in tone, because of the young age at which its writer emigrated. However, the descriptions of the physical and psychological consequences of the emigration are among the best and most memorable in the book. The most remarkable passages are those describing the deaths of his grandfather and, later, his grandmother, who raised the orphaned Eiríkur. Both were heartbroken by the immigrant experience and by not being able to have their grandson present at their deathbeds, as they had had to hand him over to the care of an Irish lady in the city to ensure his education.

Another moving passage relates Eiríkur's feelings as he returns to the Icelandic settlement in the Nova Scotian valley Mosquodoboit which had been deserted because the soil was unfit for crops. As Eiríkur sits down in the ghost settlement, he sees a squirrel which becomes the personification of the ghostly, haunted atmosphere in his mind:

> It was in high spirits. It moved about restlessly with glee and turned the nut around to all sides, looking at me at times, screeching. It was like it was telling me that now everybody was gone. "Everybody gone,—everybody gone, everybody,—everybody—everybody!" I thought I heard it say. "And why don't you go—you go—you go?" Then it finally got the kernel out of the nut and dropped the shell. It ran from branch to branch up and down the birch tree and screeched continually. It was like its screeching carried irony. "I can manage," I thought it said, "and *I* can live here well enough, but *they* couldn't—they couldn't—they couldn't—ar-r-r-r!"[64]

Jóhann Magnús' fiction is thus interesting for us in this context, partly because it contains numerous glimpses of Western Icelandic immigrant life, and partly because it voices both the problems and the ideals of Canadian immigrants in general and West Icelanders in particular. There is, however, yet another interesting feature to his fiction which enters the realm of folklore and storytelling. No doubt this feature is due to Jóhann Magnús' job as a teacher.

Apart from the influence of Dickens on Jóhann Magnús' style, we also notice in it features of a storytelling tradition. Many of the short stories contain an implication that they are actually being told as stories. For instance, "Íslenzkt Heljarmenni" ("An Icelandic Giant") begins with the statement: *Ég ætla að segja ykkur dálitla sögu frá Nýja Skotlandi* ("I am going to tell you a little story from Nova Scotia"; *VE* 139), and, a few pages later, the teller announces:

> And now I'll start on the part which I promised to tell. It is about a great feat, or rather an act of daredevilry which is surely unique in Western Icelandic history,—a foolhardy act, which no-one would have dared to risk unless he has pure Norse blood in his veins, and all the characteristics of a Viking mixed together in the right proportions.—I will now tell the story the way I have heard it, and as it is told,—as a kind of folk tale there in the East.[65]

The presence of the storyteller is here enhanced by his style, which is informal, direct and involves the audience by addressing them directly and building up tension to hold interest. Moreover, the subject matter is familiar and popular, easily recognizable to the Western Icelandic audience it addresses. Since the tale has as its subject the heroic deed of one of the group, the audience can easily empathize. The original event is exaggerated and romanticized to move and impress the listeners, but never exceeds the bounds of credibility, and hence never makes the storyteller unacceptably unreliable.[66]

The more important aspect of Jóhann Magnús' fictional tales, however, is that he creates folklore, a body of legends for the West Icelanders which has its locus in their New World experience and environment. The creation of a relevant folklore in which people recognize their own feelings and experiences greatly helps their psychological and cultural rooting in the new country, and furnishes a release for them. The idea that one of the group has performed heroic deeds in the new environment, as in the above-mentioned tale, strengthens a sense of place and continuity: the ancient heroic deeds are performed in Canada. The Icelandic culture-based imagination is adapted to the circumstances of the present. The fable "Sigurvegarinn" ("The Winner"), for example, begins thus: "Once upon a time, longer ago than anybody can remember, there was a young prince who was so wise, sweet and just, that there was nobody like him in the whole wide world. He lived in a big, beautifully decorated palace which stood on a fertile, vast plain."[67] Jóhann Magnús must soon have realized that children could not really relate to stories and fairy tales set in Iceland. Accordingly, he relocates them in a world familiar to them.

The same is done much more elaborately in the fantasy story "Karl litli—saga frá Draumamörk" ("Little Karl—A Story from Dream Forest"). This tale is a magnificent blend of Icelandic, Canadian and archetypal folklore and fairy tale motifs and elements. Karl travels by train into Dream Forest (there have never been trains in Iceland). There he meets his parents, grandparents and nanny who quarrel over the question after which famous Icelander Karl should be named. Next, he embarks on an adventurous journey as his nanny shows him stories, accompanied by Icelandic nursery rhymes. Thus he enters, for instance, an originally Icelandic giant story which has been adapted to New Iceland circumstances. He also meets Santa Claus, who refuses to be related to the Icelandic *jólasveinar*, who are troll-bred. Santa Claus travels in an airship which is named after one of Odin's travelling ravens, Huginn, while his telescope bears the name of the other raven Muninn (in Norse mythology, the two ravens, Thought and Remembrance, bring Odin intelligence). On his trip with Santa around the world, they also land in Iceland, where the children are dressed just like ordinary people in England and North America, and where Karl tells them: "I am an Icelander just like you. I live in Manitoba in Canada. I will live there all my life, and yet I always want to remain an Icelander."[68]

The climax of the story has mythological dimensions as Karl enters the land of the light elves across the rainbow-bridge, where he has to save Nanna, Baldur's bride, from a curse, and help the King and Queen of the light elves in their annual chess competition against the dark elves, while the elf-fool ironically sings the ancient ballad (*sagnakvæði*) of Ólafur Liljurós who did not want to be tempted into a heathen life by the elves and was killed by them. *Bifröst*, the rainbow bridge in Norse mythology, joins the world of the Æsir gods with the other worlds. Baldur was the god of light, fertility and goodness. He was killed through the machinations of the trickster god Loki.[69]

Thus Jóhann Magnús transmits traditional Icelandic folklore and mythology, but in a Canadian form, adapted to the circumstances of the West Icelanders. Similarly, he tells a fable which briefly relates the history of the West Icelanders in a symbolic fairy tale about a Queen in whose realm disasters such as eruptions, bad weather and starvation rage. She gives her youngest son into the care of the young noble lady who lives in the country of "Wide-Plains." He grows up in prosperity and soon makes for himself an outstanding reputation in that country. When he comes of age, he returns to his native land, where his mother asks him to move back and participate in the government of his country. He refuses with the following words:

"I can best show and prove of what ancestry I am born in this way, that I am a good son to the woman who took my mother's place when I was still a voiceless child."
The Queen smiled, pleased. She now knew that he was a good son.[70]

Not only does Jóhann Magnús fictionally replace and adapt Icelandic folklore, he also attempts to give the Icelanders a place in local folklore. An example can be found in the novel *Í Rauðárdalnum*, which is a story set in Winnipeg at the end of the last century, and revolves around the search for a treasure. The buried treasure, which belonged to an Icelandic sailor who ended up and died in Canada in the decade before the emigration, symbolically gives the Icelanders a history on the prairies preceding the actual emigration. Moreover, in the legends told by a native Canadian and a Canadian Mountie, Icelanders play an important role. The native folk tale revolves around three white men who, one may safely assume from all the allusions, are Icelanders who came to Canada during medieval times, in the wake of Leifr Eiríksson. The fates of the Icelanders and the natives are closely bound up in the tale. Moreover, some of the story's more supernatural aspects closely resemble Icelandic folklore motifs and beliefs, but this might just as well be due to a lack of knowledge on Jóhann Magnús' part with regard to Indian beliefs, as an attempt to link Icelandic folklore to the native folklore of Canada.

Similarly, the treasure hunt and the fate of the Icelandic sailor are closely associated with métis history and the Riel rebellion. It is, perhaps, only natural that Jóhann Magnús looked to native history and legends to establish a link between Icelandic and local Canadian folklore. After all, Canada's history was native history, factually so but even more mythologically so. In native folklore and history, the Icelanders recognized a similar feeling of heroic, proud ancestry as well as a close relationship with the natural world around them. The Icelanders could relate to the native Canadian position of being threatened by a foreign majority culture. Moreover, the Icelanders did settle in Canada, if only for a brief period of time, long before the English colonized it. Jóhann Magnús' view of the Indians may have been somewhat European-biased, but nevertheless his fables and tales speak for a lot of respect and a sense of kinship with native Canadians.[71]

GUÐRÚN H. FINNSDÓTTIR

With the short story writer Guðrún Helga Finnsdóttir (1884-1946) we have moved both into the era of a later generation of writers and into the realm of women writers. While it is true that Guðrún was a first-generation immigrant, she emigrated at a relatively late point in time, in 1904. At the time of her emigration she was twenty years old, but only seriously embarked on writing more than a decade later. Her first story, published in 1920, was "Landskuld" ("Debt to One's Country"). It appeared in the second volume of the annual magazine of the Icelandic National League (*Tímarit Þjóðræknisfélags Íslendinga í Vesturheimi*). Her first collection of short stories, *Hillingalönd* ("Lands of Mirages"), was published in 1938. Her second collection appeared posthumously in 1946 (*Dagshríðar Spor*, "Tracks of Day's Struggle") and was followed four years later by a collection of speeches and articles (*Ferðalok*, "Journey's End").

By the time Guðrún came to Canada and became acquainted with the West Icelanders and their history, the pioneer years were mostly over. Many of the West Icelanders of Guðrún's age were of the second generation, and Guðrún's children grew up with third-generation immigrants. Accordingly, Guðrún did not participate in the pioneer experience. Instead, she could look back on it with the eyes of the later generation, with involvement yet from a distance in time.

In this respect, Guðrún's fiction can be compared to Guttormur's poetry: they share the historical perspective, that is the conscious awareness of the link between generations and the feelings of alienation among the later generation, and the awe for the achievement of the pioneer generation, which were analyzed by Mossberg as being characteristics of the writing of later immigrant writers. However, Guðrún still has clear memories from Iceland, the country which had already moulded her before she went to Canada. In this respect, although she is further away in time from the initial Icelandic settlement in Canada, she is closer to her Icelandic roots than Jóhann Magnús Bjarnason. This difference between the two fiction writers is noticeable in their stories. Another important difference between Guðrún on the one hand, and Guttormur and Jóhann Magnús on the other, is that through Guðrún's fiction we get the female perspective of the pioneer and immigrant experience. Most of her stories revolve around female characters and their experiences. Even in the few stories which have men as their protagonists, we invariably hear the female voice.

Guðrún's fiction is far more introspective than that of Jóhann Magnús. It is also much more realistic, in that it is not nearly as much informed by the romantic ideal of the revival of the ancient Icelandic heroic past in the New World. While she was equally concerned with the preservation of the Icelandic cultural heritage and influenced by its literary tradition, Guðrún was, at the same time, all too intimately aware of the reality and the problems which faced the second generation and its Icelandic heritage. She lived at a time when Icelandic as a first language was quickly losing ground, as Canadian values, points of view and loyalties became prevalent. In her fiction, we find her own sadness over these developments as she describes the pioneer achievements and sacrifices of a generation that is now left to see the heritage of their native country greatly endangered. On the other hand, she understands the younger generation which knows Iceland only from stories. For them, Iceland is far away and in the past, whereas Canada is their reality and their future. As she balances the viewpoints and values of both, she seems to see only one way to unite the two: through the inevitable succession of generations and their dreams for a true civilization which "is ruled by a healthy intelligence and humanity. The ideals of the past and the dreams of the future could then somehow become one reality instead of just empty words."[72]

The immigrant duality between the old and the new is very much present in Guðrún's stories, but it is not posited as a tragedy. The tone is generally realistic, yet optimistic. The story which has this duality for its major theme, "Fýkur í sporin" ("Forgotten Footsteps") parts I and II, poignantly express the emotional battle which this duality causes, both in members of the first and the second generation. The ending, however, voices an optimistic faith in the future. The first story was one of Guðrún's earlier stories and originally conceived of as one independent whole. It is a tragic story which revolves around the losses of Ingólfur, one of the original pioneers, but could easily be seen as the story of his whole generation. Ingólfur contemplates his pioneer life and achievements and the costs at which they were achieved, as he attempts to deal with the loss of his last hope: his daughter Ragnhildur is going to marry an English-Canadian. To Ingólfur, this means that she will be lost not only to him, but also to the Icelandic community and heritage. Ingólfur's love and respect for his daughter finally convince him that she is of a new generation and has to make her own decisions in life. However, the story ends thus:

The life's wages of the immigrant are usually meagre, and always the same: He is given land, it is true, but in return he gives his life, his health and all his workpower. Yes, the land absorbs him, body and soul, and his children in a flock of thousands.[73]

Here, we get the same view as that expressed in Guttormur's "Sandy Bar": the pioneers pay an almost inhuman toll for a dream which they do not live to see fulfilled. At the end of their road they only find loss and death. But whereas Guðrún empathizes with the tragic fate of the pioneer generation, she looks further ahead to a way out of the tragedy and towards a future with promise, even though it may take on a different shape from what was expected.

In "Fýkur í sporin" part II, which was written much later and partly in response to the popularity of the first story, Guðrún describes the inner struggle of Ragnhildur, Ingólfur's daughter, as she is torn between her love and loyalty for her husband and those for her father, which is in fact the struggle between the Canadian and the Icelander in her. The struggle is intensified by the fact that her husband's parents are representatives of that aspect of Canadian society which so many older immigrants feared: outer snobbishness and materialism masking an inner emptiness and a contempt for "foreigners." The struggle reaches a climax when her father-in-law scolds Ragnhildur for raising her daughter bilingually and biculturally, and demands that she bring their granddaughter up as an Anglo-Canadian girl. Ragnhildur's first reaction is to flee to the Icelandic community and her father, all of whom represent a life largely devoid of material wealth but rich in genuine human kindness and in spiritual values. There, she comes to realize that by opposing the two realities inside her, she will never come to terms with her self and her life. Her solution is one of love and reunion and of faith in the future:

Ragnhildur still loved her nationality and her language; but she had obtained that farsightedness and tolerance that only the years and experience can give. And she had to admit in her mind that the course of fate had changed her whole view. The young, developing Canadian nation was probably about to swallow up her nationality, herself and her child; but she and her husband had succeeded in saving in time from shipwreck that which was most valuable to them—their love and relationship.... And the generations continue to come and go,—like the wind that whistles in one's ears—like the leaves that float on the flow of the riverstream.... The wind blows—the dust of the ages blows into the tracks—and before one realizes it not a trace of them is left to see. But the dreams of mankind continue to appear and disappear—and re-appear—and with each new dream a new hope is kindled, and—with the hope a new life.[74]

Guðrún wrote more stories which deal with the duality of the immigrant experience. Sometimes the theme takes on the shape of an outer, generational struggle which represents the old values against the new (see for instance "Dyr Hjartans," "Door of the Heart"), sometimes it is represented in the form of an inner struggle between ethnic and Anglo-Canadian nationality (as in "Sárfættir Menn," "Footsore Men"). Her solution, however, is always the same: a reunion of the polarized selves through affection, understanding and tolerance taught by life and through faith in the future.

Moreover, Guðrún has a strong belief in ancestral continuity. This enables her to look to the future with confidence: she feels that ancestry inevitably resurfaces in later generations. As a result, she believes that nationality cannot be denied. After all, ancestors live on in people's blood as well as in a people's culture, and denial will only lead to a spiritual death. Haraldur Bessason has explained this Icelandic belief in the continuous life of ancestry thus:

A close connection with the past is without doubt the principal cause for the tendency of Icelanders to see the life of the nation as a vertical cross-cut from ancient times to the present, rather than a cross-cut of the present alone. The vertical lines increase not a little the size of this peculiar if not unique picture of a nation's life where departed generations make up for the fewness of the living.[75]

As a result, Þórunn in "Ekki er alt sem sýnist" ("Deceptive Appearances"), who has tried to avoid the Icelandic community as well as her Icelandic ancestry, has to learn that she is a true granddaughter of her grandmother. Similarly, Arnold in "Sárfættir menn" must learn to accept that the Icelander in him will follow him like an *afturganga*, a persecuting ghost, whether he acknowledges this ghost or not. In fact, Arnold, who desperately wants to become a 100 percent Canadian author, only succeeds once he has come to terms with his ethnic past. Old Rannveig in "Dyr Hjartans," after an inner struggle, finally comes to see that

heredity follows the generations, whether or not the older people think of trying to deprive the younger of their right of inheritance, or the younger think of refusing it. Heredity is the unbreakable bond of the living blood-stream. Flowing along with this stream come personality, looks and character to a larger or lesser extent. The generations hold hands, whatever people say.[76]

In one of her stories, this unbreakable bond of blood is imagined as "The Voice of the Caller" ("Rödd hrópandans"), which invariably calls one back to one's family, nationality and history: "And I heard countless voices that became to my ears as one clear voice, that voice of the caller, which calls to us from our own songs and stories and over the centuries has talked vigour, reason and generosity into us."[77]

Guðrún also hears this voice calling in the literature and lore of her people. The deeper meaning of folklore and traditions, and the importance of passing them on, play an important part in many of her stories. Guðrún came from a family well-versed in literature, history, genealogy and folklore. Stefán Einarsson (1947: 13) recorded how the young Guðrún in Iceland would write down family trees dictated by her grandmother, who also left her share of tales in the folk tale collection of Sigfús Sigfússon. The influence this left on Guðrún is clear in her own stories. No character is so widely present in her fiction as the older woman rich in worldly wisdom and lore. Usually, this woman is also the storyteller within the story, as Guðrún's stories mostly take the form of a story within a story.

In her presentation of Icelandic folklore, Guðrún often hastens to explain the hidden meanings and truths behind the tales, beliefs and customs, as if to reassure her readers that Icelanders really are not superstitious. This may be due to the time in which she wrote, when technology and science made rapid progress and psychological studies included such "supernatural" phenomena as dreams and superstitions, which make up a considerable part of Icelandic folklore. In addition, Magnús Einarsson concludes in his study of Western Icelandic folklore that accounts of supernatural events in Iceland tended to be treated with whimsy among West Icelanders (1975: 21). It is not unlikely that the West Icelanders, who nurtured and guarded their reputation among the Canadian majority, had come to feel self-conscious about something so prone to outside ridicule as folk-beliefs, especially when based on supernatural features. Moreover, the West Icelanders might have sensed that certain folk-beliefs which were firmly rooted in the Icelandic environment, such as the belief in ghosts, seemed out of place in the new environment.

Guðrún realizes the deeper value of folklore, however, and is determined to transmit its significance:

Ibsen knew how to describe those dangers which confront people and their ideals, knew how to tell stories that had a meaning to them. The old women in Iceland, our foremothers and grandmothers, also knew how to tell stories which had a hidden meaning—the stories about poor cottagers' sons who always gained a victory in their dealings with kings; because the cottagers' sons exceeded the kings in cleverness and human virtues. They told stories, like Ibsen, about people who got into troll's hands, lost their freedom and were all put in the same chains and tortured. The trolls had the powers and the strength; the people the cleverness and bravery—and they won.

The old women, who told the children these stories in the dusk, while others slept, were moulding the children's souls—the future of the nation—teaching them admiration and respect for cleverness and human virtues, teaching them to watch over good heredity. Thus, good people watch over the future hopes and the future good of the nations.[78]

Considering Guðrún's statement about the meaning of another folk-genre in Icelandic literature, the *vikivaka* dance songs, we may have a description of what Guðrún tried to express with her own Western Icelandic stories: "There we hear beautiful voices reciting, there it is possible to listen to the heartbeat of the nation, read about the ways of the times and see the cultural situation."[79]

In her stories, Guðrún sets out to give expression to the collective voice of the West Icelanders as the folklore and sagas had done for the Icelandic people over the ages: she records their cultural situation, their heartbeat, their dreams and ideals and the price they had to pay, the time and place in which they live and what lives among them as an ethnic-Canadian group. She relates from the collective memory and consciousness of the West Icelanders, thus giving memories and events a meaning that often does not seem to be present in daily life. By doing this, she attempts to continue the Icelandic folk tale tradition among the West Icelanders.

In the story "Frá kynslóð til kynslóðar" ("From Generation to Generation"), old Rannveig remembers how she learnt from her grandmother the meaning behind the custom of leaving some of the New Year's food for the *huldufólk* who are moving house during that night. Rannveig had called her superstitious, but her grandmother looked at it a different way:

I love all true progress and am glad to know that the nation is becoming conscious of the fact that misery is not something that is intended to last. But there is no progress in throwing thoughtlessly onto the dung-heap all good and beautiful ways and national customs. Icelandic hospitality is one of those good customs, by which I do not mean invitations or parties of the sort that you were going to have here tonight, but rather to receive well and be good to hungry and tired travellers of whatever class.[80]

When Rannveig retorted that *huldufólk* were simply the imaginative personification of the splendour, dignity and power of the nation that had been forced into hiding by centuries of misery and oppression, but that had now been liberated and belonged to the nation itself again, her grandmother answered:

Folk-tales relate so much that people nowadays have difficulties understanding, and there is a wide variety of them from which one can learn a lot, among which this, that those who prefer the material over the spiritual and sell their soul for outer glitter shall receive stones for bread.[81]

Rannveig then considers the life and customs of the younger generation in the light of this memory, and realizes that the present generation in the New World has nearly all the attributes of the *huldufólk*. They have all the splendour, freedom and power at their disposal, although they run the risk of becoming the victim of their own attributes: they are in danger of losing their humanity as they risk losing their spiritual life to material wealth. Thus, the old *huldufólk*-tales still carry a message for the immigrants' children.

In the story "Skriflabúðin" ("The Junk Store"), Guðrún has a Western Icelandic woman, nicknamed Scheherazade because of her storytelling abilities, recreate a modern Canadian version of a folk tale, told in the form of a dream. The dream symbolically describes the history of an old Québécois church which is now only used as a junk store. It is in this store that "Scheherazade," under the influence of the haunting atmosphere of the place, had her dream. The church once contained a beautiful altar-painting of a Mother and Child, the "soul" of the church, which had been donated by the Icelandic wife of a local, one of the richest men of the area. When the man discovered that the painting was valuable, he decided to take it from the church and sell it to the highest bidder. In the dream, the Mother and Child, symbolizing selfless, true love and future hopes, walk off with the painting. In reality, the church, along with the painting, burnt the night after the painting had been sold. At the end of "Skriflabúðin," the narrator expresses her doubts whether "Scheherazade" had really had this dream or whether she tried to convey something with her story. While the "moral" or hidden meaning of the story is roughly as that of the *huldufólk*-tales, it is here told in a Canadian historical and geographical context by a Western Icelandic storyteller.

Guðrún's concern with the deeper meaning of folklore produces mildly moralistic fiction, especially since, unlike most tellers of folk tales, Guðrún often explains the message. She wishes to ensure that the wisdom amassed not only by the storyteller herself, but by a succession of generations, is transmitted. One of her major themes in this connection is that of the opposition between outer and inner values, outer and inner beauty and wealth. As I mentioned above, this theme is common in Western Icelandic literature. Uprooted from their country and its values, and lured by the promise of a wealthy future, many immigrants tended to lose themselves in a quest for riches and thereby often replaced their nationality and cultural heritage with a life of glitter, materialism and inner emptiness. Many writers reacted to this tendency by warning against the psychological consequences of the discarding of cultural and spiritual values.

Often, the ethnic culture is presented as containing the spiritual and cultural riches which the New World, for all its wealth, cannot provide. An example is the story "Fýkur í sporin" part II, which was discussed above, and the story "Bálför" ("Funeral Pyre"), which contains fierce criticism of the North American emphasis on a deceptively impressive superficiality, publicly encouraged by books and journals. However, sometimes the solution is also found in the New World itself, as in the story "Salt Jarðar" ("Salt of the Earth"). Kelly has renounced his past after a bad childhood with his foster-father. His mother, his only link with his ethnic past, died when he was very young. He turns to a life which brings him riches but no satisfaction; accordingly, he feels empty and unhappy. Not until he finally returns to his old Ontarian foster-mother, who has preserved an appreciation of the beauty of life and a peace at heart in spite of a bitterly disappointing life does he regain an understanding of the true values of life:

> He had found in the words of the old woman the yearning of all people—the longing for beauty and peace. She had succeeded in keeping warmth in her soul and gold in her heart—she had been brought up in the bosom of the earth, and from her she drank deeply for her strength. She had brought gold and fire—the autumn-colours of the woods—with her, as her inheritance, that treasure which would last her until the end of her days. She dreamed about going back east, to beauty and flower fragrance. That dream he would fulfill for her.[82]

Because Guðrún's moralism is so strongly embedded in the accumulated wisdom of individuals and generations, it hardly ever becomes annoying. The stories are human, and the appeal of their human interest exceeds the tediousness of the moral.

The figure of the storytelling woman brings us to the female perspective in Guðrún's fiction. Guðrún's greatest concern is the collective wordly wisdom of love, beauty and high ideals that was amassed by succeeding generations, and her concern for the position of women in society is secondary. As a result we find in Guðrún no militant feminist. She believes in the value of human kindness, not in militancy. However, Guðrún is obviously concerned with the importance of the female voice in human history and she sees the future of the human race as being moulded by women through the transmission of their individual wisdom and experience as well as that of preceding generations. Women thus fulfill a most important function, if not the most important function, in life. Although Guðrún strongly believes in equality, it may well be that she implicitly adhered to the latter view, as is suggested by her delightful re-telling of the story of Adam and Eve: "But it was known to him [Satan], that of all that Jahve had created, Eva was his favourite, and that she had been chosen for the responsible role of becoming mother and protector of the young and upcoming life of future generations."[83]

In the New World, the transmission of lore gains a new dimension: not only does it involve the transmission of collective experience and wisdom, it also implies a continuation of the cultural heritage. The preservation of the Icelandic cultural heritage thus depends largely on women. In nearly all stories, the link with Iceland centres around the mother or grandmother figure. However, Guðrún does not merely see women in the light of their roles in society, but also voices their own feelings and ideas as well as their fate. In her stories, we often find the urge for freedom. In this respect the Old World, with its rigid social orders, is often placed in opposition against the New, with its promise of freedom and possibilities for all.

In the story "Utangarðs,"[84] the female narrator, a young girl, has come from Iceland to her relatives in Canada because she desperately wants to be free, live her own life and see something of the world, instead of accepting the arrogant proposal of marriage from the district officer's son, which her family views as a rare opportunity to secure her future. This view becomes understandable when we read what kind of future would have awaited most girls, including her aunt Una's daughters: "And my girls,—at a time when they would have been doing odd jobs around the country district on lousy terms, looked on in disdain, they might have regarded it a godsend if it would have suited one of the farmers to employ them as farmworkers. I have seen it all."[85] It is interesting to see how in this story the roles of the two countries are reversed: it is not Iceland that is here the "land of mirages," the land of dreams and the object of longing, but Canada. The girl realizes that if she goes back to Iceland, she will always long nostalgically for her days of freedom in Canada.

Guðrún's favourite female character is one that is built on the type of women we find in Old Icelandic literature, in the Eddas and sagas. This is understandable, as the pioneer experience is one which is favourable to women's status in society: settling a country demands strength, determination and hard work from everyone involved, from women no less than from men. Because everybody helps in building up the country, the climate becomes favourable to social equality rather than social stratification. In Chapter I we saw that this was the case when Iceland was settled, and in the case of the settlement in Canada, women again found an opportunity for more equality and freedom.

The type of woman, then, which we find both in Old Icelandic literature and in Guðrún's stories, is described by Guðrún herself in one of her lectures:

And not less admirable are the ancient women who stood by the side of their husbands, strong and free, holding the hands of their children, following the affairs of relatives and friends, and ruling their households with noble vigour and hospitality. The difficulties of pioneer years had developed their independence, and a free upbringing increased their beauty and abilities. Indeed the ancient men admired influential women; that is made clear widely in the sagas....

The vigour, generosity and nobility of our foremothers is so widely apparent from the sagas that it is obvious how general those character traits were. Indeed the ancient women genuinely contributed in the moulding of their society. They raised clever men and women who showed in various ways, with their conduct, domestic appearance and upbringing the influence of their mothers.[86]

These women, strong, honest, independent and loyal, are widely represented. In more than one story, men acknowledge this unfailing strength and support of the women at their sides as a force without which they would never have survived. For instance in "Traustur máttarviðir" ("Trusted Pillar"), a couple are watching how one brief thunderstorm destroys their first and almost-ripe crop that was supposed to pay off their debts, when the man grabs for his wife's hand and says:

You have a strong hand, Þórhildur, there is a life force in it, I have known that for a long time. Once I was almost dead, but your warm hand would not let me go.... I grabbed that straw, which was your hand, and the strength that called me back to life, that was you.[87]

Similarly, Ingólfur in "Fýkur í sporin" part I, feels lost in his dilemma without the strength and sympathy of his wife, for whom the pioneer trials eventually mean her death. At the same time, Guðrún points to the price that women often have to pay for their strength and loyalty. In some cases it means an untimely death. In others, their husbands take their qualities for granted, as, for instance, Ófeigur has to realize when he is suddenly confronted with his approaching death and, looking back, sees how he has neglected his wife and how she has lost her former youth and vigour because of it ("Undir Útfall," "At Low Tide").

This particular theme is dealt with more elaborately in "Á Vegamótum" ("At Crossroads") and "Enginn lifir sjálfum sér" ("No one lives for himself alone"). Steinunn decides to leave a marriage that has become meaningless due to incompatibility of temperament and her husband's sprees of drinking and adultery. As a result, she is the one shunned and slandered by the community and publicly condemned by the new pastor, who is inexperienced, orthodox and inflexible in his opinions. Steinunn succeeds in overcoming her isolation and bitterness by managing on her own through her work as a district nurse. When she saves the pastor's son, she regains her former stature in the eyes of the community, and is esteemed even by the pastor. However, it is when she manages to be so impartial in her work as to deliver the baby of her husband's mistress and, later, nurse her ex-husband and alleviate his time of death, that she overcomes her own feelings of bitterness and resentment. Having achieved this victory over herself, she regains her peace of heart.

Another common theme is that of repressed creativity among women. Guðrún herself did not start writing for publication until relatively late in life as she had to manage a household and bring up children, and often also had to work along with her husband to be able to afford the education of their children. In the story "Traustur máttarviðir," Þórhildur briefly mentions her early dreams and attempts to cultivate her talent for writing. However, she married and emigrated, and there was no more time for writing. Steinunn, in "Enginn lifir sjálfum sér," finds an outlet in her work, but her work is a source of dispute between her and her husband, and she does not find an opportunity to extend her professional knowledge until she is on her own.

Women also play a significant role in Guðrún's stories which have war as their central theme. Participation specifically in the First

World War was an extremely controversial issue among the West Icelanders, and Guðrún treats this topic in several of her stories. Some of these are concerned with the women who stayed behind while their loved ones were on the battlefield and point to the courage and strength it takes to be left behind and manage a household ("Jólagjöfin," "The Christmas Gift"), or to the emotional struggles involved in losing loved ones in a war. Other stories tell of women who cannot see the point of these wars or of participation in them ("Úr Þokunni," "Out of the Mist").

One of Guðrún's best-known stories, "Landskuld" ("Debt to One's Country"), locates the actual controversy among the West Icelanders. A newly-engaged young couple break up during a bitter encounter when Sigríður learns that her fiancé Einar has enlisted in the army in spite of the fact that he knew how much she was opposed to participation in a war which she regards as a political power-game. Sigríður's argument is very much like Stephan G.'s, and one might well wonder if Guðrún used his standpoint as a model. Einar's argument is that he cannot live with the shame of sitting by and seeing both younger and older people signing up to do their duty for the country which had received them with open arms and given them a better life than they would have had in Iceland.

Guðrún refrains from adhering to either of the two viewpoints. Her point with this story rather seems to be to bring out the extra pain which the controversy caused on top of all the slaughter on the battlefield. Once again, her solution is one of mutual tolerance and understanding. It consists of respecting the other's differing views without necessarily giving up one's own, rather than polarizing the two, and thus causing grief and separation. As is evident from the above discussion, she favoured this approach in order to preserve the Icelandic heritage among later generations as well. One may wonder if this is not implied in her speech about the wars when she remarks in one of her lectures:

If a permanent world peace is to be something else and more than just a beautiful ideal, the nations, each and every one, have to see to it that the individuals within their society reach a cultural maturity that will prevent them from looking askance at the inhabitants of other nations, with disdain and suspicion, but rather with a friendly understanding of their conditions and customs, and with respect for their culture.[88]

Tolerance, understanding and union rather than polarization is the message of Guðrún's fiction; it is thus very likely that this is how Guðrún ideally saw the future within Canadian society as well as the future of the whole world. We have here, in other words, yet another Western Canadian author who envisions a Canadian mosaic society long before this concept was ever formally introduced in Canada. This vision is based on both a healthy ethnic pride with a respect and understanding for other ethnic groups, and a natural degree of adaptation to the new country. The fiction of Guðrún H. Finnsdóttir provides us with a female perspective on the pioneer experience, the price women had to pay and the small deeds of heroism they performed within their sphere of work and possibility. This female perspective is firmly linked in her stories both to the Icelandic past and the Icelandic folk tradition, and, through women's role as mothers of future generations and transmitters of culture and wisdom as well as strong and independent individuals, to the future of Icelandic Canadians.

THE MOVE FROM ICELANDIC TO ENGLISH: LAURA GOODMAN SALVERSON

In 1922, the Western Icelandic journalist John G. Holme wrote in his article on "Iceland's Younger Choir" about the Icelandic immigrants in Canada:

They have not begun to create. Was the gift lost in the process of transplanting or has not the second generation caught the genius of the English language? I believe there are today some tow-headed youngsters, whose parents emigrated from the saga island ... who inside of fifteen or twenty years will be piping some interesting lays in the language of this land. (553)

We have seen that the immigrants had in actual fact begun to create, and were, to be sure, publishing avidly. However, none of these creations was accessible to the Canadian public, for Western Icelandic literature was written in Icelandic. The transition from Icelandic to English had not yet taken place, even though the children of the earliest immigrants had by this time reached maturity. One such child, Guttormur J. Guttormsson, had already published his first volumes of poetry which were, however, still in the (Western) Icelandic language and tradition rather than in the English.

Two exceptions should be noted, however. A certain Christopher Johnson published poems in English in the weeklies *Lögberg* and *Heimskringla*, and, according to Beck (1951: 70), poems by Johnson also appeared in various American and Canadian newspapers, although I have been unable to trace any. Second, Baldur Jónsson, an immigrant who received his education and learnt English in Canada, submitted columns in English to the Saskatchewan paper *The Wynyard Advance* while fatally ill in a sanatorium. After his death, the editor of the newspaper published Baldur's writings under the name *Leaves from the Unwritten Notebook of an Idler, together with Letters written in a Cloister and Dedicated to the Hearth* (1918). The slim volume of *Leaves and Letters* contains personal thoughts on general subjects. They make pleasant reading but are otherwise unremarkable, except perhaps for the writer's excellent command of English. They have been forgotten in the course of time, an inevitable fate perhaps, but possibly also due to their uncertain generic status: to what literary genre did they belong? Were they to be classed among Western Icelandic, immigrant, or Canadian writings? What was their audience?

The uncertain status of immigrant writing would soon become an acute problem which still remains topical and unsolved. It importantly moulded the authorship of one "tow-headed youngster" who, about two decades before Holme's exclamation, received a vision of her destination in a public library at the age of ten:

"I too, will write a book, to stand on the shelves of a place like this— and I will write it in English, for that is the greatest language in the whole world!"[89]

LITERARY PIONEER OR MINOR IMMIGRANT WRITER?

Laura Goodman (i.e. Guðmundsson) was born in Winnipeg in 1890 to Icelandic immigrants who had left their native country in 1887. She spent her youth travelling with her parents across the North American continent as a result of her father's idealistic *wanderlust*. From her autobiography we learn that her parents were a rather mismatched couple. Against her pragmatic mother's better counsels, her father would never give up the quest for a better life in a better place for his family, and so they never settled anywhere for very long. Strenuous labour and great poverty was the common fate of immigrants in those days, and the Goodmans were no exception. The resulting unfulfilled potential of her intelligent parents, deceived by the lies of immigrant agents and having come to Canada with the conviction that they would be able to make a decent living, left an indelible impression on Laura. Nevertheless, her parents made sure to pass on their heritage, in which they took great pride, to their daughter, and instilled in her traditional Icelandic values. Laura was weaned on stories from Icelandic literature and history, and learnt the rudiments of reading and writing from her parents. She was also stimulated early in life to formulate her thoughts on all kinds of topics and to participate in discussions, a favourite Icelandic pastime. Laura did not learn English until she was ten years old and started school. There was no money to be had for more than rudimentary schooling. Instead, she continued her avid reading after work hours. Her marriage to the Norwegian immigrant son George Salverson did not bring her alleviation from long work hours or from regularly having to move house, yet she was still determined to become an author. After having had some stories accepted for publication in journals, one of which ("Hidden Fire") won her a prize, she embarked on her first and probably most popular novel, *The Viking Heart*, which was published in 1923.

The Viking Heart tells the story of the Icelandic pioneers from the moment they leave Iceland until the end of the First World War, focussing on a few families. Her purpose in writing this novel, as she says herself in her autobiography *Confessions of an Immigrant's Daughter*, was

to write a story which would define the price any foreign group must pay for its place in the national life of the country of its adoption. I wanted this payment to express spiritual values, which, to my way of thinking, are the true measure of national greatness, the only riches that abide, and which make a nation endure. (405)

This purpose is not far removed from the main ideology which informed much contemporary Western Icelandic literature. Although the theme of the immigrant had been introduced into Canadian literature by Ralph Connor in his novel *The Foreigner* (1909), Laura Goodman Salverson was the first novelist to introduce the Canadian public to the insider's viewpoint of the immigrant fate.[90] Whether it was in spite of or because of this, *The Viking Heart* earned Laura great popularity. The novels which she wrote after *The Viking Heart* all deal with Norse subjects with the exception of one, *Black Lace*, but none of them quite lived up to the standard set by her first novel. It was only when she returned to her original subject of immigrants on the prairies that she regained some of her earlier verve. *The Dark Weaver*, published in 1937, won the Governor General's Award for fiction, and her autobiography *Confessions* earned her the Governor General's Award for non-fiction in 1939.

The initial popularity of Laura's fiction among readers and critics quickly faded after the 1950s. Nowadays she is mentioned only occasionally in surveys of Canadian literary history that include literature before 1960, and her name is also largely absent from Western Icelandic records. In my following discussion of Laura Goodman Salverson in the light of both Western Icelandic and Canadian literature I will argue that Laura Goodman Salverson's motives, both as an immigrant writer and as a Canadian writer, have been largely misinterpreted. Consequently, her works have been placed on the periphery of Western Icelandic and Canadian literary history, in spite of the fact that this author is the very embodiment of important features which characterize both literary traditions. For reasons of availability as well as scope and relevance, I will rely mostly on *The Viking Heart* and *Confessions of an Immigrant's Daughter* with an occasional reference to *The Dark Weaver*.

SALVERSON AND THE WESTERN ICELANDIC TRADITION

As Lára Guðmundsson only published in English under the anglicized version of her name, she has almost solely been regarded as a Canadian writer, an immigrant writer to be sure, but Canadian nevertheless. Consequently, the fact that she was raised in the same immigrant environment that produced writers like Stephan G. and Guttormur J. Guttormsson is often ignored. Nonetheless, she has a great deal in common with Guttormur, much more so than with writers like Nellie McClung, Martha Ostenso or Frederick Philip Grove, in the shadow of whom she is most generally discussed. And yet, Lára Guðmundsson/Laura Goodman is a writer of two worlds, and should be seen in the light of both rather than one.

Like Guttormur, Laura was born in Canada shortly after the immigration of her parents. But unlike Guttormur, who was raised in the geographical isolation of New Iceland, Laura spent her youth in different areas across the North American continent, and this difference is probably largely what determined the different choice of language. The two authors shared the same concern for the future of their Icelandic heritage that characterizes other Western Icelandic authors as well. As second-generation authors, however, Guttormur and Laura have as their theme not so much the pain of leaving Iceland, the pangs of homesickness and how to survive in an alien environment, but rather the process of settlement. According to Mossberg's analysis, second-generation authors share a more historical perspective which is at the same time deepened by a first-hand knowledge of both the achievements and the sacrifices of the pioneer generation.

In poems like "Jón Austfirðingur" or "Sandy Bar" and in *The Viking Heart*, the same awe of the pioneer generation is evident, as is a similar sense of filial obligation to document its fate and transform it into art so that it will never be forgotten. The approach, however, is different. Whereas Guttormur addresses a Western Icelandic and, possibly, an Icelandic audience, Laura decided to direct her writing first and foremost at the Canadian public. Consequently, where Guttormur could assume a sense of shared knowledge and experience, Laura had to explain and justify as well as record. As a result, Laura had to distance herself from her subject in order to be able to explain it, thus adding to the distance already created by her much larger exposure to North American culture because of her father's wandering.

In "Sandy Bar," the pioneers could naturally be identified with Icelandic heroes through allusions to Old Icelandic literature and mythology. In *The Viking Heart*, such references do not, indeed cannot, occur so naturally, for no familiarity at all could be assumed with the Icelanders' pride in their heritage and the important function this heritage had played in Icelandic daily life for centuries. Instead, Laura had to turn to explanations such as the following:

Out of her greatest misery Iceland's songs have risen. It is as natural to the Icelandic heart to turn to poetry in times of stress as for another to search his Bible.[91]

To die in the arms of the Valkyrie—victor in a glorious cause—such was ever the Norseman's ideal!   (320)

Laura had made a very conscious decision to address a Canadian audience. Her main goal, apart from documenting the achievements of the Icelandic pioneers and the price they had to pay, was to make the Canadian public aware of the nature and the rich cultural heritage of her people. The reason why she felt compelled to "explain" her nation and its culture to Canadians is well expressed in the bitter words of Bjorn Lindal, an Icelandic immigrant and one of the main characters in *The Viking Heart*:

When I remember the wild plans I had in youth of gaining recognition and position after a few years in this country, it seems a huge joke. You know the attitude that the people had towards us. Suspicion, distrust and contempt. A little of that faded when we proved our worth in the rebellion—it has never been said or ever will, I hope, that a Norseman can't defend his home. But we Icelanders are still a curiosity to many. They think us creatures of doubtful habit and uncertain intelligence. They tolerate us because we are useful— because we are doing what they refuse to do, being of such superior clay. (107-08)

In *Confessions* Laura relates how she herself experienced the ignorance and contempt regarding her "peculiar nationality" (195).

The basic structure of *The Viking Heart* follows the same pattern as Guttormur's "Jón Austfirðingur" and many other immigrant novels, such as Jóhann Magnús Bjarnason's *Eiríkur Hansson*. The story begins with a pastoral, idealized description of the homeland which corresponds to the idealized image many immigrants' children had formed of "home." Lies on the part of immigration agents then lead to the decision to emigrate. Journey and settlement in the New World are described next. They are accompanied by the death of an Old World child, symbolizing the severed ties with "home" and the sacrifice that is demanded for a good life in the New World. Harmony and hope for the future are finally re-established through the birth of a New World child after a period of conflict and suffering. But whereas in "Jón Austfirðingur" this child is born from a union between Old and New World, destructive though this union was in other respects, in *The Viking Heart* little Thor the second is the son of two West Icelanders. The marriage of Ninna to an Anglo-Canadian, on the other hand, is portrayed by Laura as purely destructive. The reason for this difference could well lie in the different audiences that are addressed. Guttormur seems to say that from such intermarital unions, which were becoming increasingly frequent among West Icelanders, hope could still spring for the preservation of the Icelandic heritage, provided the children were brought up in an Icelandic atmosphere. Laura, however, is justifying the right of her people to cherish their heritage by suggesting that it contains great spiritual values which her people are offering their adopted country. In this light, someone who marries out of the group for material reasons can only be regarded as destructive to the spiritual heritage of her people. Although both works end on a positive note, Laura's work carries a much more optimistic tone. In spite of the many tragedies, optimism always prevails. In his Icelandic survey of Western Icelandic prose writers, Stefán Einarsson sees this as a flaw, and the main reason why her work is not on a par with that of her ancestors or of Rølvaag, the Norwegian author who wrote the American immigrant classic *Giants of the Earth*, all of whom wrote in a tragic mode (1951: 37). Interestingly, Einarsson praises, rather than criticizes, Salverson's romantic work in his English survey (1948: 253-55).

If optimism is the flaw preventing Laura from receiving recognition, then Jóhann Magnús Bjarnason should be criticized for this same flaw. As mentioned earlier, the romantic, optimistic tone had its parallels in the Icelandic tradition as well as the tragic one. The similarities in tone between Laura and Jóhann Magnús are striking, as are many other aspects of their writing. They share, for instance, a tendency towards verbiosity as well as a profound interest in the human heart and a talent to create animated, sympathetic characters. To achieve this, they both employ a Dickensian way of characterizing people through personal quirks or ways of speaking. Thus Finna in *The Viking Heart* comes alive almost entirely through her particular expressions which Laura captures and translates very well, as for instance in the following:

"Well, and isn't that the truth! You that made that coffee that day and me to forget. Picture it! What a dullness!" (190)

"Good evening, friend. It's sorry I am not to remember where I met you. But you know how it is in this world—so much to think of and me with a head so queer-like." (190)

Both Laura Goodman Salverson and Jóhann Magnús Bjarnason are deeply concerned with the immigrant fate which they portray very realistically, although they generally tend towards romanticized descriptions. Along with the concern for immigrants goes a concern with the preservation of heritage, which both regard as a spiritual enrichment to the developing Canadian nation. Although their main interest is, of course, with the Icelandic immigrants and heritage, we

find in the works of both a range of immigrants of different nationalities who all contribute to this enrichment. Laura gives, for instance,
as the reason for having written her autobiography:

It may be that, like myself, some child of immigrants longs to justify her race
as something more than a hewer of wood; dreams in the starlight of the
lonely prairie of some fair burnt offering to lay upon the altar of her New
Country, out of the love of a small, passionate heart.
      How to do it, in a strange, new language? How to do it, in the face of
poverty and isolation, and the cold indifference of an alien people? How to
hold fast to a purpose that no one counts as precious as a new-turned furrow,
a pelt of furs, or a load of grain.
      It can be done....   (414)

As much as she sets out to explain the immigrant's position to
Canadians, she wishes at the same time to stimulate immigrants
themselves to regard their heritage as a precious gift to their new
country rather than a burden.

      Like the other Western Icelandic authors discussed above, Laura
seems to have strongly believed in a mosaic Canada, made up of the
best in the heritages of all immigrants. This belief is expressed most
clearly in her editorial to the first issue of *The Icelandic Canadian*, the
first Western Icelandic magazine in English. In this editorial, she
points to the progressive and open nature of the ancestral Viking
spirit:

With a zest and a hunger for a richer way of life those incorrigible adventurers
braved a thousand dangers and by their daring broke forever the traditional
mold of the past. The kingdoms they carved for themselves were not
patterned upon preconceived concepts; they were evolved in accordance
with the growing stream of human consciousness; an organism that was
fed by new ideas drawn from innumerable strange sources; but the sustaining
soil was the Norse heart, the Norse nature.

She then envisions the contemporary frontier to tackle for the Viking
descendants as the realm of the mind, a "wilderness" of "mental
weeds and misconceptions": "Racial hatreds, racial pride, ignorance,
superstition, bigotry, these are the shoals the adventurer must cir-
cumvent or die." Finally, she states:

It is our conviction that the time has come to cut ourselves free of the
fallacious idea that our duty to the past must constrain us to the old Icelandic

mold. We believe that our first duty is to Canada and to the world of tomorrow. In that new world ethnic differences must not prevail as they have hitherto prevailed. Our divergent cultures must be freely spent in building a co-ordinated and greater civilization sincerely and sanely devoted to the common good of this country.... Iceland will still live in our hearts; what is more, all that is good and great and treasurable in her ancient traditions will be transformed into living reality. As Canadians, and only as Canadians will it be possible for us to orient our Norse heritage in the New World of Tomorrow. (1942: 1-3)

Laura was a pioneer in expressing this idea of a cultural mosaic through her fiction to the Canadian public at a time when most Canadians still entertained assimilationist ideals. Terrence Craig acknowledges this achievement in the following passage:

With the work of Grove and Salverson before 1940 ... the entire set of assumptions that English-Canadians had publicized about aliens were challenged. These prejudices were not quickly overturned, but they were so sufficiently discredited that they played less of a role in Canadian society and appeared less openly in Canadian literature than before. (1985b: 93-94)

However, Craig himself is perhaps the best example of his own statement that the prejudices were not quickly overturned. He gives Grove all the credit, Laura only following in his shadow, and neglects to mention that Laura Salverson's *The Viking Heart* appeared before Grove's first novels. He admits that Grove assumed an English-Canadian point-of-view rather than an immigrant or ethnic one, and seems to regard this as a good thing, accusing Laura of "narrow ethnic reclamation" (99). One wonders if Craig is not falling victim to his own argument when he applauds Grove's so-called "pioneering" contribution to Canadian multiculturalism because of that author's assumed Anglo-Canadian voice. By praising Grove's voice over that of Laura he is suggesting that multiculturalism should be cast in an Anglo-Canadian mould to make it more palatable to the Anglo-Canadian. At the same time the real literary pioneer is deflated by Craig, who regards the insider's view as "narrow ethnicity." Craig, in other words, seems to think that the goal of multiculturalism is better served by picturing all immigrants as "pioneers" whose ethnicity exists mostly in introductory adjectives than by stimulating ethnic pride in the face of assimilation.

Recognition of Craig's double-edged argument should not, how-ever, blind us to the fact that, for modern readers, Laura's national-ism seems rather overbearing at times. In this, she is following in the footsteps of her fellow Western Icelandic authors, and, like them, she is reacting to developments within the Western Icelandic com-munity. Assimilation was fast becoming the rule rather than the exception due to Anglo-Canadian pressure. It presented a desire for upward mobility, and a desire to fit in. In *Confessions*, Laura recorded her observations when she moved with her family back to Canada: "Having suffered ostracism and condescension because of their for-eignness, it seemed as though all the national energy of the people had been expanded to acquire a blameless Canadian skin, Canadian habits, and Canadian houses" (357). This was not just a Western Icelandic problem, but a problem in all immigrant communities which has found expression in most immigrant literature. As Linda Hutcheon remarks:

No immigrant could ever underestimate the psychological need to belong, to fit in, despite assurances that difference is part of the mosaic.... In their desire to make good and forget, many immigrants found that their primary aim in life, of necessity, became financial success. As a result, their main values became, again of necessity, increasingly materialistic. (1985: 34)

Similarly, Tamara Palmer, in an article on ethnic prairie writing, notes that the ambivalence towards intermarriage, such a basic theme in ethnic literature, "reflects the intensity of the conflict between the strong impulse ... toward cultural maintenance and the even stronger impulse toward a New World synthesis" (1987: 62).

As a Western Icelandic author, Laura felt a keen sense of respon-sibility towards her authorship. After all, in the Icelandic tradition, being a *skáld* meant much more than just a writer of stories.[92] A *skáld* was a wizard of words, a prophet of the people. In *Confessions*, Laura describes her difficulties in having to write with such a heavy respon-sibility on her shoulders. Part of the description runs:

The second, and greater obstacle, was my conception of the purposes of fiction. Old-fashioned Icelanders did not look upon the sagas as something to kill time. They had, indeed, no predilection for such a curious desire. Even as an old woman my mother hated to go to bed—sleep seemed such a waste of life! To our way of thinking, even light fiction failed of its purpose to interest or amuse if it did not in some way extend the mental horizon. If there was nothing in the story to provoke a novel train of thought, nothing that gave you an intriguing glimpse of human foibles, nothing that touched on the springs of beauty in nature or in man, then why trouble to read the thing? A cup of coffee would do just as well if all you wanted was mental oblivion. (401)

She concludes:

The fact remains, that to the immigrants to Canada this need to justify their race was a powerful and ever-present incentive to courageous effort. It did not surprise me, therefore, that papa's first comment upon being told that I intended to write a book was not very flattering.

"My dear," said he, "are you sure it will be a good book? There are so many bad books the old bards must shudder to see!" (403)

Being a Western Icelandic *skáld* in those days, as we saw earlier, entailed the responsibility of guiding the people through their bewildering experiences as immigrants, not only by writing "handbooks" on how to survive these experiences, but by the depiction of noble ideals, lofty purposes which recalled the proud deeds of their ancestors. One of the most immediate problems the community was facing at the time of Laura's writing was the danger of losing the Icelandic heritage through assimilation. Consequently, Western Icelandic *skáld* felt it their responsibility to point to this danger and to use their writings to turn the tide. One popular way of doing this was to depict the Icelandic cultural heritage as functioning as a priceless valuable in a New World context.

This feeling of responsibility, widely found among Western Icelandic authors, received expression in the construction of ethnic myths. Laura Goodman Salverson, however, was not only creating "in-group" literature, but had also set out to "justify her race" to Canadians outside of that group. To achieve this, she attempted to translate and recreate the Western Icelandic self-image and myths for a Canadian audience in a Canadian idiom. Seeing that this group self-image was a response to hostile ignorance and prejudice as well as the result of a sense of inferiority, Laura fell into the same trap as Jóhann Magnús Bjarnason, namely that of over-compensation. In her eagerness to deconstruct the stereotype of her people as pagan northern savages, her characters tend to become idealized stereotypes instead. Hutcheon has noticed this tendency in other immigrant literatures as well:

The question of national stereotyping in immigrant novels is a real and important issue, given every culture's resentment of what seems an inevitable simplifying process.... Not all stereotypes are created by others, however: sometimes it is the immigrants themselves who want to create an idealized self-image....

There is sometimes a fine line between realism and stereotyping.
(1985: 36)

The continual identification of the main protagonists with Norse gods and heroes, and the repeated references to the highly-developed Icelandic culture and the pre-Columbian settlement in North America must seem overly romanticized to modern readers. They served a purpose, however, and do not deserve to be misinterpreted as stemming from a sense of ethnic superiority, as Craig implies in an article devoted to Laura's Canadian work (1985a: 86). Critics like Craig do not seem to understand the background, the intercultural tensions and cultural need, from which immigrant literature springs. The following characterization of Eric Thompson in his "Prairie Mosaic: The Immigrant Novel in the Canadian West" provides a much more accurate picture:

Salverson and Kiriak excel as "folk novelists," writers who can tell uplifting stories of simple people whose ideal (and ordeal) of group settlement is crowned by success. They also use the novel in an unaffected manner to portray with charm and sentiment the lore and customs of their people. (1980: 246)

The strain of romanticism in Laura's works, then, reflects a constructed ethnic self-image as well as the ambitions of her people in the new country: it shows the continuation of a heroic past with established values in a new world. In other words, Laura sought to do with her fiction in English what her fellow Western Icelandic writers did in Icelandic: they chose from their literary past those elements that were relevant for their present situation in order to create meaning and a place for their people in their new, alien environment. The difference is that Laura chose to address both an Old World and a New World audience, in order to try to create a place for immigrants in Canadian society and literature. As a result, Laura had to balance the needs and demands of her two audiences. She does not sustain that feat continually throughout her works, but perhaps those occasional imbalances show better than any description could, the precarious position of the immigrant and the immigrant's child, eternally poised between two worlds.

Laura Goodman Salverson's motives were, however, misunderstood. Her name is suspiciously absent from most Western Icelandic records. She is included in the Western Icelandic collection *Vestan um Haf* (1930) with a translated short story, and the *Tímarit Þjóðræknisfélags Íslendinga í Vesturheimi* and *Lögberg* each published a brief laudatory review when *The Viking Heart* came out. In addition, she is included in Stefán Einarsson's survey of Western Icelandic prosewriters (1948; 1951). Last, in an article on Rølvaag's *Giants of the Earth* (1935), Richard Beck expresses his regret that no Icelander should, so far, have produced a work of similar artistic mastery in the service of his people in North America. He grudgingly gives Laura the credit that she has "set a foot in that direction" and leaves it at that one short remark.

Its silence about Laura Salverson's accomplishments seems an anomaly for a group that produced so many newspapers and magazines, and was so keen to list its achievements in its adopted society. In her autobiography, Laura herself attributed her rejection by the community to the introductory chapter to *The Viking Heart*, which she wrote at the advice of Nellie McClung and which, according to Laura, caused a small outrage in the Western Icelandic community. Laura had meant the chapter to be symbolic: it shows the immigrants content in their homefields before they are cruelly driven into the sea by a volcanic eruption that caused the death of one of their children. This symbolic picture, however, required that the volcano, which in reality is situated in the interior of Iceland, be "moved" to the coastal area. Laura says:

> The Icelandic people were so indignant that I should have played fast and loose with their landscape, shrinking it, so to speak, until the volcano came down to the sea, that the story itself had no merit. That I had tried, to the best of my ability, to represent those spiritual qualities of the people themselves, which must commend them to their brethren, was completely discounted. I had made a fool of myself by not invoking a verbal map of the country for a frontispiece! (*Confessions* 408)

The few Western Icelandic reactions to her novel that have appeared in print indicate that the main objection was to its optimistic romanticism. Einarsson briefly mentions the negative reactions of Western Icelandic readers to Laura's style (1948: 253-55). Western

Icelandic poet Jakobína Johnson voiced her dislike of Laura's perceived lack of feeling for what constituted the Icelandic national heritage or "tradition and values," as she calls it (Guðmundsson, 3, 1975:
36; trans. Wolf 1994: 188), and Stephan G. considered her work to be
inferior to contemporary Icelandic writing.[93] While such objections
were never raised against Western Icelandic authors writing in Icelandic, they were voiced with great indignation in the case of Laura
Salverson who had opted to write in English. This can be explained
by extreme sensitivity rooted in the deep-seated self-consciousness of
a minority culture. The fact that Salverson had depicted the Icelandic
immigrants and their culture and customs to the larger Canadian audience in a way that did not conform to the Western Icelandic self-
image in its attempts to explain the group's trials and sacrifices, made
her a virtual outcast of the Western Icelandic community. Laura
concludes somewhat bitterly:

However, although I and all my works have been tacitly repudiated by my
own people, with but few exceptions, it has not changed my own affection,
which is all that matters. There are no losses, except they rob the heart. (408)

Thus, the author who introduced the immigrant theme, seen from
the immigrant's point of view, into Canadian literature, and for the first
time "justified her race" to the Canadian public, was rejected by her
own people. Her immigrant works conform to the Western Icelandic
literary tradition, but were pushed back to the margins of that tradition. Lára Guðmundsson the West Icelander became a marginal figure
in an ethnic community which refused to acknowledge her.

SALVERSON AND CANADIAN LITERATURE

At the same time when the West Icelanders were waiting for "the
great Western Icelandic epic" to immortalize their immigrant experience (Beck 1935), Canadians were anxiously awaiting "the great
Canadian novel" (Pacey 1970: 665-66). The time between the two
World Wars was an important one, for it was then that Canada as a
nation began to come into its own. Its contribution to the Great War
had launched Canada into the international scene and had given rise
to a national awareness. Canada's position in the world became a
much-debated national issue, and the development of a Canadian
culture a general, topical concern. Canada's status as a colony and the
cultural isolation of Canadian writers before the arrival of modern

communications had hampered the growth of a Canadian literature. Unlike Americans, Canadians still looked to Britain as the centre of power and tradition. As a result, rather than come to terms with their Canadian environment, most writers modelled their works on British literature. Canadian reality was not given imaginative form, for the prevalent view was that culture had to be "imported" from Britain. This deeply ingrained colonial mentality, with its sense of inferiority and great regard for (British) tradition, had hindered the development of an indigenous literature such as had come into existence in the United States. Now, Canada felt ready to move away from a largely British to a more North American context.

It was for this reason that during the decades when modernism was at its height in other parts of the world, the pioneering Canadian writers were less concerned with experimental techniques than with shaping a literary image of Canada. As MacLulich points out:

> Instead, the task was to define the principal features of the Canadian social world and to articulate the typical ways in which Canadians were responding to that world. One important result of this fictional scrutiny of society was the creation of a literary consensus about the prevalent attitudes, the most common situations, and the principal conflicts that prevailed in Canadian society. These writers, then, created the first fully developed tradition of Canadian fiction. In recent years, their work has provided a context that later novelists have variously endorsed, modified, or reacted against. (1988: 89)

It was at this time that Canada began to take on a fictional identity of its own and a national literary tradition started to develop. This meant, too, however, that Canadian literature was still in its infancy, and Canadian writers, rather than being able to write within or against an existing tradition, had to create one. MacLulich explains that, because of the absence of a tradition, the distinction between popular and serious art was blurred: "since there were no established standards for them to uphold, Canadian writers allowed themselves to accept popularity as a measure of merit" (1976: 45).

All the while, the most debated issue in literary circles was the form and direction a Canadian tradition should take. MacLulich suggests that in Canada "the most conspicuous literary debate during the twenties was, in effect, a continuation of the argument between realism and idealism" (1988: 89). This debate, he has argued, reflects the tension which is revealed in the development of Canadian fiction between romance and realism, "between romantic and realistic ways of portraying the world" (1976: 43). MacLulich diverges from the view of Desmond Pacey in the *Literary History of Canada* that in the period between the Wars, a few novelists began "the process of turning the eyes of readers and fellow-writers from a fabled past or a romanticized present towards the actual conditions of Canadian life," leading Canadian writing in the direction of realism (1970: 658). I would, however, agree with MacLulich that Canadian fiction has never moved away from romance in favour of realism, but has rather developed a fusion of the two. Such a fusion explains the role that nostalgia, tradition and respect for the past have been allowed to play in the development of Canadian culture, a role that has also allowed for the development of a multiculturalist policy which stimulates the preservation of Old World heritages other than the British.[94]

It was in this literary climate that Laura Goodman Salverson wrote her fiction. Indeed, Salverson's writing poignantly reflects the literary situation in Canada at the time, with Canadian literature still in its infancy and at a crossroads. Nobody knew as yet in which direction it would develop. Thus, Salverson's writing is marred by "beginner's flaws," and, as a consequence, has become largely ignored, just like this whole initial period in the development of Canadian literature. After all, no one engaged in an obsessive search of international recognition and national identity, as the participants in Canadian literature have been since, is eager to be reminded of his relatively late development and growing pains. In this initial period one can nonetheless already see, sometimes clearly, rudiments of the traits basic to its nature. Salverson's work contains the traits belonging to what has come to characterize Canadian literature, in a rough form it is true, but also in a very profound way, as the experiences of duality and alienation so essential to Canadian literature are deepened by this author's immigrant background.

Salverson, like most Canadian authors in the 1920s, was caught in the tension between romance and realism. Characteristically, she was not able to find a perfect balance between the two. Bobak (1981) points to the confusion which existed about realism in a Canadian context. About *The Viking Heart* he says: "In the context of the period, the realistic sections of *The Viking Heart* set it apart from the bulk of literature being published, but at this distance in time, the book clearly is a romance" (95-96). One can detect, however, a fairly consistent pattern in the way Salverson used the two different modes. Whereas she romanticized both her Old World heritage, as it had been passed on to her by her parents, and her hopes for the future of Canada, she employed the realistic mode for the descriptions and dramatization of her immigrant present and the immigrant experience in general. This could, of course, be explained simply as a result of the aims of her fiction: she tried on the one hand to recreate the immigrant suffering and achievements for an audience directly familiar with it, while on the other hand she sought to provide her Anglo-Canadian audience with an insight into the immigrant experience. To achieve both aims, Salverson elevated the trials and deeds to a level of heroism and offered rewards in the form of success, as a psychological comfort and a lofty ideal for the future.

However, in *Confessions*, which is much darker in tone and more realistic in description than Salverson's earlier fiction, we receive glimpses suggesting a much deeper-lying reason for the pattern in which romantic and realist modes are employed. As an immigrants' daughter who grew up in an immigrant milieu, Laura Goodman Salverson was a child of two worlds. The outside world was a prairie landscape, which, to Salverson, seemed to embody all the sunshine, the promise of success and a glorious future connected with the New World:

There is a sunset never seen beyond the confines of Alberta and Saskatchewan, a conflagration of golden flames, that sets the whole heaven afire—a sort of jubilee of light, that cannot be confined to one small horizon, and flings its lambent banners across the entire sky.... For that, I love the prairie. In that, I place my faith. Dreams never die. (*Confessions* 360)

The prairie functions as a faithful reminder of dreams and possibilities, and the freedom to realize them, in both *The Viking Heart* and *Confessions*. In the latter, the prairie is also present as a refuge and comforter, a living being that listens to and moves with Salverson's joys and sorrows.

In this respect, the impact of the prairie landscape on Salverson as an author is not that of Man the Giant who is dwarfed by the powerful presence of the landscape and forced to tame his free spirit and passions, as analyzed by Kreisel (1986). Rather, it is the popular image at the time of the prairie as the new Garden of Eden, as analyzed by Harrison (1977). In his article, however, Kreisel does remark on the obvious, and for Salverson important similarities between prairie landscape and seascape: "Only one other kind of landscape

gives us the same skeleton requirements, the same vacancy and still-
ness, the same movement of wind through space, and that is the sea"
(7). Interestingly, the similarity of the sea and the prairie seems to
provide the linking element between Salverson's Norse imagination,
stimulated by the tales of her parents, and the New World. For her
Norse ancestors, the sea, apart from being a provider, held the possibilities of pursuing freedom and ideals, and of new regions to
explore. In *Confessions*, she describes how the prairie seems to speak
out to her in the same voice which beckoned her ancestors through
the sea:

> There is another mood of the great plains that invades the heart with tender
> melancholy.... That, too, belongs to the voice: ... lamenting the golden age
> when deeds of daring were to do. Life was so barren now. So safe! Sold to
> prosperity and commercialism. A man should be master of his own fate, the
> captain of his own soul. Grey rain, and a quiet field, and somewhere, in the
> misty dawn, the clear voice lingers. (360)

Opposed to the promise of the prairie was the misery at home:
"Back of the brightness lay a grim shadow as was ever the case in my
childhood" (1930: 69). At home were the shadows of immigrant suffering, the unfulfilled potential of intelligent parents who struggled
to keep the family alive, and Salverson's own illnesses and difficulties.
Endowed with a lively imagination, and having been raised on Icelandic literature and history by her parents, Salverson escaped from
daily miseries in Norse fantasies or fled to the prairie to dream. The
tendency to seek refuge from reality in dreams is described by
Einarsson as a familiar phenomenon among Icelanders: "The ambitious dreamer with no means to realize his ambition, no means to
develop his talents, is not an uncommon phenomenon in the small
Icelandic society.... [A]mbitious dreams the Icelanders have enough
of, a heritage from the Viking age no amount of Christendom has
been able to suppress" (1948: 206). In Chapter I we saw that, after the
great saga-writing age, deteriorating economic and social conditions
fostered the popularity of the *fornaldarsögur* and the *riddarasögur* as
escapist literature. Dahlie explains Salverson's view of the prairie as
a result of the "tension inherent in the complementary actions of
searching for a paradise and being threatened by eviction from it"
(1986: 31).

If the contrast between the two worlds in which Salverson had
grown up had not been great enough in itself, there was always the

similar contrast between the two natures of her parents, which undoubtedly emphasized the sense of dualism in her. Whereas her father's irrepressible idealism enforced her dreams of the New World's endless possibilities and her ancestors' glorious past, her mother's pragmatism and stern pride in the face of long suffering were a continual reminder of her immediate reality. Salverson noted in *Confessions*: "I had reached the stage where mamma's practical wisdom overrode all papa's idealism. It would be years until I should see any possibility of compromise between such extremes of opinion" (319). The duality of Salverson's experiences is revealed in her works through an alternately optimistic and fatalistic tone of voice, and a style, now lofty, embellished, tending towards the cliché and the melodramatic, now suggestive, detailed, powerful and realistic. Compare, for instance, the difference in tone and style in the following two passages from *The Viking Heart*:

As the sun set, bathing the river in crimson and amber, casting a ghostly glimmer over the ragged autumn woods on either side, there flashed into sight from beyond a bend in the river, a craft, long and slender, cleaving the water with the swiftness and silence of thought. And the foreigners from the far north country saw their first red man. A splendid native, straight and supple, like some bronzed god baring his copper chest indifferent to the elements, he bore down upon them. (26)

The hours that followed were bitter. Borga sat between her mother and her little sister on a grimy bench against a grimy wall. About them tobacco smoke and stale air swirled in snake-like wreaths. Children cried and called for bread. Men and women rushed about nervously with the terrible, tense energy of caged animals. The place buzzed with ceaseless noises. People stumbled over and against bundles and boxes. They whispered and they talked at the top of their voices. They coughed and they sneezed. They implored silence of their babies and were themselves more noisy than the infants. Altogether the place was hideous, humid with the heat and the indescribable odor of humanity. (32)

Reading the two passages, we sense the experience behind the second one, as Salverson conjures up the scene in the immigrant barrack in short, powerful sentences which make us part of the experience. The first one, however, is a hopelessly dramatic and romanticized picture which conveys little else than bathos. Her own experiences as an immigrants' child, it would seem, forced her to tone down her romantic imagination in favour of realistic details when dealing with topics with which she was directly familiar. Moreover, she reveals a sharp eye and a strong sense of justice when dealing with social conditions, and no elevated talk can close that eye nor keep her from criticizing both the social systems which caused such misery and the people who condoned them. "What struck me like a blow was the obvious injustice of a society which exacts the letter of the law only from the less fortunate," she notes in *Confessions* (333). During her job as a domestic servant she explains her revolt at the inequalities of life:

It was the atmosphere these things created, the sense of security and well-being, that made gracious living a matter of course. It was the contrast of this home as against Laura [her friend]'s dead dwelling that set me thinking. Laura had brains and ability and a burning desire to better herself. To what good? She was starving in a cheap little room, for the sake of peace! Exaggeration? Well, I wondered how Miss Vera would manage her placid graces on ten dollars a month, six of which went for a bed.... I wondered then, as I wonder now, how the fine moralists expect a girl to feed and clothe herself on ten dollars a month, in honour!.... There was something terribly wrong in attributing such contrasts to the dispensation of the Almighty Providence. Something blasphemous in preaching a religion that laid such evils on the shoulders of God. Not so long as I had wit to judge for myself of the boundless riches of the earth should I be persuaded to believe that these natural resources were solely designed for the enjoyment of the few who invested their money, which, without the labour of the disinherited, would have been as worthless as charity. (327-28)

Confessions was written almost fifteen years after *The Viking Heart*, during the time of the Depression, when social criticism began to be heard more determinedly and widely. Salverson must have felt the climate was ready to hear her insider's accounts of the urban poor. Whereas the Icelandic pioneers in *The Viking Heart*, in spite of their struggles with a hostile environment, still attained a relative degree of self-sufficiency and therefore retained some dignity, the immigrants in the city were exploited and often ended up dependent on somebody's charity (Palmer 1987). In her critical passages Salverson reveals a more "modern" sensibility as described by MacLulich: using a sceptical tone which at times borders on irony to expose the "underside" of prairie city life (1988: 107). A good example of this more modern tone can be found in the chapter of *Confessions* which is appropriately called "Exile," where Salverson describes the conditions in "the Saddlery" where her father worked. It seems that New is the only critic who has given Salverson credit for this social aspect of her writing when he mentions her in the chapter dealing with social protest (1989: 155).

The same experience which awakened Salverson's social protest and kept her close to reality also brought about her acute desire for escapist fantasy which led her to romanticize her Norse background and the North-American prairie with its promise of freedom and endless possibility. These fantasies, however, bring out very clearly her position. As an immigrant she fantasizes about what she feels alienated from: her Old World background as well as the possibility of success in the New World. *The Dark Weaver*, which was published two years before *Confessions*, breathes an even more pessimistic atmosphere. All characters are weighed down by an oppressive determinism. Indeed, the omnipotence and omnipresence of Fate, "the Dark Weaver," is reminiscent of the mythic Norse fatalism which pervades Edda and saga literature. Whereas *The Viking Heart* ended on an optimistic note about the future of immigrant cultural heritages in Canada, *The Dark Weaver* focusses on the inevitable reappearance in the New World of all "follies and evils" of heritage and civilization, shattering every illusion of a truly new beginning. The past cannot be left behind, but always resurges when least expected. As a result, the hero, young Canadian-born Manfred, dies in battle in the Old World, fighting the "follies and evils" of the First World War.

Salverson never resolved the battle waged within herself between the Old World and the New. Her reality is a split identity that is poised between two worlds but belongs to neither. The duality of Laura Goodman Salverson's experience as it appears in her *Confessions* has been more elaborately discussed by Kristjana Gunnars (1986). Gunnars analyzes *Confessions* as being at the same time the success story of a self-made woman and a story of the struggles and failures of a non-British immigrant. In one respect it can be regarded as an autobiography which is a New World comedy with a happy ending, and in the other as a confession and an Old World tragedy.[95] Gunnars further argues that the act of writing her autobiography can be seen as an attempt to heal the divisions within Salverson herself. This argument is in agreement with Daphne Marlatt's conclusions in her discussion of the immigrant imagination:

> It seems to me that the situation of being such an immigrant is a perfect seedbed for the writing sensibility. If you don't belong, you can *imagine* you belong and you can construct in writing a world where you do belong. You can write your way into the world you want to be a part of ... even as, from outside, you witness its specific characteristics. (1984: 222)

Marlatt sees the immigrant imagination as one which seeks to "enter into" the new place. By this she means that "it genuinely struggles to pierce the difference, the foreignness, the mystery of the new place with its other culture" (219). At the same time it desires "to knit the two places together, two (at least!) selves somehow" (223). Salverson's desire to "knit" her two selves together and to imagine she can enter the New World through her writing can be read in her childhood identification with the *huldufólk*, believing herself to be a changeling. This is a fitting metaphor indeed for her dual reality. The identification not only provided a viable explanation for her early feelings of alienation, but also validated her secret ambitions for adventure and success so far removed from her daily life in the immigrant ghetto. As we saw in Chapter I, the *huldufólk* are beautiful and successful creatures that live in splendour, and the belief in *huldufólk* has often been explained as deriving from a deep desire for companionship and dreams of happiness that are denied fulfilment in reality. Salverson herself links this "discovery" about her changeling ancestry to her first attempts at storytelling, thus establishing a connection between her authorship and her dual identity (*Confessions* 25).[96]

Marlatt concludes her discussion of the immigrant imagination by saying:

> I think that writers who feel this way are often interested in myth and symbol which are common to disparate phenomena and form a universal language underlying the specifics of the local—which is why, perhaps, so much early Canadian literature is full of myth and symbol. (223)

These concluding words are important in two ways. First, they show a connection between the dual sensibility and a preference for the romance, since myth and symbol belong to the literary genre of the romance more than to any other. Second, they place the immigrant imagination almost naturally in the framework of Canadian literature in general. It is my conviction that the "immigrant" sensibilities of dualism and alienation are not immigrant sensibilities exclusively, but characterize the Canadian literary sensibility in general. Moss (1974) discusses "immigrant exile" as one among four main types of exile found to characterize Canadian fiction. Robertson has elaborated on Moss's analysis (1976). He finds that:

All Commonwealth literature comes from two tremendous human experiences ... the experiences of the Great Frontier. One is *migration*, that of leaving the home of one's ancestors to make oneself at home in the new land; the other is *occupation*, that of having to come to terms with or perish at the hands of the migrating culture. These two historically and necessarily related experiences provide the immediate and raw material for the first period in Commonwealth literature—the Colonial Period—and all later periods, movements, themes, mythologies inherit the effects of that first and often dual experience. (77)

These two experiences involve what Robertson calls "that Middle Passage," when one wanders between two worlds. He differentiates two different kinds of wandering, called exile and alienation:

Exile may be taken in Commonwealth literary studies to mean the sense of existing in two worlds, the physical here, the mental or ghostly there. Which is my own and only country? Alienation means being lost between two cultures, part of each residing in oneself so that one becomes a kind of cultural half-breed or *méti*[sic], living spiritually in a no-man's land. Which *is* my own real country? (79)

Whereas exile is found mostly in migration literature (i.e., settler literature) and alienation in occupation literature (i.e., immigrant literature), "both are inevitably intertwined parts of the phenomenon of the Middle Passage or slow metamorphosis; their twinning is an indication of the double helix that lies at the heart of Commonwealth literature" (79).

Robertson maintains that the added difficulties of immigrants as opposed to settlers, such as a new language and an unfamiliar culture, violently transform exile into alienation, a transformation which forms the plot of much immigrant fiction. In *The Viking Heart* this violent transformation is symbolized by Thor's death. However, the hope of identity remains: "The source of identity lies not in the environment nor in the society but in the historical process of the intertwining of exile and alienation" (84). Robertson concludes by suggesting that the way out of the Middle Passage and into identity is for writers to face the vacuum of this Passage and to create an imaginative framework in the form of a literature which cherishes the national memory of "that shock of migration or occupation" in order to come to a reconciliation with the alien environment. Dahlie acknowledges Salverson's contribution to this task when he says: "Perhaps her main contribution to the literature of exile in Canada is her depiction of immigrants who successfully embrace two worlds: they retain their original language and culture, yet they partake fully of those of the New World, and this sounds a new note in Canadian literature" (1986: 64).

In this respect, Salverson's work conforms to Eli Mandel's definition of ethnic literature as "a literature existing at an interface of two cultures, a form concerned with defining itself, its voice, the dialectic of self and other and the duplicities of self-creation, transformation and identities" (1977: 65). Mandel, like Robertson, envisions ethnicity as a state "in between," the loss of self and its recovery. Mandel's emphasis is on the creation of the self, the "writing into existence" of a self that has become lost in the process of being translated into another culture, for ethnicity, Mandel argues, "sets into motion for the writer a whirligig or duality that can only be resolved in a myth, a restructured self, a fictional being" (61). However, Mandel himself does not recognize Salverson's as a Canadian ethnic voice, but rather classifies her among those authors who still belonged to an integrated community that regards itself as an authentic culture instead of an ethnic group. Mandel probably based his judgement on a reading of *The Viking Heart* and, like many other critics, mistakenly read Salverson's attempts at translating her Icelandic background into a Canadian idiom in order to resolve her duality as an authentic cultural account. Moreover, as I have tried to show in this and the previous chapter, even the Icelandic immigrants, who still possessed a sense of "authentic culture" and "integrated community," had already entered the process of self-definition through the creation of mythic self-images and writing, so that Mandel's classification, at least in the case of Icelandic immigrant writing, appears to be at fault.

In her article on ethnic prairie writing, Palmer also concludes that the thematic preoccupations of immigrant literature echo those found in Canadian literature in general. The outsider's sensibility of the immigrant merely adds an extra dimension, an intensity. She defines the sense of alienation, especially strong among the second generation, as marginality, "the result of being socialized into two different, often incompatible worlds." Palmer finds:

a frequent response portrayed in ethnic fiction to tensions inherent in the
uneasy relationship between the impulse to preservation and that to synthesis:
the marginal man, a second-generation version of the uprooted immigrant
character who appears in various guises in fiction about ethnic experience on
the Prairies. (1987: 67)

The clearest example of "the marginal man" in Salverson's works
is Salverson herself, the "heroine" of *Confessions*. Her social alienation, her marginality, she tried to "cure" with her writing: her fiction
reveals both her sharp awareness of immediate reality and her dreams
of an eventual release from alienation into identity, of entering into
the New World. Her romantic strain shows her urgent desire to
envision through fictional creation the possibility of release from that
wandering between worlds. At the same time she cannot escape realism, not even in her fiction, as she realizes that the experience of
alienation may not be forgotten but should be recreated in Canada's
literature to become a national memory, an imaginative framework.
Moreover, Salverson is caught in that very Canadian problem of
cherishing the past as well as the future, of cherishing both worlds
that keep her in "that Middle Passage." In spite of her marginal position and in spite of her rejection by her fellow West Icelanders,
Laura Goodman Salverson was not willing to give up her hopes for
a Canadian future in which the heritage of her people would play a
role along with the heritages of other immigrant groups.

Interestingly, Laura Goodman Salverson's position of being
poised between two worlds shows us the extent to which this position makes her a Canadian writer. As critics have pointed out since,
Canadian writers have come to accept marginality as their identity.
Marshall McLuhan (1977) has pointed out that Canada has never
been able to centralize because of its vast size and its small and culturally diverse population. It has never had a clearly defined national
identity or national goals. Instead, it can be characterized by its marginality: "[Chester] Duncan found the key with 'between-ness,' the
world of the interval, the borderline, the interface of worlds and situations" (233). McLuhan concludes: "Yes, Canada is a land of multiple borderlines, of which we have probed few. It is these multiple
borderlines that constitute Canada's low-profile identity, which, like
its territory, has to cover a lot of ground" (246). More recently,
Dahlie has come to the same conclusion, although from a different
vantage point. He regards the immigrant exile to the New World, like
Ovid regarded his, as a "removal from the centre of civilization to its

periphery" (1986: 10). Hutcheon, too, has emphasized McLuhan's view: "Since the periphery or the margin might also describe Canada's perceived position in international terms, perhaps the postmodern ex-centric is very much a part of the identity of the nation" (1988: 3). Moreover, her assertions show that Canada's identity of marginality is now felt to be a positive identity, and the periphery to be the place of possibility:

The ex-centric is a mirror of Canadian marginalization—but as more a privileged than a denigrated position. It both challenges the general notion of centre and, at the same time, undoes that particular idea of the possibility of a centred, coherent subjectivity. (175)

Salverson was right, then, to dream about the possibility of entering into the New country from the margin where she found herself, although she might never have dreamed that the release from the Middle Passage would turn out to be for Canada to claim the Passage as its own.

Laura Goodman Salverson created an insider's fictional image of immigrant Canada at a time when Canada needed writers to define a fictional image of its society and reality. At the same time, her fiction clearly reflects the concerns of both Western Icelandic and Canadian literature at the time of her writing. Most importantly, however, Salverson herself embodies both the peculiar Western Icelandic identity characterized by Matthiasson as "assimilated ethnic," and the Canadian identity of marginality, while she continually set herself up as a mediator between the two cultures and tried to come to a self-definition through her writing. Her marginality, however, has been intensified poignantly by the fact that she has been rejected by the two groups that she was so desirous to incorporate and unite within herself. Her rejection among the West Icelanders I discussed in the previous section. After her initial popularity among Canadians, her name quickly receded into the background. It is now only occasionally mentioned in a literary survey, with the exception of a few more elaborate discussions by McCourt (1970); Thompson (1980); Stuewe (1984); Moss (1974; 1981); Dahlie (1986); and by Gunnars (1986) and Craig (1985). Out of these critics, only Gunnars, Stuewe, Dahlie and Moss take the trouble to view her work in the broader framework of her background and her motives. Other critics simply dismiss her work as immigrant literature of negligible artistic interest and quality.[97]

It is rather surprising to find that even today Salverson should remain ignored, especially since marginality and ethnicity have become fashionable concepts in Canadian literary criticism. One can only guess at the underlying reasons. A few critics have pointed to the neglect to which immigrant literature has been subjected (Robertson 1976: 81; Palmer 1987: 50-51; Thompson 1980: 237; McKenzie 1961: 33). The most generally suggested reasons are that the works are not held to be of any artistic merit, that they pose generic problems, and that they are not Anglo-Canadian. As Palmer puts it:

> Literature by ethnic writers has generally been regarded as outside the
> literary traditions of French and English Canada. This has not made for easy
> recognition and acknowledgement of those ethnic writers who wrote of
> their experiences of the New World from the perspective of "the other"....
> Indeed, out of the history of English Canada, with its evolution from British
> Empire to Commonwealth, and the accompanying assimilationist policies
> of Canadian governments toward ethnic groups, emerged a mainstream
> literature of Anglo-Celtic voice which reflected an assimilationist bias. (64)

It is true that most of the critics who have discussed Salverson's work, have done so only in a context of "immigrant literature." It is also true that such chapters on "immigrant literature" are set apart from the rest of Canadian literature and are usually discussed in either an apologetic or a dismissive way. The inclusion of immigrant literature in courses on Canadian literature still constitutes the proverbial exception to the rule. An apparent exception, Frederick Philip Grove, of course chose to assume an Anglo-Canadian voice. This exclusion occurs in spite of the fact that immigrant novels continue to be, in Hutcheon's words, "very Canadian investigations into the nature of national and cultural identity" (1988: 194).

Apparently, the Anglo-Celtic voice of Canadian mainstream literature prefers to ignore those other voices for which it has no genres and which do not fit its established profile of literary merit, even when those voices sound truly Canadian. Some writers are more marginal than others, it seems, even in an open and ex-centric postmodern age. Thus the voice of a writer who represents both the Icelandic-Canadian and the Canadian identity is muted, victimized by what it characterizes. In Margaret Atwood's analysis of Canadian literature, Canada is the land of victims which both manufactures and attracts failure and provides it with an appropriate setting. Unfortunately, Laura Goodman Salverson is one of the victims for which Canadian literature seems to have no place, as it continues to be dominated by its Anglo-Canadian mainstream. Whether Salverson ever realized it or not, her fate as an author turned out to be very similar to that of Ninna, the anti-heroine of *The Viking Heart* who marries an Anglo-Canadian: slapped in the face and considered dead by West Icelanders, who regarded her as having "sold herself to the fleshpots," and yet never truly acknowledged and accepted by the Anglo-Canadians, she is out of the story.

NOTES

1. Stephan G. Stephansson, "Bragamál," trans. Kristjana Gunnars (Guðmundsson 1982: 58).

2. "But lost is not the language, / although difficult to recognize, and mixed, / among a people who have to find their soul / in their native country. / Although here are our work and welfare / our hope, progress, and profit, / there are our beginnings, strength and courage, / and our youth, history, and poems." Stephan G. Stephansson, "Særi eg yður við sól og báru," *Andvökur* 1: 228. Where I could not find an existing translation of the poetry discussed in this chapter, I have used my own. As my translations, however, make no claim to poetic value but merely serve to make the contents of the poems understood, I have included them in a footnote and left the originals in the text.

3. This impression was initially stimulated by the argument of Matthiasson (1974), to the effect that the Icelandic Canadians were keen to achieve the amount of assimilation which would enable them to move freely in the social and economic spheres of Canadian society: "They wanted to hold on to certain Icelandic traditions, and particularly literary ones, but they refused to be identified as 'ethnics' or 'hyphenated' Canadians" (58). The connection, however, between the desire for accepted assimilated social status and the preference for the preservation of literary rather than other Icelandic traditions, is nowhere directly made in his article, and I, therefore, assume responsiblity for it.

4. *Ég á orðið einhvern veginn / ekkert föðurland* ("Útlegðin"). Trans. Paul Sigurdson (Stephansson 1987: 6). The original text was taken from Stephansson (1939: 91). All further references to Stephan G. Stephansson's poetry in the text, unless otherwise indicated, will be to this edition.

5. This had been suggested earlier, for instance by Lindal (1969: 2), who partly attributes the outburst of literary activity to tensions within society, and partly to the blended heredities of Norse and Celtic people

who were both of high-standing literary cultures. Johnson mainly adheres to the latter assumption, and speculates a little on it in his article "Our Heritage" (1950: 13-16). The assumption is an interesting one, which has recently been more carefully and elaborately studied by Sigurðsson (1988). Western Icelandic writers do indeed display a fond awareness of affinity between the Icelanders and the Irish and Scottish (see e.g. Jóhann Magnús Bjarnason, *Í Rauðárdalnum*, and Stephan G. Stephansson, "Patrekur frændi," ("Cousin Patrick"). In the latter, Stephan draws on the analogy between the Icelandic and the Irish immigrant experience and hardships in the Western hemisphere. There are strong indications in Western Icelandic writing that the Icelanders also looked to the Scottish and Irish groups in Canada as an example of how to assimilate into Anglo-Canadian society but maintain a distinct cultural identity within that society. This subject deserves further study, but is, unfortunately, beyond the scope of this work.

6. Stephan G. Stephansson's poem "Á Ferð og Flugi" ("En route"), for instance, which deals with the early immigrant experience on the prairies, is written in light-flowing lines, whereas his poems "Kolbeinslag" ("Kolbein's metre") and "Sigurður Trölli" ("Sigurður the Troll"), which deal with the Icelandic past, are in very strict, traditional metres.

7. *Íslendingar verða ætíð hrifnari af umgjörð myndarinnar heldur en af myndinni sjálfri....*(quoted in Skúlason 1967: 33)

8. See Mowat's interview with one of the last living *alþýðuskáld* in Canada, Franklin Johnson, who composes both in Icelandic and in English (1992: 69-85). See also Jónsson (1940) for a discussion of an earlier Western Icelandic farmer-poet.

9. "My poems are not remarkable, / my dear friends! / But often I compose / differently from the others." "Ávarp" ("Address"; Júlíus 1945: 5). All further references in the text will be to this edition unless otherwise indicated.

10. "Although the Atlantic ocean parts our estates and our lands / you young man and well-born maiden, / we now shake hands and strengthen bonds of affection / and connect the nation with home 'brú'." The pun in the final sentence does not translate well: the Icelandic word for a bridge is *brú*, which is (approximately) pronounced as the English word "brew," so that for Icelanders the last sentence suggests both a connection through a home bridge as well as through home brew.

11. In Paul Sigurdson's translation: "Warm of heart and coiffed in style /
Close by me sits (the) frúin*; / Were she not a married gal, / There'd
be 'something duin.'"
  * Translator's note: "I have used the Icelandic word 'frúin' which
    means 'wife' to rhyme with the English word he himself [i.e. Káinn]
    has blended into the Icelandic." *Lögberg-Heimskringla* 18 Jan. 1991: 4.

12. "Ah, here's a heavy theme that needs attending, / I cannot say just
where it might be ending. / Watch your necks, dear fellows, joy is
dying, / Here I sit alone with sorrows, sighing. / Gudmund*, one of
Iceland's trolls is raving, / Sailing west intent on language-saving. /
I'm told he hates the trend to English slanging, / And those who
mix the tongues will soon be hanging. / Perhaps he thinks that I'm
the one who's sinning, / But let me ask on whom he is beginning? /
Sure Paul and I will meet our final hour, / Bedangling from the highest gibbet-tower. / He should be dangled for such nonsense, prickly, /
I think 'tis best to hang him also, quickly."
  * Translator's note: "Gudmundur Finnbogason ... one of Iceland's
    foremost scholars, a man with great personality and sparkling wit."
    Trans. Paul Sigurdson, *Lögberg-Heimskringla* 14 Dec. 1990: 6.

13. "So dream about your lovely Island Fjord, / And childhood haunts
upon the upland run; / Where nowhere do the colors of the land, /
Shine fairer in the glory of the sun; / As shepherds halloo from the
mountain passes, / Their flocks descending to the valley grasses."
Trans. Paul Sigurdson, *Lögberg-Heimskringla* 22 Feb. 1991: 3.

14. "To remember you, settlement so dear to me, / is well-deserved,
although the time be short; / this is what an Icelandic woman
demanded yesterday, / who came to me only in a dream. //
Although you lack the waterfalls, fjords and much, / which the
Mountain Maid* could offer us, / this is compensated for by the
shining ornament of your fields / and the forest wide and mighty. //
You do not starve your children, my dear countryside, / and let them
have the sunshine for sale; / all they need grows in your gardens, /
and God has blessed it all. // You gave us the handsomest maidens
and men, / whom our times admire most, / and still the wind whis-
pers in the oak trees, / that the top has not yet been reached."
  * Mountain Maid: Iceland.

15. "Yes, Icelandic we want to be / on the beautifully green prairies of the
Western hemisphere; / and carrying one another's burden / we reach
out a brotherly hand to each other; / even if it could cost us at times
/ a blow in the face or a beating up; / with nationalistic chauvinism
and arrogance / people fight and tell each other off at meetings."

16. "This is not nationalism / and thence even less religion, / but Icelandic spitefulness / and damned bloody implacability."

17. "All forgot is Iceland's saga glory, / Buried, shovelled deep, I tell the story. / Here the English tongue is silent never. / Icelanders should shut their trap forever." Trans. Paul Sigurdson, *Lögberg-Heimskringla* 18 Oct. 1991: 4.

18. "Now the poetic urge / of our countrymen is disappearing / Hardly any inherit the thirst for knowledge / from their fathers and mothers. / When I came with my slim volume / he bought it unwillingly / did not read one line in it / but put it on a shelf." See also his "Islendingsminnin 1922" (139).

19. "As time goes trotting on I feel / There's something awful funny; / They would have given me a horse, / Had I but stacks of money." Trans. Paul Sigurdson, *Lögberg-Heimskringla* 15 Mar. 1991: 7.

20. "I took the creed of a heifer's rump, / And I've found that it doesn't fail; / In the futter floor I have to stand, / For the holy spirit's mercy-grail." Trans. Paul Sigurdson, *Lögberg-Heimskringla* 1 Mar. 1991: 4.

21. "The church was clergy-consecrated; / Women kept sinning unabated; / The dance-hall portals opened wide, / And Icylanders [sic] thronged inside. / On Sunday morns they slept and snored, / Uncaring of redemption's word. / The devil strove to get his dues, / And capitalized on empty pews." Trans. Paul Sigurdson, *Lögberg-Heimskringla* 15 Mar. 1991: 7.

22. "I feel content that you would grin with me / Could you but witness what I hear and see. / For you were not accustomed — not your fate — / To be thus borne along by friends, in state. / But death has changed your status, so that now / Your friends assemble in your honor, bow / Their heads in faith, in grief, humility, / And all unite in speaking well of thee!" Trans. Bogi Bjarnason (*Icelandic Lyrics*: 237).

23. "Old Bacchus gave me a taste / of the best quality, beer and spirits, / and it is thanks to him, / that you are not my wife!"

24. "Gunnar would rather go to hell / Than to be home on native shores / There he had polar bear and seal / Swarms of shark and eiderduck on the sands. / Living dead both long and well / He cheerfully played with sky-born ducks. / In America he endured tormenting snows, / slavery and privations with numerous countrymen, / 'And yet I hold Gunnar's saga dear'." The last line is a parodic reference to a famous poem by Jónas Hallgrímsson, "Gunnarshólmi," which had been inspired by the same scene from *Njáls saga*.

25. Jóhannessen (1958: 106-08) has pointed out that Káinn is only one among very few Icelandic poets whose poetic reference to *Njáls saga* is irreverent.

26. "I do not have to hide the fact / that at times it got cold / but joy enveloped our bones — — / and God knows what I mean, / for hope warms everything."

27. See, for instance, his letter to his father-in-law Jón Jónsson in 1891, and his letter to Jónas Hall, 15 April 1907, both in *Bréf og Ritgerðir* (1:1938) 39, 156 (further references to this collection of letters and essays will be to *BOR* and to this edition). See also the "Autobiographical Fragments" (Stephansson 1988: 17, 20).

28. For the influence of socialism and the American freethinkers on Stephan G. see Halldórsson (1961: 69-74). Shorter studies which discuss the influence of the freethinkers are McCracken (1983); and Jóhannesson (1966: 231-37). For discussions of socialist and Marxist influences on Stephan G.'s work, see Mowat (1990); Kristjánsson (1953); and Jóhannes úr Kötlum (1936).

29. For an elaborate and informative explanation of the relationship between Stephan G. and the Western Icelandic community see McCracken (1982).

30. "Somehow it has come upon me, / I've no fatherland; / Though my heart with love is bounded / With a lasting band / To my native soil that blessed me / As a growing boy, / When the world its shining glory / Gave me hope and joy. // Never could my foster mother / Take my mother's place; / Always there was something lacking, / She could not replace. / I have yet to know the meaning / Of her legacy, / Always there's an awkward feeling / 'Twixt herself and me."
Trans. Paul Sigurdson (Stephansson 1987: 6).

31. "We're enriched by our vision not stories, / And mostly the truth is obscure, / But there is one standard prevailing / Which tells if an age will mature; / To live not for years but for ages / And not to claim all of one's wages / For man's greatest good to endure. // Through seasons of winter and summer, / This truth we instinctively see, / To make what is good into better / And strive for the best that can be. // It isn't the unfulfilled present / But the future more noble and pleasant, / That world which the prophet can see."
Trans. Paul Sigurdson (Stephansson 1987: 53-54).

32. *Það er satt, að það, sem þið kallið 'óljóst' hjá mér, er 'torf.' Ég þreytti við að rista það betur, en þá hékk hugsunin ekki í því.* Stephan G. uses a metaphor here that does not translate well into English: he describes the

unclarities in his poetry as "turf" or "sod," and maintains the metaphor by describing the polishing process in terms of turf cutting.

33. "And finally, as you had loosed yourself, / You settled down the same as before / So clear and pure into a well-cleared path / As a bright blue silk thread — / As a great thought, strong and free, / which strengthens and gladdens me / Yet struggles in the breach between rhyme and tongue / And heaps up wrong alliterations."

34. "So warm then, Canada, in your lap / The chilled kinship and memory of the native country! / Protect the freest, the well-willed young ideals, / protect the home country of each and every nation and language! / A new-coming flatterer may extensively overpraise you, / If he denounces his native land, do not believe him, / Because he would sell your honour if it came to the test, / His horizon is easily got profit — / Such a disposition flows with an assassin's blood."

35. "Because the ways and thoughts of today / reign there with unlimited power, / as the settlement springs up without a past / and is brought up by the present. / And the great progress and culture here / are not delayed by memories / if you finish ploughing, you get a field, / if you give up, a nameless grave."

36. *Ég þykist hafa sett þá litlu mynd, sem ég dró af "landnáms-konu" íslenzkri, inn í ramma landnámssögunnar, lands-náttúru og nýbyggða-lífsins, eins langt og hægt er í stuttorðri ljóðagjörð....* (BOR 1: 346).

37. *tilfinningin, sem okkur flestum er sameiginleg, að reyna að standa sem fjærst þeim, sem orðið hafa þjóð sinni til minnkunar....* (BOR 1: 106).

38. "To strands held by strangers I come with a love / That streams in the tenderest tones, / Yet green are far hillocks that grip at my heart / The graves of my ancestors' bones. / I know why that homeland has held me so close; / For hued with the mem'ries of yore / Each vista of earth bears a voice from the past / By valley and mountain and shore; / And out of those voices comes strength for the strife, / The strain that man's living requires; / Even so is the sanction that every land gives / Long sacred to mothers and sires."
Trans. Watson Kirkconnell (Stephansson 1987: 10).

39. "Land to which is hallowèd / My toil, my children's cradle-stead! / Put have I in lay and line / Mid thy grasses poems mine; / Later will thy grass for me / Make o'er my head poetry. / With thee as home my mind / And hearth are intertwined. / I do not in millions measure / At how much thy worth I treasure, / Nor do I in verse enfold / All thy praises hundredfold." Trans. Skuli Johnson (1950: 51-52).

40. "But I esteem you more for your ice and snow, / because I am ice and snow's adopted child. / And in my life I have often been closer to winter / than to my summers, whatever way things go. // I know it is fortune's game to live and enjoy, / to play and rest is what the mind chooses. / But I think it is greater to struggle and break / the ice of human experience in the blizzards of life."

41. "And the people with Icelandic progressiveness / reconciled themselves to the outlook of the future, / and the settlement grew day by day, / and their dream gradually came true. / — Although many realizations were shipwrecked, / it is hidden in one's experience: / that one never struggles for nothing / in the wilderness of the Northwest country" (Guttormsson 1947: 80). All further references to Guttormur's work will be to this edition, unless otherwise indicated.

42. The complete text of "Sandy Bar" can be found, together with two different English translations (by Paul Sigurdson and Kristjana Gunnars) in *Aurora*, a collection of poems and translations recently published by Guttormur's granddaughter Heather A. Ireland (1993).

43. "Indian summer is a woman / with an abundance of black hair, / a copper-coloured face, youthful / and mild, dark eyelashes. // Her hair is the dusk of winter's short days / that falls with a starry glow / her complexion is the autumnal / bleached straw-colour of the fields. // With leaves of rainbow colours, / colours of the most precious poetry / this beauty props herself up, and decorates herself / with the pearls of dew and rime // And then she throws off her leafy dress / — cold is close at hand — / In a chalk white polar bear cloak / she dresses herself and disappears."

44. "Two vagrants are bumming support / friends of the masses and the rich. / They cheat, betray and swindle / sons of politics."

45. "He always will prosper, in trade and in craft, / with mansion and grand summer cottage. / The rights of the first-born, embezzled by graft, / Are his for a poor mess of pottage. / He only will thrive and be happy in soul, / As fat as his black heart is clever — / The grain and the seed merchant who cunningly stole / The blessing of farmers forever." Trans. Watson Kirkconnell (1939: 116).

46. "Such are our Indians: tattered wrecks, / In exile from life's busy strand; / Held in this limbo by law's checks / That will not let them roam the land — / Land, where their fathers used to play, / Land, that is theirs no longer now, / Land, that at best they may survey / With silent grief and gloomy brow. // A roasting-stake above the fire / Is bending, spitted through a cur / (Shot with an arrow when desire

/ For dinner smote the reveller). / Low on their haunches they devour / The reeking fragments, loath to wait; / This white dog over which they glower / Stands for the White Man, whom they hate." Trans. Kirkconnell (1939: 117).

47. "Honey-bees of my high ideals / Have I imprisoned in this my winter, / Night and day in the chilling darkness / Down in the cellar beneath my spirit." Trans. Kirkconnell (1939: 113).

48. *Í ljóðagerð Guttorms kennir margra grasa, sem okkur hér heima á Íslandi eru lítt eða ekki kunn. Það eru bæði yrkisefnin sjálf og skilningur höfundarins og skoðanir, er okkur koma ókunnuglega, líka blærinn, sem um efnið og meðferð þess leikur.* (1947: 32)

49. *Skáldin eru að lýsa þessum mönnum, lífinu, sem býr hið innra með þeim, kjörum þeirra og umhverfi. Þau standa eftirtakanlega föstum fótum í veruleikanum. Lýsingar þeirra eru látlausar, ljósar og sannar.* (1930: xl)

50. Beck mentions Jóhann Magnús' diary as having been submitted for publication just before his death (1977: xxi-ii). Short passages from it have been published by Hrund Skúlason (1967). Nevertheless, I have not been able to find a published copy nor any bibliographical references; so far, it remains unknown to me whether the complete diary actually appeared in publication.

51. *Það sem heillaði hann, mun hafa verið mannkærleikurinn og hin réttláta reiði Dickens, gagnvart rangsleitni og miskunnarleysi þjóðskipulagsins; með öðrum orðum, raunsæi þess höfundar.* (1946: 12)

52. Technically, Jóhann Magnús' first publication came out in 1887, called *Kvæði* ("Poems"). This 15-page volume, however, contained only one poem by Jóhann Magnús himself.

53. *Börn geta stundum fengið undarlegar hugmyndir um það, sem ber í kringum þau, og að þau álíta þessar hugmyndir sínar áreiðanlegan sannleika. En þó að þau gæti ekki að því, þá eru þó þessar hugmyndir þeirra byggðar á glöggri og skarpri eftirtekt. Eg hefi iðulega tekið eftir því, síðan ég komst á fullorðinsárin, að flest börn leita betur eftir orsökum viðburðanna í daglega lífinu, heldur en flest fullorðna fólkið.... Eiríkur Hansson—skáldsaga frá Nýja Skotlandi* ("Eiríkur Hansson, A Novel from Nova Scotia"; Bjarnason 1973: 31). This book will henceforth be referred to as *EH* after quotations; all references will be to this edition.

54. *enginn Víkingur, sem býst að sigla hvert haf og taka strandhögg á hverju nesi. Hann er frumbýlingur sem ræktar blómsturgarð inni í skóginum á vatnsbakkanum....* (Guðmundsson 1982: 44).

55. *Vel veit ég, að sögusögn Dickens er ekki góð norræna; hann er of langorður, smásmugulegur, veigalítill og ópolandi tilfinningasamur fyrir marga. Það var þessi*

tilfinningasemi, sem skarpari "kritík" vœmir nú við, sem einmitt hreif hversdags-mennina mest. Ég er ekki heldur hrifinn af þessum kostum eða ókostum ykkar; ég er of norrænn (quoted in Skúlason 1947: 35).

56. *Við urðum undir eins beztu vinir. Ef til vill drógumst við svo fljótt hvor að öðrum af þeirri ástæðu, að við vorum báðir að miklu leyti útlendingar, og fundum svo fljótt til þess, að hinir innlendu skólabræður okkar litu á okkur sem blátt áfram útlendinga, þó að þeir á hinn bóginn væru okkur jafnan alúðlegir og góðir.* (EH 332)

57. *Hendrik Tromp var sannur Hollendingur og unni af hjarta feðrajörð sinni og þjóð, og áleit móðurmál sitt og bókmenntir þjóðar sinnar framar öðrum tungumálum og öðrum bókmenntum. Hann var stoltur af herfrægð forfeðra sinna og gat rakið ætt sína til afa Van Tromps, hins mikla hollenzka sjóliðs-foringja. Hendrik kunni fádæmin öll af hollenzkum þjóðsögum, og þreyttist aldrei á að segja þær...* (332)

58. *Þú átt meira krafta og hæfileika en þú hefir sjálfur hugmynd um. Gamla hrjóstruga Island hefir búið þig út með gott veganesti, sem þú hefir aldrei notað, síðan þú komst til þessa lands,—það hefir gefið þér dýrmætan fjársjóð, sem þú hefir aldrei kunnað að meta. En þessi huldu öfl vil ég nú vekja hjá þér, þetta veganesti og þenna fjársjóð verðurðu nú að nota, í hvert sinn og tækifæri sem gefst. Vornætur á Elgsheiðum—sögur* ("Spring Nights on Moose Heights— Stories"; Bjarnason 1982: 104). All further references following quotations will be to *VE* and to this edition.

59. *Í Rauðárdalnum* (Bjarnason 1976). All further references following quotations will be to this edition.

60. (Bjarnason 1977). This collection will henceforth be referred to as *Gim* following quotations in the text; all references will be to this edition.

61. *"Ertu þá ekki Eskimói?"*
"Nei, ég er Íslendingur."
"Vildirðu ekki heldur vera Eskimói?"
"Eg vil helst vera það sem ég er, nefnilega Íslendingur."
"Ja, hérna!" sagði litla stúlkan. "Eg hélt, að öll börn vildu vera Eskimóabörn. —Ja, hérna!"
"Eg veit samt, að þú ert góður drengur," sagði Eskimóadrengurinn, "ég veit, að þú sért ósköp góður drengur, þó þú sért ekki Eskimói." (*Gim* 122-23)

62. *Þó Magnús vænti góðs af öllum mönnum, án hliðsjónar af þjóðerni þeirra eða hörundslit, báru Íslendingar ægishjálm yfir annarra þjóða menn. Það lét nærri að hann skoðaði íslenzkt þjóðerni sem meðfædda dyggð.* (1946: 5)

63. *Og það, sem mig rekur minni til frá þeim árum, finnst mér nú að hafi verið svo skemmtilegt og bjart, allt svo **einkennilega** skemmtilegt og bjart, en ekkert*

óviðfelldið né ljótt. Og þegar ég renni huganum til æskustöðvanna ... þá finnst mér það hljóti að vera langfegursti bletturinn, sem til er undir sólinni, og Ísland langtilkomumesta landið á allri jörðinni. (EH 9-10)

64. *Það lá vel á honum. Hann iðaði allur af kæti og velti hnotunni til á allar hliðar og horfði á mig með köflum og skrækti. Það var eins og hann væri að segja mér, að nú væru allir farnir. "Allir farnir,—allir farnir, allir,—allir— allir!" heyrðist mér hann segja. "En því fer þú ekki—þú ekki-þú ekki?" Svo náði hann loksins kjarnanum úr hnotunni og lét skelina detta niður. Svo hljóp hann grein af grein og upp og ofan björkina og skrækti óaflátanlega. Það var eins og sá skrækur væri háði blandinn. "Ég get bjargað mér" heyrðist mér hann segja, "og **ég** get vel lifað hér, en það gátu **þeir** ekki—þeir ekki—þeir ekki ar-r-r-r!"* (EH 179-80)

65. *En nú er að byrja á því atriði, sem ég hét að segja frá. Það var þrekvirki, eða öllu heldur ofdirfskubragð, sem er áreiðanlega einsdæmi í sögu Vestur-Islendinga,—ofdirfsku-tiltæki, sem enginn hefði vogað að gjöra, nema sá, er hefir alveg óblandað norrænt blóð í æðum sínum, og öll einkenni víkingsins sameinuð í réttum hlutföllum.—Eg segi nú söguna, eins og ég hef heyrt hana, og eins og hún er sögð,—sem nokkurs konar þjóðsaga þar austur við sjóinn.* (VE 143).

66. For a closer examination of the folk tale elements in Jóhann Magnús Bjarnason's "Íslenzkt heljarmenni" see D'Arcy and Wolf (1992).

67. *Einu sinni fyrir aldaöðli var ungur kóngsson, sem var svo vitur, ljúfur og réttlátur, að hans líka var hvergi að finna í víðri veröld. Hann bjó í stórri og skrautlegri höll, er stóð á frjósömu, víðáttumiklu sléttlendi.* (Gim 233-36)

68. *Ég er Íslendingur eins og þið. Ég á heima í Manitoba í Canada. Ég ætla að vera þar alla mína æfi, en samt vil ég ávallt vera Íslendingur.* (Gim 141)

69. In his account of Norse mythology, Snorri Sturluson mentions a distinction between light and dark elves (*The Prose Edda* 1966). As he is our only source on this distinction, it is not clear whether such a distinction ever existed or whether it should be regarded as a Christian influence.

70. *"Með þeim hætti get ég þó bezt sýnt og sannað af hvaða ættstofni ég er kominn, að ég láti mér farast eins og góðum syni við þá konu, sem gekk mér í móður stað, þegar ég var ómálga barn." Drottningin brosti ánægjulega. Hún vissi nú, að hann var góður sonur.* (Gim 256-57)

71. See, for instance, also "Indíánahöfðinginn" ("The Indian Chief"); "Ráð hins eirrauða manns" ("Advice of the Red Man"); and "Ættarfylgjan" ("The Family Fetch"), all in *Gimsteinaborgin*, and the poem "Haugur hins hvíta manns" ("White Man's Grave Mount"), *Vestan um Haf* 96-100.

72. *stjórnist af heilbrigðu viti og mannúð. Hugsjónir fortíðarinnar og draumar*
    framtíðarinnar gætu þá að einhverju leyti orðið að veruleika, en ekki eingöngu
    innantóm orð.... "Úr Þokunni," *Dagshríðar Spor* (Finnsdóttir 1946: 70).
    All further references to this collection will be to *DS*.

73. *Ævilaun útlendingsins eru oftast rýr, og ávalt hin sömu: Honum er gefið land, að*
    vísu, en hann gefur í staðinn ævina, heilsuna og alla starfskraftana. Já, landið
    tekur hann sjálfan, líkama og sál, og börnin hans í þúsund liðu. (*DS* 205)

74. *Ragnhildur elskaði enn þjóðerni sitt og tungu; en hún hafði öðlast við það*
    víðsyni og umburðarlyndi, sem árin og lífsreynslan ein geta veitt. Og hún varð að
    viðurkenna í huga sér, að rás örlaganna hefðu breytt öllu viðhorfinu. Hin unga,
    uppvaxandi Canada þjóð var að líkindum á leiðinni með að svelgja upp
    þjóðerni hennar, hana sjálfa og barnið hennar; en þeim hjónunum hafði auðnast,
    að bjarga því í tíma frá skipbroti, sem þeim var dyrmætast—ást sinni og sam-
    búð.... En kynslóðir halda áfram að koma og fara,—eins og vindurinn, sem
    þýtur um eyru manns—eins og laufblöðin, sem fljóta á fallandi árstraumi....
    Vindurinn blæs—ryk aldanna fýkur í sporin—og áður en varir sjást þeirra
    engin merki. En draumar mannkynsins halda áfram að birtast og hverfa—
    og birtast á ný——og með hverjum nýjum draum kviknar ný von, og—með
    voninni nýtt líf. (*DS* 229-30)

75. *Náið samband við fortíðina er vafalaust meginorsök þess, að Íslendingum er*
    gjarnara að sjá sitt eigið þjóðlíf sem lóðréttan þverskurð frá fornöld til nútíðar
    heldur en sem þverskurð af nútíðinni einni. Lóðréttu línurnar auka ekki lítið á
    stærð þessarar sérstæðu, ef ekki einstæðu, þjóðlífsmyndirnar, þar sem horfnar
    kynslóðir eru látnar bæta upp fæð lifenda (1965: 26). Trans. Einarsson
    (1975: 31).

76. *erfðirnar fylgja kynslóðunum, hvort sem eldra fólkinu kemur til hugar að reyna*
    að svifta þá yngri erfðaréttinum, eða þeim yngri að neita arfðinum. Erfðirnar
    eru óslítandi bönd lifandi blóðstrauma. Með þeim straumi fljóta skapgerð, útlit
    og eðli að meira eða minna leyti. Kynslóðirnar haldast í hendur, hvað sem menn
    segja. (*DS* 118-19)

77. *Og ég heyrði ótal raddir, er urðu fyrir mér sem ein röddin skýrust, sú rödd hró-*
    pandans, er til okkar kallar úr okkar eigin söngvum og sögum og öldum saman
    hefir talið í okkur orku, vit og mannlund. Hillingalönd (Finnsdóttir 1938:
    201). All further references to this volume will be to *HL* and to this
    edition.

78. *Ibsen kunni að lýsa þeim háttum, er mætta mönnum og hugsjónum þeirra, kunna*
    að segja sögur, sem höfðu meiningu. Gömlu konurnar á Islandi, formæður okkar
    og ömmur, kunnu líka að segja sögur, sem höfðu dulda þýðingu—sögurnar um
    fátæku kotungssynina, sem ætíð báru sigur úr býtum í viðskiptum við konunga;
    því kotungssynirnir báru af konungunum að viti og mannkostum. Þær sögðu

sögur, eins og Ibsen, af mönnum, sem lentu í tröllahendur, töpuðu þar frelsi sínu og voru allir settir í sama mót, hlekkjaðir og kvaldir. Tröllin höfðu bolmagnið og kraftana; mennirnir vitið og hugprýðina—og þeir sigruðu.

Gömlu konurnar, sem sögðu börnunum svona sögur í rökkrinu, á meðan að aðrir sváfu, voru að móta sálarlíf barnanna—framtíð þjóðarinnar—kenna þeim aðdáun og virðingu fyrir viti og mannkostum, kenna þeim að gæta góðra erfða. Þannig vaka góðir menn yfir framtíðarvonum og framtíðarheill þjóðanna. "Erasmus frá Rotterdam," lecture, *Ferðalok* (Finnsdóttir 1950: 64).

79. *Þar heyrast kveða fagrar raddir, þar er hægt að hlusta eftir hjartaslætti þjóðarinnar, lesa um aldarháttinn og sjá menningarástandið.* "Um Vikivaka," lecture, *Ferðalok* 107.

80. *Ég ann öllum verulegum framförum og er glöð yfir því að vita, að þjóðin er að vakna til meðvitundar um, að vesalmenska er ekki til frambúðar. En það er engin framför í því, að öllum góðum og fögrum siðum og þjóðháttum sé kastað hugsunarlaust á sorphauginn. Íslensk gestrisni er ein af góðum siðunum, þar með meina ég ekki heimboð eða veisluhöld, eins og þú ætlaðir að hafa í kvöld, heldur hitt, að taka vel á móti og gjöra gott hungruðu og þreyttu ferðafólki, af hvaða stigum sem eru.* (DS 129)

81. *Þjóðsögurnar segja frá svo mörgu, sem fólki nú á dögum gengur illa að skilja, og þar kennir nú margra grasa, og af þeim má margt læra, þar á meðal, að þeir, sem taka efnið fram yfir andann og selja sál sína fyrir ytra glit, fá steina fyrir brauð.* (131)

82. *Hann hafði fundið í orðum gömlu konunnar þrá allra manna—löngunina eftir fegurð og friði. Henni hafði tekist að halda hlýju í sál sinni og gull í hjarta— hún var alin upp á brjóstum jarðar, og frá henni teigaði hún krafta sína. Hún hafði flutt gull og eld—haustliti skóganna—með sér, sem heimanmund, sá sjóður mundi endast henni til æviloka. Hana dreymdi um, að komast aftur austur í fegurð og blómailm. Þann draum ætlaði hann að láta rætast.* (57-58)

83. *En honum [Satan] var kunnugt, að af öllu því, sem Jahve hafði skapað, var Eva uppáhaldið hans, og að henni var ætlað hið ábyrgðarmikla hlutverk, að verða móðir og verndari hins unga og upprennandi lífs komandi kynslóða.* (DS 191)

84. "Utangarðs" means "outside the fence"; however, it is also often used as a figurative expression referring to someone who is regarded as a social misfit.

85. *Og stúlkurnar mínar—um það bil að þær hefðu verið búnar að vera léttakindur hér og þar um sveitina við lélegan kost og lítilsvirðingu, hefði þeim ef til vill fundust þær hafa himin höndum tekið, ef einhverjum bóndanum hefði þóknast að taka þær fyrir vinnukonur. Ég hefi séð þetta alt.* (HL 23)

86. *Og engu minna aðdáunarverðar eru fornaldar konurnar sem stóðu við hlið manna sinna, sterkar og frjálsar, héldu í hönd með börnum sínum, fylgdu að*

málum frændum og vinum og stjórnuðu heimilum sínum með skörungsskap og risnu. Erfiði landnámsáranna þroskaði sjálfstæði þeirra og frjálsmannlegt uppeldi jók á fegurð þeirra og atgerfi. Enda dáðust fornmenn að atkvæðamiklum konum; kemur það víða í ljós í fornsögunum....

Skörungsskapur, höfðingsháttur og drenglyndi formæðranna kemur svo víða í ljós í fornsögunum, að auðsætt er hversu almenn þau lyndiseinkenni hafa verið. Enda lögðu fornkonurnar ósvikinn skerf til að móta þjóðlífið. Þær ólu snildar menn og konur, sem sýndu á margvíslegan hátt, með framferði sínu, heimilisbrag og uppeldis áhrif mæðra sinna. "Minni Íslands," lecture, *Ferðalok* 12.

87. *Þú hefir sterka hönd, Þórhildur, það er lífskraftur í henni, það hefi ég lengi vitað. Ég var einu sinni næstum því dauður, en hin hlýja hönd þín sleppti mér ekki.... Ég greip í þetta strá, það var hönd þín og það afl, sem kallaði mig til baka, til lífsins, varst þú.* (DS 33-34)

88. *Ef varanlegur alheimsfriður á að verða annað og meira en fögur hugsjón, verða þjóðirnar, hver og ein, að líta eftir því, að einstaklingarnir innan þjóðfélagsins nái þeim menningarþroska, að líta ekki annara þjóða íbúa hornauga með lítilsvirðingu og tortryggni, heldur með vinsamlegum skilningi á högum og háttum, og virðingu fyrir menningu þeirra.* "Þakklætishátíðin," lecture, *Ferðalok* 129.

89. Laura Goodman Salverson, *Confessions of an Immigrant's Daughter* (1981: 238). This book will hereafter be referred to in the text as *Confessions*. All references will be to this new edition.

90. F.P. Grove's novels about pioneers in Canada did not appear in print until 1925, two years after the publication of *The Viking Heart*.

91. *The Viking Heart* (1975: 322). Further references to *The Viking Heart* in the text will be to this edition.

92. In fact, the word *skáld* in Icelandic is exclusively used for a poet. In Canada, however, its meaning was extended to writers of poetry and/or fiction.

93. Stephan mentions having been contacted by a Mrs Winifred Reeve, a literary critic, novelist and head of the Calgary branch of Canadian authors, who wanted to hear his opinion on *The Viking Heart*. According to Stephan, he answered by declaring the novel far inferior to the best that was being written in Iceland at the time, and added that Canadian literature was nothing much to write home about either (BOR 3: 140). In an earlier letter, Stephan writes that, although he has not read *The Viking Heart* yet, he considers Laura's use of Icelandic saga names unpoetic and weak (*óskáldlega veimil-títuleg*) and enough to make one unwilling to pick up the novel for reading (117).

94. Other critics adhering to this view are Clara Thomas (1987); Moss (1974); Godard (1977); Harrison (1977); Dahlie (1986). The main

argument on which the belief in a Canadian predilection for romance is based is that the settlers and immigrants in Canada looked back to their European past with nostalgia and a sense of exile. This is also the basis for Northrop Frye's famous analysis of the Canadian "garrison mentality," according to which Canadian settlers enclosed themselves away from Canadian reality in a garden-like nostalgic enclave (1970; rpt. 1971). Staines, in his introductory essay of *The Canadian Imagination: Dimensions of a Literary Culture* (1977: 73), has put it thus: "The basic purpose of the early literature of any colonial culture, like the basic purpose of transplanted peasant folk arts, is not to define the future but to consecrate the past. Faced by the wilderness, man seeks to assert the familiar, not to evoke the unknown..."

95. For her argument Gunnars defines autobiography as "an attempt at constructing a self out of the bits and pieces of a life seen from the inside" and a confession as "an opposite attempt at dismantling the self that has been created from without, by others" (148).

96. Interestingly, contemporary Icelandic-Canadian immigrant writer Kristjana Gunnars uses the same *huldufólk* metaphor in her poetic cycle *Wake-Pick Poems* to give expression to her dual sense of self and her search for belonging (see Chapter IV).

97. Apart from the issue of ethnicity, there is, of course, in Salverson's case, the factor of gender to be considered. The fact that she was a woman undoubtedly contributed to the lack of serious critical attention for her work by the Canadian literary establishment as well as the Western Icelandic writing community. With the recent upsurge of women's studies and feminist literary criticism, however, this particular aspect of Salverson's authorship has become the subject of several critical discussions. See, for instance, Wolf (1994); Powell (1992); Buss (1993: 170-79); Gunnars (1991); and Fairbanks (1986: 29-30, 174-75 and 202-18).

IV

"YOUR PEN IS YET A POWER IN YOUR HANDS"[1]
ICELANDIC-CANADIAN LITERATURE IN ENGLISH

CANADIAN AND ICELANDIC-CANADIAN LITERATURE
1940-1970

WITH THE FOUNDATION that had been laid for the development of a
Canadian literature in the 1920s and 1930s, the growth of fiction and
poetry which would give expression to Canadian reality and experience from a modern sensibility was accelerated in the following
decades. Canadian poetry saw a flowering of more experimental
techniques in an effort to find its own poetic voice. Unlike novelists,
the poets in Canada had already embarked on a more modernist
course in the 1920s, albeit cautiously, and thus removed many of the
remaining Victorianisms in Canadian poetry. Canadian fiction, however, was still engaged in its struggle out of the large body of popular escapist literature which held the market. Whereas poetry had
entered its course in search of its own voice, truly imaginative fiction
was written by a few individuals whom it was difficult to view in the
light of any particular development until much later. The Icelandic-
Canadian literature written at this time is very small in quantity and
belongs to the popular mass of literature.

CANADIAN POETRY

After the poets in the 1920s had cleared away the most important remnants of Victorian poetry and introduced free verse, contemporary subject matter and an ironic stance into Canadian poetry, there was more room for the poets of the next generation to start on the experiment of animating and giving voice to the Canadian world that was theirs but that had thitherto never found expression in its own terms. The first patriotic wave between the two World Wars had given way to a less vocal but more ingrained Canadianism. Moreover, Europe, which to Canadians had remained the centre of culture and civilization, lay in ruins after the barbarities of the Second World War. The poets who turned from Europe to their own country, trying to view it without the perspectives and prejudices of a colonial mindset, found they had to grapple with a vast, silent landscape. They faced the task of having to give that landscape a voice. Other poets turned instead to questions concerning civilization, the modern world and social issues. The Montreal poets, among them A.J.M. Smith and A.M. Klein, revolted against the colonialism, puritanism and Victorianism which they still saw as ruling Canadian society and art. Dorothy Livesay was one of the poets who wrote poems of social protest that were an outgrowth of the social problems resulting from the Depression.[2]

The difference in focus of these poets has given rise to a clash which still persists in the field of Canadian poetry: that between the so-called "cosmopolitans" or "internationalists" and the "regionalists" or poets who prefer indigenous subjects.[3] What they had in common, however, was a lack of audience. For the time being, these poets were too experimental for the taste of most Canadian readers. After all, as Munro Beattie wrote, being experimental was very "un-Canadian." It was not until the end of the 1940s and into the 1950s that periodicals were founded specifically as a forum for poetry, and that modern poetry came into its full force. Ironically, it was the poet Irving Layton who presented the poet figure as an outsider pitted against a bourgeois and hypocritical society, yet also he who gained Canadian poetry a larger audience through his public performances.

A poet who was very much on the borderline between the poetic tradition that went back to the Victorian age and the modernist movement was E.J. Pratt. He was very influential, especially in the way he reinvigorated Canadian poetry. Although he worked in a rather conventional mode and style, preferring narrative poetry of epic sweep and length, his work showed new faces of Canada from a modern, ironic perspective which appealed to the twentieth-century reader (Berg 1988: 60-61). Pratt always remained primarily a storyteller, and his myth-making powers, through which he linked prehistoric images with the contemporary technological, and the documentary impulse in his poetry, set an example which was to be followed and become a characteristic feature in later Canadian poetry.

The 1950s were very productive for Canadian poets, the wider publication of whose works indicated that they were now taken seriously. This decade saw the rise of the so-called mythopoeic poets, who employed myth as poetic structure and thus offered a way to combine myth and the modern world. These poets were mostly academics who had been influenced by the ideas on myth in literature by Northrop Frye. At the same time, we find a clearer sense of place developing in Canadian poetry. Many poets started to map out their own localities and communities.

The great and final breakthrough occurred in the 1960s. Poets were now not only articulate but also embarked on more original courses. This was a new generation with a new awareness of a Canadian history and heritage, no doubt emphasized by the 1967 Centennial celebration of Canada's Confederation. Canadians no longer needed to look to Europe for a past; they had their own. The great name of this decade is Al Purdy, the poet who in his poetry established a continuity between Canada's past and present: through his imagery and topics he shows history to be alive in the present. Purdy's work shuns stylistic conventions but is more a poetry of direct, daily speech. Purdy has been of tremendous influence, also on later writers such as W.D. Valgardson. His work set the tone for much Canadian poetry, especially with regard to his direct style and his explorations of landscape and recovery of history. In her introduction to *The New Oxford Book of Canadian Verse* Margaret Atwood remarks:

One cannot have flowers without roots. New cultures—made uneasy, perhaps, by their sensed absence of substructures—are constantly grubbing around in the soil. In English-Canadian poetry, geology and archeology are far more dominant as motifs than is botany: the images of permafrost and granite bedrock, blizzard, mountain, and glacier are repeatedly set against the state of being human and made to take its measure.... Like the poetry of Al Purdy, which in so many ways epitomizes it, English-Canadian poetry has been very fond of digging things up. (1982: xxx)

Atwood herself made her appearance as a poet during this period. She did not share Purdy's plain speech, but was more his academic counterpole. A pupil of Frye, she continued rather in the mytho-poeic mode, although she did share Purdy's interest in the recovery of Canadian history. Her style of cool detachment has found many followers. At the same time, Elizabeth Brewster continued in the more local vein, concentrating in her poetry on community life in the Maritimes. Her documentary style and her mapping out of local vil-lage life and characters have become a characteristic feature of much Canadian verse (Keith 103).

During this decade Canadian poetry embarks on its course of map-making, naming, recovering the Canadian past and exploring local and social landscapes, a course which it has continued to follow since. Important in this development is the increasingly conspicuous use made of the documentary long poem, a poetic form of which Dorothy Livesay remarks: "That this genre is particularly Canadian I would not dare to say. But it is a genre particularly suited to poetry throughout this vast and varied land" (1985: 127). Livesay argues that the three main elements to describe this genre are documentary, drama (dramatic or speaking voice) and political relevance. Stephen Scobie points to two main attractions of this form: "a fascination with the interplay between fact and fiction, history and imagination; and the attempt to define the identity of the self by a dialectic process of contrast to the other" (1984: 270). The documentary long poem can be seen to develop from E.J. Pratt's narrative long poems, and to gradually incorporate a growing interest in local history as well as self-discovery, both perhaps indicative of a "grubbing around in the soil" for roots. Moreover, the dialectic of fact and fiction, and of "self" and "other" mentioned by Scobie reflect the ongoing effort in Canadian poetry to recover a true inner voice and past through the deconstruction of the colonial voice and history which had muted the native.

Broadly typifying post-war Canadian poetry up until the 1970s is a predominant desire for recovery, of the past and the present, of an inner voice or "self." Canada shares this desire with other (post-)colonial countries, who all face the problem of "how to find an indigenous voice when the language and literary forms one has inherited have developed elsewhere in response to another environ-ment" (Brydon 1981: 278). Brydon argues that in order to address this problem the writer must be an interpreter rather than a creator in order to learn a new language to perceive the new reality: "the rational, masculine and European intelligence must die before an indigenous imagination may take shape." The colonial consciousness along with a language and imagination, imposed on a landscape it regarded as wild and hostile, must be silenced "until in nakedness and silence a new consciousness is born" (288). The general awareness among Canadians of this "dissociation between mind and environment," as John Moss calls it (1984: 26), is obvious from its expression in many articles by critics and writers alike, especially since Dennis Lee's article on "Writing in Colonial Space" (1974). Canadian poets have, however, since 1920 made a considerable start with the "re-invention" of language in Canada. Moss seeks to show that, with the poetry of Purdy and Atwood, word and element and word and experience have become one (1984: 41).

Regarding tone in Canadian poetry, Atwood notes that it is the elegiac and the satiric tone that have become most deeply embedded in the Canadian tradition. In a discussion of the Canadian imagination, David Stouck leads the elegiac tone back to what he calls the "instinctive quest for pastoral retreat and innocence," and the satiric tone to "the critical, self-conscious intentions of much Canadian art" (1972: 22). This self-consciousness can be attributed to the fact that the Canadian consciousness "was born literate and historical," as Peter Stevens points out, unlike the European one which goes back to ritual and myth (1977: 63). For Stevens, this explains why the figure of the explorer has become so important in Canadian poetry. The records of explorers and settlers, he claims, are the "proto-forms" of Canadian poetry, the texts on which the Canadian voice "can base its own language": "the search for roots within the continent by settlers is seen as a search for the roots of a true Canadian poetry, divorced from an alien past, ready to settle into indigenous patterns out of which might spring the material for ritual and myth" (65).

The pastoral strain in Canadian poetry, and indeed in Canadian literature as a whole, is most likely to have its roots in the fact that the settlers and immigrants were, as one critic puts it, "bounced from the Garden of Eden (even when in reality it was the slums ...)" and thus lived with a sense of exile in the new country as well as a feeling of self-blame for a lost world (Sutherland 1985: 38). Moreover, once in Canada, they had to come to terms with an alien landscape and people from both of which they sought shelter and refuge in community and domestic life; or, since this analysis by Northrop

Frye known as the "garrison mentality" no longer enjoys unanimous agreement, Canada itself was the pastoral refuge from Europe's industrial mud-pool, where Goldsmith's "The Deserted Village" could become "The Rising Village" again to combine rural virtues and urban wealth (Jones 1983: 257-59). As the settlement age was past and Canada became increasingly urban and industrialized, country-life became both a lost reality and the symbol of a lost childhood and innocence as writers went on journeys of self-discovery to a personal past. As Eli Mandel points out:

> The pastoral takes its shape as a contrast of complex and simple, in *all* the contrasts of complex and simple: the city as opposed to the country; the past (always ideal, golden, better) as opposed to the present (always crass, vulgar, worse than it was); the age of childhood as opposed to the adult world; innocence as opposed to experience.
>
> So it is that in Canadian writing the figure of the child assumes exceptional importance. (1971: 20)

The importance of the child in Canadian writing is perhaps hardly surprising in a culture that has only just reached maturity itself.

Finally, it should be noted that the contrast mentioned by Mandel as the shape of the pastoral can also be seen as the general shape of Canadian writing. Repeated evocation of a theme of marginality was mentioned earlier in this chapter and has frequently been commented upon as a characteristic both of Canada's position and of Canadian writing. As Sherrill Grace observes, modern Canadian writers often deal with "fundamental dualities thematically, but also create forms, or patterns, that self-consciously mirror duality" (1980: 438). Wallace Stegner has explained this phenomenon as stemming from the divided identity of a French and English Canada (1974: 300); Robert Kroetsch has suggested that Canada is a borderland between a dialectic of a wild, "uncreated" North and a technocratic and powerful South (1971: 46); and Donna Bennett has pointed out that Canada saw herself as a silent, mute minority removed from Britain and on the edge of the United States, a country which has been defined in terms not her own (1987: 17-19). Additionally, as in the case of Laura Goodman Salverson, there is the duality implied in the immigrant experience.

This sense of duality has become recognized as being so much part of the Canadian experience that, rather than wanting to discard it, Canadians have chosen to turn it into something productive.

Moreover, Canadians have developed a distrust of centralization. Both Kroetsch (1971) and Matthews (1979) have claimed that the sense of duality and marginality has been essential to Canada's survival. Grace concludes: "it seems our fate to be caught between opposites, unwilling to choose one and relinquish the other, desiring to bring the opposing realities of life together in a productive way" (1980: 442).

CANADIAN FICTION

Canadian fiction writers were not as quick as their poet colleagues to assimilate new international techniques in order to create a fictional image of their country. Perhaps it was more difficult for novelists to be experimental in a climate where popular escapist novels dominated the market. The first steps had been taken in the 1920s and 1930s, when Canada became a literary subject for some writers, and attempts were made by writers like Salverson to combine the wide predilection for the romantic and pastoral mode with a more realistic approach. However, novelists who attempted to grapple seriously and imaginatively with the problems and concerns of their country remained a lonely few for the next two decades to come. The post-War literary climate in Canada was a conservative and traditional one that shunned controversy, regarded serious ideas as eccentric and is characterized by a "sententious moralism" (Staines 1983: 260).[4]

The next step to take necessarily involved leaving behind the pioneer experience for more topical concerns. Hugh MacLennan is often called the father of Canadian fiction not only because he fictionalized scenes which were unmistakenly Canadian (others had taken that step before him), but also because he introduced as fictional subjects the consequences of the First World War for Canadians and the technological and social changes that were taking place in Canadian society. He was, for instance, the first to dare turn one of Canada's touchiest political problems into fiction: that of the division between a French and English Canada. Interestingly, however, he remained close to the popular fiction of the time in form and style: MacLennan was a moralist who never strayed far from the romantic mode. Contrary to what MacLennan's honorary title as father of Canadian fiction may lead us to assume, there is no really discernible fictional tradition or even movement of the 1940s and 1950s, although amid the continuing large-scale production and publication of popular writings, isolated authors created individual works of more lasting quality in different parts of Canada. These authors continued to lay the foundations used by the following generation to create a sudden wealth of Canadian fiction.

A number of writers created works with a distinct local flavour, in which the local environment is not only mapped out but also plays an important part in the story itself. Canadian regions and communities are imaginatively recreated. Thus, in Sinclair Ross' *As for Me and My House* the looming prairie is perhaps the most conspicuous presence in the book: its dust and dry winds continually threaten to wipe out the small village, and the villagers' hopes and creativity shrivel. In W.O. Mitchell's *Who Has Seen the Wind*, young Brian has an almost mythical relationship with the prairie. In Ernest Buckler's *The Mountain and the Valley*, there exists an analogous relationship between budding writer David Canaan and the mountain north of the Nova Scotian Annapolis Valley which symbolizes his creative vision.

Other writers were less concerned with locale and more with deeper structures and patterns in life. Howard O'Hagan and Sheila Watson each explored indigenous mythical patterns and their workings in Canadian lives in their strikingly original novels *Tay John* and *The Double Hook*. This is, however, the only real similarity between them. Both books still remain as original and elusive today as when they came out. Writers such as Ethel Wilson and Mavis Gallant on the other hand were more international in outlook and mainly interested in human and social issues. Gallant is also a prime example of the development of the short story in Canadian literature. Whereas many other writers published one or more full length novels along with short fiction, Gallant applied herself solely to the short story. By the 1950s, short stories had reached a prominent position in Canadian fiction.

Such fictional explorations opened up by the various writers during the period 1940-1950 bore fruit of unexpected quantity and quality in the following decade. Keith (1985: 157) remarks:

The Canadian writers who came to prominence in the 1960s and 1970s, though as varied as their immediate predecessors, are linked by a common energy, confidence, and sophistication. This is, I believe, indisputable, even if cultural historians comparing this fiction with the work produced at the same time in Britain and, especially, in the United States discern what might be regarded as a typically Canadian cautiousness.... [M]ost contemporary Canadian writers have found an abundance of promising material to be presented within technically complex but none the less traditional modes. This is a paradoxical result of the late development of the country's fictional potential. Subjects and methods of approach virtually exhausted everywhere were found to yield (and are still yielding) fresh and original results.

It is only with these writers that we can begin to note certain recurring features characteristic of what has now, at last and with sudden force, become a tradition. Much fiction from the 1960s shows similarities with the poetry of that time: a recovery of the past, a mapping out of space and time and a preoccupation with self-examination and self-discovery. Urban fiction is gaining ground fast while regional fiction remains a strong and prominent counterpole. Short fiction, at least for a while, is supplanted by longer fiction. The documentary impulse is importantly present in the fictional field as well as the poetic, especially in the form of storytelling and the transmission of oral traditions, legends and myths. Realism is often combined or subverted with romantic, mythic, pastoral or supernatural elements, not least in order to recover a muted or denied history.

If we look at the tradition that has emerged with these writers through their own original achievements as well as through the influence of earlier writers, certain characteristics come to the surface which can help us get a clearer idea of what makes up this Canadian tradition in fiction. First, there seems to be a definite tendency toward a narrow focus; that is to say the focus tends to be on one particular locale or community and even one particular family or household. Seeing that Canada is so vast in size and made up of regions which are very different, it is perhaps little wonder that writers prefer to remain close to home, to the region and the people that have moulded them. This tendency has been the reason for some critics to argue that Canadian literature is and should be regional. The debate between the so-called "regionalists" and "internationalists" who believe that regionalism is too narrow is still topical. It has also been one more reason for some Western writers and critics to regard Western, and especially prairie literature, as a separate branch within Canadian literature. Other reasons are that prairie writers have been prolific from the very beginning and have produced some of the finest fiction, and that the West's feeling of domination and marginalization by Eastern Canada has fostered among some a tendency to be aggressively Western. Moreover, since Henry Kreisel's influential article "The Prairie: A State of Mind" there has been a belief that of all landscapes the prairie is especially powerful in the way it influences its inhabitants.

Canadian literature shows a great concern with domestic and small town settings and with the position of the individual within these communities. The struggle between a sense of duty and moral responsibility towards the community and of suffocating repression and hypocrisy forms the subject of much Canadian fiction, and the individual *in caso* is often a budding artist. That the Canadian sensibility is more community oriented than the American is shown by the fact that in nearly all cases the individual returns home. Freedom is ultimately not a solution, and criticism is offered from within rather than without. As Donna Bennett points out:

In place of the primary American values—liberty, happiness and freedom, Canadian writing affirms more Canadian characteristics such as duty, and its accompanying sense of a weblike complex of social relationships. The Canadian perception of a complex, hidden, and often labyrinthine existence leads to writing that is both dense and serial. (1987: 22)

Both Robert Kroetsch (1986: 535) and Verna Reid (1973) have pointed to the frequent occurrence of the small town in Canadian fiction as a reflection of Canada's position: it is situated on the margin, on the edge of the wilderness, removed from the centre and the scene of action, and yet is significant. Its significance, Reid argues, lies in the fact that it is usually also the scene of childhood and the place where the protagonist was moulded: "The small town setting, then, becomes significant because, ... it contains our roots and a key to self-understanding, and ... it is invested with an aura of innocence that clings to an earlier and seemingly better world" (181).

The significance of the small town setting is indicative of the way in which Canadian writers recover Canadian history: through a journey of self-discovery. They find, moreover, that it is through personal and family history that a continuity of past with present can best be established. The search for a continuity through history has been an important concern in Canadian poetry as well, as we saw earlier. This concern gave rise to the use of more experimental techniques also in Canadian fiction during the 1960s and 1970s. George Woodcock has explained that writers

introduce a new sense of history merging into myth, of theme coming out of a perception of the land, of geography as a source of art. In the process they break time down into the nonlinear patterns of authentic memory at the same time as they break down actuality and recreate it in terms of the kind of non-literal rationality that belongs to dreams. (1979: 147)

What we see as emerging in Canadian fiction during the period 1940-1970, then, is a concern for the past which assumes mythical forms, along with the significance of the small town setting, with a vestigial romantic and pastoral character, as the scene of both child-hood and self-discovery.

ICELANDIC-CANADIAN LITERATURE

During the period 1940-1970, the last West Icelanders were still publishing works in Icelandic, among which were not just the more famous Guttormur J. Guttormsson and Guðrún H. Finnsdóttir but also lesser known figures such as Helgi Einarsson whose autobiog-raphy was published in 1954. At first glance, it looks as if Laura Goodman Salverson's example of writing in English was hardly fol-lowed up, and the descendants of the once so prolific immigrants were assimilated and not heard of again until recently. A closer look reveals that there were indeed a few people who did publish works in English, but of these, the ones who have become canonic did not write fiction or poetry but works of history, and the others either had a very limited audience or quickly sank back into oblivion after a short period of popularity.

Rannveig K.G. Sigbjörnsson was an immigrant writer who pub-lished two short story collections in English: *Pebbles on the Beach* (1936) and *In Days Gone By* (1955). Her writings, however, still belong to the Icelandic tradition. The stories published in English bear the marks of having been conceived originally in Icelandic, indeed some of them are translations from the Icelandic. All stories are set in Iceland and are very Icelandic in outlook and style. Canada or the Western Icelandic experience play no role in Sigbjörnsson's fiction. Obviously, these stories were aimed at an audience with an Icelandic background but no reading knowledge of Icelandic.

The poet Paul Bjarnason, an immigrants' son born in North Dakota and raised in Canada, has become known for his excellent translations from and into Icelandic. He also composed poetry, how-ever, both in Icelandic and in English. The volume *Odes and Echoes* (1954) contains original poetry (the "Odes") and translations from the Icelandic ("Echoes"). Bjarnason's poetry shows him to be a true descendant of the Icelandic *alþýðu*-tradition as it was continued among the West Icelanders: his conservatism in form is quite rigorous, and the strongly individualist spirit and radical political views expressed in the poems are unmistakably akin to the poetry of Western Icelandic *alþýðuskáld* such as Guttormur J. Guttormsson, Stephan G. and Þorskabítur. Paul Bjarnason's poetry, however, like so much writing by immigrants' bilingual children, hovers on the margins of two traditions, the Western Icelandic and the Canadian. His publications were all private ones and reached only a small audience.

Another poet of Icelandic extraction who falls outside of the general development of Icelandic-Canadian writing from the period 1940-1970 is Helen Sveinbjörnsson. In 1973 her collected poems were published under the title *Cloth of Gold and Other Poems*. Many of these poems had appeared in newspapers and journals all over Canada during the 1940s and 1950s under the anglicized version of their half-Icelandic/half-Scots author's name: Helen Swinburne Lloyd. Her collected poems, however, were published under her original Icelandic name. Helen Sveinbjörnsson was raised in Scotland and did not speak Icelandic, so that the form and style of her poetry do not bear the marks of the Icelandic literary tradition. She was, however, very interested and knowledgeable in the classical Icelandic literature which forms the theme and subject matter of some of her poems.

Two Icelandic-Canadian poets publishing during the 1950s and 1960s are Gus Sigurdson and Elma Helgason. Gus Sigurdson is probably the better known of the two, although both have a local appeal only. Both are also from the prairies, Sigurdson from Manitoba and Helgason from Alberta. What their work has in common is its "folk" nature. Their poems are about the joys and sorrows of daily life and daily people on the prairies, usually optimistic and moralizing in tone, and marked by the brand of "folksy cracker-barrel-rustic philosophy" and humaneness bordering on sentimentality that Keith noticed in W.O. Mitchell's fiction as well (1985: 148). This type of folk-literature seems to have found fertile soil in the prairie region with its strong populist traditions. Laurie Ricou is one of the very few critics who has discussed this literature which he terms the "Meadowlark Tradition." He points out that this folk-poetry "expresses the strong needs and deeply felt beliefs of the people" and predicts that "[t]he prairie poetry still to be written will be assimilating and transforming the meadowlark tradition" (1980: 162-67). The truth of his prediction is seen in Kristjana Gunnars' and David Arnason's works, which

I will discuss below. The lasting popularity of Sigurdson's and Helgason's verse among Icelandic Canadians and local people, small as this audience may be, is attested to by the fairly recent published collections of their work: in 1979 Elma Helgason's *Songs for All Seasons* came out[5] and in 1987 Gus Sigurdson's collected works appeared under the name *Seven Books between Two Covers*. In this same popular prairie tradition of storytelling and versifying we may also include Art Reykdal's *Autobiography of a Damned Fool*, published by Reykdal's own company called "Pauper Press" in 1955, and obviously aimed at a local audience.

One other author should be mentioned here, a competent writer whose works unfortunately are not readily available. Albert L. Halldorsson published at least two books, one "Selection of Poems and Essays in continuous form" called *Wings of the Wind* (1948) and a novel called *Fruits of the Valley* published in 1950. Both were private publications. Halldorsson's name itself is absent from records of Icelandic-Canadian writers. His *Wings of the Wind* is comparable to the poetry of Helgason and Sigurdson in spirit, but it is more accomplished. It lacks their strong strain of sentimentality and moralism, and, moreover, his combination of poetry and prose is an interesting, early manifestation of what was to become a favourite Canadian poetic form. Halldorsson's "historic novel" *Fruits of the Valley* tells the story of the birth of Jesus from the point of view of a young shepherd. While there are no direct references to Halldorsson's Icelandic background, the tale is constructed in such a way that it is easy to recognize in it the history of Western Icelandic religious factionalism. The plot is well-conceived and carried out, but the style and structure are marred by Halldorsson's inexperience as a writer.

The writings of Halldorsson and Helgason share the absence or near absence, of ethnic reference or influence, while the style and tone in Helgason's and Sigurdson's poetry has very little in common with the Icelandic or Western Icelandic poetic tradition. His Icelandic background is however used as the subject matter of some of Sigurdson's poetry. Sigurdson could still read Icelandic and, in his introduction to *Seven Books Between Two Covers*, he acknowledges the influence of several Western Icelandic poets on his work. Moreover, he calls himself a "traditional poet," because, as he says, "that was the style I grew up with." What Sigurdson presumably refers to is the Icelandic-Canadian folk-tradition of versifying, which had its roots in traditional Icelandic poetry (*rímur, lausavísur*). Sigurdson does indeed stick to conventional rhyme patterns and rhythmical schemes, but, although strict formal rules regulated traditional Icelandic poetry as well, his style has much more in common with prairie folk-poetry than with Icelandic poetry. While it is possible that the traditional active interest in reading and writing poetry stimulated the poetic activities of Sigurdson and Helgason, the form and style are too simple to have sprung from the complex Icelandic poetic patterns, and the moral didacticism too sententious. Halldorsson is closer to the gentle strain in Western Icelandic poetry, at least in spirit and intention. His poems display a romantic communion with the prairie landscape which gives rise to philosophic thoughts in a manner that recalls Western Icelandic poets such as Kristinn Stefánsson or Þorsteinn Þ. Þorsteinsson, although there is no reference to or evidence of this influence. Similarly, Reykdal's *Autobiography* shares certain characteristics with Icelandic-Canadian oral verses and narratives, and even displays a polemic strain reminiscent of the *alþýðu*-poetry. The name of his private press attests to this link as well.

The only work of Icelandic-Canadian literature to reach a large audience for a time was the novel *Tanya* by third-generation writer Kristine Benson Kristofferson from New Iceland, published in 1950 by Ryerson in Toronto. Although *Tanya* cannot be regarded as a balanced artistic achievement, lacking all pretension to be more than a conventional story, it does rise above the average second-rate popular novel of the time by virtue of its subject matter and the craft and insight with which it is handled. The novel is set in a small multiracial community on the shore of a lake in northern Manitoba. Its main themes are racial intolerance, symbolized by the broken relationship between part-native Canadian Joe and Anglo-Canadian summer tourist Tanya, and the consequences of war. When the former lovers return to the isolated community after participation in the war, they cannot avoid having to deal with their physical and psychological scars as well as with the reasons underlying the breach of their relationship, as violence erupts in the community.

The most striking aspect of *Tanya* is probably its genuinely Canadian atmosphere, or, as one contemporary critic called it, "its singularly Canadian aroma" (Farquharson 1951: 22). The sad, yet realistic, problems inherent in a cultural mosaic become poignantly clear to the reader in the story of this small and isolated mosaic colony, and in this respect the novel has lost none of its actuality. The reader looking for clues revealing the Icelandic-Canadian heritage of the author, however, will be disappointed. If the works by Helgason, Sigurdson, Halldorsson and Reykdal can still be considered Icelandic-Canadian although they were written within a larger prairie Canadian tradition, then *Tanya* is a very Canadian book without any ethnic hyphenation attached to it.

The literature produced by these second- and third-generation Icelandic Canadians is, in other words, not only nearly all in English, it also has little or no "ethnic" content as such. Instead, it is characterized by its local Canadian flavour, although traces of the underlying Western Icelandic tradition can still be detected in some instances. This raises questions with regard to the continuing role of the Icelandic literary heritage for Icelandic-Canadian authors. Is the Icelandic voice gradually being exchanged for an Anglo-Canadian one among later generations, or is it in the process of a more complex acculturative transformation? It is only now that a few solitary literary critics have begun to address such questions as what defines "ethnic" literature, if not easily identifiable ethnic markers such as language and content. In his article on Canadian minority writing, Enoch Padolsky (1990) has pointed out that literary texts reflect the acculturative stances of ethnic authors in various, complex ways, such as the choices made with regard to form, genre, theme and outlook, in which they will differ from majority writers.[6] For instance, the awareness of a multidimensional sense of self (of being, for instance, Canadians of Icelandic or part-Icelandic descent) is often extended to the social and geographical environment. As Padolsky notes:

Minority writers and readers ... are more likely to be aware experientially of the nature of acculturation for minorities than majority writers and readers. It is this which in my view contrasts, for example, the sympathetic portrayal of aboriginal situations in the works of Ryga, Wiebe, Suknaski, Gunnars, Valgardson, etc. with the equally sympathetic (but majority) portrayals of the aboriginal situation in Laurence or Roy. (62)[7]

This is demonstrated in early Icelandic-Canadian literature in English, which expresses a celebration of things Canadian that reveals an outlook founded upon the sacrifices with which they were won. The outlook and choice of that Canadian subject matter, too, in many cases reflect a more recent, non-British immigrant past, in that its interpretation of what constitutes "Canadian" is wider than that found in most Anglo-Canadian writings of the time, as in Kristine Kristofferson's novel *Tanya*, which focusses on interracial tensions, in the celebration of prairie life and landcape found in the works of Helgason, Sigurdson and Halldorsson, and in Vilhjálmur Stefánsson's descriptions of the Canadian North and its native inhabitants.

The famous arctic explorer Vilhjálmur Stefánsson, an immigrants' son and former classmate of Paul Bjarnason, wrote many books about his findings and experiences in the northern Canadian wilderness. His autobiography, *Discovery*, was published in 1964, and is an entertaining and well-written book which has enjoyed popularity. Stefánsson's works bear witness to his writing talents, and although technically they do not belong to the realm of creative writing, they did open up a largely unknown territory to the field of Canadian literature. His contribution to Canadian literature in this respect has been acknowledged by several critics such as MacLulich (1985) and Keith (1984), who credits Stefánsson with having shown the North in his writings from the point of view of adaptation rather than of conquest or biased interpretation.

In *Discovery*, Stefánsson displays great pride in his heritage and ancestry. He elaborates on the culture and history of his ancestral country and its influence on his person, his life and his explorations. He appears to have found himself rather exceptional in this respect, as he chides his fellow West Icelanders in the following, somewhat sarcastic recollection:

It might seem ... that Lord Dufferin wanted the Icelanders to retain their national character, to adhere as steadfastedly to their language and culture as had the French settlers in Canada. But other counsel prevailed. Instead of clinging to their own customs and traditions, the Icelanders shed them, rapidly becoming English in language and Scottish in names, Scots then being the most fashionable of nationalities in Manitoba. (6)

Obviously, the Icelandic cultural heritage was in the process of being transformed from a national attribute to a more complex, private, and indirect influence in people's daily lives as Canadians. However, the apparent lack of creative involvement in the Icelandic heritage may have had other reasons as well. Kristine Kristofferson wrote another novel after *Tanya* called *The Rugged Oak*, which is set completely in New Iceland. As she could not find a publisher for the work, it only exists in manuscript-form in the University of Manitoba Archives. I mentioned earlier that Halldorsson's, Reykdal's and Bjarnason's were all private publications, probably for the same reason.

Poets could at least publish their works in local or ethnic newspapers, although the collected works of Sigurdson, Helgason and Svein-björnsson were only published after 1970. Sveinbjörnsson, who was the only poet with a more widely spread audience, published under the anglicized version of her name until her collection appeared in 1973. If there was little interest among Icelandic-Canadian authors in the literary involvement of their ethnic background during 1940-1970, it is equally the case that there was little enthusiasm for "ethnic" literature among Canadian publishers at that time.[8] Instead, Canadian authors of Icelandic descent were gradually developing different ways in which to express creatively their Icelandic-Canadian reality in a Canadian context.

With Stefánsson ends the list of Icelandic-Canadian writers who were active between 1940 and 1970 in so far as I have been able to trace them. With the possible exception of Stefánsson their works have gone unnoticed among most of the Canadian public. The silence was not to last long, however, for during the following decades the next generation of Icelandic Canadians would let themselves be heard again.

CONTEMPORARY ICELANDIC-CANADIAN WRITING: THEMATIC AND STYLISTIC CONCERNS

In 1969, the Royal Commission on Bilingualism and Biculturalism published its report on *The Cultural Contributions of the Other Ethnic Groups*, in which it recommended to the Canadian government a number of actions to preserve cultural heritages other than those of French or English-Canadians. On 8 October 1971, the federal government announced the cultural policy of bilingual multiculturalism. This policy was to commit Canada, amongst other things, to the preservation and enhancement of the multicultural heritage of Canadians. When Bill C-93 was passed in 1988, this commitment became the duty of all Canadians.[9]

Perhaps as a result of the simultaneity of the Canadian Multiculturalism Act and the general interest in Canadian history and roots dominating Canadian writing around this time, Icelandic-Canadian literature received a new impetus during the 1970s. W.D. Valgardson began publishing poems and short stories in magazines during the late 1960s, and in 1973 his first book came out. His publications were followed by a series of privately published autobiographies and family or community histories by a variety of Icelandic Canadians; although none reached the larger Canadian public, they attest to a revived interest among Icelandic Canadians in their ethnic history and identity.[10] 1980 saw the first publications in book form by David Arnason and Kristjana Gunnars, the latter with no less than three books of poetry published during that year.

Since then, many publications have followed and new names have appeared on the literary scene. In the remainder of this fourth chapter, the works of contemporary Canadian writers of Icelandic descent will be the subject of discussion. Taking into consideration the questions that were raised by early Icelandic-Canadian literature in English, the main goal of this discussion will be to determine whether or not contemporary Icelandic-Canadian writing can be considered a continuation of the Western Icelandic literary tradition. If not, the qualifying adjective "Icelandic" will be subjected to closer scrutiny in order to determine whether it really applies only to the ethnic background of the authors, as Wolf suggests in a recent article (1992: 452), or whether the ethnic heritage receives thematic and/or stylistic expression. If it does receive literary expression, I will examine this element more closely in order to see whether it remains a nostalgic but static stereotypical image, or whether it is effectively integrated into the imaginative conception of the works.

Since most of contemporary Icelandic-Canadian writing has come from the pens of three Icelandic Canadians, their works will be discussed in detail. The first of these is W.D. Valgardson, a native of the New Iceland area (Gimli, b. 1939) who currently resides in Victoria, British Columbia. His great-grandfather, Ketill Valgarðsson, immigrated from Snæfellsnes to Canada in 1878.[11] Valgardson grew up in the Icelandic-Canadian community, and began his writing career by publishing poems and short stories. In 1980, his first novel, *Gentle Sinners*, came out. His second novel, *The Girl with the Botticelli Face* was published in 1992.

David Arnason is also a native of the Gimli area (b. 1940) whose first publication, a cycle of long poems, appeared in 1980. Since then, he has published five collections of short stories, two collages and one collection of poems. His first novel to date, *The Pagan Wall*, was published in 1992. David Arnason is a descendant of Árni Oddson (from Þingeyjarsýsla) and Guðrún Jónsdóttir (from

Eyjafjörður) who came to Canada in 1876, and of Johann Árnason and Dorothea Soffía Abrahamsdóttir, both from Eyjafjörður.

It must be emphasized that Kristjana Gunnars' situation is different from that of Valgardson and Arnason, in that she is not a native Icelandic Canadian but Iceland-born (1948). She is the daughter of an Icelandic physicist, the late Gunnar Böðvarsson, and his Danish wife Tove Christensen. She grew up in Reykjavík and spent part of her youth in Denmark. She moved to the United States in her teens and has lived in Canada since 1969. Her status as a recent immigrant who has spent her life in various cities in Europe and North America makes it interesting to compare her works with those of Arnason and Valgardson, both of whom are from a rural Icelandic-Canadian background and are four generations removed from the immigration to Canada. Gunnars knew next to nothing about the Icelandic Canadians when she came to Canada and cannot really be regarded as a member of the Icelandic-Canadian community. Rather, being an immigrant herself, she became interested in Icelandic-Canadian immigrant history, which she studied and made the subject of several of her works. Gunnars has been very prolific. Her first three collections of poetry from 1980 have been followed by four other poetry collections, two collection of short stories, three novellas, and a novel published in 1989. She has also edited a collection of Icelandic-Canadian short stories, and translated and edited a selection of Stephan G. Stephansson's works.

Other publishing Icelandic-Canadian writers include Betty Jane Wylie, Paul Sigurdson, Martha Brooks, Marion Johnson and Eleanor Oltean. Wylie has been most active in the fields of self-help books, children's stories and drama, all of which are outside the scope of this study. However, she has also published one collection of poetry called *Something Might Happen* (1989), which I have taken into consideration in the following discussion. Brooks and Johnson are fairly new writers on the Canadian scene. Brooks has published three works of fiction and Johnson one, which have been included as primary sources. Oltean, Helen Sveinbjörnsson's daughter, has published a collection of poetry called *Earth and Sky* (1987). Sigurdson, a gifted translator as well as a writer in his own right, had not published anything in book form nor in any larger Canadian magazines up to his untimely death in 1991. A private publication of his collected work, called *Not of an Age*, appeared in 1992. It was, however, a limited edition and had extremely small distribution. As a result, I have not included Sigurdson in the following discussion.

A special case is Bill Holm, an Icelandic American, who has many ties and much in common with the Icelandic-Canadian tradition and history. He is a well-known and popular figure and writer in the Icelandic-Canadian community. The Icelandic-Canadian community specifically and prairie culture generally tend to regard the national border as trivial because of a shared history and influential geography, reason enough for Gunnars to include Holm in her collection *Unexpected Fictions: New Icelandic Canadian Writing.* Holm's writings, however, cannot, strictly speaking, be regarded as a contribution to Canadian literature. He, like Sigurdson, will therefore be excluded from consideration here.

THE THEMATIC ROLE OF ETHNIC HERITAGE

One striking aspect in any comparison of Western Icelandic and Icelandic-Canadian literature is the absence of the immigrant theme in its widest sense in all Icelandic-Canadian works except those of Kristjana Gunnars. Characteristically, of course, she is an immigrant herself whereas the other writers are not. With the immigrant theme has gone the strong, immediate social function which literature provided for the newly uprooted immigrant community. In spite of Gunnars' immigrant status, this social function is not found in her works either, since her position is one outside of the Icelandic-Canadian community. Instead, contemporary Icelandic-Canadian literature is more introspective. Rather than providing a code of how to survive in the new environment, this literature is concerned with the role that ethnic heritage plays for the contemporary individual in Canadian society. Connected with this concern is, naturally, the search for and articulation of identity, a dominant theme in Canadian literature in general.

Whereas Anglo-Canadian writers have been exploring their personal past as well as their common Canadian past for a few decades, it is only since the 1970s that "other" Canadian voices are heard more strongly in their explorations of past and identity. The Multiculturalism Act has probably been a strong stimulus in this direction, as well as the recent fascination in Canadian literature with the marginal, the muted, what Hutcheon has termed the "ex-centric" (1988: 3). This has no doubt helped stimulate ethnic voices to become heard in Canadian culture. In fact, it has even helped to make "ethnic" fashionable.

Ethnic heritage, then, has become a subject of close literary scrutiny, also in the works of Valgardson, Arnason and Gunnars. For Valgardson and Arnason, Iceland is not a reality, although it is part of what makes up their heritage and carries strong emotional connotations. Their focus is, therefore, not on Iceland as an outsider might see it, but on the Iceland that remained part of the essence of the immigrants and their descendants. In their writings, we find a questioning of what ethnic identity actually is, how the Icelandic and Canadian consciousnesses have blended and whether the result has any role to play in Canadian daily reality other than possessing the status of a myth or even a burden.

For Gunnars, Iceland is still a reality. Her works are therefore different in various respects. Her immigrant status makes the themes of loss and alienation very acute for her, and in this sense her works are closer to the Western Icelandic tradition. Indeed, loss, alienation and estrangement have been recognized by more than one critic as the major themes in her work. Gunnars, however, differs from Western Icelandic writers not only in time but also in the fact that, for her, there is no longer an Icelandic-Canadian immigrant community with which to share the immigrant experience and of which she can articulate and validate the griefs and difficulties. Instead, we see that she universalizes these themes, aligning them with the feelings of alienation and estrangement experienced by contemporary men and women in every part of the world. Moreover, Gunnars has a keen interest in Icelandic-Canadian history, especially the immigrant history, and in the Icelandic-Canadian identity that has grown out of this history. As the only bilingual Icelandic-Canadian author, she also has direct access to the early immigrant history, whereas Valgardson and Arnason learnt their history by way of oral transmission. This provides for an interesting difference in perspective between a recent immigrant author and two Canadian authors of immigrant descent.

W. D. Valgardson has imaginatively recreated the Interlake area (the area between Lake Winnipeg and Lake Manitoba, where most Icelanders settled) and its people in his first three collections of short stories *Bloodflowers* (1973), *God is not a Fish Inspector* (1975) and *Red Dust* (1978). Not all stories in these collections are set in the Interlake, and not all of them feature people of Icelandic descent. However, most stories, even those without Icelandic-Canadian setting and characters, breathe an overall atmosphere which Valgardson portrays as characteristic of the rural Icelandic immigrant communities where he grew up. Valgardson himself says:

I believe that the immigrant experience and its aftermath work together to create within individuals, an inner landscape. That inner landscape, that view held by the implied author rather than the external landscape beheld by the actual author, is what the artist finally creates or recreates in his art. For that reason, it is important to understand the influences which created that landscape. (1987: 1)

Among those influences he mentions the land, the lake, and the harsh climate, the beginning of a new life in the immigrant experience of death and exploitation, the struggle to survive, and the bleakness preached by strict Lutheranism and the stoicism taught by the sagas and Eddas. If we replace the lake with the ocean, the themes could be those of Icelandic literature. There was, however, also the experience of chaos, since Valgardson was not a full member of an Icelandic-Canadian community: he had a half-English grandmother and an Irish mother: "Perhaps if I had been born into any one of these communities, secure in my identity, I would not have begun a lifelong quest to try to make sense out of what, for me, was chaos" (1987: 6). Moreover, there existed tensions between the Icelandic Canadians and other ethnic groups which had come later to settle in the Interlake area, notably the Ukrainians. Hans Norman and Harald Runblom have pointed out that earlier ethnic groups tended to erect barriers towards newly-arriving ethnic groups as a form of ethnic self-protection (1987: 273). Valgardson's experience of growing up among such cultural tensions, of which he was often a victim, has been an important influence on his fictional explorations into the nature of and search for ethnic identity.

These explorations, however, do not really occur as a theme in his first two books. In these he creates his fictional territory which Margaret Atwood names "Valgardsonland" in her review of his third book *Red Dust*: "He's staked out his territory, and now it exists" (1979-80: 190). In *Red Dust* we find the first story which deals with the theme of ethnic heritage: "Skald." Alma is of Icelandic descent, but knows very little about her heritage. In the beginning of the story, she is a rather submissive girl, easily intimidated and bossed around by her husband Junior Boys. Her life changes when she independently decides to buy a puppy-dog which she, significantly, names

Skald. Skald leads Alma onto the road towards independence and maturity, which coincides with her rediscovery and interest in her ethnic heritage. When Skald contracts a disease, Alma turns to the three Icelandic brothers whom she has met on one of her walks with Skald and who have made her aware of her heritage and ancestry. From them she obtains a rifle. Alma faces up to the consequences of her neglect to get Skald his shots with a new sense of self-responsibility, and is determined to shoot the dog herself. Rather than constituting its end, this is the beginning of a new life for Alma. Having acquired maturity through the discovery of her true identity, she will not turn back:

> She would, she promised herself, get another dog and name him the same name. She would see that she got him whatever protection he needed against disease and then, if he were run over or killed by other dogs or shot for any hundreds of reasons that people have for killing, she would get another, and, if necessary, another and another. (*Red Dust* 32)

In Valgardson's following work, the novel *Gentle Sinners*, the quest for identity is the main theme. The main protagonist, Bobby, is a teenager who has lost the link with his heritage. He is the child of parents who have exchanged ethnicity for assimilation, and culture for cult and materialism. They are Christians and capitalists of a fanaticism that borders on the grotesque. Bobby runs away from them in despair at not being allowed any room to develop his own identity and at being denied information about his family and descent. His goal becomes the killing of these forces of blind assimilation and materialism in the name of religion. Bobby escapes to the countryside, to his uncle Sigfus, whose existence he has had to trace without his parents' knowledge. There, he is symbolically baptized into a new life and renamed Eric, a name much more resonant of his Icelandic heritage. However, he still has to undergo several trials. Sigfus, who has lost his wife and son, decides to take Eric on as an apprentice. Eric's apprenticeship serves, of course, also a symbolic function in this highly symbolic novel: from Sigfus, the wise old man, he learns about his heritage and, by extension, a new set of values.

The opposition between heritage and materialism, one we have also encountered in many Western Icelandic works such as Guðrún H. Finnsdóttir's stories and Stephan G.'s poem "Á Ferð og Flugi," is made quite clear in the beginning of the book when Eric and Sigfus meet:

That the boy should have come was not strange to him. Sigfus had always believed that the pull of blood was the strongest force between people, drawing those together who belonged together. What was strange to him, what was beyond the bounds of the natural, intended order, were those people who, like his sister, did not feel the pull of blood. They were lost, without a place.... From such loss came the frantic struggle to acquire goods at any cost. The individual who knew who he was could be stripped of all but his mortal flesh and lose nothing of consequence. (*Gentle Sinners* 22-23)

Eric feels the lack of contact with his past, which has been kept hidden from him, very keenly. When he finds out his mother's true Icelandic name, it becomes "his portal into the past": "He repeated the names over and over to himself like a chant" (11). When he decides to leave, his choice of Eddyville as a destination, where his uncle lives, "was both an act of desperation and an act of faith" (13).

The connection between Eric's past and his ethnic identity is made in several ways. He is given a more Norse, even Viking-like name (cf. Eric the Red). The connection of Eric with his Viking ancestry is extended as he stands before Sigfus, and his hair "might have been a helmet of beaten bronze" (10). His Viking temperament is shown during his initial confrontation with Big Tree, one of the twin villains who terrorize the town, and his obsession with revenge on his parents, whom he is determined to kill. If Eric is the impetuous young Viking warrior, Sigfus is connected to the ancient figure of the *goði*, the priest-chieftain. He is the wise and respected leader who has to teach Eric the proper Viking ethics, a time-honoured moral code of honour and conduct. That his leadership is of both a secular and a religious nature, like that of a *goði*, is indicated by the fact that Sigfus has his own church building on his land. The code of honour and the roles of Eric and Sigfus as warrior and chieftain will be discussed in more detail below.

From Sigfus and his brother-in-law Sam, Eric also learns about the *huldufólk*, which are here connected to boulders in the Canadian prairie landscape (84-85), and is taught the traditional Icelandic-Canadian profession: lake-fishing. However, he is not solely engaged in his ethnic culture. He also has to pass through a Jungian journey of individuation, during which he has to deal with his Shadow Larry, and his Anima Melissa, whom he has to save from the claws of the Tree brothers.

Towards the end of the book, Eric's parents find out his whereabouts and come to take him back. This confrontation forms the beginning of a spiritual death-phase for Eric: as Sigfus prevents him from killing his parents, he puts a gun to his own mouth. His uncle, however, has taken out the bullets, and Eric runs away. A long, stormy night begins during which Larry and the Trees must be beaten, and Melissa saved. Eric experiences a rebirth in the river as he conquers his fear of water. Significantly, at the end of the night and the book, Eric leaves Melissa in the care of Sigfus, as he has decided to go back to finish his education. He is now ready to face up to his own life and responsibilities, and no longer needs to be on the run. Sigfus, in turn, gives Eric the silver watch of his Icelandic grandfather who immigrated to Canada.

Gentle Sinners thus ends with a positive affirmation of ethnic identity. Eric has been given his heirloom, has given his Anima into the care of his uncle Sigfus, and intends to turn back. He is now rooted in his past and ready to face and take on his future, a future he could not face earlier when he lacked a past, an identity, a heritage, and was plagued by fears and rootlessness. As in "Skald," the recovery of one's Icelandic-Canadian identity is presented as necessary to achieve a healthy maturity, necessary to face up to oneself and one's future. It is indispensable to selfhood.

After *Gentle Sinners*, Valgardson did not publish a book for ten years, when another short story collection appeared under the name *What Can't Be Changed Shouldn't Be Mourned*. In this collection, two stories, one of which is in two parts, are concerned with the theme of ethnic heritage, this time with more implied autobiographical resonances. In "The Cave," the narrator begins a search into the past of the girl he loves. Interestingly, this girl, Sigga, was brought up in Iceland but is of Icelandic-Canadian ancestry, rather than being an Icelander who has come to Canada. The narrator's discoveries become increasingly more ominous as the past becomes more and more connected with and eventually takes on the shape of a cave. This cave is only the entry to a maze of other caves, underlying the surface and roots of the area: "The surface looked, from above, impervious, solid, real, but although it supported infinite trees, marshes and animals, its solidity was only an illusion. It was a secret world discovered by dreams, a secret world that altered his whole concept of reality" (111-12). The Icelandic past thus receives expression in a very Canadian metaphor taken from a prehistoric landscape. Along the lines here established, the past is envisioned as belonging to the subconscious, the world of dreams. It becomes the "other" reality.

The increasingly ominous aspect of the past in the form of the cave lies in the fact that it is closing in on the narrator. The deeper he seems to dive into the past, the closer its implications for his future become, although for the longest time he cannot see the pattern that is developing. In the end, a vision comes full circle in which time is cyclical and the future is embedded in the past, exactly according to the thesis of the essay written by Gunnar, the first in the row of ancestors in this story, and based on his research in the cave.

Although it does appear from this story that the past teaches one about oneself, there is a haunting overall picture created by this story, that of an inevitable, fateful past turning up and determining our future lives whether we admit it or not. This is, of course, in line with the connection between the past and the subconscious, but it makes for a more forceful and less positive affirmation of heritage where heritage becomes a matter in which we do not have a choice. "The Cave" also makes one wonder if the domain of the "other" reality, to which the past belongs in this story, is meant to have connections with the past and reality of the "other" Canadians, only now being discovered and written into Canadian literature.

In "The Man from Snæfellsness" part one and two, the atmosphere is hardly less oppressive, although here the tension is relieved and absolution received in the end. Axel Borgfjord, a writer of Icelandic descent, receives an invitation from Iceland to come to the country of his forebears and discover it for himself. The unexpected invitation disrupts Axel's peace of mind. It brings back memories of his embittered great-grandfather Ketil, who had been forced to emigrate because he was a *hreppsómagi*, a man so poor that he and his family were dependent on the care of the community. The proud and stiff-necked Ketil, "Icelandic to the core" (121), never forgave this deep offense to his pride and dignity, and refused to go to the annual Icelandic Celebration until the day he died.

The invitation also brings back memories of Axel's own youthful trials. As a boy, he was rejected by the other Icelandic children for not being Icelandic, as his mother was Irish:

"You're not Icelandic."
"I am so."
"My mother says you're not. She says your mother is an *utlander*."
"She is not. She is not," I yelled back, but it did no good. The others took it up. *Utlander.* Foreigner, outsider, other than us. None of the English words do it justice. Not wanted, perhaps." (124)

At the same time, the teacher in school used the strap on him and others for remembering their heritage, for using their language. "It did no good, of course" (126): being more English than the English still left them foreign and shunned by the Anglo-Canadian summer tourists on the lake. After his mother had managed to secure an education for Axel from her knitting money, he definitely did not belong to the community, made up of fishermen, anymore, for his further education had removed him from their sphere. As Axel struggles anew with his ancestral and personal memories of rejection, of confused and laden identity, his girlfriend Helen's curiosity about his ethnicity forces him to see the other side of the coin:

She was vaguely WASP, but not in any connected way, no accent, no relatives in the British Isles, no Christmas customs except for a tree imported from the U.S. She missed what I had, she said, belonging to a specific place. (120)

She was always hunting for ethnic experience. Odd words, bits of information.... She considered people with roots to be the most fortunate of creatures. (123)

Moreover, Helen voices what Axel has felt all along: that he can go back on behalf of his great-grandfather Ketil and come to terms with the past.

"The Man from Snæfellsness" part two, is set in Iceland. Axel views the land of his forefathers and hears the explanations of his guide Fjola with rancour. He is being haunted by a dream in which he fights shoulder to shoulder with his Viking-ancestors to avenge the injustice of their rejection, and a bloody dream it is. Iceland has not kept even the traditions with which he grew up in the Icelandic-Canadian community. Against his will, he slowly begins to identify himself with the country. He recognizes the features of different families also in Iceland, and his irritation over the critical remarks he overhears among Americans eventually cause him to introduce himself as an Icelander. Slowly, he is beginning to acknowledge the various motives behind his trip:

He had not known what to expect, but somehow, fantastically, he had hoped to set things right, to obtain revenge, to undo injustice, somehow to drive his sword through the body of Ketil's enemy and even the balance with blood. As they drove, he brooded, still not certain that he should have come, if even now he should not return the trip's cost, pay for everything with his own silver. *Vergild*, he thought. They were paying him *vergild*. They had asked for nothing in return; the payment for his fare, for his apartment, the food, was for nothing in the present. It was reparation for past injustice. (140)

By the baptismal pool, where Icelanders accepted Christ, Axel finally comes to terms with his past and his ethnicity. As he descends into the pool, suit and all, he washes off the cancerous burden of rejection and bitterness of four generations as he learns how to forgive.

In these later stories, then, the attitude towards ethnic identity becomes more complex. It is no longer merely a good thing to be recovered, it also carries serious psychological implications. Nevertheless, there is still the conviction that the Icelandic heritage cannot and should not be shaken off. It is an inevitable part of one's self and needs to be acknowledged and dealt with in order for a healthy sense of complete selfhood to be reached. Affirmation of one's ethnic identity entails a sense of being rooted in place and time, whereas its rejection or loss results in alienation and fragmentation of the self, with destructive psychological consequences.

An interesting link to ethnic heritage can be detected in Valgardson's stories about this subject: the role of the Icelandic language. Three times the protagonist is asked, in Icelandic, *talið þér Íslensku?* ("do you speak Icelandic?"). All three times the answer is *nei*, "no." This indicates both the situation of loss of the ancestral language among most Canadians of "other" descent and the cultural dispossession of the characters in the stories. The question always occurs before the character starts a quest into the ethnic past, and it seems as if the negative answer forced by this question makes the protagonist particularly strongly aware of the loss of the link with his/her heritage.

Valgardson is not alone is his use of loss of language as a metaphor for loss of heritage. Beckmann makes the following observation:

Language conditions the way people perceive, the way they think, and in many works of Commonwealth fiction, language becomes the symbolic representation of ancestral heritage and home. Thus to lose one's language is to lose touch with one's ancestors. Yet loss of the ancestral tongue is all too often a hallmark of the multicultural situation, and this loss or threatened loss is reflected in the style, and becomes a significant thematic concern. (1983: 66)

In "The Man from Snæfellsness" part one, Axel has painful memories of his Anglo-Canadian education where he was cruelly "taught to forget":

> "*Hestur.*" The word was as thin and faint as monofilament.
> "It is not," she screamed. "It is a horse. Horse, you idiot. Class, here is a horse, and standing in front of the picture of a horse is an idiot. Hold out your hand!" She grabbed my wrist and dragged me to the desk, raised the strap above her shoulder. (129)

By the time an ethnic identity becomes something to be desired, as Axel's friend Helen does, the harm had often been done and the language lost. But language can still play an important role in matters of identity, even when the active knowledge of it has receded into the depths of one's being. An example is Axel's answer to the Americans who have just been uttering criticisms of Iceland. In spite of Axel's personal rancour, the criticism irks him, and when they ask him a question in English, he replies in the same words which have so often before signalled dispossession: "*Hvat? Tala thu Islenzku?*[sic]" With those words he excludes the Americans while including himself in the ethnic group. By using them in this context, he has reversed their meaning for himself: here, they signal possession. It is his first, although almost unconscious affirmation of where he feels he belongs. Thus, even though the active knowledge of the language is lost, its power and connection with heritage and identity remains.

In David Arnason's works, ethnic identity occurs as a theme only in his first two books. *Marsh Burning* (1980) consists of a cycle of long poems and prose poems, in which the author deals with his personal and ethnic past. *The Icelanders* (1981), in co-operation with the visual artist Michael Olito, is a book which commemorates the Icelandic Canadians of the Interlake area, and may be seen as a tribute to Arnason's heritage. His later works show the influence of his Icelandic descent, but are no longer thematically concerned with ethnic identity. In view of Valgardson's observation about his own fascination with the quest for identity being the result of his mixed origins, the reason may be that Arnason was born into the Icelandic-Canadian community, and was thus "secure" in his identity. For Arnason, Icelandic Canadians of his generation are "simply Canadians with a special set of memories" (*Icelanders* 7). *Marsh Burning*, Arnason's first published work, deals imaginatively with this "special set of memories," along with other personal memories. The metaphor he uses for his Icelandic memories is *Ragnarök*, the end of the world in Norse mythology. In accordance with this pagan vision, cyclical images and patterns dominate the poems which are simultaneously moving toward an acceptance of mortality and loss of heritage and toward rebirth and the forming of a new vision which incorporates the old.

In the first part, images of *Ragnarök* abound as the narrator comes to the realization that his vision is oriented to the past. He needs to shed the skin of his Icelandic heritage, which has become too tight: it needs to incorporate the new, the future. Thor has warned him of the approach of the end of his world:

> you spoke to me Thor
> saying
>> *Baldur is dead/slain*
>> *Baldur*
>>> *who was white as the snows on Hecla*
>> *Loki is free*
>> *Fenrir prowls   just beyond the horizon*
>> *somewhere over Fundy*
>
>> *the world ash is rotting*
> you said   *eaten from without and within*
>> *Nidhogg gnaws at the roots of Yggdrasil*
>> *the reindeer in the branches paw and fret* (9)

Signs of the narrator's own personal *Ragnarök* appear everywhere around him. Odin, unmistakable in his blue coat and with only one eye, comes to him in the form of a Jehovah's Witness (11). Later, he appears as his neighbour. Significantly, in this instance the lost eye has been replaced with a glass eye showing a clock which runs backward, indicating the past and Old World orientation of the vision which the Odinic neighbour represents: he "sets the clock so that the time it shows / is right in Sussex" (13). As the poem moves toward its climax, the narrator is beginning to connect the struggle that is being waged to that waged by his "twinned soul," represented by the twin gods of fertility Frey and Freyja:

> I was born under Gemini
> and I should have been twins
> my twinned soul wars in my single body
> Frey and Freya have been here
>> *Baldur is dead* (20)

A character named Mike is the last Odinic messenger. Like Odin, he hanged himself and thereby obtained hidden knowledge. He tells the narrator:

> *words*
>
> he says   *are what the world is made from*
> *and when I learned this*
> *I could move in time*
> *backwards and forwards*
> *until I met the wolf*
> *and was made prisoner* (23)

The narrator's creative powers are being kept prisoner by a stifling old culture, his heritage. To be able to integrate past and future, he must free himself first. At the end of this first part, the narrator leaves his house with the voices "speaking a language that I know / but can't quite understand" (24). As he leaves, he notices for the first time a pattern in the tiles of broken circles: he has broken free and enters the future.

In the second part of the cycle, the narrator returns to the prairies. He is a new man this time, but only to discover cyclical patterns in modern city life as well:

> and again that year the world failed to end
>
> the randomness of order
> bud leaf stalk and branch
> circling the seasons (27)

In this part, the narrator learns to deal with decay and mortality and the rebirth embedded in them. As he looks at his books he realizes they are "filled with lies / about beginnings and endings" (35).

Parts three and four are journeys into personal memories, textual reflections of the mind trying to take hold of early memories. In part four, the Icelandic heritage is slowly finding its way back into the narrator's creative pattern: the names of natural objects, remembered from his earlier prairie days, are followed by self-coined kennings. Towards the end of part four, he affirms the power of words to take on the shape of the mind and the world, which can be conjured up by naming: "out of all the lost worlds the lost words / say it and make it happen" (64). Although wordplay and the fascination with naming are very popular postmodern subjects and Arnason a postmodern writer, we sense here, too, a residue of that long-standing Icelandic belief in the power of the word which persisted in Icelandic-Canadian folklore.

The "lost words" from "lost worlds" form a bridge to the fifth part in the cycle, in which the narrator dreams of the Icelandic-Canadian immigrant past. Through dreams, his heritage is making its way back into his life and vision, as he acknowledges in the prologue to the part: "We bury too deep, denying each corpse its vegetable renewal until it is leached by groundwater and seeks the surface" (70). As with Valgardson, the Icelandic heritage and history are here represented as something that will inevitably resurface. The remaining part of the poem shows that Arnason, too, sees ethnic heritage as something fruitful if it is dealt with and affirmed. It is, in other words, seen as part of the cyclical pattern of death and rebirth. The dream journey through the Icelandic-Canadian past in part five is one through death: it recovers the smallpox epidemic which ravaged the immigrant communities, the starvation and suffering, the deaths on the lake. However, the part ends with the promise of rebirth and fertility: the rainbows which in part one were connected to *Ragnarök* are now connected with spring. There is a note of care and love: the promise to tend a garden and the newly-found love of a widower.

The concluding part of the cycle is the closing of the circle. Fragments of the Old World and fragments of the New are combined and reborn into one fertile, creative vision. They are positively affirmed as being:

> fragments
> of a vision
> fragments of a life (88)

Again, as with Valgardson, ethnic heritage is seen as something that has to be dealt with and affirmed. It is an inevitable part of one's self which can only be fertile if it is allowed to be.

The Icelanders is in many respects a continuation of the exploration of ethnic heritage we find in *Marsh Burning*. In between the many anecdotes are pieces containing the author's own memories and views. These show a similar tendency toward wholeness as the movement of the *Marsh Burning* cycle. Here, however, the author's view on how to achieve this wholeness is quite clear: ethnic heritage is something personal, "a different set of memories," which, if allowed to become a social phenomenon that creates barriers between people, can be destructive: "This is why I am against this ethnic stuff always, of segregating, and dividing and destroying the country, which can be done by different languages" (116).

Like Valgardson, Arnason also remembers and documents the tensions that used to exist between different ethnic groups, between the Icelanders and the Ukrainians: "But that's all broken down now— then, if you went some place you were either Icelandic or Ukrainian, and today you are a Canadian and nobody knows whether you're Icelandic or Ukrainian or what the heck you are" (116). To be Canadian, for Arnason, is to resolve the predicament of a fragmented identity. And yet, there remains the resonance of ancestral sounds. Arnason experiences along with Valgardson the complex power of language in ethnic matters: it excludes, but it also includes. It is dispossessive as well as part of a sense of belonging in space and time:

My friends didn't speak any better Icelandic than I did. We assumed that it was a language spoken only by adults, and used particularly for secrets or for things we weren't supposed to know about, and I, at least, believed that I would naturally speak it when I grew older. All I had to do was wait. Of course that didn't happen, but I've lost none of my love for the mystical language that drifts at the edges of my comprehension. When I hear Icelandic spoken, I am warmed. I feel an instant kinship with the speakers.... The lilting singsong rhythms of that ancient language are the beat my heart moves to when I am happy. (112)

In Gunnars' works, we find a different focus on the theme of ethnic identity. As an immigrant who is forever on the move, she is not so much concerned with the recovery and affirmation of heritage. Ethnic identity for her is not an extra dimension of the self, but an experience of duality. Her focus is not so much on dispossession and affirmation, but on dislocation and integration. Her comments on Salverson (1986) could be applied to Gunnars herself as well: her writing is both an expression of and an attempt to unify a divided self. The two works in her oeuvre which are most concerned with the theme of ethnic identity are the poetic cycle *Wake-Pick Poems* (1981) and the short story collection *The Axe's Edge* (1983).

Wake-Pick Poems imaginatively represents a journey from birth into womanhood and identity. As in many of Gunnars' works, the main theme receives expression through the adept use of images, traditions and beliefs taken from Icelandic folklore. Interestingly, like Salverson, Gunnars uses the image of the changeling to represent the experience of a divided self: the first part of the cycle is called "Changeling Poems." Straight away in the first poem, dislocation, the loss of home and the confusion of identity feature prominently:

> i want to be an elf myself
>
> but they send me away
> paper strapped on my back
> boots on, away
> for a changeling dream & then
>
> an imp goes home
> an old crone goes home
> a gnome goes home
> & I go into mountain

The little elf-girl is sent to live with the "mountain folk," the trolls. She feels out of place and alienated: "i'm a stranger here" (8) and "i insist / i'm a foreigner" (9). However, she knows that once she is baptized, she cannot go back anymore: "they've got me hooked," "i'm theirs" (14-15). She receives great-grandmother's name, and is thus placed in the community of the trolls and their ancestors. Realizing she can now never belong with the elves anymore, she turns around and tries to fit into her new community. She desires no less than complete assimilation, willing to give up her elf-gift of being able to see into stones, into the invisible world of the *huldufólk* in order to belong with the trolls:

> huldufolk are after me
> they press their faces on the window
> i can tell they want me back
>
> but i've turned loyal to mountain-folk
> i'm a mountain-folk myself
> ...
>
> & when elves knock at the window sill
> huldufolk line up for me
> folk from the egyptian desert
> folk from jupiter
> folk from atlantis
> whisper "come home, come home"

> i'll take part
> in getting rid of them.... (22-23)

Slowly, she learns to adjust, learns the ways of the trolls, although "it isn't easy to be troll / trolls take everything you got / take away your innocence" (27). She succeeds in creating a place for herself in the troll community:

> i've been given
> the key to the kingdom
> i come & go as i wish
> i surpass mountain-folk
>
> at being mountain-folk
>
> ...
>
> i don't need to be
> accepted now
> i accept them
> help the younger ones walk.... (29)

However, the joy of finally belonging does not last. She is sent away to be a foreigner again. She remains a changeling, being neither one nor the other, everywhere the stranger:

> ...
> hosted my innocence away with elves in the scrub
> gave myself away to you
>
> kick me out of mountain
> kick me out the door
> live me among foreigners again:
> & if my shadow crosses foreign deserts
> if foreigners see my shadow dig up
> desert treasures
>
> it isn't me
> it's my changeling they see (32)

In the next part of the cycle, called "Monkshood Poems," the girl moves from Iceland to Denmark, where she learns about her ancestry on her mother's side. Being half-Icelandic and half-Danish, she again goes through the experience of being an outsider. Home and roots become unclear, alien concepts, no longer located in place or time:

> i want to go home, when i'm home
> i want to go home too
> you always want to (59)

> it's clear, roots exist
> but in what sense i don't know
> i see them
> where i least expect them (70)

Finally, she comes to the conclusion that you "can't go home again / except the way you left" (73). Home has become a feeling, a moment in time to which you cannot return. The only alternative is facing the future and going into the future:

> now that i have to go, take me away
> feet first
> so i won't see which way we go
> take me through the walls
> so i'll never return
>
> ...
>
> i want to break down the wall
> get going into open death (74)

In the last part of the cycle, "Wake-Pick Poems," a woman emerges who struggles for survival. Under the most elemental, inhuman conditions this woman suffers in order to revive "the dead babes of my nation" (79) as she pleads: "leave me with hands to tie / love for my people" (90). The struggle is no longer to find an integrated identity, but for life. And it is through this heavy task that an integrated identity is achieved. The love and responsibility this woman feels give her the strength to continue her fight for life by working day and night:

> my work is my life
> with it i pay (87)

She has joined the long tradition of her country to struggle for survival under the most miserable circumstances. Her work is also in the Icelandic tradition: knitting at home, keeping the eyes open with so-called wake-picks. She has found her place within the community of her people. She has created that place for herself this time, on the basis of her work and her love. She gives this place to the service of life and the future:

> if i fail now
> when i'm dead i'll be bait
>
> ...
>
> for them all to gain life (96)

The immigrant experience is one that begins in suffering and death, but it is also one that holds great hopes for the future. The profound sense of dual identity, a divided self, is at the same time one that will give birth to new, integrated life in which the two worlds within the self become one.

Whereas *Wake-Pick Poems* deals with a personal immigrant experience, *The Axe's Edge* is a collection of short stories which, taken together, portray the course of the immigrant experience of the Icelanders at various stages. The stories are told by individual narrators whose names are given with the title of each story, so that this collection provides us with a fragmented history of the Icelandic Canadians in various voices. As it moves from pre-emigration Iceland to Canada and eventually back to Iceland with a fourth-generation Icelandic Canadian in search of her roots, we move along with the gradual and painful transformation of the characters as they adapt to the New World. This collection gives us an idea of how Icelanders became Canadians, and how some of their heritage was left behind and some kept and adapted to new circumstances. Gunnars states in her prologue to the book:

I feel more like a rescue worker than a writer, only it is hard to tell exactly what is being rescued. It may be a certain form of experience: the way in which the undefended exposure to an overwhelmingly new world of ice, dust, forest, blizzard and sun has penetrated the way in which a people thinks.... The Icelanders had this one beauty in their response to Canada: they spread out, like a fan, to the full weather of the new environment. And when they survived, they did so as a transformed people.

Something more may be undergoing rescue: the way in which memory preserves ideas during this transformation. I think of these stories as records of how old lore reaches its own joints and bends under alien pressures. Humour and bizarre bits of ancient lore become strange news in another country. What was dead has a chance to live again, acquire a new kind of meaning. (2-3)

The first two stories in the book are set in Iceland, providing glimpses of people still firmly rooted in their country and traditions. The third story is in the form of a letter from Canada to Iceland, expressing a profound sense of bewilderment and disillusionment. Through the comparisons made in the letter between the Icelandic addressee and the Canadian girl Gabrielle, each being representative of her country, we are given to understand how incompatibly different the two countries seemed to the first immigrants, and how they felt caught between the attractions of the two. Páll Thorláksson, the writer of the letter, says: "It was almost impossible to imagine that this earth created both you and Gabrielle" (28). He is even convinced that the Icelandic girl could never live in North America: "You would lose your falcon clutch on life, the mid-sun heather in your cheeks would fade among these violet perfumes and tachinids. You were made for hailstorm, not sweet pea vines" (26).

As the stories move on, however, the transplantation does take place. The following three stories show how immigrants are trying to survive and make sense of the New World with the means they have at their disposal: their Icelandic lore and traditions. In trying to fit old and new together, they develop adaptation strategies. Halldór in "Crossroads," for instance, is trying to make the lore he knows from Iceland relevant in his new context. While talking about his harvesting work in North Dakota he ponders about the latest story he has read in Jón Árnason's collection of folk tales, the only book he has from home. Slowly, similarities begin to develop, and the ritual of lying at the crossroads to call up your dead ancestors appears to hold a message for the harvester: "A harvester has to know the right time and the right signs in the crop; I'm learning fast. That's another thing you also learn at the crossroads: sensitivity of this kind is a form of patience" (53).

The following story, "Grasses," takes us into the next generation. Sveinborg, the narrator, desperately wants to recapture the lore of her dead mother in order to learn more about her, but finds that she cannot because she lacks the belief in it. Although her ancestors are part of her mental territory, there is a cultural difference which separates her from her parents and ancestors. Nevertheless, she observes her parents' traditions: "It's the least I can do, even though it is too late to respect that old vision. I know I have failed no matter how I twist and turn the grasses. Somehow it is too late" (68).

Kolla, in her story "Ticks," shows us that in spite of the differences, the Canadianization, things live on: "They say things don't last in Canada. They're wrong" (69). Some tales and superstitions become rooted in the new land. Sometimes also the ethnic heritage comes out in more elusive ways. Tómas, in "Jazz," is the son of an Icelandic-Canadian fish-dealer and an English mother, although "Mom sort of disappeared in the mass of fishermen's wives and smithy sweepers of the Canadian Prairie Icelanders" (78). Tómas has lost contact with his heritage, living in New Orleans as a jazz musician. He says:

The Tómas-Jónas clan originated in the East-fjords they tell me, in a district called Múlasýsla. I can't think of a more unlikely combination of jazz and Múlasýsla. And yet. The mental framework is there, the crazy swing in the mind that says "to hell with you all." (78)

For Tómas, his heritage is no longer something according to which he should arrange his life. It is, however, something he uses creatively because it is still part of his identity: "If you're a mixture of molasses and cod-liver oil then that's what you are. Make your music out of fish gills and saxophones if you have to, with a touch of old-country wrestling. It can all work, because nobody takes it seriously anymore" (81).

In the last story, Ása goes to visit the country which her great-grandparents left in 1876, because she wants to discover her "Icelandic bones" underlying her Canadian identity: "To do that, I will have to immerse myself completely. You can't be a part-time student of a culture. You have to dive in with both hands and feet" (86). Although she admits that she would rather be somewhere else than in Reykjavík, she feels that's not possible:

But that's out. My mom taught me something of a verse on this by Stephan G. I can't remember it exactly, so I'll reword it:
  You can go as far as you like,
  walk in any place,
  but you'll never tear your roots
  from the soil of your own race. (90)

In the end, Ása quite literally dives into her ancestral culture with hand and feet, as she immerses herself in the Reykjavík harbour:

To feel yourself falling. It's like releasing something you've had tied up all your life. There must be something underneath all this. In the dark water that's so smooth you can see your own reflection. So cold you can feel the skin peeling back, exposing the bare skull. (93)

With this last act, she has not only discovered but also proved her "Icelandic bones," which in her family were linked to a suicidal tendency (88).

The last story, then, is much like Valgardson's "The Cave," in the unexpected ominous twist that heritage can take in one's life. However, Gunnars and Valgardson as well as Arnason all seem to agree that the Icelandic heritage inevitably forms part of their identity. There is a general tendency toward positive affirmation of ethnic identity in their works, and an interest in exploring either this identity itself (Gunnars and Valgardson) or in the past that gave birth to it (Arnason).

For Gunnars, the only native Icelander with Icelandic as her mother tongue, the Icelandic language does not play the exclusive or inclusive role that it does for Valgardson, nor is it a divisive or resonating medium from the past as with Arnason. Instead, Gunnars appears to feel as torn on the linguistic level as she does on a cultural and psychological level. On this level, too, she strives towards integration. Fully aware of the immigrant past and present of Canada, she promotes the adoption of words and speech rhythms from the ancestral languages of Canada's many immigrants:

Certainly we base our understanding of literature and narrative on the Canadian English that is rooted in English English. We derive our literary history from Britain. My sense was that much of Canadian language is rooted elsewhere. I wanted, since I had that kind of ear, to hear what a *Canadian* story sounded like. (*Axe's Edge* 2)

Elsewhere, Gunnars has explained her ideas and motives on this subject more elaborately:

What fascinated me when I began was the possibility of escaping the unilingual mode, expanding the language I wrote in by pushing out the boundaries. I made cracks on the surface of the English I wrote in by shifting into an Icelandic phrase or changing the structure of an English sentence in accordance with Icelandic sentence structure. This is possible in poetry and it is good to be able to let your language be informed by other modes of thought.... In Canada it should happen with the native tongues and languages of the immigrants. Those rhythms should be allowed to enter, to alter the rhythms of English so we can start thinking in other ways. (Demchuk 1984: 32-34)

In her writings, the reader can feel how Gunnars tries to push the limits of English by incorporating Icelandic words, concepts, turns of phrase and rhythms. Especially in *The Axe's Edge*, the voices of the narrators have a quality about them that is not quite English. They speak in a slow-paced, ponderous way, with an openness toward the supernatural and the unexplainable that is unusual in English. David Arnason remarks on the "odd formality" with which the narrators speak, "as if they were not quite expert in a foreign language" and concludes: "With the publication of *The Axe's Edge* we can all hear what a *Canadian* story sounds like. It sounds slightly foreign" (1984: 110).

STYLE

We will now shift our focus to aspects of intertextuality which show influences from Icelandic literature on the works of Valgardson, Arnason and Gunnars, who write within a Canadian context and framework. I am here using the concept intertextuality as defined by Linda Hutcheon: the intervention of other works or artistic conventions (1988: 28). Can textual evidence be found which would validate the qualifier Icelandic in Icelandic-Canadian literature, and show that the authors are indeed writing from more than than just the one (Anglo-)Canadian culture?

With regard to style, there is a great difference between Western Icelandic and Icelandic-Canadian works. Whereas especially Western Icelandic prose writers tended towards a romantic style far removed from the traditional style in Icelandic literature, the prose writings by Gunnars and Valgardson exhibit a style which in many respects closely resembles the traditional saga prose. Arnason, on the other hand, writes neither in a romantic mode nor in the style of the sagas. His stories have much more in common with Icelandic folklore and the Icelandic storytelling tradition.

Valgardson has become known for his characteristic prose style. His prose is powerfully terse, dramatic and suggestive. Characters are described through actions and brief sketches rather than elaborate descriptions. It is a sparse style which fits the bleak, tragic atmosphere found in many of his works, and which effectively heightens the tension. Many critics have commented upon it. Atwood, for instance, makes the following observation:

> Valgardson's world is easy enough to label part by part, but harder to convey. Finally it is made with language. The technique—laconic, flat, but with breathtaking twists and plummets and sudden dark gaps in understanding that open like crevasses—is hard to fault. It does what it should. (1979-80: 190)

Schoemperlen remarks that: "situations are presented so calmly that both their horror and their reality are dramatically heightened" (1978: 10) and Stedingh finds that "something is changed and finalized, but always in an undeclared, implied manner" (1977: 144). Stedingh, along with Hancock (1979-80: 130), also notices how, at the beginning of many stories, a character must quickly react to an intense situation. This sets the scene for the development of the story.

In Chapter I we saw that saga prose is characterized by a similar brevity and intensity. The matter-of-fact directness dramatically heightens growing tensions, laconic irony heightens tragedy.[12] Moreover, sagas are completely centred around action: actions speak where words remain silent; actions form the core of development and plot. Emotions, descriptions and introspection occur rarely, and only where they are necessary for the understanding of the ensuing scene. Much attention is demanded of the reader, who has to be quick and attentive to catch all the implications in order to be able to interpret later scenes.

An example of Valgardson's terse, flat prose is the following passage from the story "Brothers":

> He got up when the sky was still slate grey. The cook-shack was cold so he dressed quickly. A glance told him the child was dead. His head lay tipped back on his pillow.
>
> Alex woke Fjola. She was brisk and businesslike. Before they wakened Lulabelle, they wound the body in a blanket, which they secured with safety pins. (*Bloodflowers* 51)

The story "Celebration" (*Red Dust*) revolves around a couple and their two children who are living on the edge of the poverty line. To celebrate the fact that the social worker might be able to get them on welfare they buy a bottle of homebrew, but under the influence of the alcohol they start a fight and the woman is locked out in the freezing cold. She will have to be taken to hospital in town, but a blizzard is coming up. They manage to get a lift and reach town just in time for Mabel to be admitted into hospital. As everything is snowing in, the driver offers Eric a bed for the night, but Eric replies that he prefers a hotel. This is how the story ends:

> He felt in his pockets. "Oh, hell," he said, "I forgot my wallet."
>
> "That's okay," the truck driver replied. "My old lady will give you some supper, then we'll get some sleep. You can have the kids' bed. They can sleep on the couch."
>
> At these last words, Eric gave a sudden start and his eyes widened as if, without warning, a terrible vision had been thrust upon him. He took a step toward the door, then stopped. (102)

While the focus of the action has been on the couple, the reader is given to understand only now, and only by implication, the true tragedy of the story: in their intoxication and the heat of the fight the couple have forgotten their two young children who are alone at home and are being snowed-in. Yet no judgement is passed, no further explanation given, everything is left up to the reader's imagination and interpretation. There is no elaboration on Eric's emotions after this terrible discovery, nor on what he intends to do. The horror of the event is left to speak for itself, heightened by the quiet calm and unexpectedness with which it is related.

A less horrific example is the story "A Business Relationship" (*God is not a Fish Inspector*). This story deals with an older couple who have met through a matrimonial ad in the *Winnipeg Free Press*. The man, Carl, finds out that he suffers from a fatal illness. On the surface, the story tells in a matter-of-fact tone of Carl's concern that Olga, his wife, will be well provided for after his death. Only through the eloquent silences in between the practical statements does the reader come to sense the deep love that has grown between these two people, and the flat tone makes the ending the more moving: Carl leaves, supposedly to go hunting, but by implication both Olga and the reader realize that he will not come back because Carl knows that his medical expenses would leave Olga in debt.

The language used in Gunnars' works, even though most of them are poetry, also bears a close resemblance to the saga style. George Johnston, who has translated sagas into English, remarks about

Gunnars' *Settlement Poems* and *One-eyed Moon Maps*: "The style reminds me of the sagas in its dramatic immediacy, yet its incidents and observations are joined not in narrative sequence but by juxtaposition.... In all three books the language is admirably used, sparing of adjectives, adverbs, and all forms of comparison" (1982: 74-75). Other critics have noticed the level, detached voice and the sense of understatement in her works, as well as the directness and the eloquence of the silences between the words. Gustaf Kristjanson mentions Gunnars' "clean, spare prose" and its "direct quality, as well as the vivid, almost brutal imagery" (1980: 41), and Eva Tihanyi remarks on the "evocative simplicity—a kind of muted music—and the sense of understatement that pervades her work" as well as on "the detached voice of the i in most of the poems." Although Tihanyi does not appreciate this style in all cases, she does admit that "Gunnars' cool, level voice" is effective where her subject is charged: "sometimes the quietest lines can make the loudest point" (1986: 84-85).

Two examples from *Settlement Poems 1* show how the laconic style and crystallized sentences bring out the pain behind the facts, made more poignant by unexpected turns such as in line 7 where the simple adjective "pure" is deceptively placed so as to heighten its eventual effect, or the grim meaning the apparently positive "cleanly" takes on in the context of line 10 of the second example:

> unnecessary graveyards, all
> the children complain about them
> severe stomach pain
> suffocation, insects in the mouth
>
> 3 days, august 14 to 17
> on the steamboat to winnipeg
> the drinking water is pure
> poison by now, full
>
> of creatures fallen in
> ("From Memory XII" 21)

> i'm down to collecting skeletons
> bones with deeper relations
> than flesh or skin, bones that show
> how we live, seven

are dead at fridjón's, two
left, at ólafur's the third
baby swells in the gums
blood streaks the white teeth

scurvy cuts away the flesh
as cleanly as it can, removes
the skin, viscera, bones
too small, too delicate
("Stefán Eyjólfsson XIV" 51)

An example from a later work is the poem "fell down the stairs and died," in a cycle concerned with the threat of global nuclear escalation (*The Nightworkers of Ragnarök*). Here, the matter-of-fact quality serves to heighten the ominous message implied in the seemingly flat and innocent final sentence:

until further notice
one is free to go over the facts:

1951 — an atomic reactor makes electricity
1954 — in russia an atomic plant
1955 — nautilus
1956 — calder hall, england
but this is enough

otherwise
when spring is young the birds
fly weakly over the marsh
without pattern
and drop fast
their wings almost black
and collapsible

there are low rapid calls in the marsh
that cannot be heard
for the moment
one experiment follows another
and the technical difficulties sponge
into the air like summer
warmer everyday

soon we can take off our sweaters

The crystallized style in many of Gunnars' poems is also reminiscent of Eddic poetry. Not only does it share that pictorial "stone-carving" quality of Eddic poetry (indeed Gunnars has herself compared her poetry to that of a stone sculpture in an interview with Valgardson), but some of her poems also carry remnants of the Norse stress patterns and alliterative patterns:

> galdra-leifi, another wizard
> wanted a man's head
> with wine & bread
> & with it he read the future
> (*SP* 1: "Jóhann Briem IV" 31)

Although the number of stresses per line do not conform, there is the same regular, strong stress pattern governing short lines with internal rhyme. The following stanza from "drink" in *One-eyed Moon Maps* shows the stress pattern even more regularly and strongly, although the internal rhyme is almost absent:

> an uncertain space
> connects night & day
> russet & amber
> as the giant kvasir's blood
> brewed with honey
> by dwarves

Valgardson and Gunnars, then, show in their contemporary Canadian works how the old saga and Eddic style can still function effectively in a Canadian context. This stark style fits contemporary subject matter very well, much better than the romantic style of their Western Icelandic predecessors. Perhaps the conditions under which the saga authors wrote, those of the violent and disillusioned Sturlunga age, are not altogether unlike the conditions we face in the Nuclear age as we are surrounded by the threat of global destruction and are sceptically aware of our existential isolation. There may also be a relation between the use of the saga prose style charged with implications and silences, and the fact that Gunnars and Valgardson, each in their own way, are giving a voice to the largely inarticulate characters from the Icelandic-Canadian history and community. They are inarticulate because they have been muted by the dominant Anglo-Canadian history and majority, and silenced by the harshness of their environment and the struggle to survive in it. Through the artistic talents of Gunnars and Valgardson these voices have found a medium in the traditional Old Icelandic prose style.

THEME AND OUTLOOK

Similarities in style alone, however, may not be a very convincing example of Icelandic literary influence. After all, other twentieth-century writers such as Hemingway also used a very stark and direct style without there being reason to assume that they had been influenced by the Icelandic sagas (although Hemingway did admire them).[13] Icelandic influence in the case of Gunnars and Valgardson need not be attributable to their background alone. However, when we look at matters such as theme and vision, it will become clearer that there are Icelandic influences at work.

As was pointed out in the first chapter, once a culture has died it cannot be resurrected for re-use without becoming artificial. If contact with Old Icelandic literature had been lost, it could not have exerted a natural influence on later literature or even on mentality. If all cultural baggage that had been brought by the immigrants from Iceland to Canada had eventually died during the transplantation, there could have been no true influence from the Icelandic tradition on Canadian writers of Icelandic descent. It would have been possible for them to play textual games, void of all emotion and serious intention, but there could have been no dominant theme or governing vision sprung from Icelandic or even from an Icelandic-Canadian culture. The works of Valgardson, and to a certain extent those of Arnason as well, contain a particular vision and specific themes which are also dominant in the Icelandic literary tradition. This has been possible because the prevalent conditions in the rural Icelandic immigrant areas, mainly the Interlake, were very similar to conditions in Iceland. Thus a particular vision and mind-set could easily be transplanted, and specific themes have remained relevant also for contemporary Icelandic-Canadian writers.

It is inevitable, in this respect, to mention Canadian prairie culture, as the Icelandic-Canadian communities were nearly all on the prairies. The prairie landscape has traditionally been experienced as awe-inspiring and influential. At the beginning of the twentieth century, when Western Canada was being settled, the prairie was seen as a new Garden of Eden, a fertile "garden of the world," full of promise and possibility.[14] This romantic vision, which was also held by Laura Goodman Salverson, was hardly in accordance with the rough conditions the prairie land and climate imposed on its pioneers.

As a result, the pastoral "garden myth" had to give way to its opposite, which has become known in Canadian literature as "prairie realism." The fertile garden was now an ominous, flat infinity which dwarfed and reduced man and all his efforts into eventual and inevitable nothingness. In order to wrench a living from this land, man had to curb all passion and desire. Emotion and creativity shrivelled while man struggled for survival, all hopes doomed. The Garden of Eden thus became a fallen world, a barren wasteland, and the dream turned into a nightmare as man alienated himself from the land in the struggle to survive. Prairie realism is an important strain within Canadian literature, starting with Frederick Philip Grove and culminating in Margaret Laurence's *Manawaka* novels. Nevertheless, its counterpart, the optimistic dream vision of the prairie and its pastoral rurality has remained true and alive in prairie literature, from Nellie McClung and Laura Goodman Salverson in the 1920s via W.O. Mitchell in the 1940s to Robert Kroetsch and Aritha van Herk today.

Accepting such denotations as "prairie literature" and "prairie realism" means entering the long-standing opposition within Canadian literature between "internationalists" and "regionalists." Dealing with writers from the prairies, which Valgardson and Arnason are, it seems pointless not to accept the regionalist point of view, if only because it forms the basis of these authors' works and indeed belief. Prairie writers have always been painfully aware of their absence from the cultural centres in the East (Toronto, Montreal), and of the fact that they write from a different experience, just as the prairie people have always shown a different, more politically radical mentality than that prevalent in Eastern Canada.

Certain conditions, then, prevailed in the lives of the Icelandic Canadians on the prairies similar to those that had dominated the lives of their ancestors in Iceland. In Chapter II we saw how the hardships which the immigrants suffered upon arrival in Canada were hardly less than those suffered in the home country. Moreover, the struggle for survival in an awe-inspiring, harsh landscape and rough climate continued on the prairies. Fishing on the lakes was as hazardous and rough as it had been on the ocean, and the prairie land was as hard to work and unpredictable in yielding crops as the Icelandic. These conditions fostered a fatalistic and stoic mind-set, as they had in Iceland.

These conditions, however, did not nourish only bleakness. A strongly developed sense of community and kinship has always characterized the Icelanders, and it became even more important in Canada where they had to deal with similar isolation in an alien land and alien culture. Survival often depended on support from others. At the same time, the isolation, the self-reliance imposed by a pioneer history and the domination by a foreign power (Denmark) or majority (Anglo-Canadians) stimulated individualism and a democratic sensibility strongly coloured by a profound suspicion of authority.

The pronounced regional sensibility and rural orientation which characterizes prairie culture is also present in Icelandic culture. Iceland's was, until fairly recently, a completely rural economy: there was no industrialization, and farming and fishing were the mainstays. Reykjavík, although the capital, was still hardly a town, let alone a city, at the time when emigration took place. During all of Iceland's history until well into the twentieth century, the centres of civilization and authority were always somewhere else. During the period of the Old Icelandic republic, the cultural and political centre was at the Norwegian court. Later, it became Copenhagen. Iceland, in other words, was in more than just the geographical sense marginalized, just as the prairie provinces have felt themselves marginalized by the East. Dahlie has pointed to the frequent occurrence of exile in Canadian literature as a consequence of Canada's colonial status, and along with it the development of certain obvious oppositions such as that of "metropolis and hinterland"; for exile to the New World, like Ovid's exile, meant "removal from the centre of civilization to its periphery, to a region of strange people ..." (1986: 2, 10). These oppositions find their origin in the contrasts between the Old World versus the New, and the contradiction inherent in the view of the New World as a potential paradise and a place of exile. As Dahlie notes, Iceland, with its immigrant history, was once seen as a potential paradise and place of exile as well. Consequently, like Canadian literature, Icelandic literature has adopted its history of exile as a major component.

Among the oppositions that developed in the imaginative recreation of this condition of cultural exile are such themes as country versus city or rural community versus cultural and political centre, and the individual versus authority. In saga literature we often find these themes expressed in the journeys of Icelanders to the Norwegian court where they have a confrontation with the king.[15] In later

Icelandic literature it occurs in, for instance, such influential works as Jón Thoroddsen's *Piltur og Stúlka*, and, later still, many of Halldór Laxness' works.

The regional focus almost demands the universalizing of the regional for serious artists, as there is always the inherent danger of parochialism. An early awareness of this danger must have existed in Iceland, considering that the saga authors succeeded in giving the stories of their young and far-away nation a universal application and appeal which has survived through the ages. The eagerness with which the medieval Icelanders tried to remain abreast of international developments, as was outlined in Chapter I, also attests to this awareness. A similar concern to make the regional universal can be detected in contemporary Icelandic-Canadian literature.

The process of settling a country was in many cases a not very profitable business. It neither did nor could satisfy everybody's ambitions. In early Iceland, it was fairly common for hard-working farmers to turn into pirating Vikings during the off-season in order to amass riches and have some adventure. The tension this combination of peaceful farmers with violent pirates out for wordly goods must have caused within persons and within society is given form in many of the sagas.[16]

From history we know that a similar pattern developed with the settling of the New World. Most settlers had come to build up a better future, and for many a better future simply meant getting rich quickly. If the prospect of wealth included living a life devoid of culture or of Old World heritage and values, they were prepared to take that into the bargain with or without regret. That the Icelanders were no exception is clear from many Western Icelandic works. The great concern this pattern caused among many West Icelanders is easily explained by the concern for preservation of the Icelandic cultural heritage in Canada as well as by the respect for culture which characterizes many Icelanders. Interestingly, it is still a matter of concern for Icelandic-Canadian authors, especially for Valgardson, in whose works it occurs frequently.

The themes introduced above, the regionalist orientation and pioneer history which have caused such oppositions as country versus city, old versus new, individualism versus authority and farmers versus pirates, along with a tendency towards universality, still form some of the basic themes of various Icelandic-Canadian literary works. They have been important themes in Icelandic literature from the sagas onwards and could be transplanted to Icelandic-Canadian literature because the conditions that the Icelanders encountered and adapted to in Canada had much in common with those in Iceland. Moreover, these themes served and serve to order, in a literary form, the socially and psychologically chaotic effects resulting from the immigrant experience, as the environment and community life are given imaginative shape and meaning.

In his essay "Personal Gods," Valgardson states:

> Is it any wonder that having grown up in an Icelandic-Canadian community that suffered, in its migration to the new land, hardships every bit as great as those which were left behind, I write stories which have been described as being governed by a dark vision? (1979-80: 180)

Valgardson affirms the influences from his Icelandic-Canadian background and from Icelandic saga literature, and ends by saying:

> For myself, during the past (who can know the future?), I have chosen to turn away from conscious experimentation. I have chosen, instead, to use all the dramatic devices of the traditional story to counterbalance characters who, through their relationship with a harsh and unforgiving landscape, have had their emotional range severely limited....
>
> In *Njal's Saga*, which was written somewhere around the year 1280, there is a Valgardson. I am tied to an old tradition. I do not complain. It has served me well. (185)

Interestingly, Valgardson here aligns himself with the Icelandic literary tradition, although the "dark vision" and thematic concern he describes could just as easily have been taken for a form of prairie realism in the style of Sinclair Ross.

In Valgardson's fiction, we usually encounter a rural setting with a set of characters who all have their place within the community as individuals. Valgardson's characters are rough, and if they are not, they are bound for destruction or victimization: "Valgardsonland" is no place for the weak and the meek. It is a place where people have had to struggle hard for what little they have. The struggle has made some of the characters pathetic in their desperate, feeble attempts to improve or escape their circumstances (Sonny in "The Hunting"; Gregory in "First Flight"), and others either dignified in their pride and determination not to yield (Fusi in "God is not a Fish Inspector"; Ellen in "Granite Point") or insensitive and cruel in their anxiety to survive and maintain some kind of living (Valdi in "In Manitoba"; Orville in "Red Dust").

Under such circumstances, the community takes on an important function. It provides support and a form of stability in an environment where the unpredictable elements rule and it breaks the isolation imposed on people by the landscape. Huddled together, people try to protect themselves from the onslaughts of inimical forces as they attempt to find patterns with which to ward off more blows. Sometimes the community is portrayed as playing a humane and sustaining role, as in "December Bargaining" and "God is not a Fish Inspector," where the community helps to preserve a person's dignity. Valgardson, however, who has set himself up as the mouthpiece of those who have been muted and whose emotional lives have been cut off, seems more interested in exploring the role of the community as a desperate refuge for individuals battered by extreme conditions. In "Brothers," for instance, domestic and communal stability is considered so vital that it is worth the life of a child. "The Couch" describes the endless complications and domestic quibbling Ruby puts herself through just to be able to go into town and meet acquaintances. In "Bloodflowers" and "The Curse" we see how the community has put its faith in primitive rituals in a desperate attempt to ward off death, even though these rituals involve in turn the deaths of innocent people.

Although nature plays a part in moulding Valgardson's characters, it is not man's real enemy. Nature not only takes but also gives, and her ways can be learnt and worked with. In most stories, man is either man's own enemy, or man is up against elusive inimical forces of man's making, such as technology or social institutions. In the first instance, man's ultimate aloneness in the world is emphasized, whereas in the second, man's individuality is denied by impersonal forces which cannot be fought like an enemy. A chilling example of man's ultimate isolation in life is the story "An Act of Mercy." Here, two brothers confront their enemy in the form of their cruel father, thus implying that even the closest of kin can turn against one and leave one alone in times of need. This view of man's condition in life is aptly described in Neils' observations of his brother:

The lamplight distorted Helgi, making him all highlights and deep shadows so that there were no middle planes, no soft greys, only sharp angles in pools of darkness. The appropriateness of it pleased Neils for he felt it showed Helgi

as they all were—extremes created by isolation and constant struggle.
(*Bloodflowers* 24)

People can help and support each other, but in the end one can rely only on oneself: "You have to save yourself. Nobody can save you except yourself. I've found that out," says Darlene in "A Private Comedy" (*God is not a Fish Inspector* 99).

The impersonal enemy against which many Valgardsonian characters are pitted occurs in guises often connected to the city: materialism, mechanization, institutionalism and general city values. Although the picture Valgardson draws of rural life is hardly idyllic, it is at least still a place where people are regarded as people and have to be considerate of one another: "rural people are much more aware of each other as full individuals.... You accept people very much for who they are. In the city if someone offends you, you can ignore them," says Valgardson (Haglund 1981: 41). Moreover, in the country, people are faced on a day-to-day basis with the reality of elemental life without being able to look comfortably the other way and ignore basic human problems, or seek escape in easy solutions.

In "December Bargaining," Benny always buys Solmi's fishing equipment for the season when he is not fishing, and lets him buy it back when fishing starts. Thus Solmi has some money to tide him over as he drinks his time away on land, where he feels out of place, without having to resort to begging or lending, for "[a] man's got a right to some pride," as Benny says (*Red Dust* 46). Then Benny falls ill and the family has to use up the savings with which he used to buy Solmi's fishing gear. In his despair, Solmi turns to a lawyer from the city who has bought a summer cottage on the lake. The lawyer buys the gear off Solmi for a low price and sells it for profit. When the season starts, Solmi cannot buy his equipment back. He has no money to buy new equipment nor the skills to earn money any other way. This is the price that some of the villagers have to pay for "progress": city people buying their land and their ways of living.

In "Beyond Normal Requirements," the unbridgeable gap in understanding life is portrayed through the confrontation between a high school teacher from the city and a pupil of his from the country. Gradually we come to understand that the boy's brother has committed suicide, and the teacher is driving and accompanying the boy to the funeral "on an errand of mercy" as he sees it (*Red Dust* 7). The teacher is uncomfortable with the situation and his lack of understanding why the brother took his own life. He only knows life from books, as becomes poignantly clear when he presumptiously defines the meaning of tragedy to the boy, whereas the true tragedy of the situation completely escapes him:

Angered at his lack of response, Allen said, "He was your brother. Don't you care?"
    "No," the boy answered....
In a voice at once both hollow and resonant, as though it rose from a great depth, the boy said, "For him, it's over." (14-15)

In "An Afternoon's Drive," a man is forced to realize that the ideas and qualifications which have served him so well in his city life are of no use when trying to save his pregnant wife after having got lost in the middle of nowhere with a car that has broken down. "Identities" effectively portrays the deluded sense of security that a comfortably wealthy middle-class man takes for granted. In "The Burning," an old man is forced to move from the house he had built for his bride, because the Atomic Institution wants to use it for fire practice. Unable to fight the decision because nobody claims responsibility for it, the man finally decides to set fire to the house himself.

One institution which is particularly under attack in Valgardson's fiction is that of the Church. It is not so much Christianity itself that Valgardson opposes; rather it is the cover it forms for such un-Christian motives as greed and power. Although Valgardson comes from a strict Lutheran background, he appears to share the characteristic Icelandic aversion to that inhumane by-product of institutionalized religion: dogma. In "Saved," Melissa, a run-away daughter of a fundamentalist preacher, cannot face the insecurities of a life without strict rules and flees back into the protection of the Church. "God is not a Fish Inspector" is a moving example of sheer greed and malevolence masquerading as Christianity, as Emma cruelly robs her father of his pride and dignity in the name of God.

Greed is not always linked to Christianity however, but also occurs as a form of materialism which endangers true values in life: a code of humane behaviour and honour, a belief in spiritual and cultural values, or a pride taken in work or love of the land. Materialism appears as a disruptive and destructive force in the generally peaceful routine of rural life which in itself is hard enough for most people to survive in. It is usually associated with images of decay and personified by characters bordering on the grotesque. "Capital," for instance, describes Abel Shitzer in images reminiscent of a bird of prey. His pure greed is effectively contrasted with the desperate attempts of Steini Storekeeper and his wife to make some money from their little grocery store. In the following scene both appear as grotesques, Abel horrible and Steini slightly ridiculous:

> All the time Steini struggled with the groceries, Shitzer hovered over him, a gaunt spectre enveloped in a khaki army-surplus coat that hung like a tent from his narrow shoulders. His thin, sharp face was so brown it might have been cured in a smokehouse. A purple bulge rose on the corner of his lower lip like a grape.
>
> He kept his purse crushed in the bottom of his left pocket until the total was rung up, then he reluctantly drew it out and, still more reluctantly, counted out faded dollar bills as soft as worn cotton. As he counted them, he rubbed each one between his dirty thumb and forefinger. Laying one bill on another, he kept a glittering stare fixed on Steini's face but Steini never noticed. Intent on the money, he was bent so far over he might have been prostrating himself before a god. As he tried to keep track of the growing total, his watery blue eyes screwed themselves up until his entire face was twisted and warped. (*God is not a Fish Inspector* 79-80)

Abel is a true predator who lives off other people's meagre incomes, not for survival's sake but for money's sake.

Dominic in "Trees" is another example of this type, and he, too, is presented with a dose of black humour which somehow makes him seem even more horrible:

> When disease or misfortune struck, he appeared, his profit already calculated.... No-one had seen his wife but it was said that when she died he set her up in the back seat of his car and drove her to the city in the hope of selling her to the medical school. (*Red Dust* 77)

The character of Dominic is pitted against that of the protagonist Ester. She has inherited a walnut grove which has become unproductive. However, in her life of hard work and financial straits the grove is an oasis of peace. Dominic wants to buy Ester's grove, but in spite of her financial situation she courageously decides to oppose him. She realizes that some things in life are worth more than money and need to be protected from destructive forces such as Dominic's greed.

Although Valgardson's fiction is for the larger part firmly set in the Interlake area, and for the other part in other particularized areas in Western Canada, his main concern is not with the recreation of these regions, but with the people and their human experiences:

What concerns me ... is not the retelling of history but the dramatic construction of the landscape inside my mind. Only then can I adequately express those themes which are of profound concern to me. If I were to make as my major aim a simple retelling of history, my stories would be narrowly regional. The stories would be organized, not around theme and dramatic effect, but around the randomness of life.... In discovering themes, in communicating the emotions embodied in them, I do not fear the regional because I realize that the creation of the particular does not preclude the universal; rather, it makes it possible and communicable. (1979-80: 181-82)

Valgardson uses the setting of the region he knows best to convey universal motives and themes. He explores human motives and actions and finds the drama in human experience, which is recognizable to us all: "It's that reach into humanity in which we recognize ourselves, the human condition, that makes the fiction worthwhile" (Valgardson to Gould 1979: 17). The stark life of most Valgardsonian characters may be as unfamiliar to us as the medieval Icelandic pioneer life led by Njáll in *Njáls saga*, but while they remain credible because they are set firmly in the region which has moulded them, their ordeals and attempts to give meaning to their lives are of all times and places.

Thus, at the bowling alley, Frank Labonovitch's motives in hiring his uncle Michael for a job which is too heavy for him but which he so desperately needs, and Frank's overwhelming grief rooted in fear for his own fate when he finds Michael dead by exhaustion, are timeless and universal ("The Job"). Similarly, in "The Couch," everybody can sympathize with Ruby's deep-seated need to go to town once a year to find some fellowship, or in "Skald" recognize Alma's determination to establish her own identity. We all know capitalists like Dominic or Abel. Valgardson is a clever enough writer to induce in us a growing sense of sympathy with characters whose actions we might otherwise have thoughtlessly condemned, thus forcing us to recognize how close we are to everything that is human. In this respect, Valgardson is a true Icelandic writer who likes to give his reader something to think about. Salverson once characterized this trait of Icelandic writing:

If there was nothing in the story to provoke a train of thought, nothing that gave you an intriguing glimpse of human foibles, nothing that touched on the springs of beauty in nature or in man, then why trouble to read the thing? A cup of coffee would do just as well if all you wanted was mental oblivion! (*Confessions* 401)

One book in which we can see many of the aspects discussed above at work, and which I suggest is a modern Canadian saga, is Valgardson's *Gentle Sinners*. Eric, presented as an impetuous young Viking warrior, is eager to fight his way out of captivity, prove his mettle and "gain fame and fortune" in the traditional Viking way. His judgements and actions, however, are still unrestrained by a code of ethics, an awareness of family and ancestry, and a position in the community. Sigfus is the conciliatory force, the wise and respected elder or priest-chieftain, to whom people turn for advice and who is entrusted with the task to keep violence from erupting in the rural community.

When Eric arrives, he is an outsider. He comes from the city, a cultural centre of strict authority and organized religion, into a rural community where the law of the jungle holds sway and almost pagan values rule. Although Sigfus "baptizes" him into the family, the most central unit within saga society, Eric still has to earn his place in the community. To do this, he must learn its unwritten rules, and yet he cannot prevent his coming from upsetting "the balance of things," as Sigfus says (166). Eric's fight with Big Tree, which he does not win but where he proves he can stand up for himself without flinching before a clearly stronger opponent, earns him respect and a reputation among many in the community. It also gains him the enmity of the Tree brothers, who terrorize the town by cunning (Little Tree) and strength (Big Tree).

Sigfus has to teach Eric the meaning of such crucial Norse concepts as *drengskapr* and *ójafnaðarmennska*. *Drengskapr* was considered one of the most essential ideal virtues: it comprised magnanimity and honourable, noble behaviour. *Ójafnaðarmennska* referred to a tendency to immoderate behaviour, and was considered a quality dangerous to the stability within the community. The importance of these two concepts has, of course, everything to do with the fact that early Icelandic society was based on feud: one immoderate or dishonourable act could unleash an endless chain of killings, unless generous and moderating forces would put a stop to them. As Magnusson and Pálsson point out:

Anyone who takes up the wrong sort of challenge in the sagas, as a result of responding to the goading of others, always comes out the loser in the end.

In the sagas, it is not the great warriors who are the heroes, the men who could kill the most people with fewest strokes; it is the sages, the men of moderation ... who understand the awful futility of violence and devote their lives to combating it. (1983: 33)

Sigfus considers Eric's urge to avenge himself on his parents immoderate and dangerous. First, one does not kill one's kin.[17] Second, it would be an immoderate retribution that would only cause more destabilizing ramifications. He has to make Eric understand that the consequences of an act must be in accordance with the offence, and that individual passion must sometimes give way to moderation and magnanimity. On the other hand, Sigfus shows himself perfectly prepared to kill when defending his family and protecting his property. When the Tree Brothers invade his yard in order to accuse and threaten him without grounds, it is they who are acting immoderately, and so they must be restrained, if necessary by killing them.

Although Sigfus would not have hesitated to kill in this instance, he is truly shocked when he learns that Eric stole money from his parents when he ran away. According to the Old Icelandic code of ethics, stealing was one of the pettiest and most contemptuous acts (Turville-Petre 1953: 250). In a society which celebrated generosity and hospitality as great virtues, stealing was not only unnecessary but completely dishonourable. Eric's attempted suicide is another example of his impulsive, unrestrained behaviour under pressure. In a heroic code of ethics, suicide is, of course, regarded as cowardice, which is even worse than theft; it is a negation of all heroic virtues (Hallberg 1962: 117). Sigfus points out to Eric that if he does not learn moderation, he will be a disruptive force to the community and has to be removed from it:

"Theft," Sigfus said, his voice hardening with impatience. "Threatening a social worker with a rifle. Attempted suicide. Do you know how that sounds? You run. Go ahead. They'll catch you and throw you in the nut house. They don't ever have to let you out of there." (181)

In the end, Eric learns. He runs, but does not run away. Rather, he sets out to do what he has to do: he deals with his enemies, Larry and the Trees, and frees the girl he loves from their power. Then he returns to the city to finish his education. He is no longer afraid but sure of the course to follow and determined to pursue his freedom: "He had, he thought, a year before him. He intended to survive. School would occupy most of his days. Freedom, though, could be expanded. Before he returned, he had a lot to do" (210). Thus the young Viking has learnt the values of moderation and honour, and to see the extent and consequences of his acts in a larger framework. He has been taught responsibility of action and the importance of family and community, in which he has earned himself a respected place. He has, in other words, learnt the values around which the sagas are centred. Through Valgardson, we see these values at work in a thoroughly Canadian context.

In Gunnars' work, the thematic focus is different from that of Valgardson, because she is a recent immigrant. She is not so much concerned with the opposition of city versus country, because she has never truly settled in any area, nor does she have a rural or community background like Valgardson. The concerns found in her work are more directed towards the tension between a strongly developed sense of individualism and self-reliance versus a deeply rooted desire to belong, to a community, to a place. Additionally, her childhood spent in Iceland and Denmark and her later years in the U.S. and Canada have made the juxtapositions of the new with the old and the universal with the local important motives in her work. Likewise the struggle for survival, which she knows both from childhood and ancestral experience, and is concerned with because of her interest in the immigrant history of the Icelanders.

Many of Gunnars' works carry clear autobiographical tones. She regularly explores the influences of her Icelandic childhood on her development and experiences as an adult in North America. Her frequent moving of house and country, even as a child, has made displacement and loss very acute themes for her. Owens suggests that:

The poetic cycle entitled "The Silent Hand" allows us to see the poet's hand at work, trying to draw together vastly different worlds and as well trying to pull together parts of what she feels to be a divided self.... In approaching the subject of the cycle ... the poet feels divided, between two cultures, between old and new, and, more tellingly, within herself. Her emotions pull her one way, intellect and learning another. (1990: 66)

Whereas continual immigrant experience has made the author an outsider, someone forced to rely on herself alone, this enforced self-reliance is opposed by a strong desire for the communal:

> we cannot be sure where
> we come from. all
> that matters is
>
> where we long to go
> the silent hand that draws us
> in
> (*The Nightworkers of Ragnarök* 73)

Somehow there is always a connection in Gunnars' works between community and survival. In *Settlement Poems* 1 and 2, we encounter, as one critic noted, not only "the individual wish to survive, but the wish to establish surviving communities" (Kostjuk 1982: 157). A strong sense of staying together and surviving together speaks from various poems. In "Stefán Eyjólfsson X," for instance, we see how the group helps its various members to stay alive, how individual survival is not a personal but a communal concern:

> catch 37
>
> flat-sided pike in the red
> river shallow up for dawn
> feeding, taylor tells me
> to give it to those run
>
> out of food, some have nothing
> (*1*: 47)

In "Thórgrímur Jónsson V" it becomes obvious how the individual thinks in terms of the community:

> live under dead
> leaves, my people
> without time left
> to construct (keep going
>
> on government loans)
> maybe next year, spring

leaves will stir, fish
burst out

of dead ice, dead
flakes on the ground
maybe what's left

of my people will walk
away from this place
(2: 43)

Notice the tone of despair in the following passage where one threatens to leave the group:

this insect harvesting won't
last, thórgrímur
would rather starve, or walk

to winnipeg, rather
abandon the colony than
all die together, says

he won't rub elbows

with those who suffer
because it's ugly, but if
you stay, next summer

it won't be ants
it'll be wheat, rye, barley
thórgrímur

just won't wait
(2: 26)

Wake-Pick Poems describes a young girl's journey from individualism and foreignness to acceptance of and into the community of her people. First, she claims that "i'm a stranger" (8), "won't act like one of them" (9), but slowly she gets used to her people, and "they're used to me too" (31). She eventually affirms her place with them: "i'll stay with you / anyway, my people" (25). The tension between individual and community is renewed in the "Monkshood Poems" when the girl moves to Denmark and has to deal with her kin and ancestry there.

Finally, in "Wake-Pick Poems," there is again the connection between community and survival. The girl has grown into a woman who is sacrificing her life for her people: as she knits her life away in the damp darkness of her turf hut she will not yield to exhaustion because her work is her contribution to the survival of her nation: "my life is an oath on knitting" (92). As Jesus advocated turning the other cheek, so this woman turns the other eye to save her people:

> all week i knit with the cold
> north wind between my eyelids
> between my teeth
> & when they relent & give me night
> give me darkness after the knitting wake
>
> i'll turn the other eye
> i'll give all my eye (95)

When she thinks about the long fate of her nation "where predators with poisoned claws / crawl along shrinking arms / in the tradition of my people," she pleads:

> though i be put to fulling eternity
> soak me, stiff & small
> wring me in the doorway
> but leave me with hands to tie
> love for my people (90)

In *The Nightworkers of Ragnarök*, the strength and sustenance found in community is seen first on a national and then on a global scale. "The silent hand" explores the opposing necessities of sustenance and of conservation through the subject of whaling. The poems represent the traditional necessity of the Icelandic people to use all means available to survive, including whaling, and the communal effort on a national scale that went into these means of sustenance:

> all the men and women rose to one
> purpose. to open season, to go
> *whaling* they said the way the ancients
> went to *viking*, to sub-
> sist
>
> ...

men, women and children in the water
beating in the small whales with bare
hands, herding them in
the ocean red with blood as far
as you looked. the returning
question, what is cruelty, when
you choose not to
subsist (75)

This poem raises the same problem that we saw earlier raised in Valgardson's fiction: the moral considerations connected to the struggle for survival are a luxury reserved for those who do not face that struggle daily. Icelandic traditions have, of course, been permeated with necessity and a communal effort to survive. In her novel, *The Prowler* Gunnars writes:

This was the country where people died of starvation. For eleven hundred years sheep collapsed in the mountain passes, horses fell dead in the ash-covered pastures, fishermen were too tired to drag nets out of the sea. Children faded away in the sod huts from malnutrition. Old men ate their skin jackets. (39)

In her prologue to *The Nightworkers* she explains how she tried to reconcile this tradition, in which she grew up, with what she learnt about conservation abroad. Her confusion, being caught between two sympathies, comes out well in the following passage:

when one of the crew came up, said
are you greenpeace? i guess i didn't look
like a child of this outfit. and i was
admittedly greenpeace yes but told him
no i'm a poet. which was true as far
as it went. what are you writing?
he asked, about whales or whaling or
what? yes, about that (74)

The last cycle in the collection, however, affirms the lasting, sustaining qualities of the community in the face of global movements which preach conservation while producing nuclear threats:

because i know the earth is a place
where you cannot hurt a fish-working girl
without the consequences bleeding out

like a gash in the throat
of a world that sings (103)

As forces of materialism and immoderation threaten to disrupt rural stability in Valgardson's fiction, so modern technology threatens to disrupt the peaceful routine of the rural nation without arms or armies in Gunnars' poetry. In the end, it is the small communities, Iceland's workforce trained to work on for survival under the threat of extinction, who will continue life after a nuclear escalation:

night after night in ísafjördur
they don't take off their working clothes
and they don't say anything for long
after the fire

if they prefer flowers
in the garden when the sun glows
they waste no words on what might have been
after the fire

stopping only for black
coffee by the gudný's charred hull
they think no more of soccer on the grass
after the fire

the electricians and machinists
hand to hand, before and after
the flame of midnight they keep on
After the fire, they say

she'll be rowing again in three mornings
because they stay
gutting away the burnt insides
and replacing day with day (104)

In her prologue to *The Nightworkers of Ragnarök*, Gunnars reflects on the Icelanders she grew up with: "I think now that a people's emotional makeup is molded by necessity." The final affirmation of the sustaining role of the community in the struggle to survive in the works discussed above would seem to indicate that Gunnars' own emotional life has been moulded as well by the necessity she experienced during her childhood in Iceland. She herself implies as much in the first poem of the cycle "bed of opium": "all i am is a rocky coast / nothing more" (47). For her, as well as for Valgardson with his rural Icelandic-Canadian "emotional makeup," survival is an ultimate reality which has shaped their vision, described by many as bleak, and which makes both self-reliance and a strong sense of community of the utmost importance, as it always has been in Icelandic culture.

In *The Nightworkers of Ragnarök*, the sustaining role of the community becomes of global significance. It is the members of the community, after all, who continue life "after the fire" and who "replace day with day" (104). In Gunnars' works generally, especially her later works, there is a strong tendency to make the rural, the regional, the marginal, of universal importance or application. Here she shows her affiliation with the Canadian fascination for making the marginal the centre of interest. For Gunnars, of course, the marginal works in more ways than one: within Canada she speaks from the margins of ethnicity, while her two main countries, Canada by choice and Iceland by birth, count as "marginal," away from the traditional centres of power and civilization: "Some Icelandic novels make no sense. They are not meant to make sense. They go nowhere, refuse to grasp reality. Potentially there is no reality. My father's people have always known that potentially they do not exist" (*The Prowler* 30).

In *The Prowler*, survival and, by extension, life are connected to marginality rather than community. The country that killed whales to survive in "the silent hand" has here become a country of non-killing:

I have noticed in a passive way that in literature, as well as in politics, only that which kills is thought significant. Only murder is taken seriously.

It is because the white Inuit [i.e., the Icelanders] do not murder that they are forgotten. They are the harmless people. The insignificant ones. There is no price on people of peace. It costs nothing to eliminate them. (129)

Iceland has become the centre of peace and conservation: Icelanders do not murder and they are too insignificant to be murdered. Similarly, in the cycle "north country wake" (*The Nightworkers*) the simple, daily tasks in the Icelandic countryside receive a universal dimension:

we carried winter away
where it lay in piles at the edge
of the field, in buckets

on small clogs and when summer
truly spread its fingers at the end
of the day, we received

blessings of honey cake and butter
in the kitchen where cabbage
crinkled leaves in water

we thought this a common life
the world our locale
the universe framed in our coast

shingles of rock and cliff
sands above high water mark
the margins of knowledge (67)

Gunnars succeeds in making her personal immigrant experience also a universal experience of alienation, of displacement and of division of self. In *The Nightworkers*, for instance, it is not only the author who suffers from loss and nostalgia, but the experience is subtly broadened until the reader is forced to realize that humanity as a whole has become alienated from the land and its natural patterns:

this is the tissue of
the green and blazing beating of
our hearts, the life
we pulled from the soil
the memory we now

kindle (51)

We, too, along with Gunnars, suffer the consequences of loss and displacement:

the prolific time, now
unfamiliar, unrecorded
away from the coasts

we import life itself
take pains to be distant
unbroken sod, untouched turf

> idle horses, scrapped ships
> shredded crofts. we no
> longer gather our own
>
> sustenance (69)

and:

> there is no blessing left
> in the work we do, summer
> arrives with no help from our hands (67)

Gunnars' personal memories of Iceland have become a warning, which sounds more ominous as the subject turns from alienation to the threat of destruction held by our Nuclear Age which, in turn, is signalled by a change in natural patterns: "never before have i seen the seabirds / wheel so over the waves....// and i believe the world sleeps / facing the window" (100). The invisible danger of radioactivity is effectively made clear in "those subjected to radioactivity who did not die were marked for life," in which the actual meaning of the abstract political statement in the beginning of the poem is subtly made painfully real through the innocent routine of the fishing community which spreads the contamination: "and i have come to buy it from a little girl / with folded hands" (96). The dangerous complexity of the problem is brought out well here, as political sins which threaten global destruction infiltrate the innocent routine of the workers who are our only hope of survival.

In many cases, Gunnars views contemporary global issues and problems against the background of the Icelandic culture with which she grew up. As this culture remained in many respects unchanged for centuries until fairly recently, there is an effective juxtaposition of old and new. Here, too, Gunnars explores in order to come to a connection or an integration rather than an emphasis of the opposition between old and new alone. In *The Prowler*, for instance, past and present continually interact, and although the narrator repeatedly denies that a connected story can or should be made out of the dislocated pieces, what eventually emerges is an intimately connected life story, as if her desire for connection and wholeness is stronger than her experience of fragmentation (Owens 1990: 76-77). As she says in *The Nightworkers*:

... we can-
not eradicate the past
we share, the origin of

this need, to touch
here on the stream bank
pain spun into the back of our
minds, how it borders
the field of desire (53)

In *One-eyed Moon Maps* the opposition of old and new is expressed and explored through the juxtaposition of Old Norse mythology and lunar science. Continually, the two interact and show similarities. In "stone," the moon is seen hanging in the sky the way Odin hung on Yggdrasil, both one-eyed and both possessing "hidden knowledge" (11). The moon becomes the link between primitive myth and modern science: Armstrong and Aldrin pick up samples of moonrock to learn to "read," the way Odin learnt to read the carved runes after nine days of hanging. Similarly, moon qualities form the link between the grandfather who confronts the modern sensibility of the woman in "edge."

During the development of the cycle, mythology and science are continually linked and come increasingly closer until, finally, we sense that science and mythology are simply two ways to make sense of the eternal, symbolized by the moon. The two ways, rather than cancelling each other out, should complement each other, for they are, after all, both part of our whole consciousness and our total vision:

you notice, it's a matter
of putting down the telescope
& opening the other eye
at last (71)

DOCUMENTATION

As Canadian literature seriously began to discover and explore its own locale and its own past, the documentary impulse became a very strong and even characteristic feature in both poetry and fiction. In his article "Explorer/Settler/Poet," Peter Stevens points out:

Contemporary poets are trying to discover a sense of themselves as Canadian poets through the figures of explorers and settlers in such a way as to use these historical figures as part of the poet's own persona, as if these people are part of the shadow-play of the poets' own consciousness. (1977: 63)

Stevens introduces here the term "proto-forms" to refer to the older records of the poet's country: "these proto-forms serve not only as historical record but as a text on which the Canadian voice can base its own language" (69). He suggests that the lives of the pioneers are "the proto-forms of our lives; their records are the proto-forms of our poetry" (74).

Significantly, the saga authors, too, made use of earlier documents and literary forms to construct their tales of the Saga Age. They seem to have been as concerned as Canadian writers today to record a truly indigenous literature rooted in the history and soil of their newly settled land. While not discarding the fact that their traditions were Norwegian and, partly, Celtic, they concentrated most on the interpretation and imaginative recreation of their own pioneer history (Njarðvík 1979). Some of the documents used by the saga authors have been identified. It is almost certain that the most important sources were the *Landnámabók* and the *Íslendingabók*, but extensive use was also made of, for instance, Eddic and skaldic poetry. When poetry was used as a source, it is often explicitly referred to and even partly quoted in the narrative, as in the following passage from *Gretti's saga*:

"Hear now," he said, "what I tell you of my adventure. I will tell it to you in verse, and you shall cut it in runes on a staff." She did so, and he spoke the Hallmundarkvida, in which the following occurs: ... (*Saga of Grettir* 167).

Taking into account that proto-forms are used in both saga and Canadian literature, it is natural that Icelandic-Canadian authors turn to earlier documents in order to recover and explore the Icelandic-Canadian past and give expression to the silenced voices of that past, which has so long remained ignored by the official, dominant version of Canadian history. We find this interest and recreation of proto-forms in the works of both Gunnars and Arnason.

Gunnars' *Settlement Poems* are based on historical documents, referred to in the introduction to the poems. They form her exploration of a past of which she knew little but to which she was connected through her native background and her own immigrant experience. The *Settlement Poems* do not, therefore, form a historical

account. Rather, they are a poetic interpretation of the human stories and emotions underlying the historical facts. They can and have
indeed been regarded as a documentary long poem (McVey 1986: 8).
Settlement Poems contains the three main elements which Dorothy
Livesay said described the genre of the documentary long poem:
documentary, dramatic voice and political relevance. The documentary is found in the historical accounts on which Gunnars based her
poems, while the dramatic voice in these poems is actually a multiplicity of voices contained in the various parts which make up the
poems. The voices are in most cases named, for instance "Stefán
Eyjólfsson I-XVI" (*1*: 37-53) and "Thorleifur Jóakimsson, Daybook
I-X" (*2*: 21-35). Thus, the subjective experience of the Icelandic-
Canadian pioneer past is emphasized, and the evaluation and interpretation of the fragmentary points of view is left to the reader who
becomes the link between fact and fiction (Hutcheon 1988: 65).

The political relevance of *Settlement Poems* is found in the place it
claims for these marginalized immigrant voices in Canadian history.
The multiple voices in the poem contribute to make clear the subjectivity inherent in the interpretation and writing of history, including what is accepted as the "true," dominant version of history.
Works like *Settlement Poems* tell us that no one history of Canada exists,
but is made up of the various experiences, memories and points of
view of all Canadians. As the pioneer experiences of the Icelandic-
Canadian immigrants in *Settlement Poems* are related, both author and
reader join the pioneers in their explorations of the new land and
learn to see it through different eyes. Old World lore and traditions
clash with an unknown landscape and people, and out of this clash
a new consciousness is gradually born: "messy work, but you learn
how / to be born / piecemeal" (*1*: 53). Within the context and genre
of Canadian literature, this documentary long poem fulfils a function
akin to that of the sagas: the literary recreation of the birth of a new
consciousness in a new land.

In her introduction to *The Axe's Edge*, Gunnars comments on the
stories in the collection:

Stories that exist prior to being told. Not simply what has happened to
people struggling for a living, but also the voices that still reverberate in the
wind. Cries of a certain hue that resound even now. In reading letters, journal
entries, essays and poems by people who settled in the West, I became conscious of a need to listen. What I have written in this book of stories is a

record of what I think I heard, and the way individual sounds rang clear in the clamour of voices. (1)

These words might just as well have been included in the introduction to *Settlement Poems*, for the stories in *The Axe's Edge* continue, in prose, the poetic interpretation of Icelandic-Canadian immigration history begun in *Settlement Poems*. This time, however, a longer time-span is covered. Again, we have an exploration, an expression of the history "between the lines" of immigrants. There is no factual account, but a poetic record, because, as Gunnars points out, "memory distorts, 'truth' turns into a lie; facts become inaccurate and reality becomes fiction" (3). Accordingly, we also find in *The Axe's Edge* a multiplicity of named voices, for no one "true" version of any history exists. The various points of view, each linked to a name, also help to humanize the history that is related. The personalized tales become journeys into memory in which the reader is invited to participate as he must piece the bits of information together to come to an interpretation. Thus, the reader becomes involved in each personal history to an extent that dry "facts" could never achieve.

This humanization of history is exactly what Arnason's documentary collage, *The Icelanders*, aspires to as well. In this book, photos are accompanied by bits of prose and poetry from a large variety of both oral and written sources. The introduction to the collection points out specifically the personal character of the collage. This is one of the differences from Gunnars' works: Arnason is reaching back to the past of his own community as it has been remembered by that community: "This is not a history. It is a journey into memory and myth, a collage of photos, remembrances, poems, statements and fragments.... It is not representative or fair or complete. Anybody whose background was Icelandic who set out to make a similar book would perhaps make something different" (7). In his review of the book, Valgardson observes:

The first-person anecdotes may not be history but they are human, and without humanity history is meaningless....

In a larger sense, *The Icelanders* and other books like it have an important part to play in Canadian society. Ethnic groups outside the Wasp-French tradition have been denied a place in Canadian history. Their accomplishment, their triumphs and tragedies, have been ignored. (1982: 29)

In his earlier work *Marsh Burning*, Arnason used historical material in the section "out of the mysteries, dreams" for an exploratory journey into his Icelandic-Canadian past. The material consists of letters that have been kept. Although no indication is given whether the letters are literally quoted or not, they appear to be so. They are surrounded by bits of prose which, although they may not be historically "true," flesh out the bare facts in the letters and provide more points of view. History is thus turned into a moving reality which springs to life through the writer's interpretion of his sources, while the version of this chapter in history is extended to the point of view of the suffering and no longer limited to outsiders' accounts and officially documented facts:

My darling Pheobe [sic]

I am going to fulful my promis [sic]. *That was as soon as I got back to Winnipeg. I was to write and tell you all I did during the winter. I left this Sunday the 26 of November—I got up to Gimli the next day—in the evening. Next Morning, I went over with Dr. Lynch—to visit the Hospital. It was full of patients, of course all with small pox. They were to be seen in every stage, some dieing* [sic]*—and some convalescents. The next day I went to visit several houses and such a sight you never saw—Every house had somebody down with the disease—The settlement extends about forty five Miles. And the houses were of the worst description. I had to stoop to go into nearly every house—There were some doors so low, that I had to go on my hands and knees to get in—And such filth. I cannot describe it—And fancy, I had to sleep in these wretched houses. I always slept with my coat on so that I would not get lice on me....*

The baby is dead. Asdis is weeping and the cousins are huddled in the corner. Their scabs drip and they scratch and moan. I tell them not to scratch or they will leave scars. They tell me a corpse may have scars. The scent of death is everywhere, and now it is in my house. The baby is dead and now we know that we may die too. Asdis holds it to her breast and weeps. Let her weep. There is little enough left. Tomorrow I will put its body on the roof, out of the reach of wolves. I will make it a coffin with my own hands though there is little enough wood for the fire. A man may bury his dead. (71-72)

Like the saga authors in medieval Iceland, Gunnars and Arnason make use of historical documents in order to explore Icelandic-Canadian pioneer history and open it up to reinterpretation. Their works illuminate the muted stories behind the bare facts and give them humanity. Moreover, through their use of multiple voices and a fragmentary point of view, they claim a place in Canadian history and literature for those voices that have contributed to the settlement and development of Canada but whose contributions have so far been ignored. While building on an old documentary tradition in literature,

Gunnars and Arnason are contributing to a growing documentary Canadian tradition that is recovering, exploring and reinterpreting the diversity of its own past.

MYTH AND MYTH-MAKING IN THE NEW WORLD

Earlier it was noted that Western Icelandic as well as Canadian writers were actively engaged in mythopoeic activities. The West Icelanders had created ethnic myths to legitimize the history and identity of themselves as an immigrant group in Canada. Canadian artists for their part were on a quest for indigenous patterns holding the material for Canadian myths necessary to replace the European mythic consciousness with a Canadian one. The writings of fourth-generation authors Valgardson and Arnason provide an opportunity to see how the two different mythopoeic strands have developed and intertwined within an ethnic Canadian group which is concerned with both the preservation of its ethnic culture and with its participation in Canadian culture. The indigenous patterns, or "proto-forms" in Stevens' terms, of Icelandic Canadians were after all created by people with an Icelandic mythic imagination rather than a British one. In addition, the works of the immigrant author Gunnars show how a contemporary Icelandic mythic consciousness is integrated into Canadian literature today, and how it interprets the mythic history of the Icelandic Canadians.

THE ROLE OF NORSE MYTHOLOGY[18]

In Chapter I it became evident how Icelandic culture evolved in direct continuity with the Norse past, and that Christianity was slow to take hold in Iceland. As a result, Icelandic culture retained many pagan elements. These elements found expression in, for instance, the sagas and in folklore. Greenway has argued that the Icelandic sagas are *displacements* i.e., profane texts in which the structure and content, regulated by myth, took on a sacred character as revelations of heroic paradigms (1977: 25ff, 169). Although belief in the Norse gods had long been abandoned at the time when the sagas were recorded, the view that the gods had once objectified on a sacred plane is still borne out by the sagas on a human (displaced) plane.

The sagas have exercised a continuing influence on Icelandic literature and have thus passed on their mythic legacy. In addition,

other Norse literature such as the Eddic poems have preserved fragments of a pagan mythic consciousness. As a result, the Icelanders
never completely lost contact with their pagan past in the way that
the other Scandinavian and Germanic countries did. On the contrary, the sagas were regarded as sacred revelations of heroic paradigms until well into the twentieth century. The Norse gods and
mythological tales, however, survived only as profane, artistic famil-
iars. Although they make their appearance in various folk tales, they
do so mostly in distorted forms which do not attest to any belief in
them as forms or manifestations of the sacred, but rather testify to
a tendency among the Icelandic people to give an imported tradition
(Christianity) a familiar face.[19] Thus, the Norse gods retained a kind
of imaginative reality about them. Gunnars gives an indication of the
familiarity in which the ancient Norse gods were held in Icelandic
society when she says, in an interview with Valgardson:

Growing up was sandpapered with Nordic mythology but it wasn't anything
majestic or heroic. Thor and Odin were more like big versions of the broad-
shouldered woman trudging with a can of milk through the mud, or the
fisherman tying knots on the bridge, or the farmer walking across the ice.
(1981: 5)

Norse mythology survived, then, as a familiar body of tales and
characters in Icelandic culture. In Icelandic-Canadian writing we notice
that the familiarity has become lost, and that Norse mythology
merely provides an interesting body of images and original material
from an Icelandic past. Valgardson makes no use of images from
Norse mythology at all, but Arnason and Gunnars, each in a first
work, have used imagery from Norse mythology as a framework for
their poetic journeys of discovery into the lingering influences of a
distant past. Interestingly, both writers use many of the same images
which are juxtaposed with aspects from contemporary life in order
to come to a new, creative outlook. The fact that as a fourth-generation Icelandic Canadian Arnason is much farther removed from his
Icelandic mythic past than Gunnars appears to make little difference
here, since the cultural legacy they are dealing with is an ancient one.
   In *Marsh Burning*, Arnason uses elements of Norse mythology to
deconstruct a mythic past. As the narrator of the long poem deals
with his heritage, he journeys towards a more fully developed sense
of self and the creation of a personal mythology which can serve him

in the present. Images of *Ragnarök*, the end of the world, abound in the first part of the poem as the narrator describes the deconstruction of his heritage:

you spoke to me Thor
saying
>   *Baldur is dead/slain*
>   *Baldur*
>   *who was white as the snows on Hecla*
>   *Loki is free*
>   *Fenrir prowls   just beyond the horizon*
>   *somewhere over Fundy*
>
>   *the world ash is rotting*

you said   *eaten from without and within*
>   *Nidhogg gnaws at the roots of Yggdrasil*
>   *the reindeer in the branches paw and fret*
>   (*Marsh Burning* 9)

As Frey and Freyja, twin-gods of fertility, tell him how everything reflects the death of Baldur, which announces the beginning of *Ragnarök*, the narrator goes out to buy mistletoe, thereby involving himself in Baldur's killing.[20] This personal *Ragnarök* is inevitable as the mythological *Ragnarök*: it is necessary for the creation of a new, vital New World mythology.

The images are all placed in a contemporary Canadian setting. For instance, the rainbow bridge *Bifröst*, which in Norse mythology connects heaven and earth and which will break during *Ragnarök*, has become "the bridge across the Naaswaak" which "needs repairs," and "cracks in the iron form a rainbow" (17):

>   the weather is unsettled
>   rain and haze and sunshine
>   and always there are rainbows in the sky
>   never have I seen so many rainbows
>   and so much traffic in the heavens
>   they curve and bridge in all directions
>   but mostly to the north
>   and always seem to touch down on the earth
>   just at the power station
>   on the way to Maryville (11-12)

The god Odin appears in several guises, as he does in the mythological tales, but is here adapted to the contemporary setting. He appears, for instance, as a Jehovah's Witness announcing the end of the world:

> a small man came to my door
> in an old blue overcoat
> that hung around his neck like a cloak
>
> he had one good eye only
> and said he was a Jehovah's Witness
> I bought a *Watchtower* from him
> and he went away
>
> saying   *This is the God's Truth* (11)

Later, he appears as a neighbour:

> he too has lost an eye
> but has replaced it with an eye of glass
> a jewelled eye
> with a clock in the centre
> the numbers on the dial are backward
> and the hands go counterclockwise (12-13)

Odin's lost eye is here replaced by a clock eye which runs backwards. This is indicative of the emotional loss of the once vital Norse mythology during the process of immersion in the new country, and the artificial replacement of this loss with an eye that is directed towards the past, since no vital New World mythology of the future has yet developed to replace it. The movement of the whole poem, however, is, like *Ragnarök*, towards a rebirth: old and new are reborn as one vital life incorporating one creative vision.

Marsh Burning is not only a quest into the past and future. Kathie Kolybaba calls it a quest "towards poetic and mythic discovery" (1983: 57), which is interesting when seen in the light of the image of Odin's hanging as Arnason uses it. The god Odin hanged himself on the World Ash Yggdrasil for nine days as a ritual self-sacrifice and initiation, after which he obtained numinous knowledge through magic runes.[21] According to traditional interpretations of this self-sacrifice, Odin also received the gift of poetry after this trial in the form of a drink, "the precious mead."

In the first part of *Marsh Burning*, a man called Mike hangs himself and is brought back from the dead. He has acquired special insight into life and time:

> Mike lives before us
> and must come back in time
> to speak to me (23)

Mike's connection with Odin is made clear through the image of the wolf, which was one of the animals dedicated to Odin. Mike complains of a wolf "living in his head" which has imprisoned him: "*it wants my death / orders my death*" (23). The belief embedded in the image of Odin's hanging that the gifts of creativity (poetry) and special knowledge demand sacrifice and suffering have survived, although in much distorted forms, in Icelandic folklore, where it is a recurrent theme.[22] The figure of Odin as the god of poetry and sorcery occurs in these tales in the guise of the Evil One, where he bestows secret knowledge or the gift of poetry but asks a sacrifice in return.

This belief also appears in many of Gunnars' works. In *Settlement Poems* the figure of the poet says:

> to take life for life, cut
> round the middle, pull
> the fur off, chop
> the head & feet off ...
>
> ... wash away the blood
>
> of the past, take life
> stuff the inside with fresh
> sapling boughs & carry it, the rabbit
> home, life for life on my back (*1*: 48)

This skinned rabbit becomes both the source of knowledge of life in the new land, and the parchment for the poet's writings. Similarly, the knitting woman in "Wake-Pick Poems" says: "my work is my life / with it i pay" (*Wake-Pick Poems* 87). This statement, according to Kolybaba: "expresses Gunnars' conviction that the creation of art is an act of survival and that, like life itself, it is paid for through suffering" (1982: 71). In *One-eyed Moon Maps*, in which Gunnars deals with her mythic past, Odin's sacrifice forms an analogy with the moon: Odin hung on Yggdrasil the way the moon hangs in the sky, both one-eyed and both possessing "hidden knowledge." At the same time, the moon forms the link between primitive myth and modern lunar science, as Armstrong and Aldrin pick up samples of moon rock to read, just as Odin picked up and learnt to read the carved runes: the rocks and runes "reveal everything" (11).

Like Arnason's *Marsh Burning*, *One-eyed Moon Maps* also uses the image of Odin's sacrifice as part of a poetic quest for vision. Gunnars, like Arnason, fuses ancient mythology with contemporary reality in order to come to a poetic vision that incorporates past, present and future. The poem also reflects the connection between poetry and knowledge, in this case lunar science, embodied in the one figure of Odin who is both *skáldguð* and *vísindaguð*, god of poetry and god of science (Eyjólfsson 1894: 157-58). The poetic quest in *One-eyed Moon Maps* ends in an affirmation of visionary wholeness, where mythological and technological consciousness fuse into one perspective.

Two main images from Norse mythology have thus found their way into contemporary Icelandic-Canadian writings: *Ragnarök* imagery is used by Arnason for the deconstruction of an imprisoning, backward-looking past; and both Arnason and Gunnars have used the figure of Odin, god of poetry and knowledge, and the imagery of his self-sacrifice to obtain these two gifts in their poetic quests for a creative vision. For both, that vision is ultimately born out of the fusion, through rebirth, of old and new.

MYTHICAL FIGURES: THE HERO, THE OUTCAST AND THE TRICKSTER

Valgardson has emphasized the importance of the myths embedded in sagas and folklore which, as he points out, helped the Icelanders to endure great hardship and helped the Icelandic immigrants to overcome the shock and dislocation of the immigrant experience (1979-80). Such Old World myths, however, have gradually been lost and need to be replaced by new Canadian myths that, in Valgardson's view, can provide the cohesion missing in Canada. In "The Icelandic Community and its Literature" (1982), Valgardson suggests that to achieve a healthy cohesion in Canada it is important that ethnic groups share their history and their culture with other groups, and that this can best be done through writing.

Valgardson does not make use of Norse mythological tales or imagery in his writings. He does, however, frequently create characters with clear mythical dimensions. Moreover, these characters echo figures from folklore and mythology which, although universal in themselves, carry specific Icelandic earmarks. The outcast and the trickster are two which occupy an important place in the row of Valgardsonian characters. The third one, the hero, is of course so integral to literature that he is found in any literary work, if only in his opposite guise of the anti-hero. However, the heroism I have detected in the works of Valgardson, Gunnars and Arnason is of a particular kind, which I propose is derived from the Norse view of heroism embodied in Eddic and saga literature.

In Chapter I, I discussed the role of the outcast or outlaw in Icelandic literature in the light of the development of the figure of Grettir. The mythic implications of this figure are found in the Norse creation myth and the doom of *Ragnarök*: the world and gods were created out of giants, the forces of primary chaos and destruction, and will perish at the hands of the giants (Greenway 1970: 23). The human world, *Miðgarðr*, is a reflection of the domain of the gods, *Ásgarðr*, which is a cultivated and lawfully ordered world constantly threatened by the hostile, destructive giants from the choatic wilderness of *Útgarðr*, "outside." The concept of law therefore had a particularly powerful meaning in early Icelandic society. Greenway, in his discussion of the mythical implications of the world view in the sagas, puts it this way: "Law is the symbolic assertion of human freedom in empirical time, [it] is the alternative to yielding to chaos, the disorder latent in mythic time" (1970: 25). Consequently, somebody who had caused himself to be cast out of society, out of the realm of order and law, had in mythical terms yielded to the monstrous powers of evil and destruction. An outsider was, therefore, an ambiguous and potentially dangerous figure who often became associated with the monstrous.

The conflict between society and the outcast had, of course, great dramatic potential, especially when the borders between inside and outside of society were shifting, as we saw in the case of Grettir. An outcast could become a hero or "noble bandit," and the domain of *Útgarðr* an imagined paradise in the eyes of the people once the leaders of society were considered morally unjust. Similarly, the outcast could also become an interesting focus for a changing ethos within society, as for instance in *Gísla saga Súrssonar* where Gísli is subjected to the fate of the lonely, hunted outlaw because he was somehow unable to adapt his warrior ethics of revenge to those of the settled rural society that Iceland was becoming (Byock 1982: 193).

In Valgardson's fiction, the figure of the outcast is adapted to conditions in the new land. For immigrants, dislocation is an acute and painful experience which makes the general human need for a sense of belonging all the more poignant. Those who are denied an acknowledged place, who are somehow socially inept or whose place is threatened become tragic and desperate. In some cases, they take on something of the monstrous in their despair, whereas others become tragic or merely pathetic. The theme of the outcast and his conflict with society is most elaborately dealt with in the story "A Place of One's Own." Here, the outcast appears in the form of a pedlar:

Neither Fedorchuk nor his wife approved of people not brought up in the area. Of the pedlar, they were particularly contemptuous because he had no place of his own and, therefore, no trustworthy identity. Like all people who live on the very edge of having nothing, a place of one's own was very important to them. Divorced from the land, constantly travelling, appearing and disappearing without explanation, the pedlar was no better than a gypsy. (*Red Dust* 53)

A brief look at any saga will quickly bring out the importance of a social identity, established through family and land, in Old Icelandic society: every character worthy of any mention is introduced through genealogy and geography. An outsider with no such socially established credentials is considered a potential danger to the stability of that society, just as, mythologically, the ordered society of *Miðgarðr* is continually threatened by the outside forces of chaos. Similarly, the Interlake community in Valgardson's "A Place of One's Own" regards the pedlar only as an outside force who remains nameless, his identity defined by the lack of it:

All through the Interlake he was known as the pedlar. Although no-one called him that to his face, substituting *you* and *hey, there* for his name or avoiding calling him anything at all, once he had been called the pedlar, his first identity, that fragile endowment from parents whom no-one had ever met, whose existence and place in society no-one ever confirmed, was swept away. (60)

The pedlar is barred as a member of society, although people will buy his goods, which are cheap and, incidentally, appropriately described as "the debris of ambition and greed and miscalculation and bad luck gathered indiscriminately together by misfortune" (56). The pedlar himself is a tragic figure who feels his position as an outcast poignantly: " 'You're very lucky,' the pedlar said, his voice heavy with tiredness.... 'To have a place of your own, I mean. To be able to stay in one place.' " (59). His desire to belong and his awareness of the cruel fate of the outcast cause him to accept Fedorchuk's daughter, pregnant by an unknown man, as a wife. He understands the girl's feelings better than anyone, for as the unmarried future mother of a fatherless child she is now an outcast too. In addition, the marriage provides him with a place in the community and identity which would normally have remained an impossibility for him. As Fedorchuk realizes: "In other circumstances, the pedlar would have been unthinkable as a son-in-law. Now that no-one else wanted his daughter, he was all that was available" (69). As soon as they are married, the pedlar has a name: John Crestyin. He has received a social identity. However, he is as luckless as the traditional saga outlaw, doomed to displacement. After the baby's birth, his wife leaves him, and with her go his chances for a place in the community. Mythologically, it is impossible to integrate an outsider into society without risking the destruction of that society.

The wilderness outside of civilized society was believed to be inhabited by giant elemental forces akin to the monstrous. In Norse mythology, *Útgarðr* was the domain of the giants. People from outside the boundaries of society were believed to take on qualities of the monstrous. In the discussion of *Grettis saga* we saw that Grettir incorporated certain non-human qualities, both sub- and super-human. Starkaðr the Giant and Egill Skallagrímsson are two other examples of wanderers outside their societies who take on giant characteristics (Grimstad 1977). Valgardson's short story "Wrinkles" centres around two teenage boys whose social ineptitude has made them outcasts. They do not fit in, they cannot adapt and are therefore not accepted. Consequently, they continually cross the boundaries of society and gradually lose their social consciousness and responsibility to an increasingly murderous mentality. However, the desire for a place of their own lingers:

Walking all night. Stopping periodically at donut shops, walking with nowhere to go. When it was over, when he couldn't walk anymore and they took a bus or hitchhiked back, he always felt cheated. He felt that, somewhere, if he could remember where, there was a place for him, a shack on the beach maybe, or a converted garage, a place with a stove and a bed and a table and a chair, a place where he saw it, he would know it was his. (*WCSM* 38)

In Einarsson's collection of *Icelandic-Canadian Oral Narratives* (1991), we see that the opposition of human settlement and the danger of the wilderness is retained in Icelandic-Canadian folklore, but in an adapted form: the trolls and outlaws of the Icelandic wilderness have become native Canadians, both dead and alive. In Valgardson's short story "Brothers," we find a modern Canadian retelling of the struggle of the Norse gods against the giants which incorporates this adaptation. Alex, an English immigrant, has built his own civilized garden, his *Miðgarðr*, in the northern Canadian wilderness:

Most fish camps are a motley collection of buildings thrown together from scrap lumber and building paper, and look, even when new, forlorn and dingy. Alex's camp was immaculate. All four buildings were covered with wood siding, painted white, and trimmed in blue. In the area between the buildings, the grass was kept closely cut, and the flat slabs of limestone, collected from the beach and laid down to make walks, were carefully swept. Years before, he had cut and trimmed a twenty-foot spruce tree, painted it white, and set it up outside the cook-shack. Every morning, without fail, he hoisted the Union Jack, and, every evening, he took it down. (*Bloodflowers* 35)

His camp reflects Alex's pride in his own place and his concern with retaining a certain kind of civilization rather than being swallowed by the wilderness surrounding him. The stable and orderly civilization created and run by Alex is suddenly threatened by forces from the wilderness outside: an Englishman "gone native" and his Indian family appeal for his help. At first, Alex feels unable to refuse at least some help because the man and he are fellow countrymen. However, it soon becomes clear that even this small intrusion upsets the balance and threatens to destroy Alex's creation. Even Alex himself is close to being dragged down to "wilderness" norms as his "brother" tries to convince him that he too would be regarded an outcast in England in spite of his little civilization. He is saved in time, however, by his housekeeper Fjola. In the end, an innocent child has to pay with its life for the security of Alex's civilization.

In Kristjana Gunnars' *The Prowler*, the theme of the outsider is important and pervasive. It is related to that of the immigrant as outcast, as the narrator of this autobiographical work is wandering and moving from country to country and back. As a result, she belongs nowhere:

> In my father's country I was known as the dog-day girl, a monarchist, a Dane. Other kids shouted after me: King-rag! Bean!

> In my mother's country other kids circled me haughtily on their bicycles. They whispered among each other on the street corners that I was a white Inuit, a shark-eater. The Icelander. (15)

Gunnars connects the role of the outsider with that of the writer. Her first story is written "out of longing," "about a girl who wanted to go home" (31). Consequently, the writer too becomes an outcast: "The words will not take the writer into themselves. The author is therefore locked out of the book" (93). In this novel, it seems that the text has replaced society, the social world, which is traditionally trying to live according to its own rules and lock out the chaos outside, in this case reality. However, Gunnars, whose life has been designated by "invisible social barricades" (117), is seeking escape routes from any type of borders. As an author, she refuses to acknowledge any literary rules:

It is a relief not to be writing a story. Not to be imprisoned by character and setting. By plot, development, nineteenth century mannerisms. A relief not to be writing a poem, scanning lines, insisting on imagery, handicapped by tone. A relief just to be writing. (3)

She constantly tries to evade being imprisoned by the text, just as the text seeks to elude the imprisoning interpretative expectations of the reader. Her solution is continually to cross borders so as to confuse them and thus nullify their power to exclude. The whole novel seems to work towards this obliteration of all borders, which is the author's final homecoming.

Until then, Gunnars is content to feel at home on borderlines and margins, observing them and making sure not to align herself and be caught by any one part. As a result, she feels most at home on the ship "Gullfoss" which sails between Iceland and Denmark (106). When she returns to Iceland from a stay in America, the children at school call her "American Dane":

It was not enough, I thought, for fate to place me in the ranks of our former enemies. Now that the memories of Danish colonization were mellowing out, I was just getting by. But fate has to turn around and join me up with the new colonizers as well.

There was a sense of anger, I studied methods of escape with greater intensity. If familiarity with a language determines a person's identity, I considered, I would learn Russian myself....

As time went by an even better idea presented itself.... The solution was to study more languages. I would learn French and German, Faeroese and Inuit. I would confuse them all. (133)

Accordingly, she learns to escape linguistic borders, class and national distinctions, historical and cultural boundaries, and even literary limitations: "The quest in literature is a mirror of the quest in life. It is possible to imagine where the protagonist is a reader, who is therefore also the author. It is a story where the boundary between that which is written and that which is lived remains unclear" (146).

The outsider by fate here comes to terms with this fate, not through a violent struggle with the society that has erected its borders to protect itself against disruptive elements, but through the dismantling of those excluding borders. The mythological struggle between the forces of civilization and of chaos has been ended by returning it to its own origins. After all, civilization itself was created out of chaos, and the most important gods have at least partly giant ancestry. Gunnars, using her own Canadian immigrant experience, shows us with *The Prowler* that, by dismantling artificial borders, outside forces are given a chance to become creative and dynamic forces again, revivifying a culture that would otherwise either be eliminated by destruction or wither in isolation and stagnation.

The example of Grettir showed how the outlaw figure took on more and more characteristics of the trickster. In *The Prowler*, as in *Grettis saga*, the outsider does not remain a victim of borders but retaliates by becoming a crosser of borders, thereby confusing established ideas of what constitutes "outside" and "inside." This, of course, is an important aspect of the mythological trickster, whom Karl Kerényi called "the spirit of disorder" and "the enemy of boundaries." Carl Jung points to the liberating and fertile influence of the trickster figure, who in his view is the the mythological representation of the psychological Shadow figure (1956: 209). We have seen this influence at work in two outcast figures, Grettir and the narrator of *The Prowler*.

Two representations of the trickster have been recognized in the Norse Pantheon: Odin and Loki. Davidson (1979) analyzed Odin as the cunning, scheming side of the trickster and Loki as his comical, base counterpart. According to Kerényi's analysis of the trickster figure, Odin would then approach the culture hero and Prometheus figure and Loki the Epimetheus figure (1956: 181). The close relationship between Odin and Loki is indicated by the fact that, according to the Eddic poem *Lokasenna* ("The Flyting of Loki"), they used to be foster brothers.[23] In Snorri's *Prose Edda* and in the mythological poems of *The Poetic Edda* many tales are related which involve Loki's and Odin's sexual escapades, although Odin's are on a much higher and more influential plane seeing that he is Creator and *Alfaðir* ("All-father") and not merely Phallus like Loki. Both Odin and Loki are associated with fertility, Odin in his function of cosmic father and god of death, and Loki as the generator of demons and monsters.[24]

Davidson pointed to the importance of the cunning Odinic trickster in saga literature. She found that, in accordance with the ambiguous nature of the trickster, not all of the "arch-plotters" in the sagas are evil (Njáll in *Njáls saga*) whereas others inspire laughter and respect in spite of their ruthless deceptions (Snorri *goði* in, for instance, *Eyrbyggja saga*). Independent of Davidson's findings, John Lindow has recently argued that one of the sagas (the *Bandamanna saga*) was modelled on the comic mythological trickster tales, since they were the only native literary expression of comedy (1989: 241-56).

In Icelandic-Canadian literature, the trickster makes his appearance in the fictional world of Valgardson, where living conditions, as in medieval Iceland, are generally so tough that cunning becomes a tool for survival. As Margaret Atwood worded it: "Such a world does not demand goodness as the price of survival, merely knowledge, vigilance, luck, and for some even these aren't enough" (1979-80: 189). In the short story "Brothers," which was discussed above in the context of the struggle between wilderness and civilization, Thomas, the Englishman "gone native" is, like Grettir, an example of an outcast who assumes trickster qualities. His choice to live with his native family has placed him outside society and in the wilderness. Thomas continually crosses the border between the two worlds, however, in his dealings with Alex, whom he reminds of their mutual cultural background. In his and his family's need to survive, he refuses to be victimized by acknowledging any borders. Instead, he uses guile and cunning. He ruthlessly deceives Alex who, at first, is willing to help Thomas as long as he stays away from his camp. Characteristically, Thomas does not stay away but shrewdly intrudes more and more, blurring any borders between their two worlds through the sexual favours offered by his wife and daughter to the men in Alex's camp. A true Odinic trickster, Thomas is clever enough to try and trick people with their own weaknesses. He is only defeated when he loses his son in the game, but even then he does not leave without stealing Alex's provisions.

"On Lake Therese" features another such mischief-monger, Jack Spitzer. Out of nowhere he suddenly appears on Earl's isolated territory, which, like Alex's camp in "Brothers," is a carefully tended place in which Earl takes much pride. We learn that Jack comes from another world, from the city: "'This isn't like the city,' Spitzer continued. 'I sure can tell you that. There you've got to be sharp. Sharper than your neighbour.'" (*Bloodflowers* 113). Again we have two opposing worlds, one civilized and one where the law of the jungle rules. Although Earl does not trust Jack and his mate Henry and tries to keep them away, it quickly becomes clear that he is still too trusting and slow to tackle Spitzer's guile and experience at crossing borders. Once Spitzer discovers Earl's weakness for alcohol, he easily makes use of it and succeeds in making the wary Earl tell where he keeps his money. The two then make off with Earl's boat, on which Earl is totally dependent. But the story has a twist at the end. Years of hard labour merely to survive have made Earl vigilant and provided him with enough knowledge to defend himself against the unexpected tricks of fate and people. In the end, it is Jack Spitzer and Henry who have been unexpectedly tricked by underestimating the wits of someone who has learnt how to survive the hard way. In Valgardson's world, only those who learn to trick the trickster can survive. Here, as in the medieval Iceland of the sagas, only those equipped to profit from situations as they present themselves can survive tough conditions by holding on to what they have. And what better teacher could they have than the clever trickster Odin, whose counsels are given in the poem *Hávamál*. Davidson has described these as, "a shrewd, at times cynical acceptance of life as it is lived in a tough competitive society, drawing a clear line between those who do not know their own limitations ... and those who are wise enough to profit from the situation as they find it" (1979: 6).

A trickster figure with stronger psychological dimensions in Valgardson's fiction is Larry in *Gentle Sinners*. Larry has obvious affiliations with the Lokian trickster figure, most importantly through his stupidity, his complete self-interest, his greed and his sexual obsession, which in Kerényi's analysis characterize the Epimetheus trickster. Larry's greed is symbolized by his warehouse in which he obsessively stores the results of his tricking and cheating. His phallic adventures turn into grotesque comedy in the scene with the widow, who turns Larry's intended rape into his sexual humiliation. Incidentally, it is interesting to note here that Loki's adventures, which are often of a sexual kind, have a strong tendency towards crude, grotesque humour.

Larry's function in the book, however, seems to be more than trickster buffoonery. His role as Eric's Shadow is emphasized through the shadow imagery which surrounds him. Moreover, he seems to feed off Eric's unhappiness and frustrations, because it is then that he has influence on him: "Eric's appearance at the auction had excited Larry. From the moment he had seen the black suit and the bitter countenance, he knew that he had found someone who would be of some consequence to him" (139). When Eric is content, Larry appears as gaunt, skinny and insubstantial, but as soon as Eric's frustration or anger returns, Larry gains in appearance and energy. Like the trickster as described by Carl Jung, Larry "stands in a complimentary or compensatory relationship to the ego personality," here Eric. Jung has linked the trickster with the Shadow figure: "The Trickster is a collective shadow figure, an epitome of all the inferior traits of character in individuals" (1956: 209). Moreover, Jung points out that the personal shadow, like Larry, is "in part descended from a numinous collective figure" (202). Consequently, it is Larry who draws Eric to violence, gets him into trouble, and creates dissension between the good influence from Melissa (his Anima) and Sigfus (the Wise Old Man). However, as a trickster and Shadow, Larry's acts have positive results in the end. As Jung put it: "In the history of the collective as in the history of the individual, everything depends on the development of consciousness. This gradually brings liberation from imprisonment in ... unconsciousness, and [he] is therefore a bringer of light as well as of healing" (211). Eric needs to deal with the darker parts of his personality and his past. Through his dealings with Larry, he is able to free himself and his Anima from the unassimilated influences Larry represents. When he knows his role is finished, Larry sets his warehouse on fire and burns with it. It is a fitting ending to the

Shadow, whose death means purgation and light for Eric: "Now, in spite of his exhaustion, he was no longer afraid. It was as though, in that moment, something dark and evil had been torn away from him and cast away" (208).

In David Arnason's playful postmodern fiction, we find an interesting inversion. In many short stories, it is the women who appear as Odinic tricksters. The male narrators are weak and confused characters who are somehow not quite capable of handling the chaotic inconsistencies in the urban daily life around them. As such, they form easy prey for the clever, scheming women who are only too capable of handling everything around them. Interestingly, like the "arch-plotters" in the sagas, these women inspire awe and respect rather than bitterness and hatred. In spite of the fact that they deceive the ones who trust them—their husbands mostly—they appear as accepted leaders in today's urban world. They perform the ancient function of Creator and Destroyer, like Odin, but in a modern way, for instance in the following passage from "My Baby and Me":

She told me she'd been to see a doctor, and the baby was on its way, everything in good working order as far as they could tell at this stage. I seemed to recollect some agreement about birth control, but she said that she'd only agreed to be responsible for the first three years, and after that it was my responsibility. It was now four years, and if I'd fallen down on the job, I had no-one to blame but myself. She said if I didn't like it, I could go away and she'd live in a condominium with the baby. It would cost me thirteen hundred dollars a month and I could see the baby on alternate weekends. She'd figured it all out. (*The Circus Performer's Bar* 32)

Similar female trickster types are found in, for instance, "The Sunfish" and "Over and Over" (*Fifty Stories and a Piece of Advice*), and in "Falling in love with Alice," "Sylvie" and "The Marriage Inspector" (*The Circus Performer's Bar*).

There is, then, a close relationship between the trickster and the hero. The trickster sometimes becomes a culture-hero himself, like Odin on the mythological and Grettir on the folkloric plane; or he accompanies the hero as his Shadow or comic counterpart, thus defining both the qualities and limitations of the hero (Pálsson and Edwards 1971: 79). We saw earlier that the Norse pagan code of ethics was determined by heroic ideals which stemmed from a warrior society. However, at the time when the sagas were written, many important social developments were taking place. As saga scholars as different in orientation as Jesse Byock (anthropological; 1988) and Theodore Andersson (structural; 1970) have argued, the sagas display a society which was changing its original warrior ethics for rural ethics. The combination of these interchanging codes of ethics has greatly influenced the ensuing Icelandic concept of heroism. It is one that has found new application in the New World and, consequently, found its way into Icelandic-Canadian writing.

The heroism we find in the Eddic heroic poems is that of a warrior society. The leading concept was that of honour, and preserving and defending personal and family honour was an important duty. Such individual assertiveness, however, soon proved destructive to the agricultural society that was forming in medieval Iceland. Feuds caused endless chains of killings, robbing the vulnerable rural community of its most needed members in its struggle for economic survival. Gradually, a more social consciousness developed, in which survival and conciliation became more important. Limitations on individual aggression and a willingness to compromise for the restoration of social balance became widely respected qualities. Andersson discusses these changes and concludes that: "the ideal chieftain is a tireless conciliator with an uncommon sense of justice and restraint and a willingness to efface himself in the interests of peace" (1970: 584).

The heroes of later Norse literature, then, are people of restraint and moderation, arbiters rather than avengers. A similar change on the mythological plane seems to have taken place in the role of Odin, who adds the function of cosmic father ("All-father") to his original role as god of death and numinous knowledge. In this later literature, we watch the gradual development of the warrior hero to the farmer hero, who represents a combination of the individualist warrior ethics with a more social ideal. Honour remained a key-concept, but the idea of *drengskapr* in the sagas is one of honour already tempered with respect for the honour of the opponent, with fairness of conduct and with moderation (Magnusson and Pálsson 1983: 33). At the same time, the increasingly difficult circumstances in Iceland validated the continuing applicability of a concept of heroism which found its basis in each man's lonely struggle against the elements and fate. To act out one's part in life without hesitation, to preserve an undefeated spirit and to assert one's freedom of will against the powers of fate—these were crucial aspects of Norse heroism. Greenway has explained the under-

302 THE ICELANDIC VOICE

lying mythical implications of this heroism: since the essence of created matter is evil in Norse mythology, a concept of heroism which
emphasizes the assertion of individual freedom in the face of death
implies a spiritual superiority and transcendence of the "inexorable
destructive tendency in creation" through resistance (1970: 24-26). As
a result, the closer one was to death, the better chance to prove one's
worth. The way one faced death was the final and conclusive statement
of one's life, for it was the ultimate opportunity to establish honour
and reputation which lived on after death. Heroism is, after all, as Alan
Boucher put it in his introduction to the Old Icelandic hero, "the
assertion of a triumphant humanity" (1970: 45).

This combination of social and individualist ethics as it is represented by the heroes of the sagas proved a very useful example to
the Icelandic people in their four hundred years of struggle against
natural calamities, disease, poverty and oppression. The once invin-
cible Viking warriors had become a nation of farmers eking out a
meagre existence at the edge of the world. The hero became associated with the struggling farmer who no longer faced great odds in
the form of human foes, but who fought for survival and for his
independence. The changed concept of heroism helped people to
preserve both a sense of community and co-operation and an undefeated spirit and freedom of will. The most impressive example of
this Icelandic farmer hero in Icelandic literature is probably Bjartur
í Sumarhúsum in Halldór Laxness' novel *Independent People (Sjálfstætt
fólk)*. Laxness weaves all of Iceland's history into the life of this
poor farmer, who shows almost superhuman strength of will and
endurance in his never-ending battle with the forces of nature and
society. His role model is Grettir, and his determination to follow in
this great hero's footsteps is what spurs him on. Like Grettir, he too
is a tragic, lonely figure who never succeeds. The tragedy of his life,
however, does not diminish but enhances his heroic stature, for it is
in his striving and not in his fate that his heroism lies.[25]

When the Icelanders came to Canada, they encountered hardships which were hardly less than those they had left behind. These
conditions encouraged a revival of the concept of heroism that the
immigrants had brought along from Iceland. Gunnars, Valgardson,
and also Arnason in *The Icelanders*, honour the sufferings and struggles
of the poor, who acquire heroic stature in their works. Gunnars'
Settlement Poems are a poetic acknowledgement of the settlers' courage
and endurance: incredible hardships allowed for the settlement and

development of the Interlake area. The strength of will and determination to go on speak from the brief, powerful lines in these
poems. These poor Old World farmers preserve an undefeated spirit
in the face of an alien, hostile environment which presents them
with unfamiliar odds:

> i can't say
>
> it's bad, this moving over
> from old to new iceland
> a bit crowded on the boats
>
> & wagons, unusual
> food, some stomach
>
> illness, mainly
> for the kids, but other-
>
> wise i can't say
> it's as bad as the great
> smallpox of 1707
> & 1786, or the famines
>
> of 1756 & 1784 (with
> starvation on every
> farm, no one
> had anything for any-
>
> one) only
> 30 or 40 children are dead
> of the stomach pain
> going to canada (11
>
> in the first group dead
> on arrival in winnipeg)
> but it's not as bad
>
> as 1785 (...
>
> ...) not that
>
> bad
> (*SP 2*: 10-11)

By giving the immigrants the strength of will and spirit characteristic of Icelandic heroes, Gunnars raises them to a mythic heroic level. As Valgardson remarked about the author in a review of the *Settlement Poems*: "She has reached back into the past and recreated, as art, the lives of the early Icelandic immigrants. In doing this she has both made the settlers human and understandable while also raising their lives to a mythic level." [26] In other words, Gunnars is creating an indigenous Canadian mythology out of one particular branch of Canada's literary proto-forms.

Heroism in the works of Gunnars and Valgardson tends to take on the form of the struggling Icelandic farmer hero, but in several different transformations. Their heroes are struggling for survival, and it is their perseverance and spirit that elevates their miserable lives to a heroic level, whether or not they succeed in the end (and according to good Icelandic tradition, they generally do not, for their triumph is in their apparent defeat). The heroine of Gunnars' "Wake-Pick Poems" cannot save herself from a life of squalor and starvation. Yet she has heroic stature, for she transcends her own fate through sheer force of will. Travis Lane discusses her heroism in the light of the Icelandic tradition: "This woman, half-frozen, half-prisoned, almost stone in her working-place, rises above fear. Her heroism has mythic reference and literary tradition, but her power is not magic—it is only handiwork" (1985: 66).

Gunnars' collection *The Nightworkers of Ragnarök* is a poetic voyage into her Icelandic cultural past and background. As she explores her native culture she acknowledges, again, the heroism of the daily workers who are working for the nation's economic survival under the threat of destructive forces over which they have no control, whether they are fish-working girls threatened by nuclear escalation or internationally controversial whalers exposed to the forces of weather and ocean:

> 5 a.m., ready to go
> on the ship the lights
> were on, the men tightening
> leather straps around sweaters and socks
> books and oilskins, against the lamps
> on board the snow flurried
> confused and angry.

i looked at the sea, that open
black mouth of storm and
waves, then down
at the open boat rocking violently, knocking against the pier
palm of what hand is this?
slowly we saw

the boat glide, the hand
harpoons and arrows trace out the night
search for dawn and whale. the rest
had to be imagined, how
they didn't see him but sensed
the huge presence. words

voices i still hear
telling us the story of how we were
saved. we could have starved
to death. it was whale
that saw us through. i still think

this is the way mythologies are made.
(76)

For Valgardson, too, heroism is found in the struggle for survival with an undefeated spirit. In his fiction, there are no winners and losers, only people who persevere in the face of great odds and people who give up and let outside forces rule their lives. A character like Ester in "Trees" is heroic because she resists the destructive capitalist Dominic with quiet determination, even though she knows that she is in no position to defeat him. Yielding to his wish to sell him her walnut grove would free her from financial straits, whereas refusing will only make her situation worse. Nevertheless, there is never any doubt in her mind that she will resist Dominic, for she prefers to be defeated honourably than to yield with shame. Similarly, old John Stepanovich in "The Burning" burns down the house he once built for his bride. The Atomic plant wants to use it for a fire practice, and when John has tried everything to save the house "he had built ... to last," he sees no other honourable way out but to burn the house himself with dignity instead of giving it up to be destroyed in an Atomic fire practice. His last words in the story are telling, when his wife, who thinks he went for a game of cribbage, asks him if he won:

"No," he said, "But I didn't lose either."
He could hear Anna roll over in bed. "That's not so bad then."
"No," John replied as he pulled the covers over himself, "that's not so bad." (*Bloodflowers* 90)

The house is to John and Anna a monument of their survival in the New World and the honour and dignity their stewardship of it requires, rule John's motives and actions. Although he cannot save the house, he has behaved in what is to him the only possible way to resist the powers that are out for its destruction, and consequently he need not feel ashamed.

The heroic ethics represented by Eric and Sigfus in *Gentle Sinners* were discussed earlier in this chapter. Young Eric is shown to possess heroic qualities, but he exercises them with immoderation. He has the qualities, but not the ethics. He therefore becomes Sigfus' apprentice. Sigfus has much in common with the respected chieftains in the sagas who possess good judgement and a willingness to arbitrate and work towards conciliation. It is interesting to see that, like the sagas, *Gentle Sinners* seems to espouse a change from individual to social ideals: Eric, the young warrior, is taught moderation and social consciousness by the chieftain Sigfus. As I suggested earlier, *Gentle Sinners* seems to be a modern Canadian version of an Old Icelandic saga in more than one way. The change from a warrior to a more social ethos could, in the case of *Gentle Sinners* and its Canadian context, be attributed to the fact that in the Interlake area the settlement era is over, so that the emphasis can no longer be on individual survival but must move on to a more community-oriented rural economy. Thus, Valgardson has given a time-honoured Old World code of ethics new application in a thoroughly Canadian setting. The heroism entailed in the struggle for survival appears as topical and relevant for modern Icelandic-Canadian writers as it was for the old saga authors.

OTHER MYTHIC THEMES: FATALISM AND SACRIFICE

The Norse concept of heroism, as we saw above, was closely associated with the mythological implications of the doom of *Ragnarök*: Greenway pointed to the ultimate heroism as rising above the fate of "an inexorable destructive tendency in creation" (1970: 24). Fate played an all-important role in the Norse world-view: it ruled not only over the human world but the gods, too, were subject to its power. The Norse gods lived under the doom of their own destruction. The workings of fate had to be revealed to them through other means, such as the practice of magic known as *seiðr*, which were not under their control.

Much has been written about the ancient Norse belief in fate and its manifestations, but it remains unclear to us whether or what deities or spirits were truly believed in as agents of fate. Snorri Sturluson mentions the three Norns, Urðr, Verðandi and Skuld, as being the shaping forces of men's lives, and a host of other Norns who determine the fates of individuals. The valkyries, Odin's female associates who choose the ones to die in battle, and the *dísir*, a group of female deities, are often mentioned in this connection but little is known about them and they are often confused in later sources. In literary accounts such as the sagas and various folk tales, female beings often appear in dreams as messengers of fate or as personal attendant or guardian spirits but they are not clearly distinguished.[27] It is, however, clear that a strong sense of fatalism pervades Norse mythology and literature, and has pervaded Icelandic literature and folklore as well. Although this fatalism gives rise to a moderately tragic and bleak world-view, it is not unduly pessimistic. It also makes possible the victory of human will and freedom, for fate has power over physical things only, not over the human spirit. Greenway describes it thus:

Ultimately, then, the individual was a prisoner of the past and future—of mythic time—yet he was also, paradoxically, free to choose the quality of his conduct, to define himself heroically. By rising above his fate, the extraordinary man could achieve a kind of victory. (1970: 24)

Moreover, a world-view that takes the tragedy inherent in life into consideration also tends to lend susceptibility to the beauty and promise held by the small gifts that life bestows, for it is in joy in these that the strength is found to continue in the face of great odds. This tendency towards an unexpected and intense experience of beauty is found in saga literature (cf. the famous scene in *Njáls saga* where Gunnar refuses to go into exile when he looks back on his native hills and experiences their beauty), in folk tales (most clearly in the tales about the *huldufólk*), and in Icelandic literature (for instance in the tender love between the rough Bjartur and his daughter Ásta Sóllilja, his *lífsblóm* or "flower of life," in Laxness' *Independent People*).

In the works of Valgardson and Gunnars we find a similar strain of fatalism. Valgardson's work has often been described as bleak, and Gunnars has herself commented on the influence of the fatalism that she grew up with in Iceland. These authors appear to share a fatalism derived from their Icelandic background. It does not appear to make any difference whether this is the result of a direct experience, as is the case with Gunnars, or culturally inherited after several generations as with Valgardson and Arnason. Their fatalism is closely intertwined with the long history of difficult circumstances in a harsh landscape experienced in Iceland, and in Canada by the Icelandic Canadians. Valgardson remarks:

That this dark view of life was inculcated in Icelandic children from the earliest age is highly understandable to anyone who knows something of Icelandic history.... Is it any wonder, that having grown up in an Icelandic-Canadian community that suffered, in its migration to the new land, hardships every bit as great as those which were left behind, I write stories which have been described as being governed by a dark vision? (1979-80: 180)

This inter-relation between environment and fatalism has caused critics to remark that the landscape in Valgardson's fiction is inimical. The land, however, is merely subject to the workings of fate just as everything else. Valgardson himself says in an interview with Geoff Hancock: "The land is not malevolent. It's just simply there. In the Interlake area of Manitoba, and in Northern Manitoba, it's a harsh environment.... 'Valgardson makes up a stark land.' No way. The stark land is just there" (1979-80: 131). Much of Valgardson's fiction is, like the sagas, concerned with the way in which people deal with their fate, how they measure up to it. Some characters achieve a triumph of spirit and will under the most unbearable circumstances, whereas others show themselves defeated or are simply trying to survive in whatever way they can. This important aspect of Valgardson's writing has been summed up by Stedingh in his review of *God is not a Fish Inspector*:

In all of the stories the characters approach heroic proportions in their struggles. There is an air of finality, a fatalism, which has always pervaded W.D. Valgardson's work. Beneath the surface of the action, there is a metaphorical insistence, initially seen as irony, but later, as the tragic-comic essence of the stories becomes more obvious, the strivings and passions of the individual characters seem in fruitless conflict with the inexorable process of the world. (1977: 144-45)

As in Norse heroic literature, it is exactly in the course of this "fruitless conflict" with the powers of fate that Valgardson's characters have the chance to prove their mettle. In "God is not a Fish Inspector," the dignity of Fusi Bergman, determined not to be defeated into dependency and senility by old age, is memorable and moving. Even when fate seems to close in and greed strikes a final and devastating blow, Fusi's spirit will not yield. However, Valgardson also allows room for those who lack the strength to face up to the tricks of fate. Hermann in "A Private Comedy" lives as a recluse after the wartime loss of his legs, until fate brings him into contact with the waitress Darlene. Having arranged everything to make her his wife, he loses heart at the very last moment and commits suicide only just before she arrives. There is never any condemnation of such lack of courage, but rather a tendency to regard the defeated as victims of tragic fate.

In Valgardson's work we find not only fatal tragedy or heroic dignity, but also those moments of unexpected beauty which make the drab or miserable lives of many of Valgardson's characters more bearable. These moments receive their intensity from the fact that they have been snatched from the inexorability of fate. Love and true companionship are rare, elusive treasures in a world where everyone struggles to survive. They constitute the hope in Valgardson's fiction. In "The Novice," for example, the actual focus of the story is not so much on the struggle to survive a shipwreck as on the companionship among the shipwrecked people. "A Business Relationship" deals with two elderly people who unexpectedly find love after a difficult and loveless life.

A distinct sense of fatalism and the courage to face it inform a considerable number of Gunnars' poems. In "Wake-Pick Poems," the narrator moves from bitter acceptance of her harsh fate to self-confidence and a belief in her strivings. This belief allows her to transcend her fate: whereas at first she is resigned that she will "die another death tonight" (77), she gradually comes to the realization that "at my feet lie the dead / babes of my nation." Defiantly she states that she will not be reconciled:

> because i believe freedom is spun
> out of restrictions
> i won't go by the law

> i'll revive six babes
> i'll turn into a talking stone
> i'll reveal your faithlessness
> when you step on my back
>
> ...
>
> there is no law for me
> woman breaking distaff heads in solitude (81)

Her fate will not break her, she will not let it rule her spirit even if she cannot help that it rules her life. She will no longer allow herself to "turn to stone" (77); instead she has given meaning to her efforts to which fate has bound her: "leave me with hands to tie / love for my people" (90).

Fatalism plays an important part in *The Nightworkers of Ragnarök*, as the name of the poetic collection already suggests. In her introduction to these poems, Gunnars herself comments on the fatalism of her childhood in Iceland:

There was always a sense of bleakness, a fear of fate, and an overhanging premonition of death. What amazes me now is the readiness with which one was willing to accept death, for others as well as oneself. It seemed natural to die, and not at all bitter to die young. I felt that this unarticulated fatalism must have some cause, and I sought to discover the reason as I wrote the poems in this cycle.... I think now that a people's emotional makeup is molded by necessity. (3)

The first series of poems express the narrator's own sense of fatalism, the minute scope of human existence in the face of the immensity of the galaxy which holds "the chart / they refer to as fate" (17), or human insignificance measured against natural power: "so far the rock-solid river bottom has not cut me / off, but only so / far" (9).

As the narrator continues on her poetic expedition into her past, a distinct awareness of the imminence of disaster stays with her. While these poems breathe a kind of resignation, an acceptance that something will inevitably go wrong soon, there is at the same time an awareness of the danger that complete acceptance of fate without defiance holds in our atomic age:

> "glaumur will go no further
> he will hew and burrow down a thousand metres to avoid the thought of war"

> the bird of dusk is blotted out by distance
>
> that is usually when i wonder when
> the age of victory
> passed away (101)

As the focus of the poems moves away from the personal to the cultural, the awe of immensity and acceptance of fate makes way for affirmation of human strivings and of an undefeated spirit maintained under the doom of a nuclear *Ragnarök*:

> the electricians and machinists
> hand to hand, before and after
> the flame of midnight they keep on
> After the fire they say
>
> she'll be rowing again in three mornings
> because they stay
> gutting away the burnt insides
> and replacing day by day (104)

The fatalism that develops among a people who have always lived with a high casualty rate, as has been the case in Iceland, is not far removed from the belief that natural gifts require sacrifices. As Gunnars points out in her introduction to *Nightworkers*, a fishing nation knows that a certain number of deaths will occur at sea every season. It is the price that has to be paid in return for fish. In early Iceland we know that sacrifices were made for at least two main gifts: preservation of land and people (fertility and safety) and hidden knowledge (in the form of prophecy or poetry) (Martin 1972: 58-64; Turville-Petre 1964: 252, 264).

Sacrifice also plays a role in Valgardson's work, as one might expect from an author of any immigrant community. In two stories, it is explicitly concerned with fertility and death. "Bloodflowers" is, in fact, the story of an ancient fertility ritual performed in a contemporary island community. "The Curse" is concerned with drought, illness and death which are attributed to witchery. It is set in an isolated community in northern Canada. The setting of both stories seems to imply that even today, people will tend to resort to primitive rituals when isolated and severely tried by living conditions. In "Bloodflowers," a young teacher finds a job on an island where, upon arrival, he unwittingly commits an offence against fertility. The balance now has to be restored in order to ward off disaster and ensure fertility anew. Danny's book-knowledge of rituals uncannily turns into reality as he realizes that he will become the sacrifice of one such ritual himself. In "The Curse," a family finds itself stricken by drought and the unexplained illness of their daughter. The situation is attributed to witchcraft and an innocent sacrificial victim is chosen by a cow. The victim, an old woman, is to be stoned so that fertility will return and the child may live. Cows, incidentally, were closely associated with the god Freyr who received sacrifices *til árs og friðar*, i.e., for good harvests and peace. Freyr was the god of fertility and protector from harmful influences.

In Valgardson's work, there is a general tendency to portray the victims of fate as sacrificial victims rather than losers, thereby raising not only the heroic characters to a mythic plane, but also the victims. Carl in "A Business Relationship," for instance, who suffers from a terminal disease, goes out with the intention of shooting himself so as to save his wife from medical costs which he knows she cannot afford. His sacrifice of himself is an act of pure love. However, sacrifices are not always this altruistic. In "Brothers," a child is sacrificed in order to regain peace in Alex's camp. Orville in "Red Dust" offers his wife's niece to be raped in order to get a hunting dog. Sacrifices such as these attest to the harshness of life with which many Valgardsonian characters have to cope. Under such conditions, Valgardson seems to suggest, sacrifices form a natural part of the struggle to survive.

Gunnars' use of the motif of sacrifice mainly with regard to poetry is a treatment she shares with Arnason. These authors both employ Odin's sacrifice in order to gain access to magic and poetry as an image in their journeys of poetic discovery (Arnason's *Marsh Burning*, Gunnars' *One-eyed Moon Maps*). The idea of sacrifice for poetry returns in Gunnars' *Settlement Poems*, where the poet kills a rabbit for poetic creation in the new land. *Settlement Poems* is also concerned with the sacrifices made by the immigrants in return for a new life in Canada. Death and death imagery abound in these poems, as in, for instance, "Jóhann Briem VI":

> it's a lot of luggage
> i'm taking to the grave

the flatboats won't cross
all the rest of august
i'm carting trunks over

lake winnipeg, back & back
again from the rivermouth
to gimli, it's a dream

i'm settling, a little cemetery (*SP 1*: 35)

However, after their first winter the immigrants see that their sacrifices have been taken well by the new land. Both volumes end with the promise of fertility:

messy work, but you learn how
to be born
piecemeal (*1*: 53)

and

a beginning: the first
thundershower, the first
wheat under the ground

the first milkweed
cow: a beginning

fish in the stream.... (*2*: 49)

MYTHS OF TIME AND PLACE

In Chapter II, I argued that the creation of Western Icelandic myths involved the re-establishment of the original settlement of Iceland as the symbolic matrix of Western Icelandic immigrant history. I will now elaborate on the role of the settlement of Iceland as *illud tempus* in the New World and the influence it has had on the Icelandic-Canadian mythic consciousness.

Chapter I demonstrated that, once writing had been introduced in Iceland, one of the first events to be recorded was the settlement of Iceland. A quotation from the preface to the *Landnámabók* showed the reasoning behind the eagerness to record native history. This quotation also shows that the time of settlement was regarded as the time of origins: "Anyway, all civilized nations want to know about the origins of their own society, and the beginnings of their own race." A similar awareness of the time of settlement as the time of origins appears in the sagas. Most sagas begin with an account of the settlement history of the main families and places that occur in the story and are interspersed with long genealogical lists which most commonly serve as an introduction to the characters in the sagas. The importance of this awareness of origins for the society depicted in the sagas is emphasized in such anthropological studies as Durrenberger (1985) and Thompson (1969), which draw attention to the central role played by founding parents and their land in establishing character, position, rights and fortune.

Greenway points to the mythic intuition of time in Old Norse literature. The genealogies, generally considered uninformative intrusions into the narrative by modern readers, in fact indicate a concern with the organic unity of time:

In the genealogies there is a mythic causal operation which implies that no character exists without innate characteristics, no character is independent of the past. In literary terms, he has a reality by accretion before he enters the action, a potential underscoring of his acts. If there is one theme running through the great sagas, it is that no event exists in isolation, that in spite of the will of the best men the slightest event can have an effect which culminates in catastrophe; past and future are an integral part of the present. (1977: 36)[28]

As Greenway remarks, the saga authors established a continuity within the narrative itself as well as an external link between past and present events by locating the place of action or by including the descendants of important characters (193n). This mythic perception of unified time transcends death. In her study of the conception of the dead in Old Norse literature, Ellis (Davidson) found strong literary indications of a belief that, through naming, certain qualities of the dead were passed on to the living. In the Sagas of the Icelanders especially, she noted a widespread tendency to name children after dead kinsmen, particularly someone who had recently died (1943: 139-42).

It is interesting to note that certain aspects of this mythic consciousness survived in Iceland, possibly through the great influence of the sagas. Icelandic folk tales attest to a strong belief in the continuing relations between the living and the dead through dreams, visions or ghosts. Moreover, many tales include characters' genealogies and relations to place-names. Haraldur Bessason (1965) discusses the extent to which the past has remained a living part of the present in Iceland through a strong awareness of the history of geographical place-names and of family histories through genealogy and other links with dead ancestors. Bessason argues that this close relationship with a living past has been a very important factor in the cohesiveness of the Icelanders and their awareness of themselves as a nation distinct from others.

The importance for the West Icelanders of this mythic sense of origins and continuity through genealogy, naming and a general awareness of the past as part of the present must have become clear to them as soon as they realized that their immigration to the New World was in fact a re-enactment of the original settlement of Iceland. Whereas it might be expected that the sense of national continuity would have been disrupted by an act of immigration, the sense of continuity was actually reinforced among West Icelanders by the strongly developed mythical perception of Icelandic immigrant history. Such consciousness of a re-enactment was probably stimulated by the fact that the Romantic movement in Iceland had pursued and given renewed literary form to the idea of the Icelandic saga past as the Golden Age of the North (Greenway 1977: 22).

With the idea of a temporal re-enactment of the original mythic beginnings of the Icelandic nation we have arrived at the basis for the development of the Western Icelandic social myth. Wrenched from all familiar surroundings, people and customs, and scorned by both the Icelanders in the Old Country and the Anglo-Canadians in the New, the immigrants fell back on a long-standing mythic consciousness. This enabled them to come to terms with their private griefs and to create a mythic awareness of themselves as West Icelanders which, in the long run, helped them to survive as a cohesive ethnic group. The need for a historical myth among ethnic groups is emphasized by Norman and Runblom:

> To conquer history is important for almost every ethnic and religious minority. Not least essential is to prove that the story of one's group goes far back in time. For this objective the recapitulation of the early settlement is a serious matter, and the group's legitimacy is strengthened if one can show evidence that one's fellow countrymen had been in the area of immigration at an early date. (1987: 206-07)

From the earliest writings on we encounter comparisons of West Icelanders with the settlers of Iceland and the explorers of Vínland.

In Chapter III, I demonstrated how the idea of the West Icelander as a new version of the old saga hero became a theme celebrated in Western Icelandic literature. The general consciousness of a re-enactment is reflected in fields outside of literature as well. Jakob Jónsson (1943), for instance, drew attention to the fact that the immigrants looked to the Old Icelandic republic for examples of social organization rather than to contemporary Iceland. From their first years in Canada there appears to have been a concern among West Icelanders with the recording of their immigration and settle-ment history, a Western Icelandic *Landnámabók*. This concern is attested to by the early foundation of community papers, for instance, their numerous accounts about facets of immigration life, and the frequent comparisons of Western Icelandic writings with Old Ice-landic settlement accounts, such as Stephan G.'s remark on the appearance of Jóhann Magnús Bjarnason's *Eiríkur Hansson* that it was "the West-Icelandic book of settlements" (Guðmundsson 1982: 48). Moreover, in the various published histories of the Icelandic immigrants and their descendants, from the first up to the most recent, we invariably find implicit or explicit comparisons of the West Icelanders with their medieval forbears. To make the link between Viking ancestor and Western Icelandic immigrant complete, a large number of these histories carry the word "saga" in their titles. Although in Icelandic the word *saga* also means "history," this can-not be an explanation for the fact that many Icelandic-Canadian his-torical accounts in English use "saga" in their titles, as the meaning of "saga" in English is restricted to an Old Icelandic literary saga narrative or a story which resembles such a saga. These Western Icelandic historical accounts, or "sagas," also emphasize the respon-sibility that history entails: the West Icelanders must prove them-selves worthy of their ancestry and prove their worth in the face of the world. The Icelandic immigrants thus tried to legitimize and val-idate their position by way of mythic consciousness, the spontaneous creation of myths which find the origins of Iceland as their symbolic matrix.

A more concrete idea of the development of the Icelandic mythic consciousness among the West Icelanders and their Icelandic-Canadian descendants is expressed in an article by David Arnason called "The Myth of Beginnings" (1994), and in Magnús Einarsson's studies of Icelandic-Canadian folklore (1975, 1991). Arnason's article especially is quite illuminating in this respect, for he shows how the mythic experience among the West Icelanders of their immigration to Canada grounds a durable Icelandic-Canadian group identity. He argues that the Icelandic settlement in Manitoba was "an apocalyptic event" (9). Because most Icelanders emigrated after volcanic eruptions, he says, the Icelandic settlement formed a representative slice of Icelandic society, not a single stratum. They had not left any specific enemies at home to oppose, and so an internal development was possible: "The Icelanders brought with them all the arguments from home, and they continued them here." They founded an exclusive republic with its own social organization and civil law. Arnason then notes:

The myth of beginnings is important to understanding the experience of the Icelandic community. Other prairie communities were named after people (MacGregor, McCreary) or old-country places (Balmoral, Sans Souci) or Indian place names (Winnipeg, Pinawa). Gimli, the site of the first settlement was named for the great Hall of Gimli in Norse mythology. The elder *Edda* tells us that after Ragnarok, when Fenrir kills Óðinn, and the wolves Skoll and Hati eat the sun and the moon, when Yggdrasil, the world ash, is shaken, and the gods are defeated in final battle, all the universe will return to fire and sea. Out of that will arise an island on which will be situated the Great Hall of Gimli. All the best of men, of giants, of gods and the creatures of outer darkness will be gathered here. (It's a tough place to get into: only a few gods will make it.) That post-apocalyptic vision is a perfect naming for people whose homes have literally disappeared under fire. (4)

He goes on to tell the history of the first years of the immigrants "as it is told to the children of the community." This story is factually true, he claims, but it is also mythically true:

Both metaphorically and literally cut adrift, the Icelanders make an accidental landing at the wrong place, which is nevertheless signalled to be the proper place by the miraculous white rock. They face a purification by disease, a testing by flood, a plague of locusts, an act of naming. They undergo the very same process of claiming a country that is described in the old Icelandic Landnámabók, the book that describes the discovery of Iceland. (5)

According to Arnason, the most important aspects of this myth of beginnings are the fact that it rooted the immigrants mythologically in their new country and that its hold on the community forms a strong facet of the Icelandic-Canadian identity which is ritually celebrated at the annual Icelandic-Canadian "carnival," the *Íslendingadagurinn*:

Where later immigrants to Manitoba such as the Norwegians, the Swedes and the Germans have largely been so integrated that there is little sign of their cultural presence, the Icelanders continue to form a significant cultural group. The source of this cohesiveness is the myth of beginnings, a myth shared by Icelandic Canadians and Icelandic Americans as well. We look back, not to some lost haven across the sea in Iceland, but to our roots as a people in the new land. When we hold our celebrations, we honour the old country but we celebrate the new as well....

At *Íslendingadagurinn*, we gather from all over the continent, we renew acquaintances, we hold family reunions and, most importantly, we renew the myth of our beginnings, and in that myth we find a sense of community that holds together a dispersed people who have entered thoroughly into the national mythologies of Canada and the United States. Because of the hold of that myth, it is possible to think of yourself as a New Icelander even if you speak no Icelandic and have never been to Iceland. (8)

What Arnason shows here is in fact how the temporal re-enactment of the mythic time of origins in the New World has become the central focus of the Icelandic-Canadian group identity. The mythic sense of continuity has been reinforced by its very transplantation.

Einarsson comes to conclusions quite similar to Arnason's. He notes the "marked historical, genealogical, biographical or personal character" of Icelandic-Canadian oral traditions, which he attributes to the immigration experience and the literary models which were in themselves results of the original immigration to Iceland, i.e., the *Landnámabók* and the sagas:

Then too it must be remembered that this is the method used in the old Icelandic historical work—*Landnámabók* (the Book of Settlement). It is thus a practice hoary with age. An Icelander would consider any work on the settlements in America which did not teem with biographical sketches of the settlers deficient indeed. The Icelander had great pride of race and in spite of the fact that he has been assimilated with surprising ease he yet possesses a keen consciousness of his racial extraction and continues to be greatly interested in the lives of his fellow Canadians of Icelandic origin and is very desirous that no achievement of his fellows pass unrecorded. (20)

Although Einarsson himself does not place these observations in a mythical framework, it is clear that they fit the mythic experience of origins and continuity. Again we have the example of the *Landnámabók*, again we notice the deep-rooted interest in family and ancestry, and again we see how it links the otherwise scattered Icelandic-Canadian community members. Einarsson, in fact, emphasizes strongly the role of Icelandic-Canadian folklore, with its distinct historical and genealogical flavour, as an agent which not only reflects but also reinforces in-group sentiments. Community, he suggests, has taken over from place in the New World folklore:

The point to be made then is that West Icelanders have enmeshed themselves in a world which is woven out of personal relationships as expressed in their concern for genealogy and local history, and in terms of folklore, the citing of anecdotes and verses. Finding themselves in a country which is not theirs, in the sense that Iceland was, it has come to be the community rather than place which is the recipient of their loyalty: not geographical features but the individuals identified in verses and anecdotes mark the boundaries of this world. (22)

As in Iceland, the sense of continuity transcends death in the folklore of New Iceland. Einarsson has noted that Icelandic-Canadian anecdotes show a great occupation with the supernatural, in particular with communication with the dead. Moreover, about the earlier mentioned article of Bessason he remarks:

The supernatural anecdotes show that death is not felt as a finality, but the reaching of firm ground—the final genealogical embrace of reunion with one's kinsmen and friends....

In other words, people die slowly to the memory of the living. The same tenacity that keeps the West Icelandic community together transcends the boundaries of death. (28)

The way in which genealogy, history and folklore work together as a bonding device for the Icelandic Canadians as a group is explained by Einarsson as their support of "a sense of the irrelevance of the outsider rather than any specifically defined racist or nationalistic notions; the integrity of the community is all important, even, or perhaps especially, in death" (28).

A mythic sense of continuity that is so strongly developed that it serves as a major preserver of ethnic identity is, unsurprisingly, reflected in the literature of that ethnic group. Indeed Valgardson's concern with continuity is closely associated with ethnic identity. In "Skald" (*Red Dust*), Alma starts off a process of retrieving her ethnic identity and acquiring maturity by deliberately naming her puppy-dog Skald. The dog brings Alma on the track of the Bjarnasons. They take her in as a friend because "your people come from around here" (23). After having asked Alma about her father and grandfather, they tell her more about her family background. For Alma this is the beginning of a different life. She gains confidence from her knowledge about her ancestors and the identity it gives her in the eyes of the Bjarnasons: it is as if she has come home. The security this gives her makes Alma a different and happier person.

In *Gentle Sinners*, ancestry and naming play a crucial role. Bobby's parents have completely broken with their past and have denied their son any access to it as well. When Bobby decides to run away, he deliberately seeks out a lost relation on his mother's side: her brother Sigfus. Earlier in this chapter I noted the importance of names in Bobby's return to ancestry and history: the original names of his parents become his "portal into the past" (11). When Bobby arrives at Sigfus' place, he introduces himself as his nephew, "giving not his name but his relationship. It was as if his name was without enough significance to gain him recognition or acceptance" (6). This is true, of course, for he has not been named into the family by his parents. Sigfus, however, has already recognized his nephew by the physical characteristics of his family, so that Bobby has at least an entry. Thereupon Sigfus rebaptizes Bobby into the family, naming him Eric. From then on there is no way back: "He looked as if he had secretly sunk his feet into the ground and was defying Sigfus to move him" (21). It is as if Sigfus always expected his sister's child to turn up, for the pull of blood represents for him "the natural, intended order" (22). For Eric, acceptance into and knowledge about his family is like a true homecoming. As in Alma's case, it is the recovering of a lost identity:

Without turning around, [Eric] said, as if astounded, "She was my aunt," then gave a little snort of pleasure. "My mother never told me anything. I never had anybody."

"Maybe she thought you weren't interested." Sigfus' voice was quiet and reasonable.

Eric gave a barely perceptible shake of his head. "I asked. You'd have thought we were all ordered from Eaton's and somebody lost the receipt."

Sigfus and Sam exchanged amused glances but Sam was quite serious when he said: "You've got to know who you are. You don't know, you're like a tree somebody planted after cutting off the roots." (157)

Eric's relation to Sigfus also gives him an identity within the community, although he will have to prove his mettle: "He'll keep to himself. That family always has" (34). The motif of kinship and ancestry is so pervasive in the novel that one feels entitled to wonder if the Tree-brothers were thus named to form a negative contrast to the positive family tree represented by Eric, Sigfus and Sam. Whereas the Vigfussons are strongly rooted in ancestry and history and are strengthened by these roots, the Tree-brothers seem to come out of nowhere, and are portrayed as perverted, grotesque, almost diabolical versions of Sigfus and Eric. Eric's parents, who denounced their family and past, are also presented as grotesques. Deracination leads to a grotesque life.

In "The Cave" (*What Can't Be Changed Shouldn't Be Mourned*) we saw that continuity through family takes a more ominous turn. A definite belief in genealogical determination and inevitability is found here. At the beginning of the story, Sigga refuses to marry the narrator because of her ancestry:

"No. I would like to live with you, but I won't marry."

"Are you crazy?"

It was not a good thing to say. I felt her stiffen. I had momentarily forgotten that her great-grandfather had been Gunnar Thordarson and that her father was Valdi Anderson. (102)

In response to her refusal, the narrator begins research into the lives of Sigga's ancestors, although he himself is not quite sure about his own motives in doing so: "To prove that they were not crazy? To reassure Sigga that if she was to have a son, he would escape the same fate?" (103) Ultimately, it turns out that in spite of all misgivings, Sigga conceives a son by the narrator who, it is implied in the ending of the story, will go the way of his forefathers. The whole story carries many references to cyclical time and the idea of the future embedded in the past. This is, of course, an allusion to a mythical perception of time and unity of reality as we find it in, for example, the sagas.

In "The Man from Snæfellsness," we encounter a grief that has been passed on over generations until, finally, an opportunity arises for great-grandson Axel to return to Iceland to set the old wrongs right. Here, too, there is an atmosphere of inescapability, of duty to the ancestors. The family line needs to be cleansed, old injustices avenged. At first, Axel has no interest in accepting an invitation to Iceland. The bitterness of his great-grandfather has been passed on to him, and he resents his ethnic identity. However, the trip to

Iceland presents an occasion to come to terms with the past, and Axel is almost made to feel this. He has no rest after the invitation:

That should have been the end of the matter, but every time I went out to cut the grass or weed the garden or trim the ivy, my great-grandfather's face appeared. At times, I could smell his pipe tobacco. More than once I was certain he was standing behind me, watching, and I turned suddenly as if to catch him but there was never anyone there. (120)

The almost tangible presence of his ancestor is much akin to the very concrete visions and supernatural visitations described in the sagas. Axel is plagued by a recurrent dream vision which takes him back to saga times: he sees himself together with his dead relatives gathered as Vikings in arms on a mission of revenge. In the end, it does not take such violence but merely the ability to forgive the wrongs done to Axel's forefather to clear the generations-old bitterness away and come to terms with ethnic identity.

These two stories from Valgardson's later work show a more ambiguous, though no less convinced, attitude towards continuity. A struggle with the inescapability and predetermination inherent in genealogical and historical continuity is being waged. There is, however, also a strong connection with home and identity in Valgardson's work. Both facets accord with earlier findings concerning the communal role of mythic continuity among the Icelandic Canadians and the fact that Valgardson is a member of this community.

In Arnason's work we find decidedly less concern with mythic continuity. However, there is one story, "The Sunfish" (*Fifty Stories and a Piece of Advice*), which is a literary recreation of "The Myth of Beginnings," Arnason's earlier discussed essay. The story represents in a playful way a founding myth of the Icelandic-Canadian community. The story begins with the fisherman-immigrant Gusti out on the lake. Almost immediately, the narrator claims kinship to Gusti: he is the "second cousin once removed of my great-grandmother" (61). Thus, continuity is established right away. Nevertheless, no genealogy of Gusti is traced back to Iceland, for this is the myth of beginnings in the new land. By supernatural means, a speaking fish, Gusti becomes involved in the mythological beginnings of the community: through his wish for a new wife, which is granted to him by the fish, Gusti becomes a founding father. Gusti's new wife, significantly named Freyja, comes to play the main part in an ancient fertility ritual of the community and is thus designated as its mother. From Gusti and Freyja all community members descend.

At the same, Arnason, a postmodernist *pur sang*, takes care to move away from myth's tendency towards a single vision. Instead, he ends the story with several anecdotes which present multiple endings: some say the people from Arborg descended from Gusti and Freya, whereas others claim the people of Gimli to be their descendants. Thus the mythic is deconstructed by the anecdotal so as to create a way out of myth's tendency to explain everything one way. Arnason also has a fascination with naming. In some cases, the act of naming is linked to mythic continuity, as, for instance, in *The Icelanders*, where he describes the events of Ragnarök:

Then, out of the final chaos will rise an island. On that island will stand the great hall of Gimli, the most beautiful of all halls, with 548 doors. Finally at peace, the best of gods, the best of men, and the best of creatures of outer darkness will dwell in eternal harmony.

And so we are named. (114)

In the section "Out of the mind's turning" in *Marsh Burning*, natural objects are named and followed by self-coined kennings and associative pieces of prose. The end of the section celebrates the power of words and names to create worlds: "say it and make it happen" (64). This belief in the power of words is reminiscent of the traditional Icelandic belief which we find embedded for instance in the phenomenon of the *kraftaskáld* and the combative use of verse, both of which have survived in Icelandic-Canadian folklore. Since *Marsh Burning* is largely concerned with ethnic heritage, it is quite likely that this use of naming was influenced by Arnason's background.

In many of his fictional works, Arnason's use of naming seems to be completely in the mythopoeic tradition of Canadian literature, where it serves to decolonize Canadian culture, deconstruct it so that it can be redefined on its own terms. In addition, there is also the important postmodernist influence on his work which likes to make readers aware of the creativity of our imaginations as we name and "make meaning" in order to come to terms with the reality around us or, in postmodern terms, "invent" reality (Hutcheon 1988: 35). This is the kind of naming we find in Arnason's later fiction, such as "Owl on Cairn":

The simplest thing is naming. I'd like to make a list of things we saw that day
we made the cairn, and say, "Look, these are the things that were there.
Stone, rock, gull and cairn. All the crawling and the flying things that leave
their signature in the sand." (*Fifty Stories* 39)

Gunnars brings a slightly different mythic perspective to Icelandic-
Canadian literature, moulded by her early years in Iceland rather than
by the history of the Icelandic-Canadian community. Whereas
Valgardson and Arnason explore the mythic dimensions of an ethnic history and identity in contemporary Canada, Gunnars goes back
to the Icelandic pioneers, and recreates the encounter of their
Icelandic mythic consciousness with the Canadian environment.
Gunnars' *Settlement Poems* speak of a definite awareness of continuity
and an almost natural urge to record the pioneer experience in the
traditional way. The poems are themselves all parts of daybooks,
diaries and other pioneer accounts. In *Settlement Poems 1*, one of the
immigrants notes during the voyage to Canada:

> have to write a daybook
> with moist scaly quills
> write a book of settlements
> on the way to kingston (13)

In *Settlement Poems 2*, the coming of spring, a symbolic rebirth and
beginning in the new land, is signalled by the founding of the printing press and the settlement government. New Iceland has become
a pioneer nation like the mother country a thousand years before,
and its settlement history can now be recorded:

> the printing house
> of lundar, east of the river
> begins: january 26
>
> 1877 (...)
> been to a meeting
> in mödruvellir on
>
> a settlement government
> (...)
> been to a meeting

on a district government
in sandy bar february
14 (...)

spring enters my house
broad-headed, the new
government emerges (44)

Names and the act of naming are important also in Gunnars'
work. In *Settlement Poems*, part of the process of learning and adaptation to the new land is the naming of plants and animals. For immigrant Stefán Eyjólfsson, this is part of the alphabet of the new
country in which the new book of settlement will be written: "coyote scats, settlement runes" he notes (*1*: 45). Names themselves are
very significant to Gunnars, as they are to Icelanders in general. In
Settlement Poems as well as in *The Axe's Edge*, each single poem or story
carries the name of the teller as its title. Givner remarks on this
feature in her review of *The Axe's Edge*: "Names for Gunnars have a
magical, talismanic quality, and she reels them off like the genealogies of the old sagas" (1984: 16). The quality of names is not merely
magical in the Icelandic consciousness, but is expressive of a vertical
(genealogies) and horizontal (community) continuity, as is evident
from the following passage from "Grasses" in *The Axe's Edge*:

My father, Sigfús Björnsson, passed this lore on to me. I know more facts
about him than my mother. He created Fagranes, which means Beautiful
Peninsula, here in Manitoba. He was born in Ketilsstadir, in Hjaltastadathigá, on
May eighteenth, 1863. His parents were Björn Jónsson and Björg Halladóttir
from Nefbjarnarstadir in Hróarstunga. She is still alive in Árbakki by
Icelandic River. My great-grandparents were Jón Sigfússon from Geirastadir
in Hróarstunga and Ingibjorg Jónsdóttir. These names are also a presence.
They are part of my mental territory and they make it difficult to fail. When I
have performed poorly I have to account for it to them all. Their faces come
out to me at such times. (62)

This passage indicates both the extent to which ancestors form a living part of the present of their descendants and the responsibility
exacted by them. To the Icelander, no individual exists in isolation:
his disposition and his actions have everything to do with relatives
dead or alive. Salverson described a similar influence exercised on
her parents and herself by her forefathers, whom she referred to as
"the august ancestors":

They too were outside my small, immediate world, but represented a ghostly court of equity, to whom it was my duty to refer the record of my deeds and misdeeds.

The old-fashioned Icelander, like the ancient Chinese, does not cherish his ancestors idly. It is not with him a question of recounting with pride achievements once illustrious and long forgotten, for nothing better than pleasurable vanity. One walked before this ghostly assembly, and shuddered to be found wanting in commendable behaviour. Consciously and unconsciously, my mother's judgements were invariably controlled by this final court of appeal. (*Confessions* 49-50)

Incidentally, her addition of "old-fashioned," implying that the deep-rooted sense of ancestry was something of the past, says more about Salverson's own self-esteem than about the role of genealogy for the Icelanders. The negative reactions that Salverson's work received from the Western Icelandic community left scars, and must have given her the idea that she had failed in the eyes of "the august ancestors."

Ancestry and naming also play an important role in Gunnars' autobiographical *Wake-Pick Poems*, which are set in Iceland and Denmark. Possibly, her explorations of the mythical dimensions of Icelandic-Canadian immigrant history opened up the possibility for Gunnars to recreate the mythical implications of her own immigrant experiences. "Changeling Poems" attests to the belief that naming after a dead relative involves a direct influence from that relative on the descendant namesake. The narrator protests:

> i, too, suffocate under my name
> i can't live
> up to my great-grandmother's ghost
> i want an easier name
>
> ...
>
> born under great grandmother's majesty
> under the white headdress
>
> don't give me a hard life
> don't make me die young
> give me another name
> more suitable

name me leech
name me woodlouse
name me a dream i dream
name me broadleaved woods (16-17)

Slowly, however, the narrator grows into her identity. In the last poem of the cycle, there is a positive affirmation on the narrator's part of her identity within her ancestry and on the part of her relatives who have accepted her into their company:

this is the end

now i recognize them
tove, gunnar, sister gunna by name
eleven hundred years of family
they're used to me too (31)

In the following cycle, "Monkshood Poems," the narrator has to come to terms with her Danish ancestry on her mother's side. Again, there is an initial struggle against the imprisonment of genealogical determination reminiscent of the struggle found in Valgardson's more personal stories discussed above. In "monkshood VII" the family line is experienced as a mosquito, "an irritant in the placid woods" which "stings / for blood — / your blood" (43). A little later, during a meeting with a relative:

i don't like meeting kirsten
in malmö for the first time
she says i'm a replica of my mother
makes me uncoordinated
i keep stumbling to the mirror
to look at myself:

...

i don't like repetitions
spots
in records, the needle
falls into again, again
but it's the same family tree ... (49)

This cycle also ends in final affirmation of ancestry, however, when the narrator has learnt to regard it as her "truth" rather than a prison:

> my great grandmother & her mother
> & her mother before her
> waited here in the ancient ruin
> of danehof castle, waited
>
> to emerge from blindness
> out of a dark time
>
> this is my icon
> my window into truth (72)

In *Carnival of Longing*, a very personal collection even by Gunnars' standards, there are not any direct references to continuity, but a distinct heavy atmosphere seems rather to suggest that the author is still struggling with the burden of ancestral and historical determination. A passage suggestive of this is the following:

in my room I had knitting needles and wool. in the evenings I knitted, the door closed. on my wall were pictures of Dimmalimm, watercolours, about a princess alone by a pond, looking into the water. and a swan. Dimmalimm was sad and cried a great deal in every picture. it was a mystery to me why she should be alone and why the forest behind her was so soggy, so dreary, so unpeopled. they said the painter Muggur was melodramatic. he was in love. he was in my family. I knitted and thought about kinship. (10)

In *The Prowler*, Gunnars continues her exploration into personal and national history in order to discover more about the patterns informing her life, for "[i]t was a small country, with a small tribe of people. Repetitions were bound to occur. It was understood" (125). *The Prowler* is really a collection of meditations out of which the narrator seems to expect a pattern to emerge. At the same time there are frequent instances where she expresses a reluctance to acknowledge any such patterns, a reluctance sprung from a hope of freedom which she intuitively knows to be a fallacy:

It was a time when the pattern was not yet clear. Stories had only begun. There had been no development of plots, no interweaving of incidents, no coincidences had meshed. There were no endings in sight.

I could afford a view of the world that was constructed out of simple chance. There was no order to history. Fate took random turns.

The longer you live, I thought much later in life, the more deliberate the pattern that emerges seems to be. If it is God's story, I considered, then it must be waited for. It is a story that is read in time. (119)

Gunnars' work, then, reflects a struggle with the sense of continuity which the author experiences increasingly as an imprisoning burden, a heritage from her Old World past which determines her outlook on life and which she cannot escape. Unlike Valgardson, she cannot ultimately find relief from this burden in the mythic sense of belonging of the Icelandic-Canadian community. Gunnars is, after all, a recent immigrant and not a member of the Icelandic-Canadian community. Her roots have not yet been transplanted, only severed. She lacks the communal mythic experience of the Icelandic Canadians, because her mythic experience goes straight back to the Old World. Thus, mythic continuity is for her an isolating rather than a bonding influence in the New.

One other aspect of Icelandic-Canadian mythology is found particularly in Arnason's work. It is, in fact, one of the few elements of his writings which clearly attest to his ethnic background: Icelandic-Canadian storytelling and myth-making. This will be our next topic.

STORYTELLING AND MYTH-MAKING

As the Icelandic immigrants settled in Canada, even the staunchest nationalists found they could not refrain from a certain degree of adaptation. Indeed, the general policy in the Icelandic communities from the beginning was one of public assimilation. At the same time, the immigrant experience and the reactions of people at home and in Canada caused an active concern with the preservation and promotion of the Icelandic heritage. This helped the healing process of their uprooted condition and their severely bruised self-image. Gradually, the Icelandic Canadians began to develop a community and culture of their own.

Norman and Runblom discuss this development of distinct immigrant cultures among Scandinavians. They note that the general pattern of fairly quick, though by no means easy, assimilation among Scandinavians was compensated among the Icelanders by an equal

330 THE ICELANDIC VOICE

pride taken in their cultural heritage. Norman and Runblom attribute this to the fact that the Icelanders were much more cognizant of their national culture than Scandinavians from other countries. As they continue to describe the growing cultural activities among the immigrants, Norman and Runblom observe:

Secular associations developed according to patterns from the respective countries, and for many the goal was to uphold traditions from the Old World. Some of these traditions were invented or reinvented overseas. Fatherland-based ideologies developed and took elements from the European cultures and adapted them to the immigrant situation. To borrow terminology from individual psychology, these institutions went through a process of separation ... but in the creation of their own individuality, they borrowed components from the mother organization and ideologies in the old country. (1987: 273)

This is what gradually happened to the ethnic culture of the Icelandic-Canadian communities. Some traditions were lost, others that were lost in the homeland were maintained, and yet others were revived, adapted or "reinvented." The mixture that eventually resulted made for a specific, individual Icelandic-Canadian culture. Its development can be traced in the folklore of the Icelandic Canadians, mostly in verses and anecdotes. Its lively oral culture reflects the way in which the Icelandic-Canadian community dealt with the immigrant experience as well as the processes of adaptation and transplantation. At the same time it is a communal cultural expression of ethnic identity.

The relevance of Icelandic-Canadian oral traditions for Icelandic-Canadian literature lies mainly in the strongly developed tendency among Canadian authors to move away consciously from Canada's colonial heritage in their works so as to be able to rediscover and recreate their country and its past in all its aspects and on its own terms. Contemporary Canadian literature clearly exhibits its inclination to create room for the retelling of Canadian history from the non-Imperial point of view and for the reinvention of a local Canada that does not stop at the borders of Toronto and includes voices other than Anglo-Canadian. Experiments with the literary representation of multiple voices and realities open up possibilities for a truer representation of the Canadian heterogeneous reality. Similarly, many authors seek literary means of de-colonizing Canadian culture, landscape and history, replacing imported myths with indigenous ones in order for Canada's own story to be heard and its own reality to be reflected on various levels.

The Magic Realist movement has been of great importance in Canada in this respect. Hutcheon calls it the "single largest international influence on Canadian fiction" (1988: 208). Magic realism provides an excellent narrative medium for post-colonial literature, with its dialectic between two different fictional worlds of realism and fantasy, since the post-colonial imagination is caught in a dialectic between the Old and the New World (Slemon 1980). According to Chanady, the frequent definition given to Magic Realism in Latin American fiction is also applicable in Canada: "Magic realism is often defined as the juxtaposition of two different rationalities—the Indian and the European—in a syncretic fictitious world-view based on the simultaneous existence of several entirely different cultures in Latin America" (1986: 55). This movement stimulated interest in oral folk cultures in Canada and the literary possibilities they offer. In Magic-Realist works, the "magic" and the "real," the mythical and the historical, the supernatural and the natural, are all interwoven and unified into a narrative by the storyteller who has to make it all believable (Hancock 1986: 42). Magic Realism exhibits the technological age's realization that ultimately reality exists only in the combination of the multifarious perspectives with which it is viewed and the various levels from which it is approached. It is a desire to return to what the Norse scholar Steblin-Kamenskij called "unconscious authorship" with its interrelation of form and content, fact and fiction (1972: 133). In its purest form, this kind of authorship is found in myth, but it has been transmitted mostly in the form of folklore. While it can never be recaptured, because we have lost that mythic perception, we still have access to it through folklore. The remarkable combination of realism and the supernatural found in Icelandic folk tales, or rather, the inclusion of the supernatural within the daily realistic sphere where the two levels of experience seem to interact harmoniously has many features in common with modern Magic-Realist writing, even more so when considering the socio-critical strain contained in them. Indeed, as we will see, Icelandic folk tale elements play a considerable role in contemporary Icelandic-Canadian works.

The literary climate in Canada offered a framework for Icelandic-Canadian authors in which to reconstruct and retell the history of the Icelandic-Canadian community as storytellers of that community. As such, their works form a bridge between a present New World identity and an untold Old World and immigration past. Moreover, the oral traditions of the Icelandic-Canadian community constitute a source for their literary myth-making as Canadian storytellers who transcend the boundaries of realism and contest the boundaries of ethnicity in their creation and sharing of indigenous Canadian myths.

Valgardson, Arnason and Gunnars are, each in their own way, concerned with their roles as storytellers. In Valgardson's case, this concern is clearest in his use of more traditional story-forms. He explains that in his fiction, he attempts to create understanding and emotional sharing, and to help people discover both their own true image and what they aspire to be. In order to get his message across, however, he feels his stories must be structured in such a way that they are sure to reach his audience:

> Having accepted the tradition of the story told or read about the fireplace during a long winter evening, I have also accepted certain goals for and restraints upon my fiction. Since my particular subject matter is taken from the same area as that which contains my audience, I must be faithful in detail to the reality of daily life. My audience could not, would not accept, an error of fact. Moreover, since they are the audience that they are, it is necessary for me to adhere to the traditional storyform. Experimental writing and discontinuous prose will not help me to create a bond of understanding between myself and my audience. (1979-80: 180)

Valgardson acknowledges here the influence of the Icelandic story-telling tradition on his role as a writer. As a storyteller, he is dependent upon the willingness of his audience to listen. To achieve this, he must ensure interest and credibility throughout. Icelandic literary critic Kristinn Andrésson has noted that "it is very much ingrained in Icelanders from the days of old that truth is closely tied to limited exaggeration, genealogy and placenames." [29] In other words, a story must be firmly situated in place and genealogy. It cannot pursue the marvellous boundlessly but has to retain credibility through the story-teller's art. Thus, Valgardson can create characters like the Tree-brothers or Annie in *Gentle Sinners*, who are obviously grotesques but not impossibilities. And while the story in this novel is clearly structured along mythical lines, it is at the same time a perfectly credible story firmly situated in an Icelandic-Canadian family in small-town Manitoba. In an interview with Kristjana Gunnars, Valgardson says that he believes all actions in his fiction should be in accordance with character and motivation:

In my belief, every action is motivated. That's why in a really good story you can't have a bunch of surprises. You can have surprises in the way something happens but not in what happens. There's a certain kind of mysticism in the psychological fatalism or predetermination I'm talking about.... People do not behave in an arbitrary fashion; they only appear to do so. (1989: 16)

In this interview, Valgardson traces his use of psychological credibility to Icelandic fatalism and mysticism, but ultimately there is also the same concern with credibility towards the audience.

Valgardson's subject matter also indicates a sense of responsibility or desire on the part of the author to be the voice of his community. As he says to Gunnars: "Perhaps I can speak for the inarticulate" (19). Valgardson has discussed this part of his authorship more elaborately elsewhere (1987). As he explains the influence of growing up in an immigrant community on what he calls his "internal landscape," Valgardson describes what he regarded as the main function of writing: to help the integration of the various communities within Canada and to help their members deal with loss of identity and the general toll that immigration exacted even of later generations. As long as the scars of these wounds have not healed and integration has not been achieved, there can be no healthy Canadian identity or nation. Accordingly, Valgardson's fiction deals largely with the underlying emotions of people who have long suppressed these emotions in their struggle in an alien and indifferent environment. He employs themes which are recognizable to his audience and help them see and judge themselves and others more clearly.

Arnason is more self-consciously the author as storyteller. While he, too, is aware of the need to maintain credibility, his concern is more focussed on the lengths to which he can take credibility and on audience participation. Rather than Valgardson, who as a storyteller aims to be a healer and a speaker for his community, Arnason is more interested in the play and craft of storytelling itself.[30] In his first volume, *Marsh Burning*, we still sense something of an incantation in the voice of the narrator. From *Fifty Stories* onwards, however, Arnason's focus is shifted towards the more formal considerations of storytelling. In an interview with Robert Enright, he says:

I'm interested particularly in solving narrative problems. How you can tell a story that has certain restraints, certain limitations. Then I start to write and whatever story comes, comes. So, the ideas for the stories come after the form for the stories. The idea is secondary—it doesn't matter what it's about. (1985: 8)

Interestingly, Arnason attributes his great formal interest to the storytelling that took place among families in the community, the same storytelling tradition that motivated Valgardson towards his more traditional way of writing:

I grew up in a family where people loved to tell stories.... The loudest storyteller, the one who could throw the best hooks, kept his story going. If the story didn't work somebody else would drown you out. So if you wanted to get your stories in you had to learn what are the hooks, what are the ways of catching people, how do you maintain suspense, how do you keep from giving away the secrets until you absolutely have to. What are the narrative traps, where can you get lost? I'm very concerned about craft, about technique. (8-9)

Whereas Valgardson is more attracted by the role of the storyteller as a seer and soothsayer who has a duty towards the community to teach as he tells, Arnason is more the storyteller as entertainer: "I'm not there to make the reader into a better person, or to reveal the fundamental human truths. If the reader finds them there, that's good for him, but that's not what I'm aiming for. What I would like to do would be to release joy" (9). However, even Arnason feels a responsibility towards his community as a writer, which is expressed in *Marsh Burning* and *The Icelanders*. In the former book, Arnason explores his ethnic past and that of the Icelandic-Canadian community, an exploration which ends in a cyclical affirmation of ethnic identity. *The Icelanders* is a communal reconstruction of the Icelandic-Canadian past. Arnason allows various members of the community to tell their memories in their own ways, and, adding his own, makes these into a collage. This book attests to a wish to preserve the Icelandic-Canadian narratives about the past that have survived. As Arnason himself puts it in the prologue: "Think of this book as a poem about ancestors." Later he notes:

Men became legends for the work they could do, and they nourished their own legends carefully. And at night there were hockey games for the young, chess for the old, and stories for everyone. New sagas were being written in the minds of a people who were in the full flourish of their second transplanting. (36)

Writers from an ethnic background naturally tend to have a greater sense of responsibility towards their communities, for they can, through literature, claim a part in Canadian history and reality on their behalf. By telling their stories, these writers can preserve and make known the experiences of their communities, where they came from, how they made sense of the new world and how they became what they are now. They speak for those who could not do so before them, they act as literary medium for the community. In the Icelandic tradition, of course, the role of *skáld* involved a similar responsibility. However, in Arnason's view, authors also have a duty "not to pummel" the past forever in the face of their readership. Consequently, after *The Icelanders* he turns to storytelling for its own sake.

In "The Sunfish" (*Fifty Stories*), we still find a residue of "ethnic responsibility" as it were, in that Arnason has created here a founding myth for the Icelandic-Canadian community. "The Sunfish" is in many ways a transitory story, for the storyteller is already present and is actively engaging his audience. The narrating voice unifies the discordant elements in the story, that is the natural and the supernatural. In this respect, it is very much in accordance with the Icelandic requisites for "truth" in a story as analyzed by Andrésson: the story is firmly situated in place (Lake Winnipeg, New Iceland), genealogy (Gusti is the second cousin once removed of the narrator's great-grandmother) and even in time (June 1878). The reference to Gusti's diaries as a source makes the setting even more believable, considering the traditional Icelandic respect for writing and literature. The marvellous in this story, a speaking sunfish, is made credible through this recognizable, realistic setting, and by the craft of the storyteller who had anticipated disbelief and cleverly put the phenomenon in a historically realistic context which appeals to communal immigrant experience:

Gusti did not answer right away. He was a man of common sense, and he knew that fish do not speak. Still, in the past three years, his faith in common sense had been somewhat shaken. Common sense worked perfectly well in Iceland, but it seemed to be of less value in this new country. Common sense had told him that when the water is covered with ice, you do not bother to fish. Here though, you fished underneath the ice, and when you pulled fish up through the ice, they gasped and froze solid in the winter air. Common sense told you that land which could grow trees fifty feet high could also grow potatoes, but that was apparently not necessarily so. (62)

The way in which the unreal is presented as real here is, of course, also a device found in Magic-Realist works, but only because Magic

Realism has for an important source local folklore, which is in this case Icelandic-Canadian (Hancock 1986).

Fifty Stories contains a few other stories which deal with the Icelandic-Canadian community, such as "The Event," where, according to Icelandic tradition, dreams and visions play an important role, and "The Body," which is almost Valgardsonian in style. "Fifty Stories and a Piece of Advice" really consists of fifty-one anecdotes, many of which refer to the narrator's Icelandic-Canadian background. Most of the other stories, however, are experimental in nature. Arnason's next volume, *The Circus Performers' Bar*, continues the story-making strain begun in *Fifty Stories*. The reader is now expected to participate actively in the act of storytelling. In "A Girl's Story," the reader is turned into the protagonist:

> You've wondered what it would be like to be a character in a story, to sort of slip out of your ordinary self and into some other character. Well, I'm offering you the opportunity....
>
> For this story I need a beautiful girl. You probably don't think you're beautiful enough but I can fix that. I can do all kinds of retouching once I've got the basic material. (123-24)

The Circus Performers' Bar is devoted to such playful exercises in storytelling and to subversive retellings of fairy tales such as Snow White and Little Red Riding Hood.

Gunnars is the author who is most obviously concerned with capturing and preserving oral narratives. In *Settlement Poems* and *The Axe's Edge*, she almost acts simply as a medium for the voices of Icelandic-Canadian history. In fact, in her preface to *The Axe's Edge*, Gunnars speaks about the stories in the volume as if they were just that: stories told by "voices that reverberate in the wind." She explains: "I wanted, perhaps, to look into what I saw, and see a living literature. One that was not really my own creation, but something I could step into and seize" (3). This could, of course, be explained by the fact that Gunnars is a recent immigrant and thus an outsider to the Icelandic-Canadian community. As a result, she can be a storyteller *for*, but not *from* the community. She has recourse only to its tales and experiences indirectly, through documentation or by acting as a literary "recorder" for the voices from the community. In *Settlement Poems* and *The Axe's Edge*, she names the tellers of each tale or section. Interestingly, the oral nature of her prose and poetry is different from that of Arnason, who also actively employs an oral style. Gunnars' is much closer to what Ong terms "primary orality," the orality of a culture untouched by writing or print, whereas Arnason's is clearly "secondary orality," an orality dependent on writing and print (1990: 11). Gunnars as an immigrant is, of course, closer to her direct Icelandic roots, and until this century Icelandic folk culture retained part of its original orality: most people could not afford writing materials while other popular literature circulated in manuscript meant to be read or chanted aloud.[31] Gunnars' prose in *The Axe's Edge* is almost formal and, as Arnason himself notes in his review of the book, it has a distinct oral quality: "Read the stories aloud. They feel good in the mouth" (1984: 110). By contrast, Arnason's prose is very colloquial and informal. This is an important difference between primary and secondary orality as explained by Ong: whereas typographic folk believe orality to be informal, oral folk believe it should be formal (1990: 136).

In *The Axe's Edge*, we encounter individuals who are obviously engaged in telling us their story. Most of them begin by introducing themselves and the situation in which they find themselves. In *Settlement Poems*, the lines sound more as if they were spoken in a nightmarish trance by voices speaking through a medium or in a dream-state. Both volumes of *Settlement Poems* also begin in death or with death imagery, which is, of course, a fitting metaphor for immigration. However, as the settlers slowly learn to survive and adapt, they become ready for the eventual rebirth in the new country. Stefán Eyjólfsson says in the last poem of volume one: "messy work, but you learn how / to be born / piecemeal" (53). The folklore and tales go through a transformation similar to that of the settlers. During the journey to Canada, the storyteller announces: "i'm forgetting fast / it's a long trip from glasgow to quebec / this is the last story i'll tell" (*1*: 9). The old stories will not work anymore in the new country; they will have to learn the stories of the new: "there's more / i may tell you more, provided / you give me a long life in canada" (10). The first words and the first stories they learn are those of survival, of sustenance. From simple naming of the various plants and insects, they slowly learn to read the stories of the new land: "coyote scats, learn to read them" (*1*: 45), and:

it's not a blank book
just another language, this map
of well-defined patches

...

this stomach reads well
defines
the sustenance of a new land (*1*: 49)

Toward the end of volume two, the settlers have reached the point where they are ready to set up a printing house. The things to be printed first are from the new land:

the wingless, eye-
bulging spiny shore
bugs, out

out of my house

begin to press them
down, on paper (*2*: 45)

In *The Nightworkers of Ragnarök*, the storyteller returns, but this time with a voice that carries echoes from a personal and cultural past in Iceland. In "the silent hand," the section on whaling, Gunnars creates poetry out of the stories of the whalers which emphasizes rather than loses the storytelling qualities of her source:

The truth is, sjana mín, that whales
are capable of love, uncle stefán
said who used to pilot the boats before his wife asked him to stay
home, she couldn't take the pain of
not knowing and his answer then, you do
everything for your wife

i've been out there, i've seen
what happens he said. we were in
the loft, the ship models he'd built
since he went on land were on the shelves
the window looking out on the fjord
always that rusty trawler lay below

in the sand, barnacles and seaweed on
the hulk at low tide

the whale knows how it is with us, how
crops won't grow, clouds won't break
the herring won't come, he knows when
the nets are empty and appears instead
i've seen that huge mass swim towards us
lift his head before the harpoon
gun and wait. there was a time when it struck me

the men shot. i couldn't have
done it. absolutely sure he had volunteered
himself, that's the truth. (82)

By structuring the story as a poem, Gunnars brings out the poetry of
a disappearing vision of life where everything is connected and inter-
dependent, a vision reminiscent of the unified perception of myth
which holds, after all, the origins of storytelling. The teller formally
ensures credibility by emphasizing at the beginning and the end that
he is telling "the truth." However, the story itself seems to address a
sympathetic audience, a shared communal experience: "the whale
knows how it is with us," for instance, does not add but almost says
"as we all do."

The poems and stories in *The Axe's Edge* and *Settlement Poems* contain many folkloric and supernatural elements, some of which are
quite baffling to the modern reader. In *Settlement Poems*, belief is sus-
pended because the incredible is connected to the Old World and
slowly gives way to the tangible and local in the New. In *The Axe's
Edge*, it is the narrator who must create and suspend belief. Gunnars
achieves this by using a storytelling voice that combines a down-to-
earth attitude with an absolute belief on the narrator's part in the
everyday reality of the supernatural. This combination is emphasized
by having the narrators alternately tell about the daily and the magical. The common sense of the narrators makes their stories more
reliable, while their belief in what they tell creates conviction. The
following example is from the story "Crossroads" told by Halldór
Thorgilsson:

We have very definite rituals at home concerning the raising of the dead. You
lie at the crossroads on either New Year's Eve or Midsummer's Eve. If it is
New Year's Eve, you run into the problem of confronting elves as well as

ghosts. I went out once on New Year's Eve. What you do is, you take a grey
cat, a grey sheepskin, a walrus hide, the hide of an old bull, and an axe to a
place where two roads intersect. That's all the gear you need....

I've often puzzled over why we go in for such impractical things at home.
People here are better at getting down to the business of living. I've learned
more about harvesting in six weeks in Dakota than I learned in ten years in
Skagafjördur. We worked the hay last week. I didn't know there were so many
kinds of hay. I've counted five so far: June grass, timothy, alfalfa, clover, and
trefoil. (48-49)

Storytelling in contemporary Canadian literature is not only used
for its more dynamic and social aspects, but also because it is closely
related to myth-making. In oral cultures, knowledge had to be gathered through experience and was preserved and passed on through
tales. Myths exist almost solely in narratives, for, as Ong points out,
it was the only way to bind thought and to structure and transmit
knowledge since oral peoples do not know abstractions (1990: 36). In
other words, narrative is how people have made sense of the world
over the ages. Once the mythopoeic movement had been born in
Canadian literature, it became obvious that truly Canadian myths
should be found in the various ways that people had made sense of
Canadian reality. Furthermore, writers themselves, as literary storytellers, could create new myths. In post-colonial Canada, writers had to
confront their country anew and make sense of it all over again from
a fresh perspective rather than through colonial eyes. Interestingly,
many Canadian writers have used the short story or long narrative
poem to do so. Valgardson and Arnason, too, are mainly short-story
writers, while Gunnars has written in various fragmentary narrative
forms (long poems, poetic cycles, a volume of short stories and an
episodic novel). New (1987) suggests that in Canada the short story
form has been one important example of a literary predilection for
fragmentary forms used for documentary narrative and to translate
experience and give cultural resonance to the here and now. If we
consider oral narratives, the traditional vehicles for human experience, we find that they are always episodic for mnemonic reasons.
Walker has demonstrated that the short story is rooted in the folk
tale and has retained many of its qualities even in its modern forms:
"They are often pointed towards the same goals, and they echo each
other in mode, motif, and myth" (1982: 24). There is, in other words,
a close connection between myth-making and fragmentary story-
forms. Thus Valgardson, Arnason and Gunnars have used Icelandic-

Canadian oral narratives and folkloric traditions for the literary creation of Canadian myths, favouring episodic forms which, on the one hand, hark back to an oral, mythical past, and, on the other hand, accommodate the Canadian tradition of fragmentary literature to translate the Canadian experience.

Gunnars uses a folkloric perspective in many of her works, notably in *One-eyed Moon Maps*, *Settlement Poems*, *Wake-pick Poems* and *The Axe's Edge*. For present purposes, her use of this perspective is most interesting in the works which deal with immigrant history, *Settlement Poems* and *The Axe's Edge*. The folkloric perception of the world which Gunnars recreates in her works is a reality for the Icelandic immigrants. When they find that their Old World perception clashes with the new environment they are rendered helpless, or, as Gunnars herself put it in her prologue to *The Axe's Edge*: they are disarmed, caught without an answer (2). Completely lost and dislocated, they persist in their own folklore at first, for it is all they have and all they know. Gradually, however, they learn to adapt and to replace old ways with new. As the Icelandic consciousness slowly blends with a Canadian, a new folklore results.

In Thorleifur Jóakimsson's daybooks (*Settlement Poems 2*), for instance, we observe a gradual transformation from old to new as Thorleifur absorbs the lessons of his new environment. In the first poem, he still perceives everything through Icelandic eyes. To deal with the new land, he naturally refers to traditional Icelandic sources, to Espólín's yearbooks and the magical book *Gráskinna*:

> ...
> 38 minus, 3 feet
> deep in march, try
> the old standby
> gráskinna: blizzard on new-
> year's day means hard winter
> snowfall on paul's mass (january
>
> 22) means hard winter
> full moon on paul's mass
> means hard winter: it works
>
> gráskinna's good as oxbladder
> hardly need to look
>
> got it by heart (21)

However, to predict a hard winter on the prairies is no indication that the old ways still work. Soon, Thorleifur realizes that he is "only just beginning ..." (22). The following poems show his learning process as he has to start from scratch: he learns names and how to hunt and fish to survive. Finally, when he describes how to make and preserve jerky, we know he has learnt the indigenous ways sufficiently not only for bare survival but to preserve food as well: he is ready to look to the future. All daybooks in the *Settlement Poems* tell of such transformations. Jóhann Briem describes these transformations thus:

> we've begun to rehearse now
> to see in the darkness, to see
> that which is hidden, to win
> the love of strangers, to understand
>
> the speech of birds, the foreign
> tongues   (*1*: 27)

The immigrants are reduced to the level of small children having to learn to see and speak all over again. Not everyone is able to start anew, and some people fall victim to their lack of adequate knowledge:

> it may not work in new iceland
> nothing works
>
> the way anna walks
> out on lake winnipeg, late winter
> 1877, the way she goes
>
> without returning
> that's how it is
> you disappear out there
>
> & depend nothing on goodness
> it will always be brutal
> with hail, blizzard
>
> strike hard as if you are   (*2*: 16)

Gunnars has Thórgrímur Jónsson use the appropriate metaphor "backswimmers" for the Icelandic immigrants at this historical moment: they are trying to move ahead, but they are still turned toward the old country. Moreover, the Icelandic anthropologist Gísli Pálsson shows how in Iceland the folkloric *öfuguggar*, that is, anomalous water beings that have reversed fins and swim backwards, gave their names to social misfits such as outsiders and eccentrics (1990: 126). Whether Gunnars took the metaphor from this folkloric creature or not, the reference is still informative, for it describes exactly the immigrants' predicament.

Part of the strength of Gunnars' *Settlement Poems*, and also of *The Axe's Edge* which deals with the same subject, is that she used Icelandic-Canadian immigrant history to give her poetry a realistic setting but at the same time she has poeticized Canadian colonial history, where everybody was an Old World immigrant, and Canada's more recent occupation with reclaiming the land. After all, post-colonial Canadians have to learn their own country from a fresh perspective all over again, and they are therefore in much the same position as the immigrants were. They have to abandon their old perceptions in order to see the country in its own right.

It is only fitting that most of Gunnars' narrators should be what Arnason aptly terms "knowing naifs" (1984: 109). While they are all very knowledgeable in magical or other exotic fields, they have at the same time a childlike view on the most mundane matters. This point of view is, of course, closely related to the Magic-Realist perspective where the marvellous is part of the real, one of the many aspects in which this movement draws on folklore and myth. By offering Canadian readers this naive yet knowing vantage point, they see their country in a new, de-colonized and different light. As Hancock points out (1986), this is exactly the reason why Magic Realism was so attractive to Canadian writers: it offered a way to see the country in a more "primitive" light, away from the rational and cultivated European perspective. Tómas Jónasson in "Jazz" remarks about the influence of his Icelandic background on his work: "Those old stories are extravagant, surrealism with a medieval imprint. Realism is only for beginners" (*The Axe's Edge* 81). In their search for their own country this is where Canadians can learn from their immigrant ancestors, whatever their country of origin: "They're especially good at believing things in the old country" (82). Through dislocation and an "other" perspective, unbiased by colonial "realism," an author like Gunnars, who writes from personal immigrant experience while recreating the Icelandic part of Canada's pioneer past, helps people experience Canada in a different, perhaps ultimately more authentic way. As Terry Goldie (1981: 100) concludes: "[Folklore] continues in contemporary fiction as the representation of that body of knowledge that always lies just beyond the comprehension of modern technological man."

In "Ticks" (*The Axe's Edge*), Gunnars shows how Icelandic folklore has gradually become informed by a Canadian consciousness. Kolla tells the story of her great-uncle Jóhannes, an immigrant who went to fish in the wilderness in northern Manitoba. She begins her tale with the following statement: "They say Canada's too new for folktales and legends. They're wrong" (70). When Jóhannes stays alone in his cabin one night, he has three encounters with a "ghost," or rather half a corpse. Later it turns out that the corpse must have been that of a native Canadian who fell through the ice and was cut in half in the process. This ghost story has a very Icelandic flavour: in Icelandic folklore ghosts are characteristically presented as mutilated corpses who cannot be laid until business unfinished during life has been resolved. The result is an interesting incorporation of native material pertaining to the Canadian wilderness into a specifically Icelandic context. Gunnars' story is another literary example of the replacement of traditional Icelandic wilderness creatures with native Canadians.

"Ticks" invites comparison with Kristine Benson Kristofferson's story "The Ghost of Warrens Landing" in the collection *Unexpected Fictions: New Icelandic Canadian Writing* (1989). Both are Icelandic-Canadian ghost stories set in fishing camps in the northern Manitoba wilderness, and in both the ghost is native Canadian. Kristofferson's story, however, displays a very different approach towards the folkloric contents. Kristofferson, whose Canadian novel *Tanya* was published in 1950, belongs to an older generation of Icelandic Canadians who were much more reserved in the public expression of their ethnic background. Kristofferson shares with the Western Icelandic writer Guðrún H. Finnsdóttir the apologetic, if not downright sceptical, attitude towards Old World folklore and what they regarded as superstition. In "The Ghost of Warrens Landing," the "ghost" turns out to be a practical joke played upon the superstitions of some of the people in the camp. The difference between the use of folkloric motifs in "Ticks" and "The Ghost of Warrens Landing" shows a change in the attitude towards Old World beliefs and traditions and the public expression of them, between the time Kristofferson wrote and the present. Whereas Kristofferson is clearly not comfortable with the use of Icelandic folklore in her fiction unless it is presented as a joke, Gunnars feels free in today's literary climate in Canada to integrate fully it in her work, where it becomes a body of perception.

Valgardson has a less obviously folkloric approach to literature. He tends to view the role of the writer as a sage and dreamer of the community. True to Icelandic tradition, dreams and dream visions are important in his fiction. In interviews, Valgardson has stated frequently that the ideas for many of his stories come from dreams or feelings. While he does not really use any folkloristic motifs, his stories are much akin to parables. Moreover, Valgardson strongly believes in the power of myth in any society. In his view, it is the duty of a writer to provide his community or society with positive myths.

In the short story collection, *What Can't Be Changed Shouldn't Be Mourned*, dreams play a prominent role. In "The Cave," for instance, Gunnar finds the entrance to the cave he has been searching for so long in a recurrent dream that he has while taken ill. Gunnar is also very much influenced by the theories of a certain Bjorn Bjornson, who claimed that the soul never sleeps but inhabits bodies in two different worlds and passes back and forth between them. In that case, dreams would simply be the "leakage" of information from one world to another. Such unconditional belief in the prophecying nature of dreams is an integral part of Icelandic culture. Icelandic folklore teems with dream-tales, and in much Old Norse literature we find characters who are visited in their dreams by prophecying visions or messengers from another world. In "The Man from Snæfellsness," Axel is plagued by a recurrent dream which connects him to his Icelandic past and reminds him of his duty to set things right for Axel's great-grandfather Ketill and his descendants.

Valgardson's work has often been described as Gothic, even nightmarish, and it has been said that many of his characters approach the grotesque. He has often expressed his concern for the fragmentation in Canadian society which he sees as resulting largely from the fact that the Old World immigrant myths have lost their potency and no new, affirmative ones have come to take their place. Harpham (1982) shows how the grotesque can be used as part of a larger attempt to re-establish a lost contact with an ancient past with examples from Nero's Rome. The grotesque then points to a modern sensibility caught in a lost mythology (49-50). Harpham argues convincingly that the use made of the grotesque in nightmarish fictions such as those by Poe, Emily Brontë and Mary Shelley finds its origins in the life-in-death ambiguity of the sacred which both gives life and takes it away. If we apply Harpham's findings to Valgardson's fiction, taking also into consideration Valgardson's own views of his role as a writer, his use of grotesque characters living in a world ruled by nightmarish fear or decay can well be regarded as an indication of modern man's alienation and need for myths.

The grotesque characters in Valgardson's work tend to be either pathetic, deformed creatures such as Annie (*Gentle Sinners*) and Hermann ("A Private Comedy"), who live on garbage outside of town, or malicious capitalists for whom money has taken the place of religion or mythology, such as Dominic ("Trees"), Abel ("Capital") and the Tree Brothers (*Gentle Sinners*). Many stories are set in an atmosphere of decay, fear, or despair. This atmosphere is, of course, influenced by the harsh conditions in rural Manitoba and the dark vision which ruled much of Icelandic history and culture. Valgardson points out, however, that it is also a legacy of the immigrant experience: new life began in death and exploitation, and was filled with mysterious tensions due to the presence of other immigrant groups. Whereas the first generation initially had their Old World myths to fall back on, these were soon no longer adequate. Nevertheless, Valgardson claims that no new national myths have taken their place, only community myths which celebrate the group rather than the whole. This he sees as a divisive development. In the context of Valgardson's views, the nightmarish atmosphere in many of his stories emphasizes the fear and decay of a world which has lost its mythical foundations: it is threatening to fall apart. With no positive myths to sustain them, people sink into despair, cruelty or indifference and become destructive towards one another. Their lives become grotesque lives-in-death.

Valgardson has always acknowledged the influence of the Icelandic respect for literature on his authorship. His own views of the role of the writer do indeed have much in common with the role of the *skáld* in traditional Icelandic society. Along similar lines, his works have shown Valgardson to be a myth-maker, a creator of modern myths and parables for a nation which he sees as divided and uprooted from the sustaining power of positive, integrative myths. That he should portray a world deprived of myth with the help of grotesque and nightmarish images in his fiction is not surprising when one views the literary tradition behind the grotesque as explained by Harpham. The Icelandic people were similarly drawn towards the grotesque during their dark ages, when they created their folk tales of black magic reflecting a distorted appeal to an ancient mythology during times when extreme poverty and religious dogma bred a mania of destruction and fear. According to Valgardson, Canada needs a mythology of its own in which every immigrant group will find its place in an integral rather than a divisive way. He sees this as the main task of Canadian writers:

These then are the mythmakers, the creators, the tellers. It is these voices which will, as they are heard, make clear our identity. And yet, being Canadian, we must fiercely defend the freedom for every voice to be different. We are not a homogeneous society. We cannot and should not have homogeneous voices. We are not a society in which every group arrived at the same time. New immigrants arrive all the time. They must pass through the process themselves. Central literary questions rise out of the necessity of identity.... That which is unresolved in reality must be transformed through the imagination. As long as we remain an immigrant society, as long as we must continue the process of creating an image of Canada large enough, complex enough to contain within it all the elements of our society, as long as it is necessary for us to invent ourselves, then our writers and what they have to say will be critical to our survival. (1987: 18)

Earlier, Valgardson had already introduced his ideas on this matter in brief. His conclusion then is a useful addition to the previous quotation:

In the immediate future, if Canada is to survive and prosper, the various ethnic groups must, while retaining their integrity, share with all the other groups, their history, their culture, their dreams. This is best done through two different kinds of writing: 1. the presentation, in readable form, of the history of its immigrant experience; 2. the translation of that experience into poetry, drama, and fiction. The Icelandic Canadians with their unique relationship to the written word are ideally suited for the task of providing the model for this type of literary leadership. (1982: 36)

Whether or not the Icelandic Canadians succeeded in providing that model is questionable, but it is certain that writers like Gunnars and Valgardson have made a significant contribution to this effect.

Of the three authors, Arnason is the most rooted in Canadian experience. While he has paid homage to his ethnic background, he always makes sure to point out that his point of reference goes no further back than the arrival of the first immigrant groups in Canada. This has also influenced his role as myth-maker and storyteller. Arnason is less interested in immigrant history and more in the applications of folkloric and mythical motifs in a modern context. In *The Icelanders*, he relates how old tales brought over from Iceland were transplanted:

It's hard for a child, and not much easier for an adult, to separate the myth from the reality, one kind of story from another, and that's why the landscape of the Interlake is forever charged for me with the unseen presence of heroes. My grandfather used to tell me stories from the Icelandic sagas but he didn't tell me that those stories were literature. What was the point? It would make no difference to a child. And so, when he told me the story of Grettir Asmundson, Grettir the strong, who swam the half-mile from the mainland to the island carrying fire and the fire didn't go out, I assumed Grettir lived on Hekla Island, and that he had swum from Riverton....

That's the way stories get rooted in a new land. Like Thorgeir's bull.... The bull vowed to haunt Thorgeir's descendants for nine generations. When the Icelanders immigrated to Canada, Thorgeir's descendants were among them, and so, of course, was Thorgeir's bull. He's mostly seen in the moonlight, running across a field, and sometimes he comes as a barking dog in the distance on a dark night. Grandpa's never seen him, though he's heard him, and he knows a man from Arborg who's seen him three times. There must be a different version of the story in Iceland, but I don't want to know about it. (110)

The transplantation of old stories or rituals in a new context recurs in *Fifty Stories and a Piece of Advice*. We saw earlier in this chapter how in "The Sunfish" Arnason recreated the Icelandic-Canadian Myth of Beginnings into a founding myth of New Iceland. The ritual described in this story around Freyja is a combination of universal motifs of fertility cults and the Icelandic-Canadian tradition of the *Fjallkona*, the Maid of the Mountain. The image of Iceland as the *Fjallkona* was coined by the poet Eggert Ólafsson and made popular by the Romantic poets. Among the Icelandic immigrants in Canada, the *Fjallkona* developed into a symbol of the mother of the community, elected every year during the annual Icelandic celebration, the *Íslendingadagurinn*. By surrounding Freyja's election with fertility cult motifs, Arnason gives the *Fjallkona* figure a mythic raison d'être in his story.

In the same collection, "The Event" is built around the traditional Icelandic and Icelandic-Canadian sense of mysticism and belief in dreams. It is also one of the few stories in which Arnason is not merely celebratory but deals with the pain inherent in the New Iceland community as well. The story is centered around Paul, an old fisherman who lost his son Helgi in a storm on the lake forty years ago. As Paul remembers Helgi's death, he also remembers the dream he had that night:

Paul remembered the urgent sense that there was something he had forgotten when they had come to tell him of Helgi's death. He had remembered then that Helgi had come to him in a dream the night of his death and told him not to worry. He had believed that fiercely for forty years, but now he wondered. Had that dream ever happened? Was the thing he had to remember something else? The news of his dream had spread through Gimli, and people had been in awe of him because of his power, because he had dreamed the dream. Now he wasn't sure that the dream had ever happened, or if it happened, when. (78)

From this moment on, all borders between dream and reality in the story begin to blur. It is no longer clear whether Paul is dreaming or not. The naked girl he finds on the beach, nameless and waiting like the little mermaid for her prince, "was like a fantasy, but she was undeniably real" (81). Here we have again that folkloric/Magic-Realist perspective of the unreal as real, set in a context of a firm belief in dreams. "Morning Letter" is a similar story of a narrator who drowns in his own vision. Dreams also play a role in *Marsh Burning*. In the section "Out of the mysteries, dreams," the narrator enters the immigrant past of his community through dream visions. Here, too, dreams are used to gain a different perspective on what we generally perceive to be reality.

In *The Circus Performers' Bar*, the context has become more urban and the folkloric motifs more universal. "The Figure Skater" is again a retelling of a fertility ritual, but this time in a decidedly modern North American context of hockey and figure skating. The hero of the hockey game, who happens to be the narrator, and the queen of figure skating mate in the back of a car at the end of the winter festival. It is as if Arnason is trying to give modern Canadian life a mythical quality by translating it into mythic narratives. Along similar lines, Arnason has created modern versions, or rather sub-versions, of fairy tales. There are no less than three rewritings of Snow White in this volume, and one of Little Red Riding Hood. In his interview with Robert Enright (1985), Arnason explains that he is interested in the underlying truths of fairy tales. In his rewrites, Arnason manages to bring these truths more to the surface and give them a modern application. "The Circus Performers' Bar," for instance, places the seven dwarfs as circus artists in a bar in revolutionary Russia. Although this setting is neither contemporary nor Canadian, it effectively emphasizes the sense of futility and powerlessness which plagues many urban males all over the western world, confronted as they are with a war-torn world that will always need women but no longer has room for heroism:

Whatever shape the new world takes, there will be room in it for her. However it is made, it will need princesses. But after this hour, nothing will ever make it whole for me. Here I sit, burning with love, aching with desire, stunted, dwarfed, and out in the street, already, the guns are beginning. (142)

Similarly, in "Girl and Wolf" we encounter a Little Red Riding Hood who knows exactly how to trap the wolf in his own lust, and before he knows it he is engaged and tied to a job at her father's petrol station:

The wolf already knows the ending. It is the last of his wolfhood. His morning runs down the winding and criss-crossing trails of the forest are over. Already, his legs ache from the concrete on which he will stand. His fur is beginning to smell of oil. And so it has always been. What is the good of cautioning young girls? Grandmothers cannot be trusted. They are always somewhere else. The woodcutter is always too late. (135)

Thus Arnason shows how old folkloric patterns and motifs are applicable in modern, New World situations. In a very contemporary Canadian way, he, too, is really an old-fashioned storyteller and mythmaker. With Gunnars and Valgardson, Arnason proves Barbara Godard wrong when she claims that English-Canadian writers have developed the storyteller but have not drawn on an oral tradition as Québécois writers have (1977). Or perhaps she is right if her use of "English-Canadian" refers to ethnic background rather than language. In that case, Gunnars, Valgardson and Arnason show that Canadian literature of a different ethnic background has a valuable contribution to make to the Anglo-Canadian tradition.

CONCLUDING REMARKS

With my discussion of the writings of Gunnars, Valgardson and Arnason I have tried to show that Icelandic-Canadian literature is a reality within the larger field of Canadian literature. While indeed their works have little in common with the Western Icelandic tradition, and certainly cannot be considered a direct continuation of that tradition, there has developed an Icelandic-Canadian identity based on a common cultural heritage and immigrant past; it is expressed in their writings in a fully integrated way. Valgardson and Arnason employ aspects of their ethnic background in a larger conception of current Canadian or universal concerns, while Gunnars uses her own immigrant experience and the Icelandic-Canadian immigrant history to reflect contemporary alienated and fragmented people, threatened with global destruction in a technocratic age. Valgardson is especially concerned with identity crises in the modern world. His portrayal of a stark, elemental land, in which people must find dignified and sustaining means of survival, is both very Canadian and very Icelandic while still universally evocative. Arnason's fictional use of his ethnic heritage seems sometimes more a filial duty, and yet the ways in which he integrates the oral traditions of the Icelandic-Canadian community into his contemporary Canadian literary interests are very successful. All three writers regard their ethnic heritage as a fertile source of alternatives to the destructive tendencies in twentieth-century society.

A different conclusion must however be drawn with regard to the Icelandic-Canadian writers who have only started publishing more recently, Martha Brooks, Marion Johnson, Eleanor Oltean and Betty Jane Wylie. Their works have remained outside of the discussion because there is nothing more Icelandic-Canadian about them than the background of their authors. These works are completely in the mainstream Canadian tradition. Gunnars comes to a similar conclusion in her introduction to *Unexpected Fictions*. She says there: "Everyone else seems pretty nonplussed by the Icelandic 'soul,' if there is such a thing, and in most stories the sensibility is decidedly mainstream Canadian. By sensibility I mean tone, emphasis, characterization, mood and even subject matter" (1989: xv). This remark has recently occasioned Wolf (1992) to question whether such Canadian writing can and should still be called Icelandic-Canadian solely on the basis of the background of the author. The Canadian direction which the more recent authors have taken raises the question whether Icelandic-Canadian writing is gradually moving away from ethnic concerns. If so, what could be the underlying reasons for such a move which occurs exactly at a time when Canadian multiculturalism is at its peak? These and related questions about the place and development of Icelandic-Canadian literature within Canadian multiculturalism will be the subject of discussion in the next chapter.

NOTES

1. Gus Sigurdson, "To a True Nobleman (An Old Icelandic Poet)" (1987: 200).

2. For this and other general information in this brief survey of Canadian poetry I rely on Beattie (1970: 724-817); and Keith (1985, esp. 74-117).

3. In *The Book of Canadian Poetry* (1943), A.J.M. Smith divided contemporary poets along the lines of a "native" and a "cosmopolitan" tradition, although he abandoned this division in the second edition (1948). That the debate did not end there, however, is demonstrated by Billings (1983).

4. In the following discussion of Canadian fiction I rely on Keith (1985); MacLulich (1988); and McPherson (1970).

5. For more information on Elma Helgason see Young (1990). Young mentions another, earlier publication of poetry by Helgason which I have been unable to trace: *In the Land Where the Peace River Flows* (1963).

6. Padolsky's analysis is one of very few that can be successfully applied in interpretations of Icelandic-Canadian literature, as it takes into account several levels, or "options," of acculturation as possible underlying dynamics of literary texts, including different levels of "transition" and "(apparent) assimilation." According to this analysis, Icelandic-Canadian literature in English would both fall under the "transition" and "(apparent) assimilation" categories, dependent on the various individual authors, with the possible exception of Kristjana Gunnars (see below), whose writings share certain characteristics with the "separation" category of writers in exile.

7. Valgardson confirmed Padolsky's analysis during a lecture delivered in November 1987 when he observed that "[t]oo often ... we acknowledge ethnic influences only when the subject matter of the art is identifiably about the immigration experience or the artist is dressed in ethnic clothes. We do not recognize that the truly profound ethnic influence, like a powerful current under a still surface, is constantly at work" (1; see also Chapter V).

8. It should be mentioned here that, during the 1950s, two children's books were published by Icelandic-Canadian writers: *Cold Adventure*, by Violet Paula Ingaldson (Vancouver/Toronto/Montreal: Copp Clark, 1959), and *Ian of Red River*, by R. Guttormsson (Toronto: Ryerson, 1959).

9. The full English text of the Canadian Multiculturalism Act is found in the Appendix to *Other Solitudes* (1990: 369-74).

10. Examples are Magnusson (1979; 1978); Stephansson (Sveinsson) (1979); Sigurgeirsson (1979); and Thorvaldsson (1984).

11. This and further genealogical data on the Icelandic-Canadian writers under discusson come from the "Biographical Notes" in *Unexpected Fictions* (Gunnars 1989).

12. For a short, informative chapter on Icelandic saga style see Hallberg (1962: 70-80).

13. Hemingway's style and that of the sagas have been compared in Hallberg (1962).

14. Here, and in the following summary of the alternating views on the prairie as "garden of the world" and as its contrast, a demonic nightmare, I rely on Harrison's analysis of prairie literature (1977). Other informative studies on prairie literature include Ricou (1973), and Kreisel (1986). These last two works, however, view prairie literature almost exclusively from the prairie realist angle, in which the prairie is a vast and inimical landscape where man has to try and stay on his feet to survive. I have found Harrison's analysis more in accordance with Icelandic-Canadian works, as it includes, like MacLulich's, the romantic and the pastoral.

15. This is, for instance, the central theme of the majority of the so-called *þættir*, also referred to as *smásögur* ("short sagas" or "short stories"), which are short narratives of Old Icelandic prose; see Harris' two leading articles on this topic (1972; 1976). The theme occurs, however, also in many of the sagas, such as *Laxdæla Saga* where Kjartan has a confrontation with King Olaf, and *Egils Saga*, where the confrontation between Egill Skallagrímsson's family and the royal family forms a main theme. Lehmann (1969) discusses the theme of the individual's role in his social group in Eddic poetry. Van Hamel (1936) has remarked on the Nordic combination of innate respect for the individual creative act and the social consciousness that fosters self-restriction.

16. Pálsson and Edwards (1984: 14) first directed my attention to the frequent occurrence of this theme in saga literature. Byock (1989) has emphasized that in medieval Iceland's increasingly rural society a socially stabilizing understanding had developed according to which honour, power and success had to be exercized with moderation.

17. Meulengracht Sørensen, in a discussion of the underlying ethics in certain Sagas of the Icelanders, says: "To kill one's own kin is one

of the most striking expressions of the non-human—it is wolf-like"
(1989: 156).

18. In the following discussion I will use the term "Norse mythology" to
indicate the Norse Pantheon and the narratives which involve them,
as preserved in the mythological Eddic poems and Snorri Sturluson's
mythological tales. I will, in other words, concern myself here with
the *imagery* of the ancient Norse world view rather than with that
world view itself, which will be dealt with later in this chapter.

19. Although it was common practice everywhere for Christian mission-
aries to portray pagan gods as devils during the time of conversion,
it is remarkable how closely the devil in Icelandic folklore over the
ages continues to resemble Odin in particular, not only in appearance
but also in familiarity. For an informative survey of the role of Odin
in Icelandic folklore see Eyjólfsson (1894).

20. Baldur was killed by a branch of mistletoe thrown by his blind
brother Höð through the machinations of the trickster god Loki.

21. This is according to the more recent analysis of Fleck (1971). Fleck
argues here that the sacrifice should be seen as a ritual initiation
process in which Odin aspires to become both creator and creation,
and to acquire numinous knowledge from the source near Yggdrasil
in order to transcend his monofunctional role as a god and succeed
to the sacred kingship. This interpretation has to my knowledge been
well accepted in scholarly circles, but has so far been of less influence
on the older and more general view that Odin sacrificed himself to
himself in order to gain magical knowledge from the runes and to
obtain a drink from the mead of poetry, i.e., Odin sacrifices himself
to obtain the gifts of magic and poetry. It seems to me that the latter
view is also the one that has influenced the imagery in the works
of Gunnars and Arnason, and I will therefore use this view in my
discussion of their works.

22. See also Martin (1972: 59-64), who suggests a link between prophecy
and sacrifice. Prophecy and poetry were closely connected in Old
Norse culture, and united in the figure of the god Odin. Martin also
mentions the sacrifice made by the poet-warrior Egill Skallagrímsson
for poetic inspiration in *Egils Saga*.

23. For a translation of *Lokasenna* see *The Poetic Edda* (1962: 90-103). See
also Turville-Petre (1964: 130ff). Turville-Petre does not agree with
the various existing interpretations of Loki as trickster, as he finds
it difficult to believe that "the father of the Death-goddess, of the
World-serpent and of evil monsters of every kind could be so light-

hearted." However, Radin's standard work on the trickster has shown that trickster's exploits, although often comical and primitive, do not make him a merely light-hearted, but, on the contrary, a quite essential mythological figure. Loki's similarities with trickster figures in other mythologies, as analyzed in Radin, are too many to ignore.

24. As the god of death, Odin was closely linked to the fertility function, and there are indications that Odin began to usurp that position which originally belonged to the twin gods Freyr and Freyja (Turville-Petre 1964: 56). Freyja took in fact a share in Odin's dues as god of war and death, and in some tales, Freyja is Odin's wife. In his function as *Alfaðir*, Odin is the generator and sustainer of human life who rejuvenates the universe after each cyclical *Ragnarök* (Martin 1972: 77). According to Fleck, Odin only achieved the status of *Alfaðir* after having usurped the place of the original fertility gods (1971). Odin's counterpart Loki represents an inverted sexuality and fertility. He was bi-sexual and could both beget and bear his progeny. He generated monsters of evil and destruction such as the death-goddess Hel, the world-serpent, and the wolf Fenrir (Turville-Petre 126ff).

25. For informative discussions of the figure of Bjartur see Hallberg (1971); and Andrésson (1976: 122-29). Elsewhere, Hallberg discusses Laxness' works specifically in the light of saga literature, where he also shows how Laxness' works reflect the role of the heroic ideal found in the sagas. He remarks: "Laxness ends his reflections on the sagas by reminding us of their importance to the Icelanders as a nation. To them the heroic ideal has not been, and still is not, an empty concept. The belief in the hero who defies wounds and death has sustained the Icelandic people through the centuries" (1982: 9).

26. Quoted in "Kristjana Gunnars" (1985: 209).

27. On this subject see, for instance, Turville-Petre (1964: 221-27); Davidson (1943); and Kelchner (1935).

28. See also Steblin Kamenskij (1973). Ong (1990: 43) has affirmed the function of genealogies in narrative as being descriptions of personal relationships, political information etc. in oral cultures.

29. *Það situr mjög fast í Íslendingum frá fornu fari, að sannleikurinn sé bundinn við eyktamörk, ættfærslu og staðaheiti.* (1976: 122)

30. This difference in approach between the two authors was contextualized for me after having heard Janice Kulyk Keefer during a lecture at the Free University of Amsterdam (May 1993). She pointed out the postmodern celebration of marginality that does not really take into account the pain that marginality can involve for those who are

not marginalized by choice. I see this as the main difference between Valgardson's and Arnason's storytelling: while Valgardson is focussed on the pain, Arnason is mostly at play.

31. Ong notes: "Manuscript cultures remained largely oral-aural even in retrieval of material preserved in texts. Manuscripts were not easy to read ... and what readers found in manuscripts they tended to commit at least somewhat to memory.... Moreover, readers commonly vocalized, read slowly aloud or *sotto voce*, even when reading alone, and this also helped fix matter in the memory" (119). I am thinking here specifically of the *rímur*, which were chanted from memory or manuscript, and the folk tales and sagas which were told during the *kvöldvaka*. Even in cases where one person read aloud from a book (the scriptures or sagas), this tended to be done only by one person known to be a good reader, while the others listened.

V

THE ICELANDIC TILE IN THE CANADIAN MOSAIC
ICELANDIC-CANADIAN LITERATURE AND CANADIAN MULTICULTURALISM

MULTICULTURALISM IN CANADA

Although multiculturalism did not become official policy in Canada until 1971, it is often claimed that it has been a social and historical fact since the settlement of the Canadian West. During the second half of the nineteenth century, the Canadian government began actively to promote large-scale immigration for the development of unsettled land, especially in western Canada. In the wake of Ontarian and French-Canadian migrants moving westwards, the first European immigrant groups followed, among whom were the Icelanders. These groups had been enticed to stay in Canada by the promise of large tracts of land for group settlement and the preservation of their own language and customs.

The example of early bloc settlement was continued during the 1880s and 1890s, when large groups of immigrants from various European countries as well as many Anglo-Canadians moved to the prairies. Friesen remarks on the settlement in groups as "discrete homogeneous units in the prairies" (1984: 186). This settlement pattern is quite unlike that of the United States, mainly because

Canada's two founding nations, the English and the French, have preferred throughout Canadian history to share their country precisely through cultural and geographical segregation. In addition, the Anglo-Canadians themselves entertained strong ties with Britain, and tended toward preservation of British customs. The large influx of non-English immigrants only reinforced their group solidarity.

Accordingly, the pattern of "discrete homogeneous units" had already been established by the founding nations and was followed by other immigrant groups. Since there was no unifying myth to rally native-born and immigrant Canadians under one banner, as there was in the United States, most people tended to stick to their own group. Under these conditions, neither the French nor the Anglo-Canadians were prepared to accommodate all the foreigners flooding the prairies. The result was a patchwork of isolated clusters where imported Old World customs and traditions of various nationalities could be and were perpetuated.

There was, however, one important difference between the situation of the Anglo-Canadians and that of the immigrant groups: as one of the founding nations, the Anglo-Canadians had been the first to settle the country, and they therefore occupied all the leading positions in a society that had been shaped according to their customs and ideas. As John Porter puts it in his ground-breaking study *The Vertical Mosaic*:

> The first ethnic group to come into previously unpopulated territory, as the effective possessor, has the most to say. This group becomes the charter group of the society, and among the many privileges and prerogatives which it retains are decisions about what other groups are to be let in and what they will be permitted to do. (1968: 60)

Apart from farming, non-British immigrants were assigned to menial and low status jobs, whereas British immigrants tended to find their way up easily because they spoke the (right) language and they were largely familiar with the customs and social systems. Other immigrants who had aspirations beyond the farm, the railroad or the construction area quickly found out that they needed to shed every trace of foreignness and become proper Anglo-Canadians to be able to achieve such ambitions.

Immigration continued during the decades preceding the First World War. The years 1901-1913 were a boom era on the prairies, when new farming methods were developed for wheat production.

The First World War launched Canada into an age of strongly increased self-awareness and nationalism. Optimists envisioned the Canadian West as a new Garden of Eden full of possibilities. Great expectations were voiced about a growing Canadian nation that would incorporate all the best of Europe's past. Mutual enrichment among immigrant groups was promoted by such enthusiastic men as John Murray Gibbon and Watson Kirkconnell, who attempted to introduce Canadians to the histories, customs and cultures of the various groups among them through publications such as *Canadian Mosaic: The Making of a Northern Nation* (1938) and *Canadian Overtones* (1937).[1] Earlier, authors like Salverson and Grove had pleaded in their fiction for a Canada that would preserve and encompass the cultural riches of all its peoples' backgrounds.

In spite of these valiant attempts, the basic picture changed little. Immigration continued. Increased urbanization led only to different immigrant "pockets" within the cities, which were generally separated from the more prosperous Anglo-Canadian neighbourhoods. John Porter's work showed in 1965 that over the decades the power structure remained largely intact: leading, prestigious and well-paid jobs were still held mostly by Anglo-Canadians, whereas people of non-English extraction had to a large extent remained in the lower economic strata. Instead of the one great Canadian nation envisioned in the 1920s and 1930s, the mosaic pattern was still predominant in 1965. New immigrants had formed new clusters, while the majority of non-British immigrant descendants, in spite of an inevitable degree of assimilation, still formed ethnic communities which had preserved many traditions.

During the revolutionary 1960s, an "ethnic revival" slowly developed under the influence of a widespread social movement for equality. The Civil Rights movement in the United States triggered off a general renewed interest among later generations in their ethnic "roots." Moreover, on the Canadian scene, the fierce wave of Québécois nationalism during this time, fuelled by Charles de Gaulle's rallying cry "Vive le Québec libre," also promoted an increased awareness on the part of Canadians of other backgrounds, who likewise felt entitled to an official recognition of their rights to cultural preservation. The idea developed that Canada's unity might be in its diversity, and that Canada's cultural reality was a mosaic. In 1969, the Royal Commission on Bilingualism and Biculturalism published volume four of its Report on *The Cultural Contributions of the Other Ethnic*

Groups, the "other ethnic groups" being those of an origin other than British or French. On the basis of the recommendations in this report, the Canadian government announced in 1971 a policy of multiculturalism in a bilingual framework.

Since then, boards have been established and funds made available by the government for the promotion of multiculturalism. It has also become a much-debated topic which has generated a lot of activity among people of "other" descents. It is now officially possible, indeed desirable, to take pride in one's cultural heritage and immigrant background and to voice this pride publicly. To introduce the Canadian public to the diversity of its cultures and promote understanding and respect for them, multicultural fairs and events as well as educational programs, research and literature were subsidized. An example in the Icelandic-Canadian field is the awarding of a "Heritage Cultures and Languages, Chairs of Study Program in the Department of Multiculturalism" grant to the Icelandic department at the University of Manitoba in 1990 in order to establish a Canadian Icelandic studies program. In 1988, the policy of multiculturalism became law: the passing of the "Act for the preservation and enhancement of multiculturalism in Canada" (Bill C-93) made it the duty of Canadian citizens to preserve and enhance their cultural heritage for a mutual enrichment of Canada's diverse cultures.

As multiculturalism became a celebrated social ideal as well as a policy increasingly used in descriptions of the long sought-after truly Canadian identity, so criticism grew alongside it. Porter was one of the first to strip the mosaic of its idealist aura by exposing it as a cover for social inequality. He has argued convincingly that the very ideal of the mosaic prevents social equality, since a reciprocal relationship develops between ethnicity and social class:

A given ethnic group appropriates particular roles and designates other ethnic groups for the less preferred ones. Often the low status group accepts its inferior position. Through time the relative status positions, reinforced by stereotypes and social images ... harden and become perpetuated over a very long time. (63)

One of the reasons why Porter's work was polemical was that he speculated openly that the ideal of a mosaic impedes the processes of social mobility. For a minority group to become distributed in the institutional structure ("structural assimilation"), it is inevitable that the group in the course of time adopts the cultural patterns of the charter group ("behavioural assimilation"):

At least differences in patterns of living between various ethnic groups will be reduced. There are some grounds for the view, although writers on the subject are confused on the point, that structural assimilation is incompatible with continued ethnic pluralism.... Where there is strong association between ethnic affiliation and social class, as there almost always has been, a democratic society may require a breaking down of the ethnic impediment to equality, particularly the equality of opportunity. (72-73)

Porter's study led him to the damning but important conclusion:

Ethnic and religious affiliation in Canadian society have always had an effect on the life chances of the individual. If not its one distinctive value, that of the mosaic is Canada's most cherished. Legitimization for the mosaic is sought in the notion of collective or group rights which becomes confused with the legal foundation of individual rights. It seems inescapable that the strong emphasis on ethnic differentiation can result only in those continuing dual loyalties which prevent the emergence of any clear Canadian identity. From the point of view of our study of social class and power, it is likely that the historical pattern of class and ethnicity will be perpetuated as long as ethnic differentiation is so highly valued. Canada will always appear as an adaptation of its British and French charter groups, rather than as one of a new breed in a new nation. (558)

The Vertical Mosaic has been very influential, at least in the academic world. Moore's sociological study *Multiculturalism: Ideology or Social Reality?* (1984) showed that fifteen years after the first publication of Porter's findings, they had lost none of their validity. She found that the measures implemented by Multicultural Boards were merely short-term, oriented towards visible entertainment and meant to keep everybody happy rather than to work any effective changes on a structural or institutional level. In Moore's view, the minority groups are given hope for change while the charter group can feel tolerant without seeing its dominant position threatened. This, of course, is hardly a scenario that invites mutual enrichment. On the contrary Moore, on the basis of her field work, suggests that the dominant group pays little more than lip-service to multiculturalism. While education programs do not obliterate prejudice but rather keep it dormant until roused to protect advantages when these appear to be threatened, evidence also suggests "that the dominant group is not even becoming more willing to make changes to accept minority groups on equal terms, or to accommodate their assimilation" (460).

Her conclusion is that "government activities in the economic sphere and in the spheres of culture and language retention have not been coordinated to promote a comprehensive social policy" (374). Instead, she sees the policy of multiculturalism as an attempt "to deflect minority discontent":

The informal ideal of Canadian society as a cultural mosaic, or a multicultural society, which was nurtured especially by groups other than the British and the French, furnished an appropriate response for the government to this discontent. It proclaimed the goals of social and cultural equality for all groups in Canada. But rhetoric must be distinguished from reality; the policy appeared to be an adequate response, but real social gains could not be provided to minorities without disrupting the whole society and alienating the dominant group. Thus the government actually emphasised programs to produce so-called "cultural equality", provided stop-gap economic programmes with limited resources to keep up hope among the disadvantaged, and meanwhile refused to aid any minority efforts to address basic economic and political inequalities. (469)

Unlike Porter, however, she believes that multiculturalism is still a promising ideal that is worthy of pursuit, although it will require radical changes in the present Canadian society.

Criticism of the multiculturalist policy has come not only from socio-economic quarters. Carole Carpenter has studied Canada's cultural mosaic from a folklorist angle; a very useful approach since minority cultures are generally delineated through folkways. Her findings are documented in *Many Voices: A Study of Folklore Activities in Canada and their Role in Canadian Culture* (1979). Carpenter's study leads her to regard the mosaic as a natural outgrowth of the Canadian garrison mentality as developed by Northrop Frye: each tile in the mosaic forms a separate garrison, guarding its own customs, privileges and culture against the wilderness of the larger society outside its borders. According to Carpenter, this creates a situation precluding a mutual and equal exchange of cultures, as happens in a truly multiculturalist society. Instead, the walls of the garrison allow the dominant Anglo-Canadian group to conveniently ignore Canada's minority cultures and maintain its position of supremacy unchallenged (377-78).

Moreover, Carpenter points out that the kind of cultural traditions that are recognized and funded for public manifestation are usually not the traditions through which a minority group retains its culture, but the kind that cater to an Anglo-Canadian view of folk-lore both as quaint and harmless entertainment, and, being inferior to "real" culture, not to be taken very seriously. Needless to say, this attitude again reinforces the assumption of Anglo-Canadian culture and traditions as normative and dominant. Given this situation it can hardly be claimed that the minority cultures are essential elements in Canadian culture, according to Carpenter. Instead, these elements are exploited commercially as an identification and display of Canadian culture (1985: 351). She concludes her study with the following statement about the Canadian mosaic:

Effectively, by those who can, or wish to, view it objectively Canadian society, and consequently Canadian culture, can be seen in the following manner. The foundations and primary determinants are the British and French social orderings and cultures, but predominantly the British due to social, political and historical circumstances. As an overlay on that basic structure, each constituent minority group and its culture might be seen as a coloured piece of cellophane, representing that group's world view, its perception of itself in relation to the larger society. If considered ethically by some completely alien observer, Canadian society and culture would appear to consist of a blur of colours over a dual but unequal foundation. In other words, Canadian culture as it exists today ought not to be described as a mosaic, but rather as a bipartite tapestry with decorative embroidery or a jumble of separate pieces loosely attached to one another with their distinct colours and designs being only a superficial layer on top of a more substantial base—in other words, a jigsaw puzzle. This description matches the prevailing attitude towards minority-cultural traditions, demonstrated by action, though generally not by belief. (1979: 379)

The only way of rescuing the potential of the mosaic ideal is, in Carpenter's view, through a break-down of garrison walls, so that each group will be open to mutual appreciation and exchange of true folk traditions.

In 1985, the psychologist/sociologist John Edwards published a study called *Language, Society and Identity*. This work contains some crucial observations on the way ethnic identity functions and is maintained, both in an individual and in a group context. He finds that identities alter and adapt and that most people are motivated by a desire for material well-being and are thus attracted by mainstream life. Consequently, those signs of an ethnic, or "other," identity that form an obstacle to social progress are, sooner or later, dropped, while the more invisible, i.e. symbolic or private elements, which do not impede success, are retained. As a result, Edwards argues, "[t]he more private an ethnic marker is, the more it is exempt from external pressure and the more likely to survive" (97). Like Carpenter, Edwards reckons that, in a social atmosphere like the present where there is a demand for a more visible ethnicity, the elements that are displayed are generally the more "colourful" ones, to be enjoyed also by non-members of the group. These are not the ones that are specifically symbolic of group identity, although in some cases the public and the symbolic may go together.

Apparently a process takes place among minority groups where the demands of modern society and material well-being, and those of individual and group identity, are carefully weighed and a selection made of those aspects of a communal past which are to be retained. These selected elements tend, of course, to be the ones least susceptible to external pressure so that they can be maintained within contemporary society. Thus, the tension between past and present is resolved. What Edwards' findings mean for the function and meaning of a multiculturalist policy is clear from his following statement:

If symbolic ethnicity and private markers are the aspects which remain, it follows that active intervention on behalf of the minority identity may be non-productive or, indeed, counter-productive. There is no evidence to suggest that meaningful aspects of ethnicity can be held in place for any reasonable length of time by such action, much less the ones that are usually dealt with (like language), which are visible and public markers highly susceptible to change. (112)

Moreover, Edwards claims that active supporters of multiculturalism are completely out of touch with the pragmatic capacity of minority group members to look after themselves: "First, supporters of pluralism often seem to want a more highly visible, distinct sense of group differentiation than is envisaged by group members themselves. Second, they wish to accomplish their ends by deliberate intervention in the social fabric" (116). In Edwards' view, such interventions threaten to become programs "in which planners try to orchestrate the lives of others": "This is usually with well-intentioned motives, but it can also be condescending and naive" (98). The critical question Edwards sees arising from his conclusions is whether minority groups consequently are on a road to complete assimilation. He suggests two possible answers:

First, even if total assimilation awaits at the end of this road, it is difficult to see how it could be avoided. Second, and more positively, there is the likelihood that private aspects of ethnicity will remain for a long time—exactly as long, in fact, as groups and individuals wish them to. (109)

No full-fledged study of the literary view and functioning of multiculturalism has, as yet, followed the works published in other disciplines. However, a few steps have been made in this direction. In 1982, a collection of papers and discussions was published under the title *Identifications: Ethnicity and the Writer in Canada*. This publication was followed by two other collections devoted to the theme of minority writing in Canada: "A/PART: Papers form the 1984 Ottawa Conference on Language, Culture and National Identity in Canada" was published as a supplement to *Canadian Literature* in 1987, and *Literatures of Lesser Diffusion/Les littératures de moindre diffusion* came out in 1990. These three collections are among the very few serious attempts in the world of Canadian literary criticism to address issues embedded in the study of "ethnic" Canadian literature.[2] Whereas literary critics have applied various postmodern critical theories to minority writing with varying measures of success, none of these theories was specifically developed in response to ethnic literature and they have left many questions unanswered. Finally, in 1990, Hutcheon and Richmond's collection of "Canadian Multicultural Fictions" called *Other Solitudes* appeared. While it is primarily a story collection, it includes an informative introduction by Hutcheon as well as interviews with various Canadian writers on the topic of multiculturalism. *Other Solitudes* was the first decisive step towards a "multicultural" anthology of Canadian writing. It has since been followed by *Making a Difference: Canadian Multicultural Literature* (1996), a long overdue, more extensive collection.

All publications listed above point to disagreement in the literary field over the view on the Canadian mosaic. Whereas many literary critics in the academic field appear to embrace the multiculturalist ideology with enthusiasm at least in theory, there seems to be less of a consensus among writers. Some authors do acknowledge that multiculturalism has provided the opportunity to create Canadian literature out of different cultural sensibilities and backgrounds (Pier Giorgio di Cicco in *Identifications* 83-84), and given minority groups the possibility to redefine themselves and their history from their own experience (Myrna Kostash in *Identifications* 143), while others completely refute it (Maara Haas in *Identifications* 135-37). More recently,

Neil Bissoondath, a Canadian writer of West Indian background, published his own damning views of multiculturalism in *Selling Illusions: The Cult of Multiculturalism* (1994). Bissoondath argues that multiculturalism promotes segregation and a racialized way of thinking and is detrimental to the natural development of a Canadian culture and identity.

Indeed, most writers on either side share a fear of the unwanted consequences of the institutionalization of multiculturalism that are making themselves felt. Such consequences include ghettoization, that is, literary works being labelled "ethnic" and only read and judged in that context. Ghettoization easily leads to marginalization, a case in which an increasing multicultural literary output would remain unread by a larger audience that is geared toward mainstream Anglo-Canadian literature. In the worst case, the result would be a mosaic culture where each writer only reaches his own group and no ethnic boundaries are transgressed. Another complaint that is frequently uttered by writers is that of external interference with the writing process. Whereas some authors identify with their ethnic backgrounds, others do not, and in either case they rightly feel that theirs is the freedom to be or not to be inspired by their cultural background. As George Ryga explains:

I don't think the question of my origins concerns anyone but myself. It's a very personal thing. As Jars [Balan] has pointed out, it's associated with things that are very deep inside you. In the agony of creative work and writing, you draw on that resource, but it's not a pudding for political consumption. It's just my own thing. (*Identifications* 148)

Since multiculturalism was made official policy in 1971, it has had both positive and negative receptions. While Canada's multicultural identity could now no longer be publicly ignored, and has indeed been promoted by government agencies in various manifestations, it has also been made clear that the reality is still far removed from the multicultural ideology rhetorically voiced by politicians and enthusiastic idealists. Some have even expressed grave doubts about the desirability and even the viability of an institutionalized mosaic. By viewing the history and role of one of Canada's cultures, the Icelandic-Canadian, in a multiculturalist framework, we might get a better idea of how multiculturalism has worked for that particular group and culture and if the criticism of multiculturalism has a case there or not.

THE ICELANDIC CANADIANS AS AN ETHNIC GROUP
IN CANADA

In order to view the place and role of Icelandic-Canadian literature
in a multiculturalist context, we need to have an idea of how the
Icelandic-Canadian identity has developed, what it encompasses and
how it is maintained in a Canadian context. We need to know by
what means Icelandic Canadians identify themselves and each other
as belonging to the same group, and how they perpetuate and express
this identity externally and internally. In the following discussion of
the Icelandic Canadians as an ethnic group I have relied on the theories of the anthropologist Fredrik Barth (1969). Barth has defined
an ethnic group as a population which (1) is largely biologically self-
perpetuating; (2) shares fundamental cultural values, realized in overt
unity in cultural forms; (3) makes up a field of communication and
interaction; (4) has a membership which identifies itself, and is identified by others, as constituting a category distinguishable from other
categories of the same order.

Barth also developed the idea of boundary-maintainance as a
determinant in the continuity of ethnic groups. It is particularly helpful in studies of ethnic groups in a Canadian context where so many
different minority groups interact while continuing to identify with
their own group. According to Barth, ethnic groups do not perpetuate their cultural distinctiveness through isolation. On the contrary,
this distinctiveness is often the foundation of inter-ethnic contacts
and is maintained through cultural boundaries by which members of
the ethnic group distinguish between insiders and outsiders. Since
the Icelandic Canadians especially have become known for their
almost complete assimilation into Canadian mainstream life while
still belonging to a recognized ethnic group, Barth's ideas about the
crucial role of cultural boundaries in ethnic group continuity form a
useful framework for a discussion of Icelandic-Canadian ethnicity.
They explain how the Icelandic-Canadian community has been able to
perpetuate itself as an ethnic group in an inter-ethnic context despite
a large degree of assimilation to Anglo-Canadian norms. First, however, we need to focus on what make up the Icelandic-Canadian cultural boundaries which have sustained this Icelandic-Canadian identity.

Two anthropological studies have suggested possible answers
to this question. John Matthiasson, himself an Icelandic Canadian,
has developed a theory of the Icelandic Canadians as "assimilated

ethnics." Matthiasson explains the paradox contained in this label as a natural outcome of what he sees as being the cultural theme of Iceland: dualism. He points out:

Its expression in personality and social and cultural forms is more one of "two-sidedness" than of contrast as such. On the social and cultural level, whenever there is one form of an institution, for example, there must also exist another, often identical in form, yet standing in structural opposition to the first. (1979: 203)

Matthiasson's theory is geographically founded: the theme of contrast in the Icelandic landscape is reflected in the people and their social and cultural structures.

The Icelandic immigrants brought the cultural pattern of dualism with them to Canada, where it was adapted to the new circumstances and continued with renewed vigour. The result was a factionalism which regularly threatened to split the community. We saw several examples in the history of the Icelandic-Canadian community: the split between the *Pálsmenn* and the *Jónsmenn* which led to the exodus of part of the community to Dakota, the split between the Lutherans and the Unitarians, the two competing community newspapers *Lögberg* and *Heimskringla*, the opposing parties who went to the celebration of Iceland's millenium on two separate ships. Whereas this factionalism has generally been regarded as detrimental to the community, Matthiasson argues to the contrary: it has kept the community inward-looking and has therefore been an important factor in the resistance of complete assimilation. The traditional Icelandic love of debate has caused factionalism to become, paradoxically, a strongly cohesive element with deep Icelandic roots. Even today, Icelandic-Canadian institutions and associations are characterized by disagreements and factions which appear to promote rather than avert intra-communal interest and activity.

Such intra-communal activity is of crucial importance to the Icelandic-Canadian identity, because it marks off an area where Icelandic Canadians can feel Icelandic and establish their sense of belonging to the community without disturbance to their lives as Canadians. Their debates and disagreements have reference to an Icelandic past, yet at the same time they are relevant to their present as Icelandic Canadians. Matthiasson's theories on this subject (1974; 1979; 1989) have drawn attention to the fact that the traditionally strong pull towards assimilation among Icelandic Canadians has caused them to cultivate, from the beginning, a very private form of ethnicity which did not interfere with their public life as Canadians. Their desire to prove themselves worthy citizens of their new country made them sacrifice those traditions in conflict with the norms of the majority and adopt Anglo-Canadian manners and customs, for they realized at an early stage that being categorized as immigrants and ethnics greatly hindered this desire for achievement. Their public assimilation eventually created a freedom which allowed Icelandic Canadians to move in socio-economic regions which were closed to other people who were more obviously ethnic.[3] At the same time, the Icelandic Canadians continued to preserve and pass on Icelandic values and a general pride in the Icelandic heritage in the privacy of their homes.

This combination of public assimilation and private ethnicity has been observed not only by Matthiasson but also by Friesen, who remarks:

Aside from its clubs and magazines and the August festival, the 5,000 Icelanders had few means of public expression. But pride in nationality remained. The Icelandic ideal was a combination of public conformity to English-Canadian cultural norms and private, family-centred efforts to retain their language and culture and to instil in their children an awareness of and pride in their national heritage. (1984: 262)

According to John Edwards' analysis of ethnicity which I outlined above, such private ethnicity tends to be more lasting since it is less susceptible to external pressure. It allows for inward-directed activities towards cultural preservation without repercussions in daily life and ambitions outside of the group. Matthiasson has shown how this strategy worked for the Icelandic Canadians: with factionalism as a catalyst to counteract the pull of assimilation into mainstream Canadian life, they have succeeded in achieving "non-hyphenated," i.e., Anglo-Canadian status, while still surviving as an ethnic group.

The second study to focus on the ethnic continuity of the Icelandic Canadians is that of Brydon (1987). Brydon uses the Icelandic festival, *Íslendingadagurinn*, as an entrée "through which the dynamics of the production, reproduction and transformation of West Icelandic identity are revealed." Her conclusions about the Icelandic-Canadian identity as it is contained in the festival largely agree with those of Matthiasson and Friesen. Brydon finds that there are, in reality, two festivals: a public and a private. The public one is a display of the success and achievements of the Icelanders in Canada since their immigration, which "signifies how the Icelanders fulfill the ideal of the immigrant: to achieve recognition within the larger society while maintaining a sense of one's heritage" (93). Here again is that combination of ambitions that was already present among the first-generation West Icelanders and was expressed in their writings: wanting to be both the best Canadians and the best Icelanders. At the same time there is also a private festival behind the scenes, invisible for everyone but Icelandic Canadians themselves, "where the actual perpetuation of Icelandic ethnicity occurs" (101). It comprises the interactions of family and friends, the interplay of memory and experience, the evocation of a community past that is not found in the official histories. This is where people affirm their Icelandic-Canadian identity and their membership in the community through symbols that are not recognized by outsiders as being "typically Icelandic" or "ethnic," and so they can remain private and meaningful to the individual. The experience of identity involved in attending the private festival Brydon likens to a spiritual home-coming:

Fragments of stories, of customs and myths are passed on from the older generation and are incorporated into the individual's own life experience. Thus memory and experience intermingle, and in the process produce a transformed notion of ethnicity. There are constraints, albeit flexible ones, on what experiences and memories can be thus labelled. For Icelanders generally, this relates to experiences related to the family, or to events occurring through Icelandic associations, or through experiences associated with the Interlake region. (107)

Although this private festival has little to do with the public one, the public festival does provide the backdrop and the possibility for the private.

The Icelandic Canadians have thus managed to perpetuate their ethnic identity through an early combination of public assimilation and private ethnicity. The desire to prove themselves an asset to their new country, to counteract hostilities and prejudice on the part of the Anglo-Canadian majority and to improve the living conditions left behind, formed a strong pull towards assimilation which was the only way towards social and economic success. On the other hand, as we saw in Chapter II, there was the urge to prove themselves good Icelanders instead of traitors and cowards who had left their native country, and a strong awareness of national history and culture.

Moreover, as Arnason argues in his essay "Myth of Beginnings," a mythic sense of re-enactment helped the Icelanders to adapt and develop a strong sense of community identity. In the process of adapting and becoming Canadians, a continuous internal factionalism rooted in Icelandic culture formed a strong incentive to keep them occupied with communal matters. Factionalism has thus formed an in-group area where the Icelandic-Canadian identity could be negotiated without disruption to people's public lives.

By restricting the experience and perpetuation of their ethnicity to the private sphere, it was less susceptible to external changes and pressure. Instead, it became something that was strongly family- and community-oriented and significantly associated with personal memories and experience of a communal past. This is also the conclusion of Magnús Einarsson's folklorist studies. Indeed, Einarsson's argument is that the cultural boundaries of the Icelandic-Canadian community are made up of family and communal bonds. He concludes his article thus:

The West Icelander has to an important degree projected his basic loyalties to a non-geographical world of communal and kinship bonds which, at times, are strong enough to take him even beyond finite and secular dimensions. The boundaries of this world are found in genealogy, biography and chronicle. In terms of folklore they are found chiefly in verses, and anecdotes. (1975: 31)

Brydon has shown that the annual Icelandic festival has become a ritual during which this private experience of a personal and communal past can be re-enacted, shared and become a framework for experience in the present, while remaining largely invisible to outsiders.

Brydon's study of the Icelandic-Canadian identity also draws attention to the recent role and influence of multiculturalism on the annual Icelandic festival. In fact, this forms the main focus of her work, and her findings are enlightening and important. Brydon points out that multiculturalism draws strongly on western assimilationist ideas about culture as embedded in attributes or characteristics. As a result, ethnic culture is regarded as something that cannot change without losing its authenticity. In Brydon's words:

An assimilationist logic underlies the multicultural perspective which in turn dominates commonsense knowledge of ethnic groups. This is apparent in how culture is perceived: authentic or traditional ethnic culture is seen to exist in attributes or characteristics which are or were particular to the group upon its arrival in North America. This perspective has the effect of reifying culture and separating it from the experience of identification as it arises in everyday action.

Further, the processes of change which normally occur in any society and are generally considered to be necessary to it, are seen in the case of the ethnic group as threatening to its continued existence.   (113)

The importance of Brydon's argument lies in the fact that the criteria for ethnic identity outlined above are used by group members themselves in the definition of their own identity. Brydon shows that Icelandic Canadians, prompted by the influence of multiculturalism to display their ethnic culture, have come to believe that the existence of themselves as an ethnic group might be endangered because they feel they cannot cater to the expectations of what is thought to be authentically Icelandic.

Brydon's findings support the arguments of Herbert Gans (1979). Gans argues that ethnicity as it is experienced among later generations, is removed from its origins and is therefore a private or group feeling which takes form and expression in symbols. John Edwards, who bases part of his argument on Gans', suggests that, while sometimes these symbols may match the public ideas of ethnic authenticity, this is certainly not always so (1985: 111-12). Edwards also emphasized the fact that identities do not stay unchanged but alter, implying that the ideas of culture underlying multiculturalism have created a public pattern of expectations concerning the authenticity of ethnic cultures which makes groups whose cultures have retained little that is deemed authentic, doubt their survival.

In the case of the Icelandic Canadians the effect of multiculturalism has been a split between what symbolizes Icelandic-Canadian identity for members of the community and what is expected by the outside public to symbolize authentic Icelandic culture. The problem which this creates is that multiculturalism now puts pressure on the Icelandic Canadians as an ethnic group to display their culture for other Canadians, while that which is experienced as being Icelandic Canadian is private, largely invisible to outsiders, and not what is publicly expected to be authentically Icelandic. Brydon observes: "What is of note here ... is how Icelandicness is not something visual or objectified, but is something experienced" (42). Yet it is exactly the visual and the objectified that multiculturalism expects, as it relies on an ossified view of culture, stuck in the time of immigration, and does not take into consideration that cultures and identities change with time and circumstances.

In her anthropological study of Icelandic Canadians, Ingibjörg Ásta Gunnarsdóttir emphasizes the fact that the crucial point is not to view ethnic group members as exact copies of people in the countries of origin, but as a group of people in their own right. Icelandic Canadians should be seen for what they are: Icelandic Canadians, and not Icelanders in Canada (1987: 50). Gold and Paine (1984) have drawn attention to the fact that, for ethnic groups, it is not so much the mother country that is important, for they are far removed from it in time and place, but the mother country as an image, a symbol and a dream. This corroborates Gans' argument mentioned earlier that, for later generations, ethnicity is a feeling expressed in symbols. Through the use of such symbols, ethnicity is expressed "as part invention, and part retention of past practices and beliefs" (Brydon 49). This is where multiculturalism appears to miss its mark completely.

However, as Brydon has observed, the view of culture on which multiculturalism relies is a western, assimilationist one and hence a ruling one. Thus it affects ethnic groups like the Icelandic-Canadian, who feel that their ethnic identity existed with greater authenticity in the past. The split this has created is reflected in the Icelandic festival, where the true celebration and perpetuation of Icelandic-Canadian identity takes place behind the scenes, while the public program attempts to stage and conceptualize Icelandic culture in terms of multiculturalism (Brydon 99). Significantly, Brydon finds that, for outsiders, the Icelandicness of the festival's events was not clear. They missed the point that the Icelandicness was not in the content but in the form, in the presence at the festival and the stability of its rituals. Brydon remarks:

This says more about how in everyday sense culture is defined rather than any confusion regarding Icelandicness ... it is not the practices themselves but the uses made of them which come to be symbolic for any group. Further, ethnicity is premised on this constant referral to the past to establish cultural legitimacy and meaning. Ethnicity in this sense is conservative by definition, where the present refers to the past, and the past is made to fit the present. Thus, though there are few practices which fit multiculturalism's definition of ethnic celebration, the Icelanders are nonetheless able to define for themselves what is traditional and authentic about the Festival. (96)

Moreover, the content put on display at the public festival apparently evoked a sense of pretense and inauthenticity among Icelandic Canadians and outsiders alike, but only the former knew where to find the truly meaningful aspects of the festival. There are, however, also Icelandic Canadians who no longer find the festival relevant to their identity and have stopped attending it.

The Icelandic-Canadian community, which has survived as an ethnic group through the combination of public assimilation and private ethnicity, now finds itself caught by the demands of multiculturalism to display publicly what is deemed authentically Icelandic by the criteria inherent in an assimilationist view of culture. As the Icelandic-Canadian identity is felt to be an experience continually adapted and revitalized in the light of past and present rather than an unchanging attribute from the days of immigration, the private symbols and areas where the perpetuation of Icelandic-Canadian-ness takes place perceptively diverge from the public displays which attempt to conform to multiculturalist terms. The latter have caused confusion with regard to the Icelandicness and authenticity of the content, since Icelandic Canadians have retained few things that are considered to be authentically Icelandic. The result of the influence of multiculturalist ideas has been that Icelandic Canadians have come to believe that the authenticity of their culture is fading, although in reality they have maintained a strong sense of their own identity which is expressed through symbols and networks that are meaningful to Icelandic Canadians themselves but for the most invisible to outsiders.

The case of the Icelandic Canadians as an ethnic group in the Canadian mosaic appears to support in important ways the criticisms of multiculturalism quoted in the previous section. The conclusions of Matthiasson and Brydon about the private nature of Icelandic-Canadian ethnicity, which is continued in spite of a large degree of assimilation into Anglo-Canadian customs and society, concur with John Edwards' argument: ethnic group members are more attracted by mainstream life than cultural pluralists like to believe, but at the same time a selection takes place of relevant, private ethnic markers which do not negatively affect social and economic progress and are less susceptible to external pressure. Additionally, Brydon's findings concerning assimilationist ideas about culture underlying multiculturalism and the influence they exercise on the way ethnic groups view their own culture corroborate Carole Carpenter's grave doubts about the mosaic, which she fears consists of a strong Anglo-Canadian framework in which ethnic cultures are allowed to present themselves only the way the dominant group regards them: as harmless and colourful decorations. Finally, the fact pointed out by Matthiasson that Icelandic Canadians have succeeded in achieving remarkable social and economic success by adopting a public Anglo-Canadian face at an early stage and ignoring their place in the mosaic (1974), implies Porter's conclusion that ethnicity impedes social mobility. What these observations mean for the place and development of Icelandic-Canadian literature in the Canadian mosaic will be our next consideration.

ICELANDIC-CANADIAN LITERATURE AND THE CANADIAN MOSAIC

After a period where ethnicity hardly played a role in published writing, we saw in Chapter IV how Icelandic-Canadian authors were again creatively inspired by their cultural background. It can be no coincidence that this transformation in Icelandic-Canadian writing occurred after the 1960s, when multiculturalism had become policy. The policy of multiculturalism, after the revolutionary spirit of the 1960s, offered hope and possibilities for Canadian voices which spoke from a background different from that of the Anglo-Canadian. The cultural climate seemed ready for the expression of "other" Canadian experiences, histories and realities than that of the mainstream.

Writers such as Valgardson, Gunnars and Arnason heeded the call and took up the challenge. Their prolific oeuvre can be taken as a sign of making up for the muteness of previous generations. Suddenly they had found a medium and could turn their experiences into Canadian literature. These authors have succeeded in developing an integrated artistic vision in which Icelandic, Icelandic-Canadian and Canadian elements all find expression and function as a complete body of perception. New authors of Icelandic-Canadian background, however, are not following the example of their predecessors but, on the contrary, returned to mainstream Canadian writing. While this could be attributed to a simple difference in artistic propensity, it is striking that first Arnason and now Gunnars and Valgardson too, are moving away from their original perception and turning to mainstream Canadian writing instead. Arnason was already gradually turning into another direction with *The Circus Performers' Bar* and continued this with *The Pagan Wall.* Similarly, the latest works which have appeared by Gunnars and Valgardson indicate a move away from Icelandic and Icelandic-Canadian sources. This development cannot solely be explained by a desire on the part of these writers to try their hands at something new, although this may well have played a part. It seems too much of a coincidence that all Icelandic-Canadian writing, by older as well as younger authors, is now, with multiculturalism at its peak and made the legal duty of every Canadian, taking a turn towards the non-ethnic and mainstream.

In 1985, Hutcheon remarked in her article on immigrant literature:

> Canadians have always prided themselves on their multiculturalism, their ethnic "mosaic" that allowed the cultural diversity that the American "melting pot" did not. But the mosaic can be a tyrannical image, too: it demands that you keep your ethnic roots and become Canadian as well. (34)

Gunnars had signalled this tyrannical tendency in what she saw as the "mythology" of multiculturalism a year before Hutcheon (1984). Here, and in her interview with David Demchuk, Gunnars argues that multiculturalism tyrannizes the way in which one's own culture is experienced and, moreover, creates a self-conscious tendency among Canadian writers to be "ethnic." At the same time, she finds that multiculturalism tends to lead to the ghettoization of a writer:

> In writing, the repercussions have been interesting. I began with the idea that I could expand our English by investing it with Nordic modes of expression. In the end I felt vaguely ghettoized. Instead of expanding the language I sensed that I had given the cue to have myself confined to an "ethnic" group about which I still know precious little. I believe this is a typical experience. (1984: 8)

Gunnars refers here to the fact that she is a recent immigrant and thus does not belong to the Icelandic-Canadian community. Hutcheon's and Gunnars' observations on the implications of the mosaic are very important: multiculturalism does not really take the experience or vision of the individual member of an ethnic group into consideration but departs from a pre-conceived idea of what "ethnic" constitutes and how it should be expressed. This not only tyrannizes writers, and other ethnic group members as well, but also, in turn, provides an excuse to label any work which contains "foreign" elements as "ethnic" and thus ghettoizes the writer and the work. Ethnic, after all, still stands for marginalized, "different from us";[4] even if the current trend in literature is to celebrate difference, it is not in itself considered as part of mainstream literature.

Hutcheon's and Gunnars' observations imply that while multiculturalism appears to have opened some doors, it has closed others. On the one hand, it pressures writers into a self-conscious awareness and a literary exploitation of their heritage that corresponds to the preconceived image of that heritage. On the other hand, it promotes segregation in the way that it ghettoizes writers who have been labelled as "ethnic." As Gunnars worded it: "In Canada you sometimes need to resist being pegged out of existence by cultural assumptions if you belong to a distinct "ethnic" group. The absurdity was that I knew little about the Icelanders in Canada and was forced to make it my business to find out about these people" (1984: 32). The danger in this is, of course, that works labelled as "ethnic" are not judged according to general literary criteria, but are viewed as ethnic artifacts and curiosa which are representative of a whole ethnic group rather than the product of an individual creative imagination. The continuing lack of serious critical analyses for Canadian minority writing reinforces the impression that ethnic literature tends to be approached from a non-literary standpoint.

Not only Gunnars has spoken out against the negative influence of multiculturalism, but Arnason and Valgardson as well. In *The Icelanders* Arnason writes: "This is why I am against this ethnic stuff always, of segregating, and dividing and destroying the country" (1981: 116). He introduces the book thus: "It's about the time when they were a separate group, before they became simply Canadians with a special set of memories." While in his other works Arnason has no problems referring to himself and his background as Icelandic-Canadian, it is as if, with this book and its explicit title, he wants to avoid being caught in a specific "ethnic" corner and therefore makes a particular point of presenting himself and the Icelandic-Canadian community as *Canadians*. This impression is enforced by the fact that Arnason's second collage, a revised version of *The Icelanders* which also contains new material, received the title *The New Icelanders: A North American Community* (1994). In "Myth of Beginnings," he specifically localizes the community and its myth in Canadian history and geography:

The Icelanders continue to form a significant cultural group. The source of this cohesiveness is the myth of beginnings, a myth shared by Icelandic Canadians and Icelandic Americans as well. We look backward, not to some lost haven across the sea in Iceland, but to our roots as a people in a new land. (8)

Valgardson is also very concerned with the dangers of segregation inherent in the Canadian mosaic. His story "The Man from Snaefellsness" and his interview with Judith Miller in *Other Solitudes* (1990: 133-40) make poignantly clear how many people are excluded by the mosaic simply because they do not belong to any one particular group. Although the Icelanders considered the half-Irish boy an *utlander*, he felt he did not belong to the Irish community either, while to the Anglo-Canadians he always remained a foreigner. The experience of exclusion is an often ignored but poignant reality of the mosaic. In Valgardson's view, the struggle for integration rather than the tendency toward segregation is the truly Canadian experience:

Whenever you have a very strong ethnic community, if you are not 100 percent genetically pure you are very aware: that is the Canadian experience. The whole thing about the integration into becoming Canadian, of course, is very difficult and is most difficult in those who are the first to cross the boundary.... I have given up all the terrible despair that I felt over not being totally Icelandic and not being totally Irish. It would have been much easier if both parents had been Irish or both parents had been Icelandic. Belonging to two communities forces a kind of growth, and it forces a kind of struggle with something other people do not have to struggle with. That growth is painful, but that is part of the Canadian experience. (*Other Solitudes* 137-139)

Being Canadian, that is being integrated, is to people like Valgardson and Arnason a blessing rather than a curse. Along the same lines Gunnars, an immigrant who stands outside the Icelandic-Canadian community, has also striven towards integration in her work, as we saw in Chapter IV. Only for people who have never had to struggle with the experience of exclusion and displacement can the idea of preserving separate ethnic tiles in a mosaic be attractive.

At the same time, these three writers strongly identify with their cultural background and have integrated it into their work. We seem to have a contradiction here that resembles what Brydon and Matthiasson observed about the Icelandic Canadians as an ethnic group, and that points to where multiculturalism goes wrong. Ethnicity, at least among Icelandic Canadians, is experienced and perpetuated in the private sphere, while assimilation takes over in the public. As Matthiasson has emphasized: while being very concerned with the continuation of their ethnic heritage and identity, Icelandic Canadians have, at the same time, always refused to be publicly identified as "ethnics" and suffer the consequences of such identification, whether these be discrimination or ghettoization (1974). Similarly, Icelandic-Canadian writers are evidently unwilling to be pressured into writing "ethnic" literature and have their writing categorized as "ethnic," even though they identify with their Icelandic background and are creatively inspired by it.

The inspiration from this ethnic background, however, is not primarily to be found in the type of colourful and quaint characteristics from an immigrant past that outsiders like to pinpoint as authentically Icelandic. Rather, it is drawn from personal and communal experience and memory as it is meaningful to the individual, and as it informs and creates the present and the future. In other words, when authors write from an Icelandic-Canadian background, they do so from a cultural source that has been moulded by the New World as well as the Old. As Arnason points out, the survival and cohesiveness of the Icelandic Canadians as an ethnic group have to a very significant extent depended on the fact that they did not continue to live in a past they had left behind, but instead found a way to become rooted in the new land without discarding their cultural heritage. They did not remain Icelanders in Canada, but became Icelandic Canadians through a combination of assimilation and ethnicity. The Icelandic-Canadian culture that developed among them acknowledged the Icelandic past with its cultural riches *as it informed and created the New World present*, not as some icon from days long gone. Thus it could remain a vital culture that was meaningful also to later generations far removed from Iceland and the emigration. Valgardson has suggested that Icelandic-Canadian culture has mainly been of a literary nature and that the community sense of pride in literary accomplishment has "allowed the group to exist not just for the sake of nostalgia about the past but to take pride in its identity in the present" (1982: 36).

It is in the light of this vital Icelandic-Canadian culture that we should see the concern with integration among writers like Valgardson and Arnason. Through their Icelandic-Canadian background they are very aware of the vitality and riches of Canada's "other" cultures, and the alternative ways of perception they offer of the Canadian experience of past and present, to which their works also bear witness. These cultures, as they have developed and exist in the Canadian present, are therefore relevant to all Canadians and should be shared among all Canadians through an integrative process. Such integration will not, however, take place through the display of colourful "authentic" characteristics that belong to the past and have little or no bearing on the Canadian present other than as entertainment. Yet it is exactly the latter that the multiculturalist policy continues to promote as being representative of "ethnic cultures." Valgardson makes the following observation:

Too often ... we acknowledge ethnic influences only when the subject matter of the art is identifiably about the immigration experience or the artist is dressed in ethnic clothes. We do not recognize that the truly profound ethnic influence, like a powerful current under a still surface, is constantly at work. This influence partially determines at least the following: what kind of art is produced, what is seen, what is not seen, or, if seen, is or is not acknowledged, what is regarded as worthy subject matter, what is not, what the attitude is toward landscape and human activity and what the relationships of the two will be and, particularly, what the underlying judgements will be by which all of this is evaluated. As artists of our culture, it is important that we acknowledge this but also move beyond it, not only to enter but to create the possibility of the greater society and, as part of that creating, to struggle against all those who would deny our right to create and live within our identity. (1987: 1)

This statement provides a clear picture of what the multiculturalist policy should do but fails to: in its concentration and celebration of what is visually colourful and different, it ignores the true challenge and goal of multiculturalism, which is learning about and adopting alternative values and perceptions, and appreciating them not as interesting curiosities but as relevant and important aspects of the Canadian experience and identity. Its focus on the past and on characteristics prevents the acknowledgement of other cultures in Canada as living Canadian cultures of the present. While it is true that these cultures incorporate a significant part of their past, they have not allowed themselves to be imprisoned by it and cannot be expected to have done so.

Furthermore, in focussing on the differences between past cultures, multiculturalism as it exists now in Canada promotes segregation whereas it should promote integration. Writer and social critic Susan Crean expresses this same impression:

The liberal interpretation of multiculturalism, moreover, has taken the Mosaic literally, developing a micro approach to cultural policy, which concentrates on each ethnic community as a separate entity, treating them as shining relics from the past. Multiculturalism prohibits the interaction between the pieces, and the possibility of their so affecting and changing each other that something entirely new grows....

Yet assimilation in this country has become a four letter word whether it implies an entirely natural process or one that robs people of their past, their identity and their dignity. Governments officially recognize everybody's heritage and tell us we have the right to preserve them—a feat that's a bit like freezing a waterfall. (1986: 11)

This is also what Gunnars observed in her interview with Demchuk:

When we talk of "mosaic" culture in this country and the preservation of immigrant cultures including heritage languages, we are asking to remain shackled to the parents we killed. We become tied to something that has died. It is a dangerous business and could prevent the natural maturing of Canadian culture. (1984: 35)

Arnason gives an example of how communal myths and cultures can be shared:

Even more importantly, the myth of beginnings ties together the Icelandic community of North America with the other communities of Manitoba which help us celebrate.... As contemporary North Americans we live in many cultures at the same time. We wish to protect our own, but also to share it. *Íslendingadagurinn* and the myth of beginnings it celebrates is important to Canada. It gives us one more valid way of being Canadian without evoking ancient dreams of Empire. (1994: 8)

This is possibly the very issue behind the failings of institutionalized multiculturalism in Canada: a fear that true integration would mean replacing Canada's British-rooted culture and social structure with a "foreign" one where familiar Anglo-Canadian values and customs would be challenged and established advantages be given up for more equal sharing. As long as cultural items can still be referred to as "ethnic" because Canadian continues to mean Anglo-Canadian, multiculturalism will not make a true difference in Canada. While it has given Canadians of non-British origins the possibility to make themselves heard, it has so far failed to create audiences prepared to take the sounding voices seriously enough to recognize them as relevant to themselves as *Canadians*, so it cannot work any real changes. But, then, perhaps it was never meant to.

What this has meant for Icelandic-Canadian writers is that the abandonment of public assimilation for the expression of ethnic identity still has undesirable repercussions. While the works of Valgardson, Arnason and Gunnars have generally been well received in circles which strongly support the multiculturalist ideal for various reasons, they are seldom judged by literary standards alone. Their works are applauded by prairie critics as contributions to prairie literature. Regionalist sentiments on the prairies are strong and prairie regionalists tend to be great supporters of the mosaic, which they have adopted as one of their main images: it is regarded as an important part of prairie reality which makes the region different from that of the Canadian heartland. As a result, literary works by prairie writers which contain regional influences or ethnic influences or both are enthusiastically received as yet another proof of an independent and different prairie culture.

However, such reception has an important political basis in which literary criteria appear to play a secondary role. Moreover, while regionalist sentiments use the mosaic image, they do not really contribute to the acknowledgement of ethnic literature in the canon, but probably hinder it even more by supporting it for non-literary reasons and thus enforcing its "other" status. While literary efforts, including those on the Icelandic-Canadian front, are often subsidized, this is usually done from either specific multiculturalist or prairie funds. Consequently, works by Canadian writers who write from an ethnic sensibility are really funded for political and not for literary reasons, implying that their literary quality is only of second importance. Crean has drawn attention to this phenomenon:

Rarely, if ever, have clients of one program been shifted out of and over to another as the nature and professionalism of their project has changed. Which only reinforces my suspicion that terms like "ethnic" and "excellence" are taken by the bureaucracy to be mutually exclusive and my conviction that we do indeed have an official Culture. (1986: 11)

Once the label "ethnic" has been attached to a work of literature, it is no longer eligible for the label "Canadian." As a result, writers like

Valgardson, Arnason and Gunnars, who have won their spurs on the prairies with various prizes and medals, are rarely included in anthologies, collections or curriculums of Canadian literature. Thus, politics and institutions direct the attention which their works attract to specific, largely non-literary elements, thereby setting them apart from the mainstream. Consequently, they are almost automatically excluded from national literary recognition.

The impression articulated by many critics, that multiculturalism as a policy is used to appease minority discontent while endorsing the status quo of Anglo-Canadian dominance, is reinforced. This happens also in the field of literature, where the funding and encouragement of writers with an ethnic background leads to their ghettoization, which in turn prevents them from being taken seriously as Canadian authors and being adopted in the canon of mainstream literature. In fact, considering the situation in which Laura Goodman Salverson found herself sixty years ago, one must come to the conclusion that in spite of two decades of multiculturalism, the situation of Icelandic-Canadian and other ethnic writers has changed very little indeed.

It is little wonder, then, that, coming from an ethnic community which has traditionally kept its ethnicity private and avoided ghettoization through public assimilation, Icelandic-Canadian writers are returning to this strategy. From the very beginning, Canadians of Icelandic descent have expressed in writing their desire for a Canadian culture which would incorporate the cultures of all its immigrants. At the turn of the century, West Icelanders like Jóhann Magnús Bjarnason articulated their hopes for this ideal in their literature, and criticized prevailing Anglo-Canadian attitudes which ignored the cultural backgrounds and contributions of other Canadians. Next, in 1923, Laura Goodman Salverson voiced her views in her fiction in English. *The Viking Heart* is an optimistic account of how an immigrant culture like her own can be an enrichment to the evolving Canadian culture. However, Salverson became more pessimistic in the course of her fictional career as she felt increasingly alienated from the realization of her ideal. Her own works were read with delight but not taken very seriously, and in later works like *The Dark Weaver*, the optimistic ideal of a multicultural society is subjected to the looming shadows of inevitability. Her autobiography *Confessions* is an account of split worlds which are never integrated except in the realm of dreams. In spite of her popularity at the time of writing, her works never received proper recognition in the canon of Canadian literature still dominated by Anglo-Canadian norms and standards.

Contemporary Icelandic-Canadian writers have contributed to the multicultural ideal with works written from an ethnic-Canadian sensibility. While they are, on the one hand, thoroughly Canadian, they are, on the other, an expression of a living Icelandic-Canadian culture. This culture has preserved certain elements from the Icelandic past, has invented others, and is constantly revitalized in the light of the Canadian present so as to remain meaningful to the individual members of its community. Valgardson, Gunnars and Arnason have successfully integrated the Canadian and the ethnic perception into a whole artistic vision, and with their works have made a case for the recognition and integration of "other" Canadian sensibilities, values and experiences into Canadian culture. The reception of their works, however, indicates that two and a half decades of official multiculturalism have produced very few actual changes in Canada. Politics, funding and pre-conceived ideas about ethnic culture encourage ethnic writing, but at the same time promote evaluation by non-literary standards, thereby directing it away from mainstream literature and ghettoizing it. Valgardson, Gunnars and Arnason are therefore denied a readership and recognition on a national scale, as the literary establishment in Canada remains dominated by Anglo-Canadian norms and standards and can continue to regard Canadian literature from other sensibilities as marginal, different and thus not belonging to the canon.

As a result, Icelandic-Canadian writers are returning to the traditional strategy of their community: public assimilation and private ethnicity. Gunnars, Valgardson and Arnason, as well as more recent writers like Martha Brooks and Marion Johnson are now writing in an Anglo-Canadian tradition, thus avoiding ghettoization as "ethnics" and aiming for an audience which will judge their work on the basis of its literary merits. The development of Icelandic-Canadian literature appears to prove John Edwards right in his argument that active external intervention on behalf of ethnic minority groups may, indeed in this particular case does, work counter-productively. In the case of Icelandic-Canadian literature, multiculturalism has failed its authors by re-assimilating them into the homogeneity of Anglo-Canadian mainstream writing.

NOTES

1. For a discussion of the attempts of Gibbon and Kirkconnell and the subsequent development of the position of Canadian ethnic literatures see Andrusyshen (1975).

2. Robert Kroetsch (1985) and Eli Mandel (1977) especially have drawn attention to the need for a theoretical framework for minority writing in Canada, and have provided some helpful clues towards the study of so-called "ethnic narrative." Padolsky (1990; 1991) has made suggestions towards such a framework.

3. This also appears from Porter's analysis, where Icelanders occasionally make their appearance in high-up positions which are otherwise exclusively held by Anglo-Canadians (1968: 389, 410, 501).

4. See also Hutcheon in her introduction to *Other Solitudes* (1990: 2, 13).

THE ICELANDIC-CANADIAN CONTRIBUTION

THE ICELANDIC IMMIGRANTS to Canada brought their literary heritage as their main cultural baggage. This heritage had been the major vehicle of popular cultural expression in Iceland over the centuries, and was firmly rooted in the Old Icelandic literature which reflected Iceland's own immigrant origins. Consequently, the West Icelanders had a literary model for the expression of their immigrant experience. Literature thus became the most important focus for cultural preservation and expression in Canada as well and, as in Iceland, it was practised widely by people from all social strata. In many aspects, the literary activities in medieval Iceland and in immigrant Canada show remarkable similarities. The most important of these is probably that the voluminous literary output of both communities indicates a profound need to establish a self-image which finds recognition at political and cultural centres outside of the communities, in order to combat the feelings of alienation and inferiority inherent in the immigrant experience. Medieval Icelandic literature shows the immigrant dynamics of adaptation to the new environment and preservation of Old Norse traditions. Similarly, in Western Icelandic literature we see how authors promote a strategy of both assimilation to Anglo-Canadian society and retention of the Icelandic heritage.

The literary activities in the Western Icelandic community were essential for the development of a distinct Icelandic-Canadian cultural identity within the larger Canadian society. Western Icelandic literature constituted the main conduit and channel for communal expression, thereby drawing the community together and keeping it in touch with and involved in communal activities and interests. It provided the community with a sense of identity and expressed, validated and helped create its self-image as a group which strove to be both the best Icelanders and the best Canadians. Last but not least, it recreated in literary form the beginnings of the Icelandic Canadians as a group in Canada. In doing this, Western Icelandic literature provided both the symbolic matrix of a new beginning for the Icelandic Canadians in the New World, while at the same time firmly establishing the link between the Icelandic-Canadian community and its Icelandic past through the re-enactment of a literary recording of the community's immigrant beginnings.

The oppositional strategy of cultural assimilation and preservation, which has become characteristic of the Icelandic Canadians, has been an important factor in the contribution of Icelandic-Canadian authors to Canadian literature. From the beginning, it gave rise to a literature which was not solely caught up in nostalgic reflections of an Old World past, but opened itself to the influences from its Canadian environment as well. Works by Icelandic immigrant authors show that, at its best, Western Icelandic literature reflects a Canadian environment and a part of Canadian immigrant history in a framework of the Icelandic literary tradition. Stephan G. immortalized the Canadian landscape in which he lived in many of his poems, while other work by him preceded Anglo-Canadian literature in its poetic expression of internationally acute themes. The poetry of Guttormur J. Guttormsson is a striking example of how a transplanted cultural and linguistic heritage can be employed and combined by a Canadian-born writer to function in a Canadian reality. Káinn's humourous sketches from the Western Icelandic communities, while composed in a traditional Icelandic form, record daily life in immigrant Canada as well as offering invaluable examples of the way in which Icelandic and Canadian were mixed into a distinct Icelandic-Canadian idiom. Similarly, the stories of Jóhann Magnús Bjarnason and Guðrún H. Finnsdóttir provide sketches of life in immigrant communities of Canada. At the same time, they are fictional recreations of the concerns in the Icelandic-Canadian community how to preserve the best from its Icelandic heritage while fully participating as Canadian citizens in an Anglo-Canadian society which tacitly but determinedly entertained assimilationist expectations. Jóhann Magnús took to romantic reconstructions of an Old Icelandic code of behaviour in a Canadian context, while Guðrún employed a more realistic mode in which the inevitable integration into Canadian society is counteracted by the strong force of ancestry and kinship. Both writers, however, directed their fiction towards an eventual multiculturalist ideal, in which all ethnic heritages would be acknowledged as part of one Canadian nation.

The ideology of a mosaic culture, however, was slow to take root in the social and cultural establishment. This is well reflected in the works of Laura Goodman Salverson, the immigrants' daughter who was the first to write in English and address a Canadian audience in the 1920s and 1930s. Her first novel, while telling realistically of the immigrant hardships suffered by the Icelanders in Canada, still ends with the optimistic celebration of the place and prosperity which her people eventually find in Canadian society in return for their sufferings and the contribution of their heritage. Her later works, however, reveal a pessimism bordering on bitterness. The profound sense of duality and alienation which informs these works is an early literary manifestation of a characteristic facet of the Canadian heritage: the effects of an immigrant past. Moreover, the optimistic ideal of a respected place for her people's cultural heritage found in the first novel has made way in these later works for a melting pot in which those who refuse to discard their ethnic pride are cut off from the realization of their ambitions and remain confined to the immigrant ghettos.

Salverson's initial popularity quickly faded and since then her name has receded into the background of Canadian literary history. Nearly all Icelandic-Canadian writers who followed in her footsteps during the following four decades had a local appeal only and were generally reticent about their ethnic heritage in their writing. This changed only with the rise of multiculturalism during the 1960s and 1970s. Contemporary Icelandic-Canadian writing incorporates Icelandic and Icelandic-Canadian elements in a Canadian literary framework. While it is true that it has little in common with the Western Icelandic tradition, a distinct Icelandic-Canadian identity has developed which receives expression in this writing in a fully integrated way. Kristjana Gunnars, a native Icelander and recent immigrant, has given poetic and fictional expression to the immigrant past of the Icelandic-Canadian community as well as to her own immigrant experience. In Gunnars' work, the long muted and marginalized immigrant voice in Canadian literature has received powerful universal expression, interlaced with Icelandic speech rhythms and imagery. W.D. Valgardson and David Arnason, fourth-generation members of the Icelandic-Canadian community, explore in their fiction and poetry the role, function and influence of ethnic heritage in contemporary Canadian life. Valgardson is especially concerned with identity crises in the modern world, and his portrayal of a stark, elemental land in which people must find ways to discover dignified and sustaining means of survival, is both very Canadian and very Icelandic while losing nothing of its universal impact. Arnason's fictional use of his ethnic heritage seems sometimes more a filial duty, and yet the ways in which he integrates the oral traditions of the Icelandic-Canadian community into his contemporary Canadian literary interests are very successful. All three writers regard their ethnic heritage as a fertile source of alternatives to the destructive tendencies in twentieth-century society. Valgardson and Arnason employ aspects of their ethnic background in a larger conception of current Canadian or universal concerns, while Gunnars uses her own immigrant experience and the Icelandic-Canadian immigrant history to reflect contemporary alienated and fragmented man, threatened with global destruction in a technocratic age.

Younger writers of Icelandic-Canadian background, however, are returning to mainstream Canadian writing. Books by Martha Brooks and Marion Johnson, as well as the poetic cycles of Eleanor Oltean and of self-help and drama writer Betty Jane Wylie, show no interest in a literary exploitation of ethnic heritage and bear few marks of it. Significantly, their most recent works show that Valgardson, Arnason and Gunnars are turning away as well from ethnic influences on their writing. Seeing that multiculturalism in Canada is at its peak, this change of direction that Icelandic-Canadian writing has taken raises questions with regard to the effects of an institutionalized mosaic. The Icelandic Canadians have developed a distinct New World culture which gives expression to their identity as Canadians with an Icelandic immigrant past. A central aspect of this culture has been the Icelandic oppositional dynamics of adaptation and preservation, which among Icelandic Canadians has taken the shape of a combination of public assimilation and private ethnicity. Multiculturalism as it is presently exercised in Canada, however, appears to be based on assimilationist cultural assumptions which view ethnic cultures as quaint relics from an immigrant past rather than living Canadian cultures. As a result, apparent tolerance masks a situation where the status quo of an Anglo-Canadian establishment can be perpetuated. The true challenge of a multiculturalist society, where living cultures enrich each other, is thus warded off. The consequences for Canadian literature are that authors who write from a "marginal" sensibility or perspective, i.e., different from the ruling Anglo-Canadian, tend to become ghettoized because they are read and judged by different standards. As a result, younger writers choose to avoid the pitfalls inherent in "ethnic" writing, for as long as "Canadian" continues to mean "Anglo-Canadian," and "ethnic" as deviant from that norm, nothing is really accomplished. Instead of promoting diversity, multiculturalism is threatening to lead, in the case of Icelandic-Canadian literature, to conformity.

SELECTED BIBLIOGRAPHY OF WESTERN ICELANDIC AND ICELANDIC-CANADIAN LITERATURE

Arnason, David. *The Circus Performers' Bar*. Vancouver: Talonbooks, 1984.

————. *The Dragon and the Dry Goods Princess*. Winnipeg: Turnstone, 1994.

————. *Fifty Stories and a Piece of Advice*. Winnipeg: Turnstone, 1982.

————. *The Happiest Man in the World*. Vancouver: Talonbooks, 1989.

————, and Michael Olito. *The Icelanders*. Winnipeg: Turnstone, 1981.

————. *If Pigs Could Fly*. Winnipeg: Turnstone, 1995.

————. *Marsh Burning*. Winnipeg: Turnstone, 1980.

————, and Vincent Arnason. *The New Icelanders: A North American Community*. Winnipeg: Turnstone, 1994.

————. *The Pagan Wall*. Vancouver: Talonbooks, 1992.

————. *Skrag*. Winnipeg: Turnstone, 1987.

Bjarnason, Emil. *The Whole Truth: Sagas from the Quills*. Vancouver: The Icelandic Canadian Club of British Columbia, 1989.

Bjarnason, Jóhann Magnús. *Brazilíufararnir*. [The Brazil Farers] 1905-1908. *Ritsafn* [collected works] III. Akureyri: Bókaútgáfan Edda, 1972.

————. *Eiríkur Hansson: Skáldsaga frá Nýja Skotlandi*. [Eiríkur Hansson: A Novel from Nova Scotia] 1899-1903. *Ritsafn* IV. Akureyri: Bókaútgáfan Edda, 1973.

Bjarnason, Jóhann Magnús. *Karl litli: Saga frá Draumamörk / Ævintýri.* [Little Karl: A Story from Dream Forest/ fairy tales] 1935 / 1946. Rpt. as *Gimsteinaborgin.* [The City of Jewels] *Ritsafn* I. Akureyri: Bókaútgáfan Edda, 1977.

―――. *Haustkvöld við Hafið.* [Autumn Evening at the Ocean] 1928. *Ritsafn* VI. Akureyri: Bókaútgáfan Edda, 1971.

―――. *Í Rauðárdalnum.* [In the Red River Valley] 1914-22. *Ritsafn* II. Akureyri: Bókaútgáfan Edda, 1976.

―――. *Vornætur á Elgsheiðum.* [Spring Nights on Moose Heights] 1910. *Ritsafn* V. Akureyri: Bókaútgáfan Edda, 1970.

Bjarnason, Paul. *Odes and Echoes.* Vancouver: private publication, 1954.

Brooks, Martha. *A Hill for Looking.* Winnipeg: Queenston House, 1982.

―――. *Paradise Café and Other Stories.* Saskatoon: Thistledown, 1988.

―――. *Two Moons in August.* Vancouver/Toronto: Groundwood Douglas & McIntyre, 1991.

Einarsson, Helgi. *Ævisaga Helga Einarssonar frá Neðranesi.* Reykjavík: Ísafoldarprentsmiðja, 1954. Rpt. as *Helgi Einarsson, A Manitoba Fisherman.* Trans. George Houser. Winnipeg: Queenston House, 1982.

Finnsdóttir, Guðrún Helga. *Dagshríðar Spor.* [Tracks of Day's Struggle] Akureyri: Árni Bjarnarson, 1946.

―――. *Ferðalok.* [Journey's End] Winnipeg: Gísli Jónsson, 1950.

―――. *Hillingalönd.* [Lands of Mirages] Reykjavík: Félagsprentsmiðjan, 1938.

Gunnars, Kristjana. *The Axe's Edge.* Victoria: Porcépic, 1983.

―――. *Carnival of Longing.* Winnipeg: Turnstone, 1989.

―――. *Exiles Among You.* Regina: Coteau Books, 1996.

―――. *The Guest House and Other Stories.* Toronto: Anansi, 1992.

―――. *The Nightworkers of Ragnarök.* Victoria: Porcépic, 1985.

―――. *One-eyed Moon Maps.* Victoria: Porcépic, 1980.

―――. *The Prowler.* Red Deer: Red Deer College Press, 1989.

―――. *The Rose-Garden: Reading Marcel Proust.* Red Deer: Red Deer College Press, 1996.

―――. *Settlement Poems 1 and 2.* Winnipeg: Turnstone, 1980.

―――. *The Substance of Forgetting.* Red Deer: Red Deer College Press, 1992.

―――, ed. *Unexpected Fictions: New Icelandic Canadian Writing.* Winnipeg: Turnstone, 1989.

―――. *Wake-pick Poems.* Toronto: Anansi, 1981.

―――. *Zero Hour.* Red Deer: Red Deer College Press, 1991.

Guttormsson, Guttormur J. *Aurora/Áróra: English Translations of Icelandic Poems by Guttormur J. Guttormsson.* Ed. Heather Alda Ireland. Vancouver: private publication, 1993.

Guttormsson, Guttormur J. *Kvæðasafn.* [Collected Poetry] Ed. Arnór Sigurjónsson. Reykjavík: Iðunn, 1947.

Guttormsson, R. *Ian of Red River.* Toronto: Ryerson, 1959.

Halldorsson, Albert L. *Fruits of the Valley: An Historic Novel.* N.p.: private publication, 1950.

————. *Wings of the Wind.* Dugald, Man.: Springfield, 1948.

Helgason, Elma. *In the Land Where the Peace River Flows.* Edmonton: Applied Art, 1963.

————. *Songs of All Seasons.* Washington, DC: Review and Harald, 1979.

Ingaldson, Violet Paula. *Cold Adventure.* Vancouver/Toronto/Montreal: Copp Clark, 1959.

Johnson, Marion. *The Book of All Sorts.* London, Ont.: Nightwood, 1989.

Jónsson, Baldur. *Leaves from the Unwritten Notebook of an Idler, together with Letters Written in a Cloister and Dedicated to the Hearth.* Wynyard: Bogi Bjarnason, 1918.

Júlíus, Kristján Niels. *Kviðlingar og kvæði.* [Verses and Poems] Ed. Richard Beck. Reykjavík: Bókfellsútgáfan, 1945.

Kristofferson, Kristine Benson. *Tanya.* Toronto: Ryerson, 1950.

Magnusson, Kristiana. *Roots that Bind.* Langley: Trinity, 1979.

————. *So Well Remembered.* Langley: A & K and Trinity, 1978.

Oltean, Eleanor. *Earth and Sky.* 1987. Calgary: Unicorn Graphics, 1993.

Reykdal, Art. *Bibliography of a Damned Fool.* Winnipeg: Pauper, 1955.

Salverson, Laura Goodman. *Black Lace.* Toronto: Ryerson, [1938].

————. *Confessions of an Immigrant's Daughter.* 1939. Social History of Canada 24. Toronto: University of Toronto Press, 1981.

————. *The Dark Weaver.* Toronto: Ryerson, 1937.

————. *The Dove of El-Djezaire.* Toronto: Ryerson, [1933].

————. "Hidden Fire." *MacLean's* 36.1 (15 Feb. 1923): 14: 50-51.

————. *Immortal Rock.* Toronto: Ryerson, 1954.

————. *Lord of the Silver Dragon: A Romance of Lief the Lucky.* Toronto: McClelland and Stewart, 1927.

————. *The Viking Heart.* 1923. New Canadian Library 116. Toronto: McClelland and Stewart, 1975.

————. *Wayside Gleams.* Toronto: McClelland and Stewart, 1925.

————. *When Sparrows Fall.* Toronto: Thomas Allen, 1925.

Sigbjörnsson, Rannveig K.G. *In Days Gone By.* Ilfracombe, Devon: Stockwell, 1955.

————. *Pebbles on the Beach.* Treherne, Man.: Treherne Times, 1936.

Sigurdson, Gus. *Seven Books Between Two Covers: The Complete Poetical Works of Gus Sigurdson.* Winnipeg: Wheatfield, 1987.

Sigurdson, Paul. *Not of an Age.* Morden, Man.: private publication, [1992].

Sigurgeirsson, V.J. *The Sigurgeirsson Saga.* N.p.: privately printed, 1979.

Stefansson, Vilhjalmur. *Discovery: The Autobiography of Vilhjalmur Stefansson.* New York: McGraw-Hill, 1964.

Stephansson (Sveinsson), Edward L. *Identity: Autobiography of Edward L. Stephansson.* Belleville: Warwick and Weeks, 1979.

Stephansson, Stephan G. *Andvökur: úrval.* [Sleepless Nights: A Selection] Ed. Sigurður Nordal. Reykjavík: Mál og Menning, 1939.

————. *Andvökur.* [Sleepless Nights] 6 vols. Eds. Nokkrir Íslendingar í Vesturheimi. Reykjavík/Winnipeg: 1909-1938.

————. *Bréf og Ritgerðir.* [Letters and Essays] 4 vols. Ed. Þorkell Jóhannesson. Reykjavík: Hið Íslenzka Þjóðvinsfélag, 1938.

————. *Selected Prose and Poetry.* Trans. and ed. Kristjana Gunnars. Writing West Series. Red Deer: Red Deer College Press, 1988.

————. *Selected Translations from Andvökur.* Edmonton: The Stephan G. Stephansson Homestead Restoration Committee, 1987.

————. *Vígslóði.* [Battlefield] Reykjavík: Bókaverzlun Ársæls Árnasonar, 1920.

Sveinbjörnsson, Helen. *Cloth of Gold and Other Poems.* Ilfracombe, Devon: Stockwell, 1973.

Thorvaldson, Skapti. *Sveinn Thorvaldsson MBE: A Family Chronicle.* Manitoba: Skapti Thorvaldsson and the Canada Iceland Foundation, 1984.

Valgardson, W.D. *Bloodflowers.* Ottawa: Oberon, 1973.

————. *Carpenter of Dreams.* Victoria: Skaldhus, 1986.

————. *Gentle Sinners.* Ottawa: Oberon, 1980.

————. *The Girl with the Botticelli Face.* Vancouver: Douglas & McIntyre, 1993.

————. *God is not a Fish Inspector.* Ottawa: Oberon, 1975.

————. *In the Gutting Shed.* Winnipeg: Turnstone, 1976.

————. *Red Dust.* Ottawa: Oberon, 1978.

————. *What Can't Be Changed Shouldn't Be Mourned.* Vancouver: Douglas & McIntyre, 1990.

Vestan um Haf. [West across the Ocean; a collection of Western Icelandic writing] Eds. Einar H. Kvaran and Guðmundur Finnbogason. Reykjavík: Bókadeild Menningarsjóðs, 1930.

Wylie, Betty Jane. *Something Might Happen.* Windsor: Black Moss, 1989.

REFERENCES

Aðalsteinsson, Jón Hnefill. "Þjóðtrú." [Folk-belief] *Íslensk Þjóðmenning* [Icelandic national culture].Vol. 5. Ed. Frosti F. Jóhannsson. Reykjavík: Bókaútgáfan Þjóðsaga, 1988. 341-400.

Almqvist, Bo. "Um Ákvæðaskáld." [About poet-magicians] *Skírnir* 135 (1961): 72-98.

Alver, Brynjulf. "Folklore and National Identity." *Nordic Folklore: Recent Studies.* Eds. Reimund Kvideland and Henning K. Sehmsdorf. Bloomington: Indiana University Press, 1989. 12-20.

Andersson, Theodore M. "The Displacement of the Heroic Ideal in the Family Sagas." *Speculum* 45.4 (1970): 575-93.

————. *The Icelandic Family Saga: An Analytic Reading.* Harvard Studies in Comparative Literature 28. Cambridge: Harvard University Press, 1967.

Andrésson, Kristinn. "Sjálfstætt Fólk. Hetjusaga." [Independent People. A Heroic Tale] *Um íslenskar bókmenntir: ritgerðir.* [About Icelandic literature: essays] Vol. 1. Reykjavík: Mál og Menning, 1976. 122-29.

Andrusyshen, C.H. "Canadian Ethnic Literary and Cultural Perspectives." *The Undoing of Babel: Watson Kirkconnell, the Man and his Work.* Ed. J.R.C. Perkin. Toronto: McClelland and Stewart, 1975. 31-49.

Anon. rev. of *The Viking Heart. Lögberg* 8 Nov. 1923: 6.

"A/PART," see Bumsted, J.M.

Arnason, David. "Dislocations." *Prairie Fire* 5.2 (1984): 109-10.

———. "Icelandic Canadian Literature." *Identifications: Ethnicity and the Writer in Canada*. Ed. Jars Balan. Edmonton: Canadian Institute of Ukrainian Studies, University of Alberta Press, 1982. 53-66.

———. "The Myth of Beginnings." *Border Crossings* 7.4 (1988): 9-11; Rpt. in *The New Icelanders: A North American Community*. Winnipeg: Turnstone, 1994. 3-8.

Árnason, Guðmundur. "Arfurinn." [The heritage] *Tímarit Þjóðræknisfélags Íslendinga í Vesturheimi* 5 (1923): 97-103.

———. "Íslenzkar og aðrar útlendar bókmentir í Canada." [Icelandic and other foreign literature in Canada] *Tímarit Þjóðræknisfélags Íslendinga í Vesturheimi* 21 (1939): 30-39.

———. "Tvenn Sambönd," [Dual bonds] *Vestan um Haf*. Eds. Einar H. Kvaran and Guðmundur Finnbogason. Reykjavík: Bókadeild Menningarsjóðs, 1930. 705-17.

Árnason, Jón. *Íslenzkar þjóðsögur og ævintýri*. [Icelandic folk and fairy tales] Rev. edn. Eds. Árni Böðvarsson and Bjarni Vilhjálmsson. 6 vols. Reykjavík: Bókaútgáfan Þjóðsaga, 1954-61.

Atwood, Margaret. Introduction. *The New Oxford Book of Canadian Verse in English*. Ed. Atwood. Toronto: Oxford University Press, 1982. xxvii-xxxix.

———. *Survival: A Thematic Guide to Canadian Literature*. Toronto: Anansi, 1972.

———. "Valgardsonland." Rev. of *Red Dust*, by W.D. Valgardson. *Essays on Canadian Writing* 16 (1979-80): 187-90.

Auden, W. H. "The World of the Sagas." *Secondary Worlds: The T.S. Eliot Memorial Lectures*. London: Faber and Faber, 1968. 47-84.

Babcock, Melinda. "Icelandic Folk Tales or National Tales." *Journal of the Anthropological Society of Oxford* 7.2 (1976): 78-86.

Balan, Jars, ed. *Identifications: Ethnicity and the Writer in Canada*. Edmonton: Canadian Institute of Ukrainian Studies, University of Alberta, 1982.

Barth, Fredrik. *Ethnic Groups and Boundaries: The Social Organization of Culture Difference*. Bergen/Oslo: Universitetsforlaget; London: George Allen & Unwin, 1969.

Bauschatz, Paul C. *The Well and the Tree: World and Time in Early Germanic Culture*. Amherst: University of Massachusetts Press, 1982.

Bayerschmidt, Carl F. "The Element of the Supernatural in the Sagas of the Icelanders." *Scandinavian Studies: Essays Presented to Henry G. Leach*. Eds. C.F. Bayerschmidt and Erik J. Friis. Seattle: University of Washington Press, 1965. 39-53.

Beattie, Munro. "Poetry 1920-1935"; "Poetry 1935-1950"; "Poetry 1950-1960." *Literary History of Canada.* Ed. Carl F. Klinck. Toronto: University of Toronto Press, 1970. 724-817.

Beck, Richard. "Bókmenntaiðja Íslendinga í Vesturheimi." [The literary activities of Icelanders in North America] *Eimreiðin* 34 (1928): 41-69, 321-40; 35 (1929): 49-62.

————, ed. *Icelandic Lyrics, Originals and Translations.* Reykjavík: Þórhallur Bjarnason, 1930.

————. *Guttormur J. Guttormsson, skáld.* [Guttormur J. Guttormsson, poet] Winnipeg: Columbia, 1949.

————. *A History of Icelandic Poets 1800-1940.* Ithaca: Cornell University Press, 1950.

————. "Höfuðskáld norðmanna vestan hafs." [The pre-eminent author of the North American Norwegians] *Skírnir* 109 (1935): 118-35.

————. *Í Átthagana: andinn leitar.* [In my native region: the spirit searches] Akureyri: Bókafélag Odds Björnssonar, 1957.

————. "Jóhann Magnús Bjarnason." *Gimsteinaborgin.* By Jóhann Magnús Bjarnason. Vol. 1 of *Ritsafn* [the collected works]. Ed. Arni Bjarnarson. Akureyri/Reykjavík: Bókaútgáfa Edda, 1977. v-xxvii.

————. "Kristján N. Júlíus (K.N.)." *Kviðlingar og Kvæði.* By K.N. Júlíus. Ed. Beck. Reykjavík: Bókfellsútgáfan, 1945. xi-xxii.

————. "Kveðja og þökk: ræða flutt við jarðarför Kristjáns N. Júlíusar skálds." [Greeting and thanks: a speech delivered at the funeral of the poet Kristján N. Júlíus] *Heimskringla* 4 Nov. 1936: 2-3.

————. "Með alþjóð fyrir keppinaut." [With the whole population as competitor] *Eimreiðin* 66 (1969): 252-63.

————. "Stephan G. Stephansson." *The American-Scandinavian Review* 44.2 (1956): 151-56.

————. "Vestur-íslenzk ljófskáld." *Tímarit Þjófræknisfélags Íslendinga í Vesturheimi* 32 (1951): 39-70.

————. "Yrkisefni vestur-íslenskra skálda." [Subjects of Western Icelandic Poets] *Skírnir* 129 (1955): 95-117.

————. *Ættland og Erfðir.* [Native earth and heritage] Reykjavík: Bókaútgáfan Norðri, 1950.

Beckmann, Susan. "Language as Cultural Identity." *Language and Literature in Multicultural Contexts.* Ed. Satendra Nandan. ACLALS 5th Triennial Conference Proceedings. Suva, Fiji: University of South Pacific and ACLALS, 1983. 66-78.

Benediktsson, Gunnar. "Harmkímin þjóð." [A tragicomic nation] *Tímarit Máls og Menningar* 2.3 (1950): 229-41.

Benediktsson, Gunnar. "Útilegumennirnir og þjóðin." [The outlaws and the people] *Eimreiðin* 46 (1940): 122-28.

Benedikz, B.S. "Basic Themes in Icelandic Folklore." *Folklore* 84 (1973): 1-26.

———. "The Master Magician in Icelandic Folk-Legend." *Durham University Journal* n.s. 26 (1964): 22-34.

Bennett, Donna. "On the Margin." *Canadian Forum* 67 (April 1987): 17-25.

Berg, Arie van den. "'Ik denk dat het land weet dat we vreemden zijn': Notities bij de Engels-Canadese Poëzie." *Bzzletin* 152 (1988): 59-64.

Bessason, Haraldur. "New Light on Vinland from the Sagas." *Mosaic* 1.1 (1967a): 52-65.

———. "Where the Limitations of Language and Geography Cease to Exist." *The Icelandic Canadian* 24.4 (1967b): 47-53, 72-76.

———. "Þar sem þumlungarnir gleymast." [Where measurements are forgotten] *Tímarit Þjóðræknisfélags Íslendinga í Vesturheimi* 46 (1965): 25-28.

———, and Robert Glendinning, eds. *Edda: A Collection of Essays.* Winnipeg: University of Manitoba Press, 1983.

Billings, Robert. "Regionalism and Internationalism." *Waves* 11.2-3 (1983): 37-47.

Bissoondath, Neil. *Selling Illusions: The Cult of Multiculturalism.* Toronto: Penguin, 1994.

Bjarnar, Vilhjálmur. "The Laki Eruption and the Famine of the Mist." *Scandinavian Studies: Essays Presented to Henry G. Leach.* Eds. Carl F. Bayerschmidt and Erik J. Friis. Seattle: University of Washington Press, 1965. 410-25.

Bjarnason, Jón. "Íslands þúsund ár." [Iceland's thousand years] *Rit og Ræður.* Winnipeg: Hið Evangeliska Lútherska Kirkjufélag Íslendinga í Vesturheimi, 1946. 205-18.

Bjartmarsdóttir, Guðrún. "Ljúflingar og fleiri fólk—um formgerð, hugmyndafræði og hlutverk íslenskra huldufólkssagna." [Male elves and other folk—about the structure, ideology and function of Icelandic elf-stories] *Tímarit Máls og Menningar* 43.3 (1982): 319-36.

Björnsson, S.E. "Móðurmálið." [The mother tongue] *Tímarit Þjóðræknisfélag Íslendinga í Vesturheimi* 42 (1960): 38-39.

Bobak, E.L. "Seeking 'Direct, Honest Realism': the Canadian Novel of the 20s." *Canadian Literature* 89 (1981): 85-101.

The Book of Settlements—Landnámabók, see Pálsson, Hermann.

Boucher, Alan. "The Hero in Old Icelandic Literature." *Iceland Review* 8.3 (1970): 41-45.

Brjef frá Ameríku, see Magnússon, Skúli.

Brydon, Anne. "Celebrating Ethnicity: The Icelanders of Manitoba."
M.A. Thesis. Hamilton: McMaster University, 1987.
————. "The Icelanders of Canada." *The Peoples of Canada: An
Encyclopedia for the Country*. Multicultural History Society of Ontario.
Toronto: University of Toronto Press, 1997 [forthcoming].
Brydon, Diana. "Landscape and Authenticity: The Development of
National Literatures in Canada and Australia." *Dalhousie Review* 61.2
(1981): 278-90.
Bumsted, J.M. Ed. "A/PART: Papers from the 1984 Conference on
Languages, Culture, and Literary Identity in Canada." *Canadian
Literature* Suppl. 1 (May 1987).
Buss, Helen M. *Mapping Our Selves: Canadian Women's Autobiography in
English*. Montreal/Kingston: McGill/Queen's University Press, 1993.
Bynum, David E. *The Daemon in the Wood: A Study of Oral Narrative
Patterns*. Cambridge, MA: Harvard University Presss, 1978.
Byock, Jesse L. *Feud in the Icelandic Saga*. Berkeley: University of
California Press, 1982.
————. "Inheritance and Ambition in *Eyrbyggja saga*." *Sagas of the
Icelanders: A Book of Essays*. Ed. John Tucker. New York/London:
Garland, 1989. 185-205.
————. "Íslendingasögur og kenningar um formgerð frásagna." [Sagas
of the Icelanders and theories on narrative structure] Trans. Gísli
Sigurðsson. *Tímarit Máls og Menningar* 51.2 (1990): 21-39.
————. *Medieval Iceland: Society, Sagas, and Power*. Berkeley: University of
California Press, 1988.
The Canadian Imagination, see Staines, David.
Carleton, Peter. *Tradition and Innovation in 20th-century Icelandic Poetry*. Diss.
University of California, 1967. Ann Arbor: UMI, 1974.
Carpenter, Carole H. "The Ethnicity Factor in Anglo-Canadian
Folkloristics." 1975. *Explorations in Canadian Folklore*. Eds. Edith
Fowke and Carpenter. Toronto: McClelland and Stewart, 1985. 340-86.
————. *Many Voices: A Study of Folklore Activities in Canada and their Role
in Canadian Culture*. CCFCS Mercury Series 26. Ottawa: National
Museum of Man, 1979.
Chadwick, Nora. "Dreams in Early European Literature." *Celtic Studies:
Essays in Memory of Angus Matheson 1912-1962*. London: Routledge
and Kegan Paul, 1968. 33-50.
————. "Norse Ghosts." *Folklore* 57 (1946): 50-65: 106-27.
Chanady, Amaryll. "The Origins and Development of Magic Realism in
Latin American Fiction." *Magic Realism and Canadian Literature: Essays*

and Stories. Eds. Peter Hinchcliffe and Ed Jewinski. Waterloo Ont.: University of Waterloo Press, 1986. 49-59.

Ciklamini, Marlene. "The Folktale in *Heimskringla.*" *Folklore* 90 (1979): 204-16.

Clover, Carol J. *The Medieval Saga.* Ithaca, NY: Cornell University Press, 1982.

———. "Skaldic Sensibility." *Arkiv för Nordisk Filologi* 93 (1978): 63-81.

Clunies Ross, Margaret. "Why Skaði Laughed: Comic Seriousness in Old Norse Mythic Narrative." *Maal og Minne* 12 (1989): 1-14.

Craig, Terrence L. "The Confessional Revisited: Laura Salverson's Canadian Work." *Studies in Canadian Literature* 10.1-2 (1985a): 81-93.

———. "F.P. Grove and the 'Alien' Immigrant in the West." *Journal of Canadian Studies* 20.2 (1985b): 92-100.

Crean, Susan. "Cracks in the Mosaic." *Border Crossings* 5.4 (1986): 9-11.

Dahlie, Hallvard. *Varieties of Exile: The Canadian Experience.* Vancouver: University of British Columbia Press, 1986.

D'Arcy, Julian Meldon, and Kirsten Wolf. "The Sources of Jóhann Magnús Bjarnason's *Íslenzkt hejjarmenni.*" *Scandinavica* 31.1 (1992): 21-32.

Davey, Frank. "The Explorer in Western Canadian Literature." *Studies in Canadian Literature* 4.2 (1979): 91-100.

Davidson, H.R. Ellis. "Hostile Magic in the Icelandic Sagas." *The Witch Figure: Folklore Essays by a Group of Scholars in England Honouring the 75th Birthday of Katharine M. Briggs.* Ed. Venetia Newall. London: Routledge and Kegan Paul, 1973. 20-39.

———. "Loki and Saxo's Hamlet." *The Fool and the Trickster: Studies in Honour of Enid Welsford.* Ed. Paul V.A. Williams. Cambridge: Brewer, 1979. 3-17.

———. *The Road to Hel: A Study of the Conception of the Dead in Old Norse Literature.* Cambridge: Cambridge University Press, 1943.

Demchuk, David. "'Holding Two Ropes': Interview with Kristjana Gunnars." *Writers News Manitoba/Prairie Fire* 5.2-3 (1984): 32-37.

Derry, T.K. *A History of Scandinavia.* London: George Allen and Unwin, 1979.

Dronke, Ursula. "The Poet's Persona in the Skald's Saga." *Parergon* 22 (1978): 23-28.

Durrenberger, E. Paul. "Icelandic Saga Heroes: The Anthropology of Natural Existentialists." *Anthropology and Humanism Quarterly* 9 (1984): 3-8.

———. "Sagas, Totems, and History." *Samfélagstíðindi* 5.1 (1985): 51-80.

Edda, see Bessason, Haraldur.

Edwards, John. *Language, Society, Identity.* London/New York: Basil Blackwell, 1985.

Einarsson, Indriði. "Íslendingar vakna." [Icelanders awaken] *Tímarit Þjóðræknisfélags Íslendinga í Vesturheimi* 1 (1919): 55-65.

Einarsson, Magnús. "The Folklore of New Iceland." *Tímarit Þjóðræknisfélags Íslendinga í Vesturheimi* 50 (1969): 67-73.

————. *Icelandic-Canadian Oral Narratives.* CCFCS Mercury Series 63. Hull, Qc.: Canadian Museum of Civilization, 1991.

————. "Oral Tradition and Ethnic Boundaries: 'West' Icelandic Verses and Anecdotes." *Canadian Ethnic Studies* 7.2 (1975): 19-32.

Einarsson, Stefán. *A History of Icelandic Literature.* New York: Johns Hopkins University Press, 1957.

————. *A History of Icelandic Prose Writers.* Ithaca, NY: Cornell University Press, 1948.

————. *Íslensk Bókmenntasaga 874-1960.* [A history of Icelandic literature 874-1960] Reykjavík: Snæbjörn Jónsson, 1961.

————. "Vestur-íslensk skáldkona." [A Western Icelandic authoress; about Guðrún Helga Finnsdóttir] *Eimreiðin* 53 (1947): 10-26.

————. "Vestur-íslenzkir rithöfundar í lausu máli." [Western Icelandic Prose Writers] *Tímarit Þjóðræknisfélag Íslendinga í Vesturheimi* 32 (1951): 17-38.

Elford, Jean. "The Icelanders: Their Ontario Year." *Beaver* 304 (1974): 53-58.

Eliade, Mircea. *The Myth of the Eternal Return.* Bollingen Series 46. Princeton: Princeton University Press, 1974.

Ellis, Hilda R. See Davidson, H.R. Ellis.

Enright, Robert. "Storyforming: David Arnason's Addictive Fictional World." *Arts Manitoba* 4.2 (1985): 8-10.

Eyjólfsson, Sæmundur. "Um Óðin í alþýðutrú síðara tíma." [About Odin in later folk-belief] *Tímarit Íslenzka Bókmentafjelag* 15 (1894): 134-97.

Eylands, Valdimar. *Lutherans in Canada.* Winnipeg: Icelandic Evangelical Lutheran Synod in North America, 1945.

Fairbanks, Carol. "Lives of Girls and Women on the Canadian and American Prairies." *International Journal of Women's Studies* 2.5 (1979): 452-72.

————. *Prairie Women: Images in American and Canadian Fiction.* New Haven: Yale University Press, 1986.

Farquharson, Rica. "Northern Races." Rev. of *Tanya,* by Kristine B. Kristofferson. *Saturday Night* 3 Nov. 1951: 22.

Finnbogason, Guðmundur. *Íslendingar—nokkur drög að þjóðarlýsingu.*
[Icelanders: some sketches towards a national description] 1933. Abr.
edn. Ed. Finnbogi Guðmundsson. Reykjavík: Almenna Bókafélagið,
1971.

———. "Um ljóðin og leikritin." [About the poems and plays; intro-
duction] *Vestan um Haf.* Eds. Einar H. Kvaran and Guðmundur
Finnbogason. Reykjavík: Bókadeild Menningarsjóðs, 1930. xxvii-
xxxviii.

"Fjölnir." *Fjölnir* 1 (1835): 1-17.

Fleck, Jere. "Óðinn's Self-Sacrifice: A New Interpretation." *Scandinavian
Studies* 43 (1971): 119-42, 385-414.

Foote, Peter. "Wrecks and Rhymes." *Aurvandilstá: Norse Studies.* Eds.
Michael Barnes, Hans Bekker-Nielsen *et al.* The Viking Collection:
Studies in Northern Civilization 2. Odense: Odense University Press,
1984. 222-35.

———, ed. *The Saga of Grettir the Strong.* Trans. G.A. Hight. Everyman's
Classics. London: Dent, 1972.

Framfari 1877-1880, see Houser, George.

Francis, R. Douglas. "Changing Images of the West." *Journal of Canadian
Studies* 17 (1982): 5-19.

Friðþjófsson, Sigurður V. "Kolbeinslag Stephans G. Stephanssonar."
[Kolbein's metre by Stephan G. Stephansson] *Tvær ritgerðir um
kveðskap Stephans G. Stephanssonar.* [Two essays about Stephan G.
Stephansson's poetry] Ed. Steingrímur J. Þorsteinsson. *Studia Islandica*
19. Reykjavík: Leiftur 1961. 95-181.

Friesen, Gerald. *The Canadian Prairies: A History.* Toronto: University of
Toronto Press, 1984.

Frye, Northrop. Conclusion. *Literary History of Canada.* Ed. Carl F.
Klinck. Toronto: University of Toronto Press, 1970. 821-49. Rpt. in
The Bush Garden. Toronto: Anansi, 1971. 213-51.

Furuland, Lars. "The Swedish-American Press: the Literary Institution of
the Immigrants." *From Scandinavia to America: Proceedings from a
Conference held at Gl. Holtegaard.* Eds. Steffen Jørgensen *et al.* Odense:
Odense University Press, 1987. 290-98.

Gans, Herbert J. "Symbolic Ethnicity: The Future of Ethnic Groups and
Cultures in America." *Ethnic and Racial Studies* 2.1 (1979): 1-20.

Gibbon, John Murray. *Canadian Mosaic: The Making of a Northern Nation.*
Toronto: McClelland and Stewart, 1938.

Givner, Joan. "Strangers in a Strange Land." Rev. of *The Axe's Edge*, by
Kristjana Gunnars. *Books in Canada* 13 (March 1984): 16-17.

Gjerset, Knut. *History of Iceland.* New York: Macmillan, 1924.

Glendinning, Robert J. *"Grettis saga* and European literature in the late Middle Ages." *Mosaic* 4.2 (1970): 49-61.

Godard, Barbara. "The Oral Tradition and Contemporary Fiction." *Essays on Canadian Writing* 7-8 (1977): 46-62.

Gold, Gerald L., and Robert Paine. Introduction. *Minorities and Mother Country Imagery.* Ed. Gold. St. Johns: Institute of Social and Economic Research, Memorial University of Newfoundland, 1984. 1-16.

Goldie, Terry. "Folklore in the Canadian Novel." *Canadian Folklore* 3.2 (1981): 93-101.

Gordon, E.V. *An Introduction to Old Norse.* 1927. 2nd rev. edn. Oxford: Oxford University Press, 1957.

Gould, Ed. "Making Them Measure Up: Interview with Bill Valgardson." *Canadian Author and Bookman* 54.1 (1979): 16-18.

Gov't of Canada. Royal Commission on Bilingualism and Biculturalism. *The Cultural Contribution of the Other Ethnic Groups.* Vol. 4. Ottawa: Queen's Printer, 1969.

Grace, Sherrill E. "Duality and Series: Forms of the Canadian Imagination." *Canadian Review of Comparative Literature* 7.4 (1980): 438-51.

Greenway, John L. *The Golden Horns: Mythic Imagination and the Nordic Past.* Athens: University of Georgia Press, 1977.

————. "The Wisdom of Njal: Representation of Reality in the Family Sagas." *Mosaic* 4.2 (1970): 15-26.

Grimstad, Kaaren. "The Giant as Heroic Model: The Case of Egill and Starkaðr." *Scandinavian Studies* 48.3 (1977): 284-98.

Gröndal, Benedict. *Um vesturheimsferðir* and *Enn um vesturheimsferðir.* [About the Emigration and Again about the Emigration] Reykjavík: Ísafoldarprentsmiðja, 1888.

Guðmundsson, Bragi, and Gunnar Karlsson. *Uppruni Nútímans.* Reykjavík: Mál og Menning, 1988.

Guðmundsson, Finnbogi, ed. *Bréf til Stephans G. Stephanssonar: úrval.* [Letters to Stephan G. Stephansson: a selection] 3 vols. Reykjavík: Icelandic Cultural Fund, 1971-75.

————. *Að Vestan og Heiman.* Reykjavík: Leiftur, 1967.

————. *Stephan G. Stephansson In Retrospect: Seven Essays.* Reykjavík: Icelandic Cultural Fund, 1982.

Guðmundsson, Gils, ed. *Öldin sem leið: minnisverð tíðindi 1861-1900.* [The past century: memorable events 1861-1900] Reykjavík: Iðunn, 1956.

Gunnars, Kristjana. "Ethnicity and Canadian Women Writers." *Room of One's Own* 14.4 (1991): 40-50.

Gunnars, Kristjana, ed. Introduction. *Unexpected Fictions: New Icelandic Canadian Writing.* Winnipeg: Turnstone, 1989. xi-xx.

———. "Laura Goodman Salverson's Confessions of a Divided Self." *A Mazing Space: Writing Canadian Women Writing.* Eds. Shirley Newman and Smaro Kamboureli. Edmonton: Longspoon/NeWest, 1986. 148-53.

———, ed. Preface. *Stephan G. Stephansson: Selected Prose and Poetry.* By Stephansson. Red Deer: Red Deer College Press, 1988. vii-xi.

———. "Voyage on a Dark Ocean: Interview with W.D. Valgardson." *The Icelandic Canadian* 67.3 (1989): 14-19.

———. "Words on Multilingualism." *Prairie Fire* 5.2-3 (1984): 7-8.

Gunnarsdóttir, Ingibjörg Ásta. "Landnám og samsemd: Vesturheimsferðir Íslendinga." [Settlement and identification: the Icelandic emigration to North America] Thesis. University of Iceland, 1987.

Guttormsson, Guttormur. "Þjóðararfur og þjóðrækni." [National heritage and nationalism] *Vestan um Haf.* Eds. Einar H. Kvaran and Guðmundur Finnbogason. Reykjavík: Bókadeild Menningarsjóðs, 1930. 687-704.

Guttormsson, Guttormur J. "Frá landnámsöldinni." [From the age of settlement] *Tímarit Þjóðræknisfélags Íslendinga í Vesturheimi* 27 (1946): 36-39.

———. "Sigurður Júl. Jóhannesson og íslenzka hagyrðingafélagið." [Sigurður Júl. Jóhannesson and the Icelandic versemakers' society] *Eimreiðin* 72 (1966): 152-60.

———. "Tveir þættir." [Two stories] *Andvari* 17 (1975): 75-92.

Haglund, Diane. "W. D. Valgardson on Writing." *Alumni Press,* University of Winnipeg (Summer 1980): 40-43. Rpt. in *The Icelandic Canadian* 59 (1981): 25-27.

Hallberg, Peter. *Halldór Laxness.* Trans. Rory McTurk. Twayne's World Authors Series 89. New York: Twayne, 1971.

———. "Halldór Laxness and the Icelandic Sagas." *Leeds Studies of English* 16 (1982): 1-17.

———. *The Icelandic Saga.* Trans. Paul Schach. Lincoln: University of Nebraska Press, 1962.

———. *Old Icelandic Poetry.* Trans. Paul Schach and Sonja Lindgrendson. Lincoln: University of Nebraska Press, 1975.

———. "The Syncretic Saga Mind: A Discussion of a New Approach to the Icelandic Sagas." *Mediaeval Scandinavia* 7 (1974): 102-17.

Halldórs frá Höfnum, Sigfús. "Hagur Norðanlands við upphaf Vesturflutninganna." [Circumstances in Northern Iceland during the beginnings of emigration] *Tímarit Þjóðræknisfélags Íslendinga í Vesturheimi* 8 (1926): 79-90.

Halldórsson, Óskar. *Bókmenntir á lærdómsöld.* [Literature during the Age of Learning] Reykjavík: Hið íslenska bókmenntafélag/Sögufélagið, 1977.

———. "Á Ferð og Flugi eftir Stephan G. Stephansson." [En Route by Stephan G. Stephansson] *Tvær ritgerðir um kveðskap Stephans G. Stephanssonar.* [Two Essays on the Poetry of Stephan G. Stephansson] Ed. Steingrímur J. Þorsteinsson. *Studia Islandica* 19. Reykjavík: Leiftur, 1961. 9-94.

Hamel, A.G. van. "Gods, Skalds, and Magic." *Saga-Book of the Viking Society* 11 (1936): 129-52.

Hancock, Geoff. "An Interview with W.D. Valgardson." *Canadian Fiction Magazine* 32-33 (1979-80): 120-34.

———. "Magic or Realism: The Marvellous in Canadian Fiction." *Magic Realism and Canadian Literature: Essays and Stories.* Eds. Peter Hinchcliffe and Ed Jewinski. Waterloo, Ont.: University of Waterloo Press, 1986. 30-48.

Haraldsson, Erlendur. "Are we Sensitive or Superstitious?" *Iceland Review* 15.4 (1977): 30-34.

Harpham, Geoffrey Galt. *On the Grotesque: Strategies of Contradiction in Art and Literature.* Princeton: Princeton University Press, 1982.

Harris, Joseph. "Genre and Narrative Structure in Some *Íslendinga Þættir.*" *Scandinavian Studies* 44.1 (1972): 1-27.

———. "Theme and Genre in Some *Íslendinga Þættir.*" *Scandinavian Studies* 48.1 (1976): 1-28.

Harrison, Dick. *Unnamed Country: The Struggle for a Canadian Prairie Fiction.* Edmonton: University of Alberta Press, 1977.

Haskins, Charles H. *The Renaissance of the Twelfth Century.* Cambridge: Harvard University Press, 1927.

Hastrup, Kirsten. "Establishing an Ethnicity: The Emergence of the 'Icelanders' in the Early Middle Ages." *Semantic Anthropology.* Ed. David Parkin. ASA Monographs 22. New York/London: Academic Press, 1982. 145 60.

———. "Tracing Tradition: An Anthropological Perspective on *Grettis saga Ásmundarsonar.*" *Structure and Meaning in Old Norse Literature: New Approaches to Textual Analysis and Literary Criticism.* Eds. John Lindow *et al.* The Viking Collection: Studies in Northern Civilization 3. Odense: Odense University Press, 1986. 281-313.

Hjartarson, Paul. "Transformation of the 'I': Self and Community in the Poetry of Kristjana Gunnars." *Canada and the Nordic Countries: Proceedings from the Second Internationl Conference of the Nordic Association for Canadian Studies*. Eds. Jørn Carlsen and Bengt Streijffert. Lund Studies in English 78. Lund, Sweden: Lund University Press, 1988. 123-37.

Hofman, Dietrich. "Die Einstellung der isländischen Sagaverfasser und ihrer Vorgänger zur mündlichen Tradition." *Oral Tradition—Literary Tradition, a Symposium*. Eds. Hans Bekker-Nielsen *et al*. Odense: Odense University Press, 1977. 9-27.

Hollander, Lee M., trans. *The Poetic Edda*. 1962. 2nd rev. edn. Austin: University of Texas Press, 1990.

Holm, Bill. "Kristjan Niels Julius (K.N.): A Four-Part Project." *Lögberg-Heimskringla* 7 Dec. 1990: 2.

Holme, John G. "Iceland's Younger Choir." *American Scandinavian Review* 10.9 (1922): 550-55.

Höskuldsson, Sveinn Skorri. "Í minningu Guttorms." [In memory of Guttormur] *Andvari* 22 (1980): 71-82.

———. "Ófeigur í Skörðum og félagar." *Skírnir* 144 (1970): 34-110.

Houser, George J. *Pioneer Icelandic Pastor: The Life of the Rev. Paul Thorlaksson*. Ed. Paul A. Sigurdson. Winnipeg: The Manitoba Historical Society, 1990.

———, trans. *Framfari* 1877-1880. 2 vols. Gimli: The Gimli Chapter of the Icelandic National League of North America, 1986.

Hreinsson, Viðar. "The Barnyard Poet Stephan G. Stephansson (1853-1927)." Lecture. Nordic Experiences: Exploration of Scandinavian Cultures—Interdisciplinary Conference in Celebration of the 150th Anniversary of the Birth of Edvard Grieg (1843-1907). Hempstead, NY: Hofstra Cultural Center, 11-13 Nov. 1993a.

———. "The Power of the Word: Some Reflections on 'The Icelandic Academy'." *The Icelandic Canadian* 51.2 (1992): 90-104.

———. "Western Icelandic Literature 1870-1900." *Scandinavian-Canadian Studies* 6 (1993b): 1-14.

Hugason, Hjalti. "Kristnir trúarhættir." [Christian beliefs] *Íslensk þjóðmenning*. [Icelandic national culture] Vol. 5. Ed. Frosti F. Jóhannsson. Reykjavík: Bókaútgáfan Þjóðsaga, 1988. 75-339.

Hutcheon, Linda. *The Canadian Postmodern*. Toronto: Oxford University Press, 1988.

———. "Voices of Displacement." *Canadian Forum* 65 (June 1985): 33-39.

Hutcheon, Linda, and Marion Richmond, eds. *Other Solitudes: Canadian Multicultural Fictions*. Toronto: Oxford University Press, 1990.

Icelandic Lyrics, see Beck, Richard.

Identifications, see Balan, Lars.

Ingimundarson, Jón Haukur. "Hidden People and Social Experiences 'Remembered'." Unpublished Paper. Tucson: University of Arizona, 1988.

Ingstad, Anne Stine. *The Norse Discovery of America: Excavations of a Norse Settlement at L'Anse aux Meadows, Newfoundland 1961-1968*. Oslo: Norwegian University Press, 1985.

Ingstad, Helge. *Westward to Vinland: The Discovery of Pre-Columbian Norse House-sites in North America*. Trans. Erik J. Friis. New York: St. Martin's Press, 1969.

Islensk Bókmenntasaga, see Ólason, Vésteinn.

Johannessen, Matthías. *Njála í íslenzkum skáldskap*. [*Njáls saga* in Icelandic Poetry] Reykjavík: Hið Íslenzka Bókmenntafélag, 1958.

Johannesson, Sigurður Júlíus. "Framtíðarbókmentir Íslendinga í Vesturheimi." [The future of Icelandic Literature in North America] *Tímarit Þjóðræknisfélags Íslendinga í Vesturheimi* 33 (1951): 84-97.

Jóhannesson, Þorkell. *Lýðir og Landshagir*. [People and National Circumstances] Vol. 2. Reykjavík: Almenna Bókafélagið, 1966. 2 vols.

Johnson, O.T. "Frumbygð og fortíð." [The original settlement and the past] *Tímarit Þjóðræknisfélags Íslendinga í Vesturheimi* 17 (1935): 102-09.

Johnson, Skuli. "Einar Hjörleifsson Kvaran in Winnipeg." *The Icelandic Canadian* 7.1 (1948): 7-10, 48-52.

———. "Our Heritage." *The Icelandic Canadian* 9.1 (1950): 13-16.

———. "Stephan G. Stephansson (1853-1927)." *The Icelandic Canadian* 9.2 (1950): 9-12, 44-56.

Johnston, George. "Icelandic Rhythms." Rev. of *One-eyed Moon Maps* and *Settlement Poems*, by Kristjana Gunnars. *Canadian Literature* 92 (1982): 73-75.

———. "What Do the Scalds Tell Us?" *University of Toronto Quarterly* 52.1 (1982): 1-8.

———, trans. *The Saga of Gísli*. Toronto: University of Toronto/Dent, 1963.

Jónasson, Sigtryggur. "Are the Icelanders Born to Everlasting Hunger and Suffering?" Trans. George Houser. *Framfari* 5 April 1878: 173-76.

———. *The Early Icelandic Settlements in Canada*. Winnipeg: Manitoba Free Press, 1901.

Jones, D.G. "Canadian Poetry: Roots and New Directions." *Credences* 2.2-3 (1983): 254-75.

Jónsson, Baldur. "Guðspjöll og pistlar í *Vídalínspostillu.*" [The gospels and epistles in the *Vídalínspostilla*] *Afmælisrit til Dr Phil. Steingríms J. Þorsteinssonar, 2 júlí 1971, frá nemendum hans.* Eds. Aðalgeir Kristjánsson *et al.* Reykjavík: Leiftur 1971. 28-41.

Jónsson, Bergsteinn. "Aðdragandi og upphaf vesturferða af Íslandi á nítjándu öld." [Antecedents and beginnings of the emigration from Iceland during the nineteenth century] *Andvari* 17 (1975): 28-50.

Jónsson, Björn. "Fréttabréf frá Nýja-Íslandi." [Newsletter from New Iceland] *Andvari* 17 (1975): 64-74.

Jónsson, Einar Páll. "Í heimsókn hjá Helen Swinburne." [A visit with Helen Swinburne] *Tímarit Þjóðræknisfélags Íslendinga í Vesturheimi* 22 (1941): 85-86.

Jónsson, Gísli. Formáli. [Preface] *Ferðalok.* Akureyri: Árni Bjarnarson, 1950. 5-6.

———. "Gunnsteinn Eyjólfsson." *Eimreiðin* 19 (1913): 44-50.

———. "Hugleiðingar út af afmæli." [Reflections on account of a birthday] *Tímarit Þjóðræknisfélags Íslendinga í Vesturheimi* 30 (1949): 77-79.

Jónsson, Jakob. "Alþýðuskáldið Valdimar Pálsson." [The unschooled poet Valdimar Pálsson] *Tímarit Þjóðræknisfélags Íslendinga í Vesturheimi* 21 (1940): 75-80.

———. "Þegar Nýja Ísland var sjálfstætt ríki." [When New Iceland was an independent state] *Eimreiðin* 49 (1943): 116-26.

Jónsson frá Sleðbrjót, Jón. "Sundurlausar hugsanir." [Unconnected thoughts] *Tímarit Þjóðræknisfélags Íslendinga í Vesturheimi* 2 (1920): 74-81.

Jónsson, Magnús. "Jón biskup Vídalín og *Postilla* hans." [Bishop Jón Vídalín and his *Postilla*] *Eimreiðin* 26 (1920): 257-78.

———. *Tímabilið 1871-1903: Landshöfðingjatímabilið.* [The period 1871-1903: The Age of the Governors] Vol. 9.2 of *Saga Íslendinga.* [History of the Icelanders] Reykjavík: Menntamálaráð og þjóðvinafélag, 1958. 12 vols.

Jónsson, Þorsteinn M. *Spjall um íslenska þjóðtrú og þjóðsögur.* [Conversation about Icelandic folk-belief and folk tales] Akureyri: Prentsmiðja Björns Jónssonar, 1952.

Jung, Carl G. "On the Psychology of the Trickster Figure." *The Trickster: A Study in American Indian Mythology.* Ed. Paul Radin. New York: Philosophical Library, 1956. 195-211.

Kamboureli, Smaro, ed. *Making a Difference: Canadian Multicultural Literature.* Toronto: Toronto University Press, 1996.

Keith, W.J. *Canadian Literature in English.* London/New York: Longman 1985.

———. "Nature and the Literary Imagination." *Nature and the Literary Imagination.* Papers from the First Northern Literary Symposium. Ed. Vincent D. Sharman. North Bay, Ont.: Nipissing University College, 1984. 11-35.

Kelchner, Georgia Dunham. *Dreams in Old Norse Literature and their Affinities in Folklore.* Cambridge: Cambridge University Press, 1935.

Kerényi, Karl. "The Trickster in Relation to Greek Mythology." *The Trickster: A Study in American Indian Mythology.* Ed. Paul Radin. New York: Philosophical Library, 1956. 173-91.

Kirkconnell, Watson. "A Skald in Canada." *Transactions of the Royal Society of Canada* 3rd ser. sec. 2: 33 (1939): 107-121.

———. "Canada's Leading Poet: Stephan G. Stephansson (1853-1927)." *University of Toronto Quarterly* 5.2 (1936): 263-77.

———. *Canadian Overtones.* Winnipeg: Columbia, 1937.

———. "Four Decades of Icelandic Poetry in Canada 1922-62." *The Icelandic Canadian* 22.2 (1963): 17-27.

Kirshenblatt-Gimblett, Barbara. "Culture Shock and Narrative Creativity." *Folklore in the Modern World.* Ed. Richard M. Dorson. The Hague: Mouton, 1976. 109-121.

Kjartansson, Helgi Skúli. "The Onset of Emigration from Iceland." *American Studies in Scandinavia* 9 (1977): 87-93.

———. "Vesturfarir af Íslandi." [Emigration from Iceland] Diss. University of Iceland, 1976.

Kjartansson, Magnús. Rev. of *Kviðlingar og Kvæði,* by Káinn. *Tímarit Máls og Menningar* 7 (1946): 66-67.

Kolybaba, Kathie. Rev. of *Marsh Burning,* by David Arnason. *Arts Manitoba* 2.2 (1983): 57.

———. Rev. of *Settlement Poems* and *Wake-pick Poems,* by Kristjana Gunnars. *Arts Manitoba* 2.1 (1982): 70-71.

Kostjuk, Dwight. Rev. of *Settlement Poems,* by Kristjana Gunnars. *Canadian Ethnic Studies* 14.2 (1982): 156-58.

Kötlum, Jóhannes úr. "Hvað varðar okkur um Stephan G.?" [What concerns us about Stephan G. ?] *Skinfaxi* (1936): 3-15.

Kreisel, Henry. "The Prairie: A State of Mind." *Trace: Prairie Writers on Writing.* Ed. Birk Sproxton. Winnipeg: Turnstone, 1986. 3-17.

"Kristjana Gunnars," see May, Hal.

Kristjanson, Wilhelm. *The Icelandic People in Manitoba: A Manitoba Saga.* 1965. Winnipeg: R.W. Kristjansson, 1990.

Kristjansson, Gustaf. Rev. of *Settlement Poems*, by Kristjana Gunnars. *The Icelandic Canadian* 39.2 (1980): 40-41.

Kristjánsson, Jónas. "Bókmenntasaga 1100-1260." [Literary history 1100-1260] *Saga Íslands*. [History of Iceland] Vol. 2. Ed. Sigurður Lindal. Reykjavík: Hið Íslenska Bókmenntafélag/Sögufélagið, 1975. 147-258.

———. *Eddas and Sagas: Iceland's Medieval Literature*. Trans. Peter Foote. Reykjavík: Hið Íslenska Bókmenntafélag, 1988.

———. "Learned Style or Saga Style?" *Speculum Norroenum: Norse Studies in Memory of Gabriel Turville-Petre*. Eds. Ursula Dronke *et al*. Odense: Odense University Press, 1981. 260-92.

Kristjánsson, Sverrir. "Efnishyggja og húmanismi Stephans G. Stephanssonar." [The materialism and humanism of Stephan G. Stephansson] *Tímarit Máls og Menningar* 14 (1953): 121-32.

Kroetsch, Robert. "The Canadian Writer and the American Literary Tradition." *English Quarterly* 4.2 (1971): 45-49.

———. "Canadian Writing: No Name is My Name." *Dialog der Texte: Literatur und Landeskunde*. Eds. Franz Luna and Heinz Tschachler. Tübingen: Gunter Narr Verlag, 1986. 529-44.

———. "The Grammar of Silence: Narrative Patterns in Ethnic Writing." *Canadian Literature* 106 (1985): 65-74.

Kvaran, Einar Hjörleifsson. "Um sögurnar og ritgerðirnar og Vestur-Íslendinga." [About the stories and essays and the West Icelanders; introduction] *Vestan um haf*. Eds. Einar H. Kvaran and Guðmundur Finnbogason. Reykjavík: Bókadeild Menningarsjóðs, 1930. xxxix-lxiv.

———. *Vestur Íslendingar*. [West Icelanders] Reykjavík: Bókaverzlun Sigfúsar Eymundssonar, 1895.

Lane, M. Travis. "Troll Turning: Poetic Voice in the Poetry of Kristjana Gunnars." *Canadian Literature* 105 (1985): 59-68.

Lange, J. de. *The Relation and Development of English and Icelandic Outlaw Traditions*. Haarlem: Tjeenk Willink, 1935.

Laxness, Halldór. "Before the Sagas." *Adam International Review* 391-93 (1975): 7-19.

———. *Independent People*. Trans. J.A. Thompson. New York: Knopf, 1946. Trans. of *Sjálfstætt Fólk*. 1936.

———. *Íslendingaspjall*. [Conversation of Icelanders] Reykjavík: Helgafell, 1967.

———. "Landneminn mikli" [The great pioneer; about Stephan G. Stephansson]. *Af Skáldum*. [By poets] By Laxness. Reykjavík: Bókaútgáfa Menningarsjóðs, 1972. 7-17.

Laxness, Halldór. Rev. of *Saga Íslendinga í Vesturheimi*, by Þorsteinn Þ. Þorsteinsson. *Tímarit Máls og Menningar* 2 (1941): 83-86.

———. "Um Jónas Hallgrímsson." [About Jónas Hallgrímsson] *Af Skáldum*. Reykjavík: Bókaútgáfa Menningarsjóðs, 1972. 18-33.

Lee, Dennis. "Cadence, Country, Silence: Writing in Colonial Space." *Boundary* 2: 3.1 (1974): 151-68.

Lehmann, Winfred P. "On Reflections of Germanic Legal Terminology and Situations in the Edda." *Old Norse Literature and Mythology: A Symposium*. Ed. Edgar C. Polomé. Austin: University of Texas Press, 1969. 227-43.

Lenoski, Daniel S. Rev. of *Gentle Sinners*, by W.D. Valgardson. *Arts Manitoba* 2.1 (1982): 64-66.

Lewis Tom J., and Robert E. Jungman. Introduction. *On Being Foreign: Culture Shock in Short Fiction*. Eds. Lewis and Jungman. Yarmouth, ME: Intercultural, 1986.

Lid, Niels. "The Paganism of the Norsemen." *Studies in Folklore*. Ed. W. Edson Richmond. Bloomington: Indiana University Press, 1957. Westport: Greenwood, 1972. 230-51.

Lindal, Walter J. "Cultural Pursuits of the First Generations of Icelanders in Canada." *Canadian Ethnic Studies* 1.2 (1969): 1-12.

———. *The Icelanders in Canada*. Canada Ethnica Series 2. Ottawa: National Publishers; Winnipeg: Viking Printers, 1967.

Lindow, John. "A Mythic Model in *Bandamanna Saga* and its Significance." *Sagas of the Icelanders: A Book of Essays*. Ed. John Tucker. New York/London: Garland, 1989. 241-56.

———. "Narrative and the Nature of Skaldic Poetry." *Arkiv för Nordisk Filologi* 97 (1982): 94-121.

Literatures of Lesser Diffusion, see Pivato, Joseph.

Livesay, Dorothy. "The Canadian Documentary: An Overview." *Open Letter* 6.2-3 (1985): 127-30.

Lönnroth, Lars. *European Sources of Icelandic Saga Writing: An Essay Based on Previous Studies*. Stockholm: Lars Lönnröth, 1965.

———. "Rhetorical Persuasion in the Sagas." *Scandinavian Studies* 42.2 (1970): 157-89.

MacLulich, T.D. *Between Europe and America: The Canadian Tradition in Fiction*. Toronto: ECW, 1988.

———. "Novel and Romance." *Canadian Literature* 70 (1976): 42-50.

———. "Reading the Land: the Wilderness Tradition in Canadian Letters." *Journal of Canadian Studies* 20.2 (1985): 29-44.

Magnusson, Magnus, trans. *The Atom Station.* By Halldór Laxness. Sag Harbour, NY: Second Chance, 1982.

————, and Hermann Pálsson, trans. Introduction. *Laxdaela Saga.* London: Penguin, 1983. 9-42.

————, trans. Introduction. *Njal's Saga.* London: Penguin, 1982. 9-31.

————, trans. Introduction. *The Vinland Sagas: The Norse Discovery of America.* London: Penguin, 1965. 7-43.

Magnússon, Skúli, ed. and trans. *Brjef frá Ameríku.* [A letter from America] Reykjavík: Prentsmiðja Íslands—Einar Þórðarson, 1871.

Making A Difference, see Kamboureli, Smaro.

Mandel, Eli. "Ethnic Voice in Canadian Writing." *Identities: The Impact of Ethnicity on Canadian Society.* Ed. Wsevolod Isajiw. Canadian Ethnic Studies Association 5. Toronto: Peter Martin, 1977. 57-68.

————. "The Study of Canadian Culture." *English Quarterly* 4.3 (1971): 15-24.

Marlatt, Daphne. "Entering In: The Immigrant Imagination." *Canadian Literature* 100 (1984): 219-23.

Martin, John Stanley. *Ragnarök: An Investigation into the Old Norse Concepts of the Fate of the Gods.* Assen: Van Gorcum, 1972.

Matthews, John. "Colonial Societies in Search of Identity: Lifeboats for the Titanic." *Humanities Association Review* 30 (1979): 239-54.

Matthiasson, John S. "Adaptation to an Ethnic Structure: The Urban Icelandic-Canadians of Winnipeg." *The Anthropology of Iceland.* Eds. E. Paul Durrenberger and Gísli Pálsson. Iowa City: University of Iowa Press, 1989. 157-75.

————. "The Icelandic Canadians: The Paradox of an Assimilated Ethnic Group." *Two Nations, Many Cultures.* Ed. Jean Leonard Elliott. Scarborough, Ont.: Prentice Hall, 1979. 195-205.

————. "Icelandic-Canadians in Central Canada: One Experiment in Multiculturalism." *The Western Canadian Journal of Anthropology* 4.2 (1974): 49-61.

Matyas, Cathy. "Invoking the Dead." Rev. of *The Axe's Edge,* by Kristjana Gunnars. *Canadian Forum* 64 (June 1984): 35-36.

May, Hal, ed. "Kristjana Gunnars." *Contemporary Authors.* Detroit: Gale, 1985. 208-09.

McCourt, Edward. *The Canadian West in Fiction.* 1949. Toronto: Ryerson, 1970.

McCracken, Jane. "Stephan G. Stephansson: Icelandic-Canadian Poet and Freethinker." *Canadian Ethnic Studies* 15.1 (1983): 33-52.

McCracken, Jane. *Stephan G. Stephansson: The Poet of the Rocky Mountains.* N.p.: Alberta Culture, Historical Resources Division, Occasional Papers, No. 9, 1982.

McKenzie, Ruth. "Life in a New Land." *Canadian Literature* 7 (1961): 24-33.

McLuhan, Marshall. "Canada: The Borderline Case." *The Canadian Imagination: Dimensions of a Literary Culture.* Ed. David Staines. Cambridge: Harvard University Press, 1977. 226-49.

McPherson, Hugo. "Fiction 1940-1960." *Literary History of Canada.* Ed. Carl F. Klinck. Toronto: University of Toronto Press, 1970. 694-722.

McTurk, Rory. "'Áhrifafælni' í íslenskum bókmenntum." ['The Anxiety of Influence' in Icelandic literature] *Tímarit Máls og Menningar* 52 (1991): 74-81.

McVey, Moray. "The Emergence of a Canadian Voice in the *Settlement Poems* of Kristjana Gunnars." *Lögberg-Heimskringla* 19 Sept. 1986: 8-10.

Medieval Scandinavia: An Encyclopedia. Eds. Phillip Pulsiano and Kirsten Wolf. Garland Encyclopaedias of the Middle Ages 1. New York/London: Garland, 1993.

Meulengracht Sørensen, Preben. "Starkaðr, Loki and Egill Skallagrímsson." *Sagas of the Icelanders: A Book of Essays.* Ed. John Tucker. New York/London: Garland, 1989. 146-59.

Mitchell, Stephen, A. "The Sagaman and Oral Literature: The Icelandic Traditions of *Hjörleifr inn kvensami* and *Geirmundur heljarskinn.*" *Comparative Research on Oral Traditions: A Memorial for Milman Parry.* Ed. John Miles Foley. Columbus: Slavica, 1985. 395-423.

Moore, Dorothy Emma. *Multiculturalism: Ideology or Social Reality?* Diss. Boston University Graduate School, 1980. Ann Arbor: UMI, 1984.

Moss, John. "Landscape, Untitled." *Essays on Canadian Writing* 29 (1984): 26-47.

———. *Patterns of Isolation in English Canadian Fiction.* Toronto: McClelland and Stewart, 1974.

———. "Salverson, Laura Goodman." *A Reader's Guide to the Canadian Novel.* Toronto: McClelland and Stewart, 1981. 253-54.

Mossberg, Christer Lennart. "Notes toward an Introduction to Scandinavian Immigrant Literature on the Pioneer Experience." *Proceedings of the Pacific North West Council on Foreign Languages.* 28.1. Ed. John T. Brewer. Corvallis: Oregon State University, 1976. 112-17.

Mowat, Carol. "An Interview with Franklin Johnson: Farmer-Poet of Geysir." *The Icelandic Canadian* 51.2 (1992): 69-85.

———. "Stephan G. Stephansson: An Idealist or a Materialist." Thesis. University of Manitoba, 1990.

Munch, Peter Andreas. *Norse Mythology: Legends of Gods and Heroes.* Trans. Sigurd B. Hustvedt. Rev. edn. Ed. Magnus Olsen. Scandinavian Classics Series 27. New York: The American Scandinavian Foundation, 1954.

New, W.H. *Dreams of Speech and Violence: The Art of the Short Story in Canada and New Zealand.* Toronto: University of Toronto Press, 1987.

———. *A History of Canadian Literature.* London: MacMillan Education, 1989.

Njarðvík, Njörður P. "Creator of Documentary Fiction." *Atlantica and Iceland Review* 17.4 (1979): 34-39.

Nordal, Sigurður. "Framtíð íslenzkrar menningar í Vesturheimi." [The future of Icelandic culture in North America] *Tímarit Þjóðræknisfélags Íslendinga í Vesturheimi* 19 (1937): 5-22.

———. "Samhengið í íslenzkum bókmenntum." [Continuity in Icelandic literature] *Íslenzk Lestrarbók 1400-1900.* Reykjavík: BSE, 1931. ix-xxxii.

———, ed. "Stephan G. Stephansson." *Andvökur: úrval.* By Stephansson. Reykjavík: Mál og Menning, 1939. xii-lxxii.

Norman, Hans, and Harald Runblom. *Transatlantic Connections: Nordic Migration to the New World after 1800.* Oxford: Oxford University Press, 1987.

Ólason, Vésteinn, and Halldór Guðmundsson, eds. *Íslensk Bókmenntasaga.* [Literary history of Iceland] 3 vols. Reykjavík: Mál og Menning, 1992-96.

Oleson, Tryggvi J. "Anglo-Saxon England and Iceland." *Tímarit Þjóðræknisfélags Íslendinga í Vesturheimi* 45 (1963): 80-89.

Ong, Walter J. *Orality and Literacy — The Technologizing of the Word.* London/New York: Methuen, 1982. London/New York: Routledge, 1990.

Other Solitudes, see Hutcheon, Linda.

Owens, Judith. "'Drawing / in': Wholeness and Dislocation in the Work of Kristjana Gunnars." *Contemporary Manitoba Writers: New Critical Studies.* Ed. Kenneth James Hughes. Winnipeg: Turnstone, 1990. 64-78.

Pacey, Desmond. "Fiction 1920-1940." *Literary History of Canada.* Ed. Carl F. Klinck. Toronto: University of Toronto Press, 1970.

Padolsky, Enoch. "Canadian Minority Writing and Acculturation Options." *Literatures of Lesser Diffusion/Littératures de Moindre Diffusion.* Ed. Joseph Pivato. Edmonton: Research Institute for Comparative Literature at the University of Alberta, 1990. 46-64.

Padolsky, Enoch. "Cultural Diversity and Canadian Literature: A Pluralistic Approach." *International Journal of Canadian Studies* 3 (Spring 1991): 111-28.

Palmer, Tamara. "Ethnic Response to the Canadian Prairies, 1900-1950: A Literary Perspective on Perceptions of the Physical and Social Environment." *Prairie Forum* 12.1 (1987): 49-73.

Pálsson, Gísli. "The Idea of Fish: Land and Sea in the Icelandic World-View." *Signifying Animals: Human Meaning in the Natural World.* Ed. R.G. Willis. London: Unwin Hyman, 1990. 119-33.

Pálsson, Heimir. *Frásagnarlist fyrri alda.* [Narrative art in former centuries] Reykjavík: Forlagið, 1990.

Pálsson, Hermann, and Paul Edwards. *Legendary Fiction in Medieval Iceland. Studia Islandica* 30. Reykjavík: Menningarsjóður and Heimspekideild Háskóla Íslands, 1971.

————, trans. *The Book of Settlements—Landnámabók.* Winnipeg: University of Manitoba Press, 1972.

————, trans. Introduction. *Eyrbyggja Saga.* London: Penguin, 1989. 1-16.

————, trans. Introduction. *Orkneyinga Saga.* London: Penguin, 1984. 9-20.

————. "Narrative Elements in the Icelandic Book of Settlements." *Mosaic* 4.2 (1970): 1-11.

Pálsson, Jóhannes P. "J. Magnús Bjarnason." *Tímarit Þjóðræknisfélags Íslendinga í Vesturheimi* 27 (1946): 2-14.

————. "Bókafregn." [Book News; announcement of publication of *The Viking Heart*] *Heimskringla* 24 Oct. 1923: 4.

Pétursson, Rögnvaldur. "Að frægðar orði." [Renowned] *Tímarit Þjóðræknisfélags Íslendinga í Vesturheimi* 5 (1923): 109-11.

————. "Upphaf Vesturferða og Þjóðminningarhátíðin í Milwaukee 1874." [The beginning of the emigration and the national celebration in Milwaukee in 1874] *Tímarit Þjóðræknisfélags Íslendinga í Vesturheimi* 15 (1933): 66-78.

————. "Þjóðræknissamtök Íslendinga í Vesturheimi." [Icelandic nationalist organizations in North America] *Tímarit Þjóðræknisfélags Íslendinga í Vesturheimi* 1 (1919): 98-128; 2 (1920): 92-113; 3 (1921): 96-118; 4 (1922): 97-117; 6 (1924): 110-21; 8 (1926): 117-22.

Pivato, Joseph, ed. *Literatures of Lesser Diffusion/Littératures de Moindre Diffusion.* Edmonton: Research Institute for Comparative Literature at the University of Alberta, 1990.

The Poetic Edda, see Hollander, Lee M.

Poole, Russell. "Verses and Prose in *Gunnlaugs saga Ormstungu.*" *Sagas of the Icelanders: A Book of Essays.* Ed. John Tucker. New York/London: Garland, 1989. 160-84.

Porter, John. *The Vertical Mosaic: An Analysis of Social Class and Power in Canada.* 1965. Toronto: University of Toronto Press, 1968.

Powell, Barbara. "Laura Goodman Salverson: Her Father's 'Own True Son'." *Canadian Literature* 133 (Summer 1992): 78-89.

Propp, Vladimir. *Morphology of the Folk Tale.* Trans. Laurence Scott. 1958. 2nd rev. edn. Eds. Louis A. Wagner and Alan Dundes. Publications of the American Folklore Society 9. Austin: University of Texas Press, 1973.

The Prose Edda, see Young, Jean I.

Radin, Paul. *The Trickster: A Study in American Indian Mythology.* New York: Philosophical Library, 1956.

Reid, Verna. "The Small Town in Canadian Fiction." *English Quarterly* 6.2 (1973): 171-81.

Reykers, Hans Heinrich. *Die isländische Ächtersage—ein Beitrag zur nordischen Volkskunde.* Marburg: Bauer, 1936.

Ricou, Laurie. "The Meadowlark Tradition: Popular Verse of the Canadian Prairie." *Essays on Canadian Writing* 18-19 (1980): 161-68.

———. *Vertical Man/Horizontal World: Man and Landscape in Canadian Prairie Fiction.* Vancouver: University of British Columbia Press, 1973.

Ringgren, Helmer. "The Problems of Fatalism." *Fatalistic Beliefs in Religion, Folklore, and Literature.* Stockholm: Almqvist and Wiksell, 1967. 7-18.

Robertson, R.T. "My Own Country: Prairie Immigrant Literature." *The Commonwealth Writer Overseas: Themes of Exile and Expatriation.* Ed. Alastair Niven. Brussels: Didier, 1976. 75-85.

Ruth, Roy H. *Educational Echoes: A History of Education of the Icelandic Canadians in Manitoba.* Winnipeg: Roy H. Ruth/Columbia, 1964.

The Saga of Gísli, see Johnston, George.

The Saga of Grettir, see Foote, Peter.

Salverson, Laura Goodman. "An Autobiographical Sketch." *Ontario Library Review* 14 (1930): 69-73.

———. Editorial. *The Icelandic Canadian* 1.1 (1942): 1-3.

Schoemperlen, Diane. Rev. of *Red Dust,* by W.D. Valgardson. *Quill & Quire* 44.9 (1978): 10.

Scobie, Stephen. "Amelia or: Who do you think you are? Documentary and Identity in Canadian Literature." *Canadian Literature* 100 (1984): 264-85.

Sigfússon, Björn. "Fornklassískt siðerni og tilvitnanir meistara Jóns." [Classical religion and the quotations of Master Jón] *Nordæla—afmæliskveðja til Sigurðar Nordals.* [Nordæla: a birthday greeting to Sigurður Nordal] Eds. Halldór Halldórsson *et al.* Reykjavík: Helgafell, 1956. 29-39.

Sigurðsson, Gísli. "Gaelic Influences in Iceland: Historical and Literary Contacts." *Studia Islandica* 46 (1988).

Sigurðsson, Jón. "Hugvekja til Íslendinga." [Essay to Icelanders] 1848. Rpt. in *Hugvekja til Íslendinga.* Ed. Jakob Benediktsson. Reykjavík: Mál og Menning, 1951. 112-30.

Sigurðsson, Jónas. "Vestur-Íslendingar." [West Icelanders] *Tímarit Þjóðræknisfélags Íslendinga í Vesturheimi* 11 (1929): 186-98.

Sigurdson, Paul. "Insights into the Humourous Poetry of K.N." *Lögberg-Heimskringla* 26 Oct. 1990: 4.

———. Translations of K.N.'s Poetry. *Lögberg-Heimskringla* 26 Oct. 1990: 4; 14 Dec. 1990: 6; 18 Jan. 1991: 4; 8 Feb. 1991: 3; 22 Feb. 1991: 3; 1 Mar. 1991: 4; 15 Mar. 1991: 7; 5 Apr. 1991: 2; 19 Apr. 1991: 5; 3 May 1991: 4; 17 May 1991: 5; 24 May 1991: 4; 14 June 1991: 6; 28 June 1991: 4; 12 July 1991: 2; 6 Sep. 1991: 7; 20 Sep. 1991: 3; 18 Oct. 1991: 4.

Sigurjónsson, Arnór. "Guttormur J. Guttormsson og kvæði hans." [Guttormur J. Guttormsson and his Poetry] *Kvæðasafn.* Ed. Sigurjónsson. Reykjavík: Iðunn, 1947. 5-36.

Simonson, Simon. "Icelandic Pioneers of 1874: From the Reminiscences of Simon Simonson." Trans. W. Kristjanson. *The Icelandic Canadian* 5.2 (1946): 40-55.

Skúlason, Hrund. "Úr dagbókum J.M. Bjarnasonar." [From the diaries of J.M. Bjarnason] *Tímarit Þjóðræknisfélags Íslendinga í Vesturheimi* 48 (1967): 29-40.

Slemon, Stephen. "Magic Realism as Post-Colonial Discourse." *Canadian Literature* 116 (1988): 9-24.

Sluijter, P.C.M. *IJslands Volksgeloof.* Haarlem: Tjeenk Willink, 1936.

Smith, A.J.M., ed. *The Book of Canadian Poetry: A Critical and Historical Anthology.* Chicago: University of Chicago Press., 1943. Rev. ed. 1948.

Sollors, Werner. "Introduction: The Invention of Ethnicity." *The Invention of Ethnicity.* Ed. Sollors. New York: Oxford University Press, 1989. ix-xx.

Spoelstra, Jan. *De Vogelvrijen in de IJslandse Letterkunde.* Haarlem: Tjeenk Willink, 1938.

Staines, David. "Crouched in the Dark Caves: The Post-Colonial Narcissism of Canadian Literature." *Yearbook of English Studies* 13 (1983): 259-69.

———, ed. *The Canadian Imagination: Dimensions of a Literary Culture.* Cambridge: Harvard University Press, 1977.

Stanton Cawley, F. "Mesta skáld Vesturheims: Stephan G. Stephansson." *Tímarit Þjóðræknisfélags Íslendinga í Vesturheimi* 19 (1937): 120-26. Rpt. as "The Greatest Poet of the Western World." *Scandinavian Studies* 14 (1942): 99-106.

Steblin-Kamenskij, M.I. "Folklore and Literature in Iceland and the Problem of Literary Progress." *Scandinavica* 11.2 (1972): 127-36.

———. "On the Nature of Fiction in the Sagas of the Icelanders." *Scandinavica* 6.2 (1967): 77-84.

———. *The Saga Mind.* Trans. Kenneth H. Ober. Odense: Odense University Press, 1973.

Stedingh, R.W. Rev. of *God is not a Fish Inspector*, by W.D. Valgardson. *Canadian Fiction Magazine* 27 (1977): 143-45.

Stefanik, Heinrich. "Saga and Western." *Parergon* 15 (1976): 55-64.

Stegner, Wallace. "The Provincial Consciousness." *University of Toronto Quarterly* 43.4 (1974): 299-310.

Stephansson, Stephan G. "Um *Ljóðmæli* eftir Jóhann Magnús Bjarnason, Ísafjörður 1898." [About *Ljóðmæli* by Jóhann Magnús Bjarnason, Ísafjörður 1898] *Heimskringla* 13 Apr. 1899: 2-3.

Stevens, Peter. "Explorer/Settler/Poet." *University of Windsor Review* 13 (1977): 63-74.

Stouck, David. "Notes on the Canadian Imagination." *Canadian Literature* 54 (1972): 9-26.

Ström, Åke V. "Scandinavian Belief in Fate." *Fatalistic Beliefs in Religion, Folklore, and Literature.* Ed. Helmer Ringgren. Stockholm: Almqvist and Wiksell, 1967. 63-88.

Strömback, Dag. "Some Remarks on Learned and Novelistic Elements in the Icelandic Sagas." *Nordica et Anglica: Studies in Honour of Stefán Einarsson.* Ed. Allan H. Orrick. The Hague: Mouton, 1968. 140-47.

Stubbs, Roy St. George. *In Search of a Poet.* Winnipeg: Peguis, 1975.

———. "Paul Bjarnason, Poet and Apostle of a Brave New World." *The Icelandic Canadian* 45.1 (1986): 9-19.

Stuewe, Paul. *Clearing the Ground: English-Canadian Literature after* Survival. Part 2. Toronto: Proper Tales, 1984.

Sutherland, Ronald. "How 'Canadian' is Canadian Literature?" *English Quarterly* 3.2 (1985): 37-40.

Sveinsson, Einar Ólafur. "Íslenzkar bókmentir eptir siðskiptin."
[Icelandic literature after the Reformation] *Tímarit Þjóðræknisfélags
Íslendinga í Vesturheimi* 11 (1929): 127-71.

——. *Um íslenzkar þjóðsögur.* [About Icelandic folk tales] Reykjavík:
Sjóður Margrétar Lehmann-Filhés/AB, 1940.

Sweatman, Margaret. "Arnason's Irony and Vision." *Contemporary
Manitoba Writers: New Critical Studies.* Ed. Kenneth James Hughes.
Winnipeg: Turnstone, 1990. 31-53.

Thomas, Clara. "Some Traditions in Fiction, Canadian Style." *CEA Critic*
50.1 (1987): 26-34.

——. "Women Writers and the New Land." *The New Land: Studies in a
Literary Theme.* Eds. R. Chadbourne *et al.* Waterloo: Wilfrid Laurier
University Press, 1978. 45-59.

Thompson, Eric. "Prairie Mosaic: The Immigrant Novel in the Canadian
West." *Studies in Canadian Literature* 5.3 (1980): 236-59.

Thompson, Laura. "The Icelanders." *The Secret of Culture: Nine Community
Studies.* New York: Random House, 1969. 150-81.

Tihanyi, Eva. "Theme and/or Non-Theme." Rev. of *The Nightworkers of
Ragnarök*, by Kristjana Gunnars. *Waves* 14.4 (1986): 84-86.

Tomasson, Richard. *Iceland, the First New Society.* Minneapolis: University
of Minnesota Press, 1980.

——. "The Literacy of the Icelanders." *Scandinavian Studies* 47.1
(1975): 66-93.

Tómasson, Sverrir. "Helgisögur, mælskufræði og forn frásagnarlist."
[Saints' legends, rhetoric and classical narrative art] *Skírnir* 157 (1983):
130-62.

Toorn, M.C. van den. *Ethics and Moral in Icelandic Saga Literature.* Assen:
Van Gorcum, 1955.

"Troll Turning: Poetic Voice in the Poetry of Kristjana Gunnars," see
Lane, M. Travis.

Tucker, John. "Introduction: Sagas of the Icelanders." *Sagas of the
Icelanders: A Book of Essays.* Ed. Tucker. New York/London:
Garland, 1989. 1-26.

Turner, Victor W. "An Anthropological Approach to the Icelandic Saga."
The Translation of Culture: Essays to E.E. Evans-Pritchard. Ed. T.O.
Beidelman. London: Tavistock, 1971. 349-73.

Turville-Petre, Gabriel. "Dreams in Icelandic Tradition." *Nine Norse
Studies.* London: Viking Society for Northern Research, 1972. 30-51.

——. *Myth and Religion in the North.* London: Weidenfeld and
Nicolson, 1964.

Turville-Petre, Gabriel. *Origins of Icelandic Literature.* Oxford: Clarendon Press, 1953.

Tuttle Marzolf, Marion. "The Danish Immigrant Press: Old Friend in a New Land." *From Scandinavia to America: Proceedings from a Conference held at Gl. Holtegaard.* Eds. Steffen Jørgensen *et al.* Odense: Odense University Press, 1987. 299-319.

Valgardson, W.D. "The Icelandic Community and Its Literature." *The Icelandic Canadian* 60.1 (1982): 35-36.

————. "An Immigrant Culture: Reconciling Diverse Voices." Lecture. St. John's College. Winnipeg: University of Manitoba, Nov. 1987.

————. "Interview with Kristjana Gunnars." *Lögberg-Heimskringla* 16 Jan. 1981: 5, 8.

————. "Personal Gods." *Essays on Canadian Writing* 16.2-3 (1979-80): 179-186.

————. "True Norse." *Books in Canada* 11 (Aug.-Sept. 1982): 29.

Walker, Warren S. "From Raconteur to Writer: Oral Roots and Printed Leaves of Short Fiction." *The Teller and the Tale.* Ed. Wendell M. Aycock. Lubbodi: Texas Tech. Press, 1982. 13-26.

Wallace, Birgitta. "L'Anse aux Meadows and Vinland: An Abandoned Project." Lecture. Annual Meeting of the Canadian Archaeological Association. Halifax: 1-5 May 1996.

Wolf, Kirsten. "Heroic Past—Heroic Present: Western Icelandic Literature." *Scandinavian Studies* 63 (1991): 432-52.

————. "Icelandic-Canadian Literature: Problems in Generic Classification." *Scandinavian Studies* 64.3 (1992): 439-53.

————. "Jóhannes P. Pálsson's 'Alfur of Borg' and Medieval Icelandic Þættir." *The Icelandic Canadian* 49.4 (1991): 35-41.

————. "Looking Across Generations" (about Helen Sveinbjörnsson and Eleanor Oltean). *Lögberg-Heimskringla* 26 Nov. 1993: 4-5.

————. "Western Icelandic Women Writers: Their Contribution to the Literary Canon." *Scandinavian Studies* 66 (1994): 154-203.

Woodcock, George. "The Meeting of the Muses: Recent Canadian Fiction and the Historical Viewpoint." *The Canadian Historical Review* 60 (June 1979): 141-53.

————. *The Meeting of Time and Place: Regionalism in Canadian Literature.* NeWest Lecture Series 1980. Edmonton: NeWest Institute for Western Canadian Studies, 1981.

Young, Esther. "Profile of a Secretary—and More" (about Elma Helgason). *Lögberg-Heimskringla* 9 Mar. 1990: 4.

Young, Jean I., trans. and ed. *The Prose Edda of Snorri Sturluson: Tales from Norse Mythology*. 1954. 2nd edn. Berkeley: University of California Press, 1966.

Þorleifsson, Páll. "Meistari Jón og *Postillan*." [Master Jón and the *Postilla*] *Húspostilla -Predikanir eftir Jón Vídalín*. [A collection of home sermons by Jón Vídalín] Eds. Þorleifsson and Björn Sigfússon. Reykjavík: Bókaútgáfa Kristján Friðrikssonar Hólar, 1945. xi-xxix.

Þorsteinsson, Björn. Rev. of *Íslenzkar þjóðsögur og ævintýri*, rev. edn. *Tímarit Máls og Menningar* 23 (1962): 186-91.

Þorsteinsson, Steingrímur J. "Icelandic Folk Tales." *Scandinavica* 12.2 (1973): 85-99.

————. "Stephan G. Stephansson: Aldarminning." [Stephan G. Stephansson: centennial commemoration] *Skírnir* 127 (1953): 18-36.

Þorsteinsson, Þorsteinn Þ. "Sporin frá 1875." [Traces from 1875] *Tímarit Þjóðræknisfélags Íslendinga í Vesturheimi* 22 (1951): 5-16.

————. *Vestmenn: útvarpserindi um landnám Íslendinga í Vesturheimi*. [West Icelanders: a radio lecture on the settlement of Icelanders in North America] Reykjavík: Ísafoldarprentsmiðja, 1935.

————, and Tryggvi J. Oleson. *Saga Íslendinga í Vesturheimi*. [History of Icelanders in North America] 5 vols. Reykjavík: Bókaútgáfa Menningarsjóðs, 1940-53.

INDEX